The Aztecs, Maya, and Their Predecessors

ARCHAEOLOGY OF MESOAMERICA

The Aztecs,

Maya, and Their Predecessors

ARCHAEOLOGY OF MESOAMERICA

Muriel Porter Weaver

HUNTER COLLEGE

SEMINAR

PRESS

NEW YORK
AND
LONDON

A Subsidiary of
Harcourt Brace Jovanovich, Publishers

STUDIES IN ARCHEOLOGY

Consulting Editor: Stuart Struever

Department of Anthropology
Northwestern University
Evanston, Illinois

SEMINAR PRESS, INC.
111 Fifth Avenue, New York, New York 10003

United Kingdom Edition published by
SEMINAR PRESS LIMITED
24/28 Oval Road, London NW1 7DD

LIBRARY OF CONGRESS CATALOG CARD NUMBER: 70-183477

February 1973, Second Printing
June 1973, Third Printing

PRINTED IN THE UNITED STATES OF AMERICA

Cover and text design by Anne Hallowell

For Harold,
Jean and Leslie

Contents

List of Illustrations[*]

FRONTISPIECE. Olmec jade figurine. The left arm was sawed off in ancient times: such mutilation of objects was not uncommon. Height: 6 inches. Courtesy of the American Musem of Natural History.

Chapter Headings

Charts

[*]Figures and photos are not included in this list.

Maps

Plates

Preface

The continuing interest in the pre-Columbian cultures of Mexico and Guatemala has, over the years, led to the accumulation of a tremendous amount of literature to be found in field reports, widely scattered articles, and books by scientists, scholars, and art lovers. The student who wants to learn something of the events that took place in this region prior to the Spanish Conquest is confronted by a bewildering assortment of books and articles, some of which are hard to locate in the most richly stocked library.

This book was conceived as an answer to a frequently asked question, "Can you give me the name of a single volume that will cover the archaeology of both central Mexico and the Maya area?" The question reflects the need for synthesis, for an attempt at generalization, and to fit the scattered knowledge of pre-Columbian history into some comprehensive framework. As such this book is the first of its kind.

As the student begins to understand how the ingenious life of hunters and gatherers evolved into a complex civilization, he will also become aware of how great is our debt to archaeology; how with the increasing advantages of interdisciplinary studies, more can be learned from the past; and precisely how it is possible to combine archaeological facts and theories. This book is planned as a general introduction to the archaeology of Mesoamerica. For some students this may represent their only involvement with the field of archaeology, and if so, they will see how the evolution of one of the highest civilizations in the New World came about, as well as gaining an appreciation of archaeology as a science. For others this volume will serve as a point of departure for specialized research. It is my hope that many will be stimulated to expand their interests to examine specific field reports and monographs, to rethink theories and challenge ideas presented here. For those primarily interested in the primitive art of this area, the book will help them view their objects in a cultural context, thus giving them meaning and perspective.

Rather than deal with the sequence of events by geographical areas, I have chosen to treat Mesoamerica as a whole, emphasizing major cultural changes and trends beginning with the earliest inhabitants of 38,000 B.C. (?) and ending with the arrival of the Spanish in 1519. After some description of the physical setting, the scene is focused on the earliest known beginnings of farming in the highland area of the Tehuacán Valley, and then shifts to the lowland cultures of the Gulf Coast region where the Olmec civilization was centered. Following these remarkable developments, the key areas become central highland Mexico, which never again relinquishes its leadership, and the lowland jungles of Guatemala, followed by the Yucatán peninsula. These regions taken together provide us with a mainstream or central core of complexity to which cultures of other areas can be related, compared, and contrasted.

The absorbing history of Mesoamerica's culture, however, can be ultimately understood and appreciated only when given the perspective of other New World developments. In this regard one should remember that Mesoamerica was not a static geographical area; its sixteenth century contours do not have the same boundaries of the twelfth and ninth centuries. These fluctuations involve neighboring peoples and their interaction with those of more complex civilizations. More widespread relationships with South American cultures of Colombia, Ecuador, and Peru, that is, the role of Mesoamerica within Nuclear America and the Intermediate area, are part of this perspective. These contacts are touched on briefly, as well as current trends in Transpacific studies. Finally, I have presented my views on Mesoamerica as a civilization and mentioned some of the problems to be faced by the archaeologist in this part of the world. Many of these problems can be met and resolved by an appreciation of the past. It is here that we will begin.

Acknowledgments

I have made a conscious effort to avoid complicated terms as well as all but the most vital current debates on issues and interpretations. "Try to make it understandable" was the hope expressed at the outset by Dr. Daniel F. Rubín de la Borbolla, to whom I owe my initiation into Mesoamerican archaeology. As a founder and director of the Escuela Nacional de Antropología and subsequent director of the Museo Nacional de Antropología in Mexico, no one could have offered more encouragement, stimulation, and opportunity to a student than he gave to me. I also recognize a long-standing debt to the late Alfonso Caso, Ignacio Marquina, Wigberto Jiménez Moreno, Paul Kirchhoff, Miguel Covarrubias, Ignacio Bernal, Román Piña Chán, José Luis Lorenzo, and to all my Mexican teachers and colleagues who throughout years of intimate involvement with Mesoamerica, have treated me as one of their own. In the direct preparation of this book, I would like to extend very special thanks to Arturo Romano, who as director of the Museo Nacional de Antropología, Mexico, generously put all his resources at my disposal.

Discussions and conversations with others in this field have been invaluable, and a number of colleagues generously made available to me unpublished material. In this respect I am very grateful to Isabel T. Kelly, Robert H. Heizer, Michael D. Coe, Paul Tolstoy, David Grove, and Ellen and Charles Brush. In addition, Paul Tolstoy and Pedro Armillas read parts of the manuscript and Michael D. Coe the whole. I greatly appreciate their helpful comments and suggestions, although the responsibility for all shortcomings is mine alone.

To Mary Beth Stokes, who prepared the art work with both talent and interest, go my heartfelt thanks. I am grateful too to Frederick J. Dockstader for innumerable favors and time spent on my behalf. The photographs from the Museum of the American Indian are the work of Carmelo Guadagno, many of which were specially prepared for this text.

The art work and photography were made possible through the interest of Dean Ruth G. Weintraub and by a Doctoral Faculty Research Grant from the City University of New York. To those many institutions and individuals who provided photographs and granted permission for their publication, I am deeply grateful. Tana Agoras and Jean Kemp typed the original manuscript.

I also wish to express my appreciation to the following publishers who have graciously permitted the reproduction of figures redrawn from their publications to appear here: Alfred Knopf, Inc., American Museum of Natural History, Carnegie Institution of Washington, Field Museum of Natural History, Fondo de Cultura Económica, Instituto Nacional de Antropología e Historia, International Congress of Americanists, McGraw-Hill Book Company, Museum of the American Indian, Peabody Museum of Harvard University, R. S. Peabody Foundation, Sociedad Mexicana de Antropología, Smithsonian Institution of Washington, Stanford University Press, Universidad Nacional Autónoma de Mexico, University Museum, Philadelphia, University of Texas Press, and Wenner-Gren Foundation for Anthropological Research.

One of the most rewarding experiences in preparing this book was the opportunity to meet and work with staff members of Seminar Press. The production of this volume in an age characterized by computerized, stereotyped relationships has been a delightful personal experience. The tasteful design of the book, the very difficult task of fitting in my vast disarray of illustrative material, and the precision and detail work necessary to see Mesoamerica's past properly recorded are all very much appreciated.

I realize, however, that it was only through the encouragement, understanding, and countless considerations of my husband, Harold M. Weaver, that the long-standing desire to write this book has been realized.

Introduction

As in any area of the world, the ancient culture history of a people prior to their possession of a written language is gradually pieced together from that material evidence of their civilization that has managed to survive the ravages of weather, time, and man. The archaeologist first recovers what he can methodically and scientifically, and then interprets this material in terms of temporal or geographic change.

One admitted shortcoming of this traditional approach lies in the difficulties and limitations it poses in explaining the processes involved. There is increased interest in attempting to explain rather than merely describe. The many new approaches and trends in archaeology represent a breakthrough in both theory and scientific method. Archaeologists are becoming more aware of the importance of thoroughly understanding the environment or paleoecology of prehistory, and this is leading to unprecedented collaborations with geologists, nuclear physicists, veterinary anatomists, zoologists, botanists, and an entire spectrum of specialists in other fields. New interpretations and inferences are also being offered in such areas as ancient social affiliations, residence patterns, population densities, and political institutions, making use of both archaeology and ethnographic and historical documents. There is a new trend toward reinterpretation and reevaluation of past work. Thus, archaeological methods are being improved, a higher precision becomes possible, and the field of archaeology is branching out into new areas of investigation, which involve both cultural and noncultural phenomena such as ecological factors. All of this has been made possible, however, by years of "dirt" archaeology, which provides the material evidence for speculation and testing of theories.

Thus, the cultural evolution of Mesoamerican civilization is understood as a result of cumulative efforts from many years of digging in the field. In this case the task is very complex. In the geographical area encompassing Mesoamerica, which embraces most of Mexico and part of northern Central America, the extraordinary diversity of altitude, climate, natural resources, fauna, and flora have contributed to an equal diversity of ecological adaptations and cultural manifestations. About eighty years of intensive archaeological study have been required to reach a point where one can begin to speak about characteristics, trends, patterns, and traditions. It has taken a very long time to understand what happened in Mesoamerica and archaeologists are far from satisfied. Such explanations are just being initiated. As scientists, archaeologists are not out to defend preconceived theories, to place one site in competition with another, or to force the antiquity of remains. The goal is simply to understand what happened, and if possible how and why. I think that archaeologists are now able to see certain trends and processes, and once process mechanisms are set in motion, a course is determined which moves in a particular direction. I believe that this evolution will be self-evident in the following pages. Primarily, however, this is to be a history of cultural events in Mesoamerica rather than a testing of theories, although one need not exclude the other. Hopefully, the unfolding of sequences will help illuminate such processes and the mechanisms at work.

The history, however, is based primarily on fragmentary remains which are subject to constant revision and reinterpretation. There is also another factor of which the reader should be aware. The people who developed these extraordinary cultures lived in a world with values and ideals that differed greatly from those of modern times. By our standards, some might be classified as savages or barbarians, with complete disregard for human life. Through studying their history, beliefs, and discipline, however, one hopes to view them as human beings coping with the universal problems of mankind everywhere, but solving them in their unique way. Artists, astronomers, gifted craftsmen and architects, merchants, warriors, royalty, peasants, and slaves will be found—all with a singular dedication to their society and religion. In order to understand the complex world of the Aztecs, Maya, and their contemporaries, one must learn first about the long chain of cultural events leading up to the culmination of these great civilizations. And in the process, the oft-asked question comes to mind: "Were our American cultures developed independently in the New World, or do they owe their initial stimulation to influences from the Old?" In addition, there is much one can learn today from the evolution of a past civilization that, when viewed in perspective of its own life and times, was probably as great as one feels ours is today.

I have attempted to present a cultural history of Mesoamerica—the account of how this area of the New World reached spectacular heights of civilization from the more modest hunting and gathering base shared by most of the western hemisphere. Why did it happen here? What was the role of agriculture, of irrigation? What factors contributed to the rise of urban centers such as Teotihuacán in central highland Mexico and Tikal in the Petén region of Guatemala? How, precisely, does Mesoamerica qualify as a high civilization?

In order to understand the cultural evolution that did take place, it is necessary to consider the area as a whole. Much has been written on the Aztecs and the Maya, who occupied adjacent geographical areas connected by a narrow corridor of land, the Isthmus of Tehuantepec. A kind of dichotomy has grown up over the years between the central Mexican cultures and the Maya and their predecessors. Indeed, there are few archaeologists who have done extensive work both east and west of the "Isthmus." The complexity and extreme diversity of cultures has justified such past specialization to some extent.

On the other hand, it is generally agreed that these components form a cultural unit—hence the term "Mesoamerica." Thus, despite interior diversity, the central Mexican cultures have more in common with those of Guatemala than they do, for example, with southwestern United States or the Caribbean Islands—in fact, they have much in common. Such themes as certain religious concepts, a calendrical system, hieroglyphic writing, human sacrifice, a ball game with rings, a periodic market system, the use of lime mortar, and many other such elements constitute a common denominator uniting those people who share them, and in turn distinguish them from their "have-not" neighbors.

In working out the chronology of cultures in this area, our starting point is the year 1519, marking the arrival of the Spaniards, and from this date we proceed backwards. The Spanish Conquistadores destroyed much, but also provided excellent accounts including letters written by Cortés himself. *The General History of the Things of New Spain*, often considered to be the first full-fledged ethnology, was written by Fray Bernardino de Sahagún. A truly remarkable scholar, he trained young Aztec nobles to write their native tongue, Náhuatl, in Spanish script. With their aid and his own questioning of informants, Sahagún produced this monumental work. Another sixteenth century source is Bernal Díaz del Castillo's eye-witness account of the conquest of central Mexico. In Yucatán, Bishop Fray Diego de Landa, who gave the orders that resulted in the burning of many Maya *códices*, the Indians' native books, partly offset this great loss by accurately recording much of Maya life himself. We also rely on local native chronicles for Yucatán called the Books of Chilam Balam. Fortunately for us too, the Spanish monarchs requested detailed information about New Spain, much of which has been preserved. These sixteenth century sources by Spanish chroniclers and members of native orders of Franciscans, Augustinians, and Jesuits, as well as native documents, provide a firm cultural base from which to start. Logically it follows that cultural remains lying beneath Aztec and Maya materials are earlier, but how much? "Dirt" archaeology is indispensible for providing the relative sequence of remains, followed by the painstaking task of correlating nearby sites and regions. Even the best relative chronology, however, can indicate only that B, for example, is older than A and perhaps C older than B.

The backbone of Mesoamerican chronology is based on the correlation of the Maya calendar with the Christian calendar, thus providing absolute dates. If, for example, one can be sure that July 26, 1553 corresponds to a certain Maya date, then once the Maya system of calendrics is understood, one should be able to translate the dates of their monuments into the Christian calendar as they are found. Unfortunately it is not at all that simple. The Maya Long Count, yielding absolute dates from an ancient year 1 in the past, was discontinued before the Spanish Conquest and a more abbreviated form was substituted. The correlation with our calendar then becomes a problem of interpretation. For example, the date above is given by Landa for the founding of the Yucatecan capital of Mérida. To which date in the Maya calendar does it correspond? There are two proposed solutions to date: the Goodman–Martínez–Thompson (GMT) or 11.16 correlation and the Spinden or 12.9 correlation. The difference of opinion is one of 260 years. At present, most evidence seems to support the GMT 11.16 system, and this is followed here. Both can be justified, however, and the problem has not been definitely solved. The sequence in Yucatán would tend to support the Spinden correlation, yet if this were uniformly applied, discrepancies would crop up, necessitating adjustments in central Mexico that no archaeologist is currently prepared to make. The carbon-14 dates from Oaxaca would favor a Spinden correlation as well, but seem too far out of line with the Teotihuacán sequence. Therefore, for consistency I have followed the GMT correlation, but not without reservation.

All dating in Mesoamerica is ultimately tied in with the Maya Long Count, which is discussed in Chapter 5 as simply as possible, along with some basic information on Maya calendrics. The Long Count dates, as we will see, were recorded only between the years A.D. 300 and 900, a span of time designated as the Classic period. For other absolute dating, carbon-14, fluorine tests, and obsidian dating have been used with varying success. These are checked against relative chronologies based on stratigraphy and seriations. All are tentative and subject to change.

I should also say a word about the designation of developmental stages. The dilemma is not merely that of choosing among periods, using a block of time arbitrarily, as opposed to stages that deal with levels of achievement regardless of absolute time. Both schemes are possible and have been used with success in New World archaeology. In Mesoamerica developmental stages have been used with relatively little variation: hunters and gatherers or Paleo-Indian, Archaic or Incipient Agriculture, Preclassic or Formative, Classic or Florescent, Postclassic or Militaristic. I am painfully aware of the discrepancies that result from using the term "Classic" for the years A.D. 300–900, as based on lowland Maya development, and the subsequent effect on earlier and later periods. A given period thus may be stretched to fit all of Mesoamerica where it may or may not be applicable. As a result one is faced with such incongruities as the florescence of the Mixteca-Puebla culture occurring in the "Postclassic" and that of the Olmec civilization in the "Preclassic!" "Classic" does indeed fit the lowland Maya for which it was conceived, as well as developments at Teotihuacán, but when this term is applied generally to Mesoamerica, many instances of inconsistencies are found. As a result, it must be recognized that these terms are now used largely to denote chronological periods, and sometimes the descriptive term of the developmental stage may be appropriate. Having voiced my discomfort, I nevertheless have retained these terms here, because of the value of the system as a key to the literature.

I should also say a word about references to mounds, tombs, and monuments such as stelae and altars. In the process of identifying such objects, it is a long-standing custom of archaeologists to arbitrarily assign numbers or letters to each find in the order of its appearance at each site. Hence, the reader will come upon mention of Mound J and E-VII-sub, Tomb 7, Stela 29, and Altar Q. Such is the nature of archaeological labeling and recording.

I prefer the word *Mexica* to *Aztecs* to designate those late inhabitants of central highland Mexico. Because they are better known as Aztecs, this term is used more frequently at first, but the two words are eventually applied interchangeably.

In dealing with sequences of time, the older periods receive the most complete coverage, which means that as the Conquest is approached, the selection of material has been greater, necessitated by its sheer abundance. I have not attempted to present a complete account of sixteenth century Maya and Aztec cultures. It is the sequence of events, the rise to civilization rather than a description of its fulfillment, that is emphasized here.

IN THE COURSE OF CULTURAL DEVELOPMENT OF pre-Columbian civilizations in the western hemisphere, two areas pulled ahead of their neighbors and attained high peaks of civilization unparalleled elsewhere in the New World. These regions, roughly the Andean area and the Mexican–Guatemalan complex, together form what is called Nuclear America, implying centers of high cultural development. The complexity of these civilizations may be readily appreciated by reading first-hand appraisals of these cultures written in the sixteenth century by eye witnesses — the Spanish Conquistadores and chroniclers.

The northern center of development is called Mesoamerica. Geographically it forms part of tropical America, including, at the time of the Spanish Conquest in A.D. 1521, central and southern Mexico with the peninsula of Yucatán, Guatemala, El Salvador, and parts of Honduras, Nicaragua, and northern Costa Rica. The northern boundary at that time, drawn from west to east, begins at the mouth of the Sinaloa River in northwest Mexico, dips south in the central plateau of the middle Lerma River valley, and then climbs north and east to meet the Gulf of Mexico at the mouth of the Soto la Marina River above Tampico. The southern limits, from north to south, begin at the mouth of the Ulua River on the Gulf of Honduras, extend west to the Cholulteca River, and then south across the Nicaraguan lakes, and end at Punta Arenas on the Pacific coast of Costa Rica. On what basis were these geographical limits defined, and what makes this a distinctive culture area? In 1942 Paul Kirchhoff made a distributional study of culture traits or elements and found that many of them were restricted to the area within these limits; others were found only rarely among the neighboring groups to the north and south (Kirchhoff, 1943).

The northern boundary roughly separates hunters and gatherers without a knowledge of agriculture from their more sophisticated farming neighbors to the south. There was a direct confrontation of the Aztec and Tarascan states with these nomadic northern bands, a rather rare situation. Armillas (1969) calls this boundary a hard frontier. The southern limits of Mesoamerica are less sharply defined culturally. In the sixteenth century the higher cultures of Mesoamerica blended into those of Nicaragua and Costa Rica, which form part of an intermediate area between the centers of Nuclear America.

These boundaries of Mesoamerica were drawn up largely on the basis of ethnographic and linguistic data as known at the time of the Conquest. What were some of these diagnostic traits of Mesoamerica? A few of the most important were:

1

Mesoamerica: The Area and the People

ball courts with rings
cacao, chocolate
chia cultivation, a plant raised for food, drink, and oil

chinampa agriculture, a system of cultivation on artificial islands built of vegetation and mud in shallow freshwater lakes

clay pellets for blow tube
coa, digging stick
códices, books made of painted bark or deer skin
grinding of corn mixed with ash or lime
hieroglyphic writing
human sacrifice
labrets, lip ornaments
one-piece warrior outfits
periodic market system
polished obsidian
position numerals
pyrite mirrors

rabbit hair weaving
ritual use of paper and rubber
sandals with heels
stepped pyramids
stucco floors
turbans
use of 13 as ritual number
volador, ritual ceremony in which several men "fly" down to earth from a high pole
wooden clubs with flint or obsidian chips for blades
year of 18 months of 20 days plus 5 extra days

Most of these are in some way related to a rich complex of religious ceremonialism and interactions between groups and regions involving exchange of goods and ideas. These features and their influence on the lives of the people played a large part in the cultural development of Mesoamerica. Combined with many other factors, they gave rise to a civilization unique in content and imaginative in conception, which conforms only in part to the expected patterns and theories that have emerged from studies of other civilizations.

Mesoamerica is therefore a term that refers to this geographic region where a particular pattern of civilization is identified as prevailing in the sixteenth century. What can be said about the preceding years? How far back in time can Mesoamerica be recognized as having a pattern of its own? Does archaeology verify the study by Kirchhoff? It is not possible to reconstruct as precisely as he has done the former extensions of Mesoamerica throughout its long pre-Columbian history. Nevertheless, archaeology shows that some considerable changes took place during this time.

The northern boundary, for example, was far from stable. Pedro Armillas (1969), Beatriz Braniff (1970), and Eric Wolf (1959) all have concerned themselves with the fluctuations of the northern extension of agriculture. From about the year A.D. 1000 to 1300, during the early Post-classic or Toltec period, the boundary of Mesoamerica was pushed northward between the twenty-second and twenty-third parallels, extending from San Luis Potosí in the east to southern Chihuahua in the west (see Map 4, Chapter 7). Armillas believes that during these years a buffer belt, or soft frontier, lay between Mesoamerica and the areas to the south. In this buffer zone farming groups constructed hilltop fortresses such as La Quemada, while the outer groups on the far frontier manifested a more equal balance between hunting and gathering and farming (Armillas, 1969). This situation could reflect adjustment to a new cultural scheme as well as adaptation to a different environment. The northward push of farming peoples was, we believe, contingent on an adequate water supply; a slight fluctuation in rainfall would make the vast territory to the north alternately suitable either for agriculture or for hunting and gathering in a desert-like environment. We shall see, when dealing with the Toltecs, the importance of this fluctuating northern frontier.

For earlier times, it is questionable whether the region of west Mexico properly belongs within the boundary of Mesoamerica. The peoples living in the area of Michoacán, Jalisco, Nayarit, Colima, and Sinaloa manifested a cultural development quite unique in flavor and apparently did not share in the major events taking place in the heart of Mesoamerica. I have therefore represented this area as a peripheral region until the Postclassic period (see Map 2, Chapter 4; Map 3, Chapter 6; Map 4, Chapter 7).

The southeastern boundary of Mesoamerica has long gone unchallenged, the assumption being that traded goods or any Maya influence was sufficient proof of Mesoamerican affiliation. Recently Thompson (1970) reexamined the southern extension of Maya culture and concluded that it fell just to the west of the Ulua River and north of the Lempa River in Classic times. El Salvador is not placed directly in Maya territory. Accordingly, the southern limits of Mesoamerica would not extend to Costa Rica until perhaps Conquest times. The region south and east of the Ulua River was not specifically Maya, but it was heavily influenced by various Mesoamerican groups in the sixteenth century.

We do not know who these Mesoamerican people were. We only know what they called themselves at the time of the Conquest in the sixteenth century. In pre-Columbian times a great variety of languages were spoken. Fortunately for us, linguists have grouped them into families and have been able to study relationships and changes between them. Because changes are believed to have taken place at a constant rate, linguists, through comparing basic vocabularies, are able to estimate how long it has been since two related tongues branched off from a common ancestral form. Thus, they can reconstruct the linguistic past.

An excellent summary of languages and their history is found in the volume by Wolf (1959), which is briefly summarized here. Prior to 4000 B.C. all languages in Mesoamerica may have been related, but soon after that, the great Uto-Aztecan strain can be distinguished, which probably had its roots somewhere in western Mexico. This group in turn split into many subdivisions, Nahua being the most important, and its close relative, Náhuatl, became the language of the Aztecs and is still spoken today by many rural groups in central highland Mexico. Náhuatl is beautiful and melodious and became, as did Maya and Quechua, one of the literary tongues of ancient America used for recording epic poems, proverbs, flowery rhetoric, and hymns to the gods. Nahua speakers moved around even before the Aztecs came to power; afterward, Náhuatl-speaking Aztecs carried this language throughout Mesoamerica in the course of their late expansion. Náhuatl had great influence on speech and spelling as far south as lower Central America, though its center remained in the basin of Mexico.

Another large group was made up of Macro-Mayan speakers who spread through the southern lowlands of the Gulf Coast and the eastern highlands. Huastec and Mayan languages are closely related; available evidence indicates that these people once lived side by side along the Gulf Coast and spoke a Mayan language. A linguistic map shows a very complex assortment of tongues, which indicates much shifting and mixing of peoples. The people of the northern Gulf Coast area were separated from their Mayan-speaking neighbors by the intrusion of Totonac- and Zoque-speaking peoples, and Huastec subsequently followed its own path of development (Map 1a). Mayan languages, with the exception of orphaned Huastec, are clustered in a contiguous area, suggesting a long history in their present location. Some stimulating recent lexicostatistical studies postulate that around 2600 B.C. northwestern Guatemala may have been the earliest home of the Maya, from where they could have expanded to the Huasteca and Yucatán.

A great number of other languages are found in central and southern Mexico. The Otomian group is composed of Otomí, Matlazinca, and Mazahua. Mixtecan languages, such as Mixtec, Chocho, Popoloca, Mazatec, and Ixcatec, together with Zapotec, are all related in the distant past to an ancient Oto-Zapotecan stock. An interesting language unrelated to other Mesoamerican tongues is Tarascan, which is still spoken around the region of Lake Pátzcuaro; it formerly was the language of most of the state of Michoacán.

Today the vast majority of Mesoamerica's inhabitants speak only Spanish, but a minority is still bilingual, speaking an additional autochthonous Indian language. Though the native languages are diminishing with each new generation, a process accelerated by modern communication and mass media, the mark of the past is left indelibly on modern Mexican Spanish.

Natural Areas

The map of Mesoamerica is shaped like a tilted bow tie, with the left side slightly higher than the right. The knot in the center is the Isthmus of Tehuantepec, a narrow corridor of land uniting western Mesoamerica with the Maya area to the east (Map 1b).

In the western section, two great mountain systems run like backbones down each coastline until they are interrupted by an east–west chain of volcanoes. These mountain systems enclose the central highland plateau or the Mesa Central, one of three highland centers in Mesoamerica, the cultural and political domination of which was felt for centuries. The Mesa Central is still the focus of the leading social, political, and economic forces in Mesoamerica today. The most important area in the Mesa Central is the Valley of Mexico, more accurately described as an inland basin. At one time its waters drained off to the south into the great Papaloapan and Balsas rivers, but a chain of volcanoes rose up to cut off this flow, thus forming the only Mexican inland basin with no outlet. Five shallow lakes were created in the basin floor which were swampy at the shoreline and offered many attractions to aquatic life. East and west of the basin of Mexico lie two other river basins that figure prominently in the history of Mexico. Puebla, lying to the east over the mountains, is even more suitable for habitation than is the basin of Mexico because rainfall is more plentiful. This region drains to the east, the principal river system being that of the Pánuco, which empties its waters into the Gulf of Mexico near Tampico. In the opposite direction, the basin of Toluca is the gateway to all western Mexico and gives rise to the mighty waterway of the Lerma–Santiago, which eventually pours into the Pacific Ocean.

The volcanic chain, called the transverse volcanic axis (West, 1964), lends excitement to the landscape. Majestic and terrifying, commanding respect and awe, the great volcanoes soar upward 13,000 to over 17,000 feet and, with occasional tremors and shakes, remind those in the valleys below that they are still the older, dominating force. To them the people owe the fresh springs on the southern escarpments, the swarms of cinder cones, wide lava flows, ash falls, mud flows, and the enriched soils that

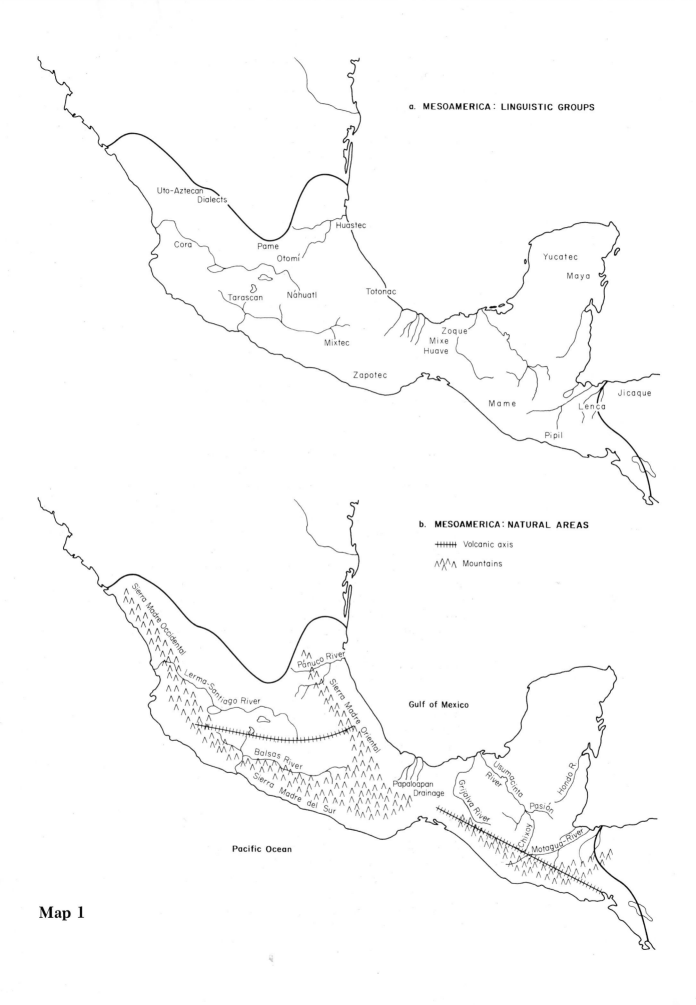

a. MESOAMERICA : LINGUISTIC GROUPS

Uto-Aztecan Dialects

Cora

Huastec

Pame

Otomí

Tarascan

Náhuatl

Mixtec

Yucatec

Maya

Totonac

Zoque
Mixe
Huave

Zapotec

Mame

Jicaque

Lenca

Pipil

b. MESOAMERICA: NATURAL AREAS

╫╫╫╫ Volcanic axis

∧∧∧∧ Mountains

Sierra Madre Occidental

Lerma-Santiago River

Pánuco River

Sierra Madre Oriental

Gulf of Mexico

Balsas River

Sierra Madre del Sur

Papaloapan Drainage

Usumacinta River

Grijalva River

Pasión

Honda R.

Chixoy

Motagua River

Pacific Ocean

Map 1

permit man to grow food more advantageously. They have also provided the volcanic glassy rock, obsidian, for man's tools and andesites and basalts for construction work. The largest volcanoes from east to west are Orizaba and the Cofre de Perote in Veracruz; the Malinche in Puebla; Popocatépetl and Ixtaccíhuatl, which guard the eastern rim of the basin of Mexico; Nevado de Toluca at the entrance to west Mexico; and Tancítaro and the Volcán de Colima in the far west. One may often be in sight of two or three of these peaks at the same time.

South of this volcanic chain, the land falls off sharply into the Balsas depression (Photo 1), an area dominated by two enormous drainage systems, the Balsas River, which empties into the Pacific, and the slower, more tranquil Papaloapan, which winds eastward to the Gulf of Mexico. The southern highland plateau of Oaxaca is the only relatively flat land in the entire depression. The western mountains, Sierra Madre del Sur, border the Pacific Ocean in southern Michoacán, Guerrero, and Oaxaca, leaving a strip of coastal plain offering a natural corridor for movements of peoples. The narrow coastal plain, backed by a wet, hilly piedmont area, continues eastward along the Isthmus of Tehuantepec and southward through Guatemala, forming a region known as Soconusco. Behind Soconusco and past the Isthmus of Tehuantepec, the Sierra Madre de Chiapas rises boldly to prominence and continues down the Pacific coast of Guatemala, bends eastward, and crosses into northeastern Honduras.

East of this range, and also sprouting at the Isthmus, are the mountains of northern Chiapas. Presenting a high and difficult terrain, this system stretches into central Guatemala and forms the highlands of Alta Verapaz and the Sierra de Santa Cruz. There are many minor ranges and intervening depressions, but these two dominant mountain systems enclose the third highland area of Mesoamerica, the plateau where Guatemala City is located today, and border the great tectonic depression from the valley of Chiapas that extends through the Motagua Valley of central Guatemala to the Caribbean. This plateau has greatly benefited from volcanic activity, which spread ash and pumice to the Pacific Coast, preserving the richness of the soils and contributing substantially to the advantages of the environment.

Like central Mexico, the highland country of southern Mesoamerica has both suffered and prospered from its volcanic setting. Human footprints in consolidated mud near Managua, human remains buried under ash fall and pumice, and the earthquakes that shatter men's plans and dwellings attest to the risks of inhabiting this area. Yet the region provides excellent materials for building and for making tools, rich soil derived from weathering of basic volcanic ejecta, and an aesthetic setting with dramatic peaks, clear blue lakes occupying collapse pits or depressions, clear fresh air to breathe, and an invigorating climate in which to live and work. These advantages perhaps outweigh the hazards.

One block of land not yet mentioned is the low-lying limestone peninsula of Yucatán. Risen from the sea in recent geologic times, this area is an almost level shelf except for the little hills of Campeche. Indeed, Yucatán is the only flat surface of any size in the whole of Mesoamerica.

Climate and Faunal Resources

Although, for the most part, Mesoamerica lies below the Tropic of Cancer, hot, humid climates do not predominate, for altitude is equally as

Photo 1. View from Mil Cumbres toward the Balsas depression. Photographed by the author.

important as latitude. Because of the physical exaggerations of the landscape, early man was offered a wide variety of environmental choices when he ceased to follow wild game and eventually settled down to raise food crops.

In the Mesa Central, an area typical of cool, tropical highland environments, man found many intermountain basins with evergreens and deciduous oaks and pines, and open woodlands abounding in white-tailed deer and rabbits. Higher on the mountain slopes were forests of firs and white pines. Since the region was volcanic, lakes and springs were plentiful and large lakes in the basin of Mexico contained a variety of fish, reptiles, amphibians, aquatic birds, and insects that provided an easy daily food supply. The climate was cool; rainfall, though mostly restricted to June through November, was adequate to produce one crop per year. This was essentially the same environment as that offered by the highland plateau of Guatemala. The southern highland plateau of Oaxaca was slightly lower in altitude and therefore warmer.

For those preferring a tropical climate, the lowlands of the east or west coasts provided distinctive choices. The Pacific Coast was favored by early peoples. The vegetation consisted largely of tropical deciduous or semideciduous forests. The northern area from southern Nayarit to Sinaloa has a coastal plain as wide as fifty kilometers in places. Many indications of human occupancy are found along the wide natural levees and flood plains. To the east lies the escarpment of the Sierra Madre Occidental. Just north of San Blas the great Río Grande de Santiago crosses the narrow coastal plain to empty into the Pacific Ocean. This is the termination of the Lerma–Santiago river system that rises in the Toluca Valley of central Mexico and is known simply as the Lerma River as it passes through the western states to Lake Chapala. Thereafter it is called the Río Grande de Santiago, but the hydrographic system is one and the same. Of enormous importance to the inhabitants of this area, it influenced settlement patterns and facilitated travel to and from central Mexico and the west coast. South of Cabo Corrientes, the alluvial plains become narrow and the coast is rugged and mountainous. The Sierra Madre del Sur gives rise to a great many rivers that carry alluvial soil across the level coastal plain, making a shoreline of marshes, lagoons, and mangrove swamps. The Balsas River, bordering the states of Michoacán and Guerrero, is Mexico's second largest river system. Its waters served as main thoroughfares for early travelers, and in later times this same route was used by those carrying tribute to the Aztecs in their central highland capital.

Throughout its history, coastal Guerrero has provided man with food from both land and sea and excellent shelter for sea-going vessels once they reached the great delta of the Balsas River. Mangrove swamps and lagoons, common from the Isthmus of Tehuantepec to the southern borders of Mesoamerica, support abundant fish, mollusks, and varied aquatic bird life and, accordingly, were appreciated as early habitation sites.

The Pacific coastal area provided a moderate annual precipitation and a long dry season. This region was heavily populated at the time of the Spanish Conquest, and Acapulco became the center of Spanish trade with the Orient and Peru. Even today this shore boasts a greater density of population than the east coast.

The eastern seaboard of Mesoamerica is more varied in land forms since it includes the Veracruz and Tabasco coasts on the Gulf of Mexico, areas with low coastal plains; the rather unique Yucatán peninsula, which forms a special subarea within the tropical lowland environment; and the coastal strip of the Gulf of Honduras, an area of dense, evergreen rain forest, characteristically hot and humid (West, 1964). This true rain forest of the east coast contrasts sharply with the Pacific seaboard, although scattered areas of savannas and tropical deciduous woodlands can also be found here. Cultural remains are most abundant along the natural levees where the land was fertile and out of the reach of floods. The east-coast rivers from south to north notable as zones of habitation are the Aguan, Ulua, and Chamelecón in Honduras; the Motagua River in Guatemala; and the Tonalá, Mezcalapa, Grijalva, Usumacinta, and Papaloapan rivers in Mexico. In these zones are found the giant ceiba tree, the mahogany tree, the rubber tree, and a great variety of palms.

An area known as the Petén forms part of this lowland rain forest environment (Photo 2). The Petén is a modern department of Guatemala but geographically and culturally includes the southern two-thirds of Yucatán and adjacent regions. It presents a series of hilly limestone formations, numerous lakes and swamps, and a lush tropical forest that, paradoxically, has both aided the preservation and speeded the destruction of archaeological remains.

Two lowland tropical east coast areas present notable variations. The extreme northern part of Veracruz has been so altered by man that it is difficult to speculate on its original state. At the present time, it offers environments ranging from savanna grasslands to tropical deciduous forests. As on the Pacific Coast, the natural levees and river terraces of the Pánuco were favorite habitation sites.

The other special situation is that provided by the Yucatán peninsula. Although lying within a tropical lowland area, it is at present characterized by a tropical scrub vegetation. The natural environment has

Photo 2. (*Right*) Tropical forest, Petén, Guatemala. Courtesy of the University Museum, University of Pennsylvania.

Photo 3. (*Below*) Xlopah *cenote*, Dzibilchaltún, Yucatán. Courtesy of the Instituto Nacional de Antropología e Historia, Mexico.

been greatly modified by slash-and-burn agricultural methods, but it is a naturally dry area with a special hydrographic pattern based on underground water channels. The peninsula is basically a limestone plain devoid of surface streams and is made habitable by natural steep-sided pockets called *cenotes*, where rain water accumulates (Photo 3), and by natural wells called *aguadas*, which are funnel-shaped sink holes. Removed from the coast is an area of small limestone hills that lacks even these natural reservoirs.

Aside from these markedly contrasting environments of cool tropical highlands and varying tropical lowlands, there are also areas of near-desert conditions such as those near the northern frontiers of Meso-america. Even in some parts of the Mesa Central, like north and south-

13   CLIMATE AND FAUNAL RESOURCES

eastern Puebla, semiarid conditions exist, the vegetation consisting largely of a thorn scrub and cactus growth.

Thus, when man settled in Mesoamerica, he could live at an elevation of 8000 feet, at sea level, or at intermediate points. He had a wide choice of dwelling sites: alluvial plains, terraces, caves, valleys, inland basins. He could choose to live near a lake, spring, or river in areas with abundant rainfall, or he could choose a dry, semidesert climate. Lush tropical forests, savannas, deciduous forests, and barren desert-like terrain offered very different opportunities for exploitation. In some regions he could live where several ecological niches were within easy reach. These are known as microenvironments (Coe & Flannery, 1964). As we shall see, groups did not fully exploit the possibilities of all or even one niche, but perhaps utilized a small selection of plants and animals ranges of which cut across several environments.

In the cool highlands of Mexico and Guatemala, white-tailed deer and rabbit were probably the most common game animals. Bears were to be found in the northern area only. Peccaries, coyotes, bats, raccoons, and a great variety of rodents and other small mammals were typical of the entire area. Especially common in the tropical lowlands were howler, marmoset, and spider monkeys and tapirs, ocelots, jaguars, and opossums. Turtles, lizards, iguanas, and many varieties of snakes were common reptiles. Common birds included ducks, geese, swans, teals, and coots, which were often a valuable addition to the food supply. Owls lived at all elevations; vultures and birds of prey were important as scavengers. Lakes and streams as well as the two lengthy coastlines afforded abundant fish, mollusks, and crustaceans; deep shell middens attest to their importance as a basic food supply (West, 1964).

Of special significance to the Indian were the rattlesnake, which was often associated with a rain cult, and the *quetzal* bird, a native of the humid mountain cloud forests highly prized for its brilliant plumage. Eagles and fish are found as recurrent themes in art. Perhaps the most important of the symbolic animals is the jaguar, a principal motif in the first great art style, which, as we shall see, influenced others that followed.

GEOLOGISTS TELL US THAT THIS VERY IRREGULAR LAND
mass, which is responsible for the great diversity of the Mesoamerican landscape, can boast of rock formations dating back
at least as far as the Paleozoic era and possibly pre-Cambrian times.
But only the approximate contours are known for these ancient geologic
periods; the really basic outlines were laid down in the Mesozoic period,
many millions of years before man was to appear. The great volcanoes
forming the transverse volcanic axis rose during Pliocene times, causing
existing animals to migrate hurriedly to the nearest zone of safety,
probably to the eastern shores. The major climatic zones were already
differentiated, but even more violent activity was to modify the landscape and environment further in the Pleistocene or Quaternary period
(Maldonado-Koerdell, 1964).

The very earliest remains of man, bones, and tools date from the
Pleistocene period, and thus the geological events at this time are vitally
important to us. About 500,000 years ago, more volcanoes erupted ex-
plosively and violently. They dammed up the river outlets south of
highland Mexico, thus creating the great enclosed basin, the Valley of
Mexico. Two great volcanic chains were then defined: one running from
east to west in Mexico, the other running diagonally from north to south
from Chiapas to Panama. Only the peninsula of Yucatán and northeastern
Honduras have no extrusive rocks, as this area was formed by a gradual
emergence of the land from the sea.

The Pleistocene period is best known as the Ice Age; in the New
World it was marked by four major ice advances, the Nebraskan, Kansan,
Illinois, and Wisconsin, separated from each other by warmer interglacial intervals. The longest interglacial interval was the second, but
the best known is the third, known as Sangamon, which lasted approximately 100,000 years and was succeeded by the final advance of the ice
caps, the Wisconsin glaciation.

In the region of Mesoamerica at the end of the Pleistocene period, the
circulation of warm southern winds led to a greater humidity, resulting
in more rain and thus ultimately causing a recession of the mountain
glaciers. As the ice melted, rivers flowed swiftly to lower levels, carrying
along all sorts of loose material swept up on the way. Winds also helped
to erode the face of the land. Today, on the volcanoes of Popocatépetl
and Ixtaccíhuatl, one can see striated rocks and terminal and lateral
moraines, visible evidence of the presence of these ancient ice caps.

When water from the melting ice flowed down the western slopes
of these volcanoes, it found no outlet, and the inland basin of Mexico
became a veritable reservoir for water and eroded materials. This central
highland area has been more thoroughly studied than other regions, but
what happened here is probably similar to the climatic and geological
events that occurred at the time of man's appearance in other highland
areas of Mesoamerica.

2

Man Arrives and Occupies Mesoamerica

Man Enters the Scene

Physical anthropologists tell us that man first entered the New World via the Bering Straits of Alaska. There are many points on which anthropologists differ, but agreement is general that man originated in the Old World and was a fully developed species, *Homo sapiens*, when he came to the Americas. No remains of any other species of man have ever been found. It is also important to note that the highest type of primate found in the western hemisphere is the American monkey, and no one places these creatures in man's direct line of evolution. Thus, fossil evidence leads one to believe that *Homo sapiens* was the original settler of North and South America.

Man had spread over all suitable areas of habitation in the Old World by mid-Pleistocene times. Having developed a taste for the meat of big game animals, he had learned how to kill them. Where the bison, the woolly mammoth, and the tundra-loving musk-ox wandered, man followed. During the height of the Wisconsin glaciation, which was marked by two major advances of the ice separated by a relatively ice-free interval ending approximately 25,000 years ago, the water was locked up into great ice sheets, and the sea level was lowered at least three hundred feet and possibly as much as a thousand. This created the massive Berengia land bridge connecting what is now Siberia and Alaska, a thousand-mile-wide strip of land that would have permitted easy access to America from Asia (Jennings, 1968). It is interesting to note that areas of central and northwestern Alaska were never covered by the ice. When Asia and America were thus united by land, the horse and camel passed from the New World to the Old, while Old World elephants, deer, elk, and moose entered the Americas. Man too, pursuing big game, could easily have passed into the western hemisphere unawares, since climate and resources presented no change requiring adaptation.

When did man first cross over into the Americas? The event is not easily estimated chronologically, for the land bridge must have opened and closed at different times. The broadest interpretation places man's entrance into the New World no earlier than 50,000 years ago, during the latter part of the Wisconsin glaciation. However, optimum conditions would have prevailed about 20,000 years ago, when the forests had retreated owing to glaciation and the resulting tundra vegetation and animal life in open country would have been more appealing to the hunter than a forest setting. We shall see that most of the absolute dates for early man in the New World fall between 12,000 and 6000 B.C., but a few are considerably older.

The Berengia land bridge in the Bering Strait region would seem to have been the only available land route for entry into the New World, but speculations have been made regarding other possible means of entry. No scientific data support any hypothesis involving a lost continent now submerged that might have furnished such a bridge. Conceivably man could have navigated by way of the Aleutian and Komandorski Islands, but this would have required considerable skill in navigation by sea, of which we have no evidence, and is hardly the way to pursue big game animals if these were the lure.

The reader may feel that the Bering Strait entrance has been accepted largely through a process of elimination of all other explanations.

This is not entirely true, although it does remain the most feasible one. There are archaeological remains from the American side to lend support to this theory. Evidence is accumulating to show that migrations passed into North America and fanned out in the south, the most traversed route being an ice-free corridor east of the Rocky Mountains. These high plains made movement easy. Where many dry lakes exist today, water was more plentiful then. There is evidence that man reached southern Chile by 7000 B.C., and new finds from highland Peru indicate that man was present around 13,000 B.C. (MacNeish, 1970). Numerous radiocarbon dates indicate human presence around 10,000 B.C., and recent excavations at Tlapacoya in the basin of Mexico suggest that man may have lived in that region 22,000–20,000 years ago (Lorenzo, 1970). How much earlier he entered the New World is a matter of speculation. If man spread out very quickly, his very wide distribution need not necessarily imply a much greater antiquity. It is usually felt that man has inhabited the western hemisphere for at least 20,000 years, and some specialists feel justified in extending this to 40,000 years.

What we know of this early Paleo-Indian is based on fragments of skeletal remains and a great many tools made to kill and dismember big game animals and to scrape their skins. Most of these stone knives, blades, scrapers, and projectile points show a technique shared by the Levallois–Mousterian tradition of the Old World. The art of shaping a tool by chipping and flaking from both sides (termed knapping) may have originated independently in America. If so, it is remarkably similar to that of the Old World. The greater Paleo-Indian antiquity proves to be, the more likely it is that this technique was developed in the New World.

Many finds of early man have been made in both North and South America. The big game animals—camels, bison, woolly mammoths, and mastodons—became extinct at the end of the Pleistocene period as the climate changed and became too warm for them. But the presence of man-made artifacts accompanying the bones of these early grazing animals testifies to man's presence here at the same time. Many "kill" sites have been found where groups of men drove the animals over cliffs, or perhaps into swampy lake shores where their movements were restricted by the deep mire and they could be killed by projectile points, darts, and, no doubt, hurled stones.

Similar scenes were enacted over and over again throughout the Americas. Everywhere man's problem was the same—to subsist. It is beyond the scope of this book to discuss even the most important skeletal remains and artifacts dating from this period. We mention only the pertinent traces of the Paleo-Indian from the particular geographic region that was to become Mesoamerica. Nevertheless, what happened in this area is probably typical of man's development throughout the western hemisphere during the late Pleistocene period.

Undisputed evidence of the presence of the first inhabitants of Mesoamerica is of two kinds: (1) human skeletal remains, and (2) tools unquestionably fashioned by man which are often associated with the remains of extinct Pleistocene mammals. Numerous finds have probably been lost to science because of the manner in which they were recovered. Since the skeleton of a Paleo-Indian is virtually indistinguishable from that of a present-day Indian from the same region, geological and

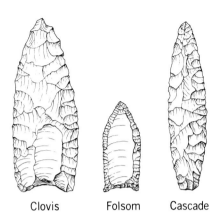

Figure 1. Early American projectile points. From *Prehistory of North America* by J. D. Jennings. Copyright © 1968 by McGraw-Hill, Inc. Used with permission of McGraw-Hill Book Company.

Clovis   Folsom   Cascade

paleontological data must usually be relied upon as the best means of authenticating the antiquity. Thus, only if a skeleton is carefully excavated and studied *in situ* in relation to the stratum in which it is found and the strata proved to be undisturbed subsequent to burial can the skeleton be accorded an antiquity coeval to that of its strata. The techniques of carbon-14 dating and fluorine analysis are the modern arbitrators of disputes, and in several cases these tests have substantiated or altered existing hypotheses. The same approach also applies to associated artifacts. Surface remains and fortuitous finds can be studied on typological grounds, but their antiquity remains strictly a matter of guesswork and opinion.

Some traces of these early hunters have been found in the present area of the United States and Canada where intensive work has been done. It is believed that the culture of the earliest Paleo-Indians was very simple. The only tools and implements used by these nomads consisted of the very crude scrapers, knives, and chopping tools that they and their ancestors had made in eastern Asia. This level of culture is sometimes called a preprojectile horizon, and it is postulated as characteristic of the very earliest migration from Asia. All authorities do not recognize this early period, but whenever man entered the New World, it is believed that he brought his current knowledge of tool making with him.

At least 20,000–10,000 years ago, these big game hunters made a great technological change in their tool production. More specialized implements have been found, among them the innovative lanceolate and fluted points. Outstanding is the fine Clovis projectile point (Figure 1), made by careful percussion and pressure flaking to form a channel or broad groove extending part way up the shaft from the base, on one or both sides. Undoubtedly derived from this is the well-known Folsom point (Figure 1), which is more refined and delicate in technique and found in a relatively restricted geographical area including eastern New Mexico, Colorado, Wyoming, and parts of adjacent states. The Clovis and related points have been found over a very large area from Alaska to Panama. The Clovis and Folsom points, together with other long lanceolate points and projectiles, make up what is called the Big Game Hunting tradition. Many of these tools have been found at kill sites near the edges of lakes and marshes where animals were butchered.

Another great North American tool complex, the Old Cordilleran tradition, probably originated in the Pacific Northwest area. A different projectile type, known as the Cascade (Figure 1), was the dominant tool. It was shaped like a willow leaf and was pointed at both ends. This point is associated with a series of unspecialized artifacts. Although there is some evidence of the Big Game Hunting tradition in Mesoamerica, the Old Cordilleran had the widest distribution in both Meso- and South America. In age, it would appear to be at least partly contemporaneous with the Big Game Hunting tradition, and probably gave rise to the Desert tradition that prevailed in Mesoamerica after 7000 B.C.

With these brief remarks on the major tool traditions that concern us here, let us examine evidence of the Paleo-Indian's occupation of Mesoamerica.

Early Man in Mesoamerica

By looking at a map of the western hemisphere, one sees immediately that to reach South America by land man must have passed through northern Mexico and squeezed through the Isthmus of Tehuantepec in order to continue his journey south. Whether this trip was made by large groups or small, it is nonetheless surprising that man left, or that we have found, so few traces of his passage.

Most of the earliest remains of man come from central highland Mexico. This area is rich in cultural remains of people from Preclassic to Aztec times, which are found in a geologic layer known as Totolzingo. It is necessary to dig down to deposits underlying this formation to find remains of more ancient occupation. To search for Paleo-Indian remains in the basin of Mexico, one may look for the Becerra formation, which is divided into upper and lower layers (De Terra, Romero, & Stewart, 1949). The Upper Becerra formation yields abundant fossils of extinct fauna dating from the upper and terminal Pleistocene. This formation is conveniently separated from the more recent Totolzingo layer by the Caliche III, or Barrilaco Caliche, a formation that effectively seals off the Pleistocene beds. Caliche III represents a severe dry period that may have contributed to the extinction or migration of many Pleistocene animals.

There is some question about how widespread this arid altithermal period was. In Oaxaca, for example, conditions may have been considerably wetter. In the Tehuacán Valley of Puebla, not much change can be seen from post-Pleistocene times to the present. It is possible that the water table was higher and, thus, that mesquite forests and some grasslands covered part of the valley, but no drastic climatic changes have been detected. The recent excavations at Tlapacoya, an ancient site in the Valley of Mexico, do not support the Becerra–Caliche–Totolzingo sequence, and its value is limited to certain localities (Lorenzo, 1970).

Human Skeletal Remains

Tepexpan man (Photo 4) presumably was interred in the Upper Becerra formation on the former northeastern shores of Lake Texcoco. The skeleton, probably that of a woman about 5 feet 2 inches tall was found face down, with the legs flexed, and is similar to that of modern Mexican Indians. There were no associated artifacts. Because of the circumstances surrounding the excavation, authorities were hesitant to accept the skeleton's Pleistocene antiquity. More recently, however, fluorine analysis bears out a date coeval with that of the Santa Isabel Ixtapan finds and other fossils of the Upper Becerra formation, roughly 8000 B.C. As a result, Tepexpan man now occupies his rightful place in the record as an early resident of Mesoamerica (Heizer & Cook, 1959). The Xico child is probably of an age comparable with Tepexpan man, as substantiated by fluorine tests. This find consists of the jaw of a human infant from Xico, a site on the southern shores of Lake Texcoco.

These are the most important human remains of the Paleo-Indian found to date (Aveleyra, 1964). Undoubtedly more will be forthcoming as interest grows in the search for early man, as dating methods are perfected, and as improved excavation techniques lessen the chances of human error.

Artifacts and Cultural Remains

Far more tools have been found than traces of man himself. Twenty-five kilometers east of Mexico City, Tlapacoya, which was an island or peninsula depending on the fluctuations of a lake, was apparently an early

Photo 4. (*Left*) Reconstruction of Tepexpan man. Courtesy of the Instituto Nacional de Antropología e Historia, Mexico.

Photo 5. (*Above*) Sacrum of extinct llama, carved to resemble the head of an animal. Tequixquiac, Mexico. Width: 7 inches. Courtesy of the Instituto Nacional de Antropología e Historia, Mexico.

living site. It has yielded some hearths and heaps of animal bones discarded by the residents. The stone artifacts from this site were made mostly of local andesite, but tools fashioned from obsidian, basalt, and quartz must have been imported, because these materials are foreign to the area. These remains are presently dated around 19,000 B.C., which, if confirmed by further research, will necessitate the modification of current theories of man's antiquity in the New World. Most other early finds, which are from Upper Becerra or Late Pleistocene formations, are therefore considered coeval with Tepexpan man.

Speculation about the existence of a preprojectile horizon is narrowed at present to two possibilities: the Diablo focus in southeastern Tamaulipas, on the northern frontier of Mesoamerica, and the rich fossil beds of Tequixquiac, just north of the old Lake Texcoco (Aveleyra, 1964). The Diablo focus consists of the oldest level of a long stratified sequence in dry caves in the present state of Tamaulipas. MacNeish, who performed the excavations, believes that these remains belong to a preprojectile horizon antedating Tepexpan man (MacNeish, 1958). No projectile points were found and the tool inventory consists of primitive pebble end-scrapers, unifacial flake scrapers with both percussion and pressure retouching, and crude bifacial tools, choppers, and ovoid blades. The case for great antiquity is based primarily on negative evidence, and the typology has been severely questioned. Supporting Mac-Neish's arguments is the fact that the Diablo focus underlies the Lerma phase stratigraphically; the latter has been dated by carbon-14 at 7000 B.C. and has yielded a tool tradition reminiscent of the Old Cordilleran.

Similarly, no projectile points are known from Tequixquiac, which promises to be a most rewarding site. It has long been known for its rich fossil bone beds of upper Pleistocene date. Of the many remains found, twenty implements are considered to be of human manufacture, including bone tools. Artifacts recovered *in situ* include a variety of end- and side-scrapers, unifacial blades with lanceolate contours retouched by pressure flaking, and bone awls. These were found in gravels and sands rich in fossil remains of mammoth, horse, bison, camel, ground sloth, and mastodon. The well-known sacrum bone of a fossil camelid, carved slightly to resemble a dog or a coyote, is also from Tequixquiac (Photo 5).

The Valsequillo reservoir, located south of the city of Puebla, may also date from this time. It is another site long known for its rich Pleistocene fossil gravels. Although large collections have come from these deposits, precise dating is lacking. Some charcoal buried by volcanic ash has yielded an astonishing carbon-14 date of 36,000 years B.C. Geologists believe that this deposit is as old as that overlying the man-made artifacts. But since the charcoal is not from the same outcrop as the tools and the date is considerably older than any others in the area, future excavations are necessary to confirm or deny the antiquity of the artifacts. A fragment of the pelvic bone of a large Pleistocene elephant bears some crude incisions or scratches that have been interpreted by some, in particular the discoverer Juan Armenta Camacho, as truly early art, representing a bison, a tapir, and mammoths. Whether or not this is pictorial art, there seems little doubt that the bone is of Pleistocene date, as are the incisions, made while the bone was in a fresh state.

The remains of two imperial mammoths (*Mammuthus imperator*) discovered at Santa Isabel Ixtapan provide undisputed evidence that these beasts were pursued by men and driven into the swampy edge of old Lake Texcoco, where they were killed and dismembered (Aveleyra, 1956; Aveleyra & Maldonado-Koerdell, 1953). A surprisingly large variety of tools was found: obsidian side-scrapers, flint blades, a fragment of a bifacial knife, three projectile points, and prismatic knives of obsidian, all of which are common in later archaeological horizons (Figure 2). The projectile points are of considerable interest, because one is a generalized knife that vaguely resembles a shouldered point called the Scottsbluff type, which is found in the Great Plains area of the United States; one is a Lerma type, a leaf-shaped projectile in the Old Cordilleran tradition; and one is a lanceolate point without a well-defined relative. The kill site setting and certain tools are in line with the Big Game Hunting tradition, but the Lerma-type point represents the Old Cordilleran tradition. This latter tradition prevailed during later times in this area.

The Lerma phase, a stratigraphic layer overlying the more controversial Diablo focus in northeastern Tamaulipas, is important for its laurel-leaf projectile points, which are similar to that just mentioned from Ixtapan. It is interesting that these points, together with other bifacial flaked tools, were found with remains of modern animals including deer but with no remains of extinct varieties. The same type of hunting culture has its counterpart in the Ajuereado complex in the Tehuacán Valley in the state of Puebla (MacNeish, 1958, 1961, 1962; MacNeish & Nelken-Temer, 1967).

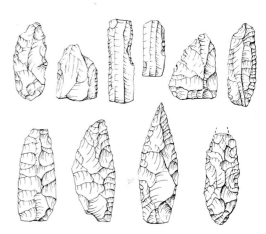

Figure 2. Tools found with Ixtapan mammoths. (From Aveleyra, 1964.)

Farther north in Tamaulipas, near the Falcon International Dam, surface finds include a Plainview and an Angostura point. These are well-known types more commonly found in the Great Plains of the United States. Specifically the Plainview point is an unfluted projectile or knife, carefully pressure flaked, with a slightly convex base, and no stem or shoulder. The Angostura is a distinctive, long, graceful lanceolate point characterized by a diagonal rippled flaking. It has no shoulders or stem but has a flat or slightly indented base. These two points together with the Scottsbluff type form part of a tool complex that followed the Folsom and Clovis. The fluting characteristic of the latter no longer is found. The Scottsbluff, Plainview, and Angostura points are thought to date from about 7000 B.C. Such isolated finds as these are relatively common, particularly on the northern frontier of Mesoamerica. Clovis-type fluted points, which should be slightly earlier than the complex just mentioned, have been reported from Baja California, Sonora, Coahuila, Chihuahua, Nuevo León, and Durango. Lake deposits in Jalisco present a geological situation similar to that of the basin of Mexico, and Pleistocene fossils abound near the lakes of Chapala, Zacoalco, and Sayula (Aveleyra, 1950).

South of central Mexico, the evidence is scanty and more questionable. Shook (1951) reports finding a fossil mylodon bone with man-made cuts or incisions from the Pasión River in Guatemala. A preceramic level at Copán, Honduras, contains charred bones and primary flakes, separated from the Preclassic Maya material by a sterile layer. From El Cauce, on the shores of Lake Managua, human and bison footprints in hardened volcanic mud have been known for a long time, but the geologists tell us that these probably do not antedate 3000 B.C.

Thus far, most of the evidence of man's occupation of Mesoamerica comes from the north and central regions. Skeletal material is admittedly very scarce, but the tool inventory is essentially similar to that of man's contemporary north of the Río Grande. Both the Big Game Hunting and Old Cordilleran traditions are represented in projectile points, and after 7000 B.C. these give way to another era in man's existence, which can best be understood as an extension of the Desert tradition in western North America and which probably developed from the Old Cordilleran and persisted in some areas into historic times.

A New Life Style

Several essential changes marked the shift to a desert way of life:

1. Hunting techniques and tools were adapted to exploit the smaller fauna that replaced the big game animals; thus, projectile points were made smaller and broader.
2. People lived in extended family groups, probably numbering no more than twenty-five to thirty individuals, who were engaged in cyclical wandering in search of food; they were not truly nomadic.
3. Few material possessions were needed; remains of basketry and milling stones predominate in the archaeological record.

What we know of Mesoamerican life during this period of incipient agriculture, which lasted approximately from 7000 to 2000 B.C., conforms very closely to this pattern, which was shared by many groups in

North America (Jennings, 1968). During these five thousand years, Meso-america gradually pulled ahead of her neighbors until by 2000 B.C. a year-round sedentary village life was possible. From this time we can begin to see the emergence of the distinctive Mesoamerican culture.

The shift from a hunting and gathering existence to a sedentary life sustained mainly by agriculture is one of the most exciting accomplishments in the history of mankind. Cultivation of plants did not, however, "produce" a sedentary way of life, for such a mode of existence could be sustained in certain regions by harvesting and collecting wild food, trapping and hunting game, or exploiting marine and freshwater environments. Indeed, it apparently took man a very long time to rely predominantly on domesticated plants. But the eventual dependence on agriculture seems to have cleared the way for a chain of events that could, and in this case did, lead to the development of a high, complex civilization. In the following chapter we shall examine the critical events that took place in the period called Incipient Agriculture and look for explanations of the processes involved in these changes.

THE ORIGINS OF NEW WORLD AGRICULTURE HAVE LONG been a subject of interest, debate, and speculation. Agreement is now general that agriculture was developed independently in the New World. The reasoning is convincing. Domestication of plants in Mesoamerica seems to have taken place as long ago as similar processes at work in the Near East, the accepted cradle of Old World civilizations. The principal New World crops, maize, squash, beans, and manioc, form an inventory differing greatly from the Old World staples of wheat, barley, and rye. Moreover, the wild ancestor of each plant was restricted to either the New or Old World, respectively. Distinctive patterns of cultivation and its accompanying technology further reinforce a belief in independent origins. This much seems clear, but in trying to answer questions of when, where, and how agriculture arose in the Americas, opinions vary.

For a very long time, little progress was made in this field. Data on primitive agriculture in Mesoamerica lagged far behind information on pottery types and ceremonial centers because visible ruins usually attract attention first. Although the importance of agricultural origins has long been acknowledged, early researchers did not know where to look or exactly what to look for. Thus, remains that could shed light on the beginnings of agriculture were generally unsought and perhaps even overlooked.

Initially there was little agreement on what crops were raised first. Some felt that root crops might have led the way to domestication because they are easy to plant and require little or nothing in the way of tools. Others felt that the answer would be found in the history of corn, *Zea mays,* because it eventually became the basic crop of much of the New World. It was felt that the beginnings of maize cultivation would coincide with the threshold of civilization, so closely is civilization linked to agriculture. In spite of this close association, we know now that maize was not responsible for agricultural beginnings, but the history of the plant is of fundamental interest. Moreover, botanical investigations of the ancestors of maize have helped to unravel the history of other domesticated plants, including squash and beans, the cultivation of which apparently preceded maize.

The Search for Corn

Many years ago Spinden (1917) suggested that the origins of agriculture most logically would be found where life was not too easy, such as in a semiarid environment. He assumed, as did many at that time, that corn was the first cultigen, and visualized this environmental hearth as a healthy setting free of dense vegetation, pests, and many diseases that would stimulate man to experiment with plants. It now seems that Spinden was correct in his choice of environment, although the rise of agri-

3

Incipient Agriculture: Man Settles Down

culture was probably due to other factors. The search for early corn has revealed much about the beginnings of New World plant domestication. Maize cultivation once was believed to have originated in South America. Attention shifted to Mexico and Central America when it was found that maize was closely related to a wild grass called *teosinte*. For many years, *teosinte* was mistakenly believed to be a wild forerunner of domesticated maize rather than simply one of its relatives. When the true relation of *teosinte* and maize was elucidated, there was even some question of whether maize was native to the New World, since no wild corn is found here today. The recovery of very ancient wild maize pollen, probably 80,000 years old, from deep borings beneath Mexico City proved that there once was a truly wild maize in the Americas. It may have become extinct as the result of continued back-crossing with domesticated varieties (Mangelsdorf, MacNeish, & Galinat, 1964).

The corn we know cannot disperse its own seeds or kernels because they are tightly enclosed within a husk. Wild corn seeds, however, must have been self-dispersing. Botanists' speculations about what form this hypothetical wild corn might have had were ended in 1948 when tiny cobs of corn were discovered at Bat Cave in New Mexico. These cobs, only two to three centimeters in length, were actually the prototype of an early race of corn known as *chapalote*; carbon-14 analysis of the cobs yielded a date of 3600 B.C. Similar cobs were found by R. H. Lister in Swallow Cave in Sonora, Mexico. These are probably of the same *chapalote* prototype, but so few were recovered that they could not be sacrificed for analysis and hence are undated.

Soon after the Bat Cave discovery, two excavations of dry caves by MacNeish in the state of Tamaulipas, Mexico, produced other remains of corn. Some of these cobs were slightly larger, later in time (2500 B.C.), and belonged to the *nal-tel* race, a variety of corn that still exists. Other cobs from southwestern Tamaulipas, dated at 2200 B.C., had some resemblance to the Bat Cave types. The search for primitive corn had started (MacNeish, 1958, 1961, 1962, 1967; Mangelsdorf *et al.*, 1967). Now one had some idea of what to look for and where. These finds directed attention to a semiarid environment and indicated that under certain conditions it was possible to recover perishable materials. Since Tamaulipas lies on the very northeastern frontier of Mesoamerica, MacNeish felt that evidence of earlier domestication might lie farther south. Accordingly, he made a survey of possible sites in Honduras and Guatemala, with disappointing results. He next excavated the Santa Marta rock shelter in Chiapas and found preceramic remains but no traces of corn prior to 1500 B.C. (MacNeish & Peterson, 1962). His efforts were finally rewarded in central highland Mexico, for in a series of dry caves in the Tehuacán Valley he found the earliest corn known.

The corn samples from Tehuacán are so well preserved that all parts of the plant were recovered including cobs. Both wild corn and twelve races of domesticated corn were found. The earliest samples date from about 5000 B.C., which is now the oldest record of corn anywhere in the world. This was either a wild maize or maize in its first stages of domestication, a form of pod corn, which, as predicted, was self-dispersing. There is definite evidence that maize was domesticated by 3000 B.C. The earliest cobs seem to be a prototype of both *chapalote* and *nal-tel*, the two ancient indigenous races of corn found previously in Bat Cave and Tamaulipas. This early corn, the cobs of which ranged from 1.9 to

2.5 centimeters in length (Figure 3), was too small to offer much nourishment as food. However, its response to cultivation is reflected immediately in a larger cob. By 2300 B.C. some hybrid corn was present, thought to be the result of a hybridization of early domesticated corn with one of its wild grass relatives, *teosinte* or *Tripsacum*. How this was accomplished is not clear, because neither of these grasses grow wild today in the Tehuacán Valley nor have they been found as yet archaeologically. Perhaps the early corn was carried outside the valley and reintroduced after hybridization. A likely area for such a development could be the region of Guerrero where these grasses grow wild. The hybridization of maize, wherever it took place, was the catalyst that initiated changes eventually altering the subsistence economy. A tremendous variability in the plant was one result, along with an increase in the size of the cob to ten centimeters in length by 100 B.C. with tougher and harder glumes and rachises. Curiously enough, in other respects, this is substantially the same corn we know today; it has maintained the same botanical characteristics for seven thousand years.

Although corn became Mesoamerica's most important domesticated plant, one surprising fact is that its cultivation was preceded by that of avocados, chili peppers, squash, and beans, which were undoubtedly more useful for food until maize was produced with enlarged cobs. Evidence on the earliest cultivated plants came to light as a result of excavations in southeastern Puebla in the Tehuacán Valley. This work was coordinated by the Tehuacán Archaeological Botanical Project (MacNeish, 1967; MacNeish & Nelken-Temer, 1967). A landmark in Mesoamerican archaeology, this project utilized the services of botanists, geologists, geographers, ethnographers, and specialists in irrigation and human and animal remains, all of whom worked with MacNeish and his team of archaeologists in a highly successful interdisciplinary study. A long stratified sequence revealed traces of cultural evolution from an early hunting-and-gathering economy to a fully agricultural village community, which in turn led to the complex ceremonial pattern achieved by Classic and Postclassic cultures.

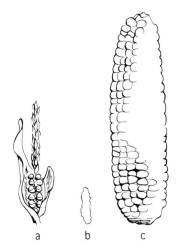

Figure 3. Comparison of wild, ancient, and modern dent corn. (a) Reconstruction of wild corn, Tehuacán Valley, ½ actual size; (b) Coxcatlán Phase corn cob, Tehuacán Valley, ½ actual size; (c) modern dent corn, ½ actual size.
(From Mangelsdorf, MacNeish, & Galinat, 1967.)

Excavations in the Tehuacán Valley

The Tehuacán Valley is located in southeastern Puebla at an elevation of 4500 feet. Long and narrow, it is almost completely surrounded by high mountains that help create the extremely hot and dry environment with rainfall limited to two months of the year. Although this is a desert environment, a close scrutiny of the immediate vicinity reveals that man actually had several microenvironments available for exploitation. The alluvial valley floor, with a spotted covering of mesquite, cactus, and spiny scrub, was adequate for primitive maize agriculture with natural rainfall. The slopes on the western side of the valley were also suitable for growing maize and tomatoes or trapping cottontails. Farther up the mountain slopes thorn and pine forests provided seasonal wild fruits as well as deer and abundant small game. Deer might also have been hunted in washed-out canyons or barrancas, which otherwise had little to offer. However, large caves in the dry vegetation zone furnished convenient shelter, and from them man could carry on his varied activities. This concentration on several ecological niches enabled man to survive seasonal variations in food supplies and therefore furnished ideal conditions for the establishment of farming communities. Botanists tell us that the beginnings of agriculture would logically have taken place in just such a setting, where dry and wet seasons were pronounced and the soil was thin and poor, giving plants such as wild corn a chance to grow without competition from perennials or lush tropical ground cover. Man's fertile rubbish heaps must have been attractive places for these weedy plants to spring up; thus man might have found food being offered to him at the very entrance to his cave.

Of the many archaeological sites located in the valley, twelve were chosen for intensive excavation. Seven were caves or rock shelters that, because of the extreme dryness, had preserved all remains of human occupation and refuse in stratified floor deposits. The other sites were located out in the open. In addition to plant and animal remains, foodstuffs, feces, and other perishables such as nets, baskets, and woven cloth were found. Utensils and tools made of stone, wood, and ceramics were also recovered. Never before had such a complete cultural record been found in the western hemisphere.

One of the most valuable results of the Tehuacán excavations was the evidence they uncovered concerning the settlement patterns and life of these early people. How much can archaeology tell us of such remote times? If harvests were seasonally restricted, plant remains may indicate a spring or fall occupation of the cave. Likewise, projectile points and scrapers indicate hunting, but if these decline in number while evidences of basketry, net making, and milling increase, we can then say that hunting was being replaced by collecting and planting. In the same way, the depth of a level and the corresponding horizontal area of occupation, together with the number of hearths, provide the basis for a population estimate. Surveys were made of floor levels both in caves and in open sites in the valleys. Three phases, El Riego, Coxcatlán, and Abejas, represent this period of incipient agriculture. They are preceded by Ajuereado, a phase during which man was still a nomadic hunter and collector.

Ajuereado (?–6500 B.C.)

Nomadic microbands engaged in hunting, collecting, and trapping moved their camps several times a year. Now-extinct species of horses and antelope were hunted, but small game—rabbits, gophers, rats, turtles, and birds—provided most of their meat. The enormous quantity of rabbit bones suggests communal drives. Tools include chipped flint knives and projectile points, choppers, scrapers, and crude prismatic blades. There are no ground stones or evidences of weaving, burials, or agriculture.

El Riego (6500–4800 B.C.)

Microbands (four to eight people each) occupied seasonal camps, but joined others in the spring to form temporary macrobands, and thus the population increased over the former Ajuereado hunters and collectors. MacNeish (1967) suggests that these people may have been organized into patrilineal bands and believes there may have been shamans who, as parttime religious practitioners, were heeded in matters of ritual and ceremony. These people subsisted primarily on plant gathering and game hunting. Deer had replaced the earlier horses and antelopes, and cottontail rabbits had become more numerous than jackrabbits. The earliest evidence of agriculture is found in this phase. Chili peppers and avocados were probably the first domesticated plants, followed by squash (*Cucurbita mixta*) toward the end of this period. Remains of amaranth (*Amaranthaceae*), a fast-growing bushy weed, well known for its brilliant red foliage, have been found, but this plant may have been collected in its wild form rather than cultivated. Although greatly in demand at later times for ceremonial and ritual uses, amaranth was utilized by the El Riego peoples for the food value of its black shiny seeds. Other important food plants were wild corn (*Zea mays*) and pumpkins. Cotton may have been domesticated but the evidence is questionable. Flint knapping continued, but the most important innovation in tools was the manufacture of ground-stone and pecked-stone implements —mortars, pestles, and milling stones. The first evidence of weaving and woodworking occurred during this phase.

One of the amazing discoveries at El Riego was evidence of ritual burials, offerings, and cremation or human sacrifice. The burials of two children were found in pits dug into a refuse layer. The head of one had been severed from the body, placed in a basket with a string of beads, covered by another basket, and buried near the body, which was carefully wrapped in a blanket and net. After the pit had been partially filled, another headless body, flexed and wrapped, was also buried in it, accompanied by various baskets. Its skull, which also had been separated from the body, was found in a basket, but this skull had been roasted, the occiput smashed, and the surface scraped clean. Another instance, the multiple burial of a man, woman, and child, makes one wonder whether they all died a natural death at precisely the same moment!

Coxcatlán (4800–3500 B.C.)

The macrobands had become semisedentary, perhaps splitting into microband camps only in the dry season, the most difficult time for survival. The occupation sites are fewer but larger, which leads to speculation about changes in the subsistence economy. Although still largely collectors and hunters, agriculture advanced significantly; the bottle gourd, squash (*Cucurbita moschata*),. and the common bean (*Phaseolus vulgaris*) were added to the group of cultigens. Wild corn is common and the first cultivated cobs appeared, followed toward the end of the period by white and black *sapotes* (*Casimiroa edulis* and *Diospyros digyna*) that produced an edible fruit. These plants are not native to the valley; their presence indicates that they had been brought in from a wetter region and must have been carefully watered. Tool changes were slight, but a new tanged projectile point, more delicate blades, and new scrapers and choppers were developed during this period. True *metates* and *manos* are found in remains of this phase.

Abejas (3500–2300 B.C.)

Some outstanding changes in settlement patterns occurred in this period. Some macroband settlements were located along river terraces, where groups of pit houses have been found. These may have been occupied year round. Caves were still used by hunting macrobands in the dry season. Corn definitely had been cultivated by this time and two new domesticated beans appeared, the jack and tepary beans (*Canavalia* sp. and *Phaseolus acutifolius*). The presence of the latter at Tehuacán at this time is of particular interest since it antedates its previous earliest known distribution in the western Mexican Sonoran desert region by four thousand years. Another possible domesticate was the pumpkin (*Cucurbita pepo*). Cotton also was widely used. Remains of dogs have been found, and although it is generally believed that dogs followed man to the New World across the Bering Strait from Siberia, these remains are the earliest found in Mesoamerica. Dogs soon became a favorite food.

The older techniques of tool manufacture were continued; new additions included a long prismatic obsidian blade, which became a favorite knife, stone bowls, and oval *metates*.

The hunting of large animals such as deer, pumas, and peccaries gradually gave way to trapping or collecting smaller game animals like rodents, foxes, skunks, turtles, lizards, and birds. This trend can be observed in the decline in arrow points, projectile points, and *atlatl* in favor of the slip noose, snares, and nets.

Through interpretation of the remains at El Riego, Coxcatlán, and Abejas, a gradual transition toward sedentary life can be seen. The subsequent phases in the Tehuacán Valley series fall easily into the Preclassic way of life, for which there is abundant material from many sites.

The Tamaulipas Remains

Although this region has provided the most complete information about the beginnings of farming life, there is promise of much more from other areas, for this was not the only scene of plant experimentation. The Infiernillo complex of southwestern Tamaulipas, an earlier excavation by MacNeish, is known from similarly well-preserved remains from dry caves in arid mesquite desert scarred by deep canyons. This site is contemporary with El Riego at Tehuacán; in both regions the people were primarily meat eaters during the early phases. Projectile points, flake choppers, and scrapers were recovered along with baskets, net bags, and twilled and plaited mats (MacNeish, 1958).

Wood seems to have been a more important medium than skin. It was used for making fire tongs and fire drills. Sticks were peeled and whittled to desired shapes and served various purposes in traps, snares, rods, and *atlatls*. Darts were the most prominent weapon.

Fibers from the yucca and *agave* plants provided the material from which the bags and mats were made. The fibers were softened and twisted into strings and woven into a great variety of these articles. Mats are so common and present such diverse patterns that "mat maker" suggests itself as a suitable designation for this horizon. The abundant bag and net containers provided means of carrying and storing wild foodstuffs such as nuts, seeds, and fruits. The gourd, of course, was an excellent receptacle. By comparison, bone and antler tools are relatively scarce, but a few were fashioned into needles, punches, and awls.

The foods are particularly interesting as compared with those of Tehuacán. Among the wild plants utilized were *agave*, *opuntia*, and the runner bean (*Phaseolus coccineus*), while domesticates included the bottle gourd (*Lagenaria siceraria*), chili pepper (*Capsicum annuum* or *Capsicum frutescens*), and possibly the pumpkin (*Cucurbita pepo*).

In succeeding phases of these dry-cave deposits in the mountains of northeastern and southwestern Tamaulipas, a greater variety of tools has been found, and stone mortars and *manos* appear in the remains.

Domesticated plants definitely include the pumpkin and red and yellow beans (*Phaseolus vulgaris*). Maize does not appear until after 3000 B.C., and thereafter the percentage of domesticated plants greatly increases.

Evidence from Southern Mexico

Also belonging to this incipient agricultural period are the remains from caves and rock shelters near Mitla in the state of Oaxaca. The oldest remains show that deer and cottontail rabbits were hunted. The tools include flint projectile points and the usual assortment of choppers, scrapers, and knives. These remains correspond to the El Riego and Coxcatlán phases of Tehuacán. The Guilá Naquitz Cave (7840–6910 B.C.) has preserved dried remains of acorns, maguey (*agave*), pricky pear, and organ cactus fruits, while toward the end of the period squash seeds and small black beans mark the initiation of agriculture. The food remains found at another dry cave, Cueva Blanca (3295 B.C.), roughly parallel those from the Coxcatlán phase. Pollen analysis suggests that the Oaxaca region was considerably wetter and more humid about this time than it is today (Lindsay, 1968).

In the state of Chiapas, the Santa Marta rock shelter near Ocozocautla has yielded preceramic remains with estimated dates of 7000–5360 B.C. These remains underlie Preclassic deposits from the cave floors (MacNeish & Peterson, 1962). The tool inventory of points, knives, and scrapers is similar to the Tamaulipas complex, but no maize or maize pollen occurs prior to the Preclassic horizon. We have found no evidence of the beginnings of agriculture here; these people seem to have eaten mostly wild foods. A nearby rock shelter at Comitán likewise has yielded preceramic tools but no plant remains, while on the Pacific Coast at Islona de Chantuto, the lower levels indicate that many shellfish were collected.

A similar pattern of life is reflected at El Viejón in central Veracruz, where preceramic remains have been found in fossil sand dunes, and by early remains from coastal Guerrero near Acapulco, where shellfish and fish were abundant. Again, mortars, *metates*, and *manos* are absent.

Life during Semisedentary Days

We can begin to distinguish certain definite trends in this transitional period. Even before the large Pleistocene animals were extinct, man was hunting small game, trapping, and collecting. It is in the highland regions of semiarid environments where evidence has been found of the beginnings of plant domestication. Although the dryness of the caves has made excellent preservation possible, something not to be expected in lowland regions, it is nevertheless true that the latter have not produced stone artifacts associated with agriculture. The adaptive process in the lowlands was characterized by collecting wild foods, hunting, and, where possible, exploiting the sea.

The early Tehuacán material and that from the Tamaulipas caves furnish the best evidence of plant domestication. It may well be that these areas were actual centers of origin for some cultigens, but they were not the only ones. As we learn more of early agriculture, it becomes apparent that there were multiple origins of New World plant domestication, and initial steps must have been in progress in many regions that interacted and stimulated each other. The dependence of lowland coastal peoples on food gathered from the sea as well as on hunting and collecting food on land reminds us that the steps toward a sedentary agriculture-based economy were not the same in every region; rather, each group developed a subsistence pattern reflecting the food available in each particular ecological niche.

Attention has been called to the similarity of this seminomadic life to that of the Desert tradition, characteristic of the Great Basin Indians who inhabited the western United States in the area of Nevada, parts of Utah, and Southern California. The semiarid environment, the tool complex including *atlatl*, a seasonal occupation of camps, and milling stones and basketry are features common to both. The Desert tradition adequately describes life in highland Mesoamerica until about 5000 B.C. After that, distinctive artifacts, along with the domestication of plants, begin to draw Mesoamerica into a unique cultural pattern.

By 2300 B.C. the major domesticated plants had probably spread throughout the highland regions of Mesoamerica. It is interesting to note that squash, avocado, chili peppers, and amaranth, followed by corn, were the first domesticates in the Tehuacán sequence, while pumpkins, bottle gourds, beans, and chili peppers preceded corn in the north. Some of these plants were probably imports to both areas. The domestication of plants was a slow unconscious process, at first merely supplementing the diet of the hunter and collector but gradually dominating the subsistence economy. There was no sudden or rapid progress, no "revolution." This transition seems to have required about 5000 years.

The adaptive processes involved in the transition from hunting and gathering to full dependence on agriculture have been the subject of much thought recently. Earlier searches for origins of events and "things" such as maize agriculture and pottery will always motivate archaeologists, but at present there is equal interest in attempting to explain cultural process. As a leader in this school of thought, Flannery (1968b) emphasizes the greater importance of studying the mechanisms of change and resulting counteractions. Seen in this light, the early Mesoamericans were not fumbling about to get through each day, but were astute, clever people who had learned how to extract a living from a very difficult environment. They lived on such foods as cactus fruits, maguey, a variety of wild plants, and deer and small animals, some of which were exploited seasonally. Other resources were continually available and, in order not to threaten any wild species, a definite pattern of utilization was employed to avoid upsetting the ecological equilibrium (Flannery, 1968b).

For example, the sap of the maguey plant may have been utilized in some form as a drink as it is today in preparing *pulque, tequila,* and *mezcal,* but there is also evidence that the plant was exploited for food. Ample remains of masticated cud or "quid" of the maguey have been found in the caves. The maguey must be roasted from twenty-four to seventy-two hours to make it edible. Not only did these Indians know how to prepare it as food, but also harvested the plant precisely at the time it began to die, when it was sweetest. This system of exploitation did not threaten the existing plant supply, but served to weed out the dying plants. Thus, collecting and hunting were carried out according to a planned schedule based on the availability of food resources.

As long as a group adhered to a pattern proven to be efficient, there was little inducement or pressure for change. Eventually, however, some genetic changes, perhaps very minor, took place in one or two species of plants useful to man. These deviations, insignificant and accidental as they may have been, nevertheless set in motion a whole series of events that eventually altered the entire ecosystem. Indeed, in the case of maize and bean cultivation, an excellent combination of starch and protein, as agriculture was intensified through weeding, back-crossing, and further genetic changes, this new way of obtaining food increased in importance at the expense of others. Planting and harvesting patterns would logically have led to grouping of macrobands and reinforcement of the sedentary village way of life. The archaeological record shows increasing percentages of cultigens in the diets of these incipient farmers and corresponding decreases in the utilization of wild foodstuffs. As each region, including the lowlands, incorporated agriculture into its local economy new techniques of exploitation were developed. These in turn permitted man to farm new lands, produce a surplus, and become involved in all the complexities of a civilization.

Probably as early as 2000 B.C. in some areas, and certainly by 1500 B.C. in most, farming villages were common. One of the most fascinating phases in the development of Mesoamerica, the Preclassic period, in which the basic cultural pattern was formed, was about to begin.

T HE SPAN OF TIME FROM APPROXIMATELY 2000 B.C. TO A.D. 300 is known as the Preclassic or Formative period. During this time the basic patterns of Mesoamerican civilization were formulated, patterns that were to lead directly to the great Classic civilizations after A.D. 300. Thus, the more we learn of Preclassic peoples, the closer we are to understanding the forces and events that created a unique high civilization in this part of the New World.

A number of cultural characteristics of Mesoamerica already have been pointed out. Nearly all made their appearance prior to A.D. 300. That is to say, the characteristic technology, architecture, ceremonialism, specialization of arts and crafts, social differentiation, and hieroglyphic writing and calendrics were initiated during this period. Agriculture was based on a variety of cultigens. Knowledge of irrigation and water control increased. Trade and commercial relationships were established. Two basic features remain to be added at a much later date: the knowledge of metallurgy and a fanatic dedication to warfare.

What happened, then, in these remarkable 2300 years to transform the Mesoamerican incipient farmer into a highly specialized, sophisticated agriculturist approaching the complications of urban life? Several factors were of fundamental importance: continual improvements in agricultural techniques, the addition of new cultigens, an increased knowlege of crop control, and an increase in productivity of plants by back-crossing. Hunting, gathering, and fishing still formed an important part of the economy, but gradually they came to occupy a position second to farming. Life in Mesoamerica was characterized by scattered village communities differing in climate, altitude, and type of ecological niche but sharing new techniques of plant control.

The most widely employed method of farming was slash-and-burn, or *milpa,* agriculture, in which trees were laboriously felled, the stumps burned, and the land painstakingly cleared. Planting was accomplished by pushing the fire-hardened end of a simple digging stick, or *coa,* into the soil. *Milpa* farming could be done in the same plot of earth for one or two years, but afterward the clearings had to be allowed to revert back to forest for several years to revitalize the soil. Thus, each family had to open up new *milpa* land at frequent intervals. If they were entirely dependent on maize agriculture, it follows that they would have to move about in search of more land to keep up production. The conditions imposed by slash-and-burn agriculture formed an ever-present problem that had to be taken into account for any community planning, and every archaeologist must allow for the effects of this system when attempting to reconstruct life at this time. Variations of slash-and-burn agriculture included fallowing systems in which only certain sections were planted, alternating with others left idle. This is known in Mesoamerica as *tlacolol* (Sanders & Price, 1968) and was practiced over large areas of the highlands. There is great divergence of opinion as to the size of population

4
_____

Mesoamerica Identifies Itself: The Preclassic Period

these systems of agriculture could support on a permanent basis. To make any meaningful population estimates based on this kind of information, we would need to know what races of maize were available, how many crops were produced per year, and what other potential food sources were available. If the Preclassic community was not wholly dependent on slash-and-burn agriculture, that is, if it had sufficient alternative food resources, then anthropologists' traditional belief in the necessity of periodic village transfers may be erroneous. As we shall see, villagers were not restricted to maize, and in some areas may have cultivated manioc, but in any case they exploited their local environments for a great variety of other foodstuffs.

In some areas, sedentary life was possible even before agriculture was known. This was especially true for the lowland settlements in Mesoamerica. As we have seen previously, people in these areas could exploit tropical forests, tidewater rivers, and lagoons and estuaries, all of which provided plant and animal resources that made sedentary life possible at a very early date. Along the Pacific, and Gulf coasts of Veracruz and Tabasco, great natural food resources of many varying microenvironments made a seminomadic life or seasonal occupation unnecessary. Thus, knowledge of maize cultivation, which came to the coasts from the semiarid highland regions such as Tehuacán in the form of a primitive pod corn of the *nal-tel–chapalote* complex, effected no immediate great change in coastal settlements. Maize was easily cultivated on the alluvial flats without causing any dislocation in an already thriving economy based on collecting and fishing (Coe & Flannery, 1967).

The appearance of pottery, weaving, and stone grinding at this time parallels developments in Neolithic settlements in the Near East during the fifth and sixth millenium B.C. Many general similarities between Mesoamerica at this time and Old World Neolithic cultures can be found. Notable differences lie in the particular food plants brought under cultivation and the presence of wild sheep, goats, cattle, and pigs in southwestern Asia, but these are specifics. The processes were comparable.

The construction of planned religious centers, which was initiated during this period, is evidence of further important changes. A sizable labor force was needed, suggesting a considerable increase in population. It also means that by this time not every man was needed as a full-time agriculturist. Farmers must have constituted the bulk of the population, but there must have been a sufficient agricultural surplus to support those engaged in religious functions, civic duties, and craft specialization. Although we know of no great concentrations of population at this time, village residents might have made pilgrimages to religious centers that represented a unifying factor in their lives. In addition to its religious function, the center could also have served as a meeting place for exchange of goods and gossip, gradually formalizing the activity into the typical market system known today, which fulfills both economic and social needs. A jungle rendezvous or marketplace leaves no such obvious traces as a temple-pyramid, but inferences can be made and tested archaeologically. We are impressed today by the size and planning of ceremonial centers, which reflect the power wielded by religious and political leaders and the unwavering devotion of the people. Perhaps the farmers' participation was greater than is often im-

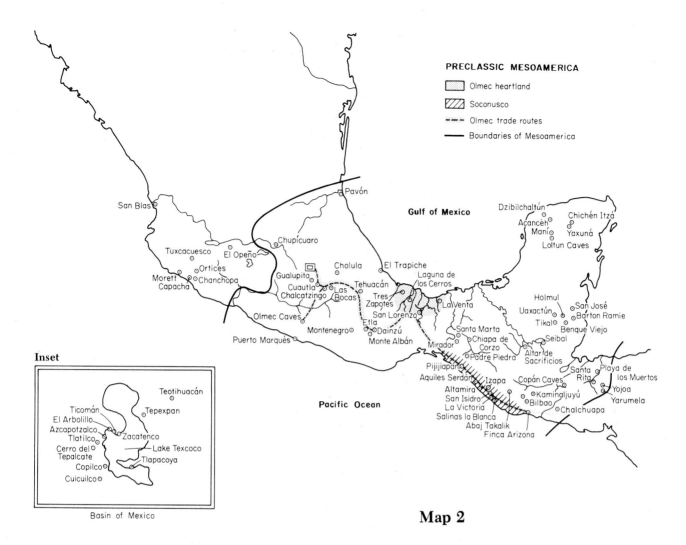

PRECLASSIC MESOAMERICA

- Olmec heartland
- Soconusco
- Olmec trade routes
- Boundaries of Mesoamerica

Map 2

plied. The ceremonial center further signifies a shift in attitude. The scattered villages no longer looked only to themselves; although the clusters of villages may still have been widely separated, they came to share a common religious and political center occupying a separate, specific, awe-inspiring place. In many areas these ritual centers did not appear until the very end of the Preclassic or the beginning of the Classic period. On the other hand, they emerged in some lowland regions around 1000 B.C.

It is helpful to think of Preclassic remains in terms of three, and in some cases four, phases of development. In the early phase man lived in settled villages and demonstrated his ability to maintain a sedentary life based on agriculture. The appearance of pottery and the very first religious centers also belong to this phase. The middle phase was rich in fine pottery, ceremonial objects, and well-stocked burials and saw the spread of mound building. The late phase was marked by an increasing amount of ceremonial architecture and greater complexity of material goods. In some areas an additional, transitional phase is justified, the Protoclassic, in which a blending with Classic period features is apparent. This term is applied to certain regions that developed more rapidly than others.

Chart 1.   Preclassic Chronology

	WEST MEXICO	GUERRERO	MORELOS	BASIN OF MEXICO	PUEBLA	OAXACA
A.D. 100	Chanchopa–Ortices Tuxcacuesco Early Ixtlán			Teotihuacán II (Miccaotli) Teotihuacán I (Tzacualli)	Early Palo Blanco	
A.D. 1	Shaft tombs of Colima, Nayarit, and Jalisco Chupícuaro, Guanajuato		Cerro Chacaltepec II	Ticomán Cuicuilco V (Patlachique) Cuicuilco IV (Tezoyuca) Cuicuilco III	Late Santa María	Monte Albán II
400 B.C.	San Blas, Nayarit	Iguala sites	Cerro Chacaltepec I	Zacatenco Atoto– Cuauhtepec Cuicuilco II Cuicuilco I Totolica– La Pastora Iglesia– El Arbolillo	Early Santa María	Monte Albán I Guadalupe
900 B.C.	Capacha, Colima (?)	Olmec cave paintings	San Pablo La Juana– Chalcatzingo	Ixtapaluca	Late Ajalpan Las Bocas	San José Mogote
1500 B.C.				Tlalpan (?)	Early Ajalpan	
2000 B.C.	Matanchén complex, Nayarit (?)	Puerto Marqués			Purrón	
2300 B.C.						

Although archaeologists are in the habit of thinking in terms of Early, Middle, and Late Preclassic, the division between phases may be meaningless in some cases but perfectly valid in others. The discussion will proceed along chronological lines, but the reader may want to consult Chart 1 often to place the material in its proper perspective.

The Earliest Sites

The very earliest material (2300–1500 B.C.) is provided by the Purrón phase in the Tehuacán Valley sequence and by sites in coastal Guerrero (MacNeish, 1961, 1962; Brush, 1969). Settled villages were well established by this time at Tehuacán, and a new hybrid maize had been added to the growing list of cultigens. The outstanding new innovation was

HUASTECA	SOUTHERN VERACRUZ	CENTRAL CHIAPAS	SOCONUSCO	HIGHLAND MAYA	LOWLAND MAYA
	Cerro de las Mesas II–Tres Zapotes II	Chiapa VII (Istmo)	Izapa	Santa Clara	Matzanel
El Prisco Chila	Cerro de las Mesas I–Tres Zapotes I	Chiapa VI (Horcones) Chiapa V (Guanacaste)	E a r l y I z a p a Crucero	Miraflores–Arenal	Chicanel
Aguilar Ponce	Palangana L a V e n t a Nacaste	Chiapa IV (Francesa) Chiapa III (Escalera) Chiapa II (Dili)	Conchas II Conchas I	Providencia–Majadas Las Charcas B	Mamom Xe
Pavón	San Lorenzo B San Lorenzo A Chicharras Bajío Ojochí	Chiapa I (Cotorra)	Jocotal Cuadros Ocós	Las Charcas A Arévalo	
			Barra		

pottery, the earliest on record for Mesoamerica. The presence of pottery indicates that man had already learned to select a clay, dampen it, add "something" to it, and fire it. This "something" is called a temper, which may consist of sand, powdered shell, or even ground-up bits of pottery. Its addition to the clay strengthens it and also prevents shrinkage in the drying process. The Purrón pottery, known from two cave occupations, has a coarse, gravel-like temper and is crude and crumbly, but its production nevertheless represents a major achievement. The two dominant Purrón vessel forms are the *tecomate* (see Figure 5m) and the flat-bottomed bowl with low, flaring sides. MacNeish (1961, 1962) draws attention to the fact that these two shapes are similar to stone vessel forms of the previous Abejas phase. Could one origin of pottery lie in a desire to duplicate in a lighter material a shape already known in stone?

Pottery very similar to Purrón and of equal antiquity has been found at Puerto Marqués, a site near Acapulco on the Pacific Coast (Brush, 1969). Here too *tecomates* are believed to be the dominant form, but the distinguishing ceramic feature common to both Tehuacán and Puerto Marqués is the pitted secondary surface on the shards, giving rise to the term "Pox pottery." Figurine fragments, both hollow and solid, make their appearance shortly after. Some of these can already be described as Olmecoid in style. As yet this early period is very imperfectly known, but coastal areas of Guerrero and Oaxaca can be expected to yield much more information in the near future. With the possible exception of early pottery at Tlapacoya in the basin of Mexico, the only other material that may be of comparable antiquity is the Lake Yojoa pottery in northwestern Honduras (Strong, Kidder, & Paul, 1938). Here, a simple monochrome horizon was uncovered that has yielded crude stone tools and figurines and tetrapod pottery with no incising and a little paint.

By 2000 B.C. pottery making was firmly established in Mesoamerica, but except for MacNeish's suggestion that earlier stone vessels may have inspired a ceramic craft, there is no evidence of its beginnings. Mesoamerica is not unusual in this regard, for nowhere in the world have the initial steps in pottery making been preserved. It is entirely possible that the invention was made at numerous times and places. In the case of Mesoamerica, the idea of making pottery could have come from cultures farther south, where between 3000 B.C. and 2100 B.C. potters at Valdivia in Ecuador and Puerto Hormiga in Colombia were already turning out ceramics.

Lowland Cultures: Early Leadership

Although the domestication of maize probably took place in the semiarid uplands, and pottery at Tehuacán is as ancient as any yet discovered, the most advanced cultural developments during the long Preclassic period took place in the lowland region of southern Veracruz and western Tabasco, an area we call the Olmec heartland. Earlier remains, however, precede the remarkable Olmec civilization and are found in adjacent lowland regions of the Isthmus of Tehuantepec and the Pacific coastal area of Guatemala known as Soconusco. It is here, then, that we will begin to trace Preclassic developments, and it is here too that excavations suggest the idea of early contact with South America.

Soconusco and Chiapas

Excavations at Altamira on the Pacific coast of Chiapas near the Guatemalan border have led to an examination of the possibility of root-crop agriculture. Altamira, in the geographic province of Soconusco, is located on the flat, hot, relatively dry coast and has a backdrop of tall rain forest. It is an area where small-scale flood-plain farming could have been practiced with ease. Marine life also was available but apparently was never exploited (Green & Lowe, 1967).

One particular mound yielded pottery and a great abundance of obsidian chips, but none of the prismatic obsidian blades so characteristic of Mesoamerican cultures after 900 B.C. Known as the Barra phase, this oldest material has been tentatively dated at 1600 B.C. The pottery forms could have been inspired by squash or gourds. Certain *tecomates* and open bowl types have counterparts among the pottery and stone bowls from the Machalilla phase at Valdivia, Ecuador. The Barra people

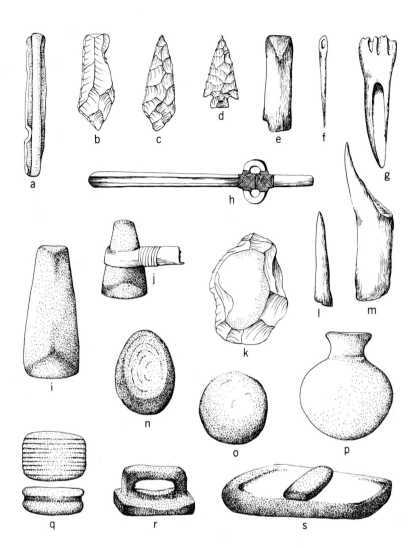

Figure 4. Man's tools.
(a) obsidian blade; (b) burin; (c) knife;
(d) projectile point; (e) bone polisher;
(f) needle; (g) bone auger; (h) *atlatl*;
(i) chisel; (j) hafted axe; (k) scraper;
(l) bone stone-flaker; (m) bone per-
forator; (n) hammer stone; (o) stone
ball; (p) pottery *olla*, (q) stone bark-
beater; (r) stone polisher; (s) *metate*
and *mano*. (Adapted from Piña Chán,
1955.)

show no indications of having exploited their fish or shellfish, nor were
they maize farmers, for none of their stone tools could be used for grinding corn. On the other hand, abundant small obsidian flakes were concentrated in habitation refuse; these flakes might have served as blades
in manioc graters, logically ending up in the household dump. Obsidian
chips identical to those reported from Altamira are also found in the
oldest phase at nearby Aquiles Serdán, along with stone vessels, mortars, pottery, and a great variety of small animal remains dominated by
iguana.

The possibility of manioc cultivation is a stimulating one and would
explain how settled communities such as these could have sustained
themselves without relying on maize, fishing, or shell gathering. Although manioc is usually considered to have originated in the tropical
forest areas of South America, botanists tell us that the Central American
tropics are an equally likely source (see discussion in Green & Lowe,
1967).

Both the Barra phase and succeeding Ocós phase at Altamira reflect
this economy, but thereafter the abundant obsidian flakes sharply decline and true *metates* (Figure 4s), announcing maize agriculture, appear
around 1100 B.C. There may have been two basic economic systems,
one based on root-crop agriculture or manioc cultivation and the other

on maize. We do not yet know how extensive manioc cultivation may have been, if indeed it did exist in Mesoamerica at this time. Assuming for the moment that both manioc and maize were known in the lowlands, the question arises of whether they were always mutually exclusive, as appears to have been the case at Altamira. Speculation is our only recourse at present, for root crops leave little surviving evidence in the hot tropical forest environment. There are some indications that manioc cultivation reached Tamaulipas by 1000 B.C., probably via the coastal lowlands, but not until 400 B.C. is there any trace of the plant at highland Tehuacán (MacNeish, 1967). In both these areas maize had been farmed for many years. At Tehuacán, *manos* and *metates* were in use as early as 4000 B.C., and they appeared in the southern Veracruz lowlands by 1400 B.C. Thereafter they were generally very widespread throughout all Preclassic settlements. The history of manioc cultivation is still unclear.

Not far east of Altamira, just over the border in Guatemala on the hot Pacific Coast, is the related site of La Victoria. It lies on a narrow strip of coastal plain of savannas crossed by sluggish rivers, creating an alluvial zone. Inland lies an elevated sloping region or piedmont with a luxuriant rain forest. This coastal site, located between two rivers three kilometers north of the fishing village of Ocós, furnishes a good example of an early Preclassic village that, in contrast to Altamira, did exploit its rich coastal environment (M. D. Coe, 1961). Such foods as clams, oysters, turtles, crabs, iguanas, and a variety of fish were supplied by the brackish water estuary system, while maize was cultivated in the alluvial flats. Maize was probably first traded down from the central Mexican highlands prior to 2000 B.C. in the form of a primitive pod corn, and adopted by the lowlanders without upsetting their already existing economic

Figure 5. Preclassic period vessel forms.

(a) simple bowl, La Venta; (b) flat-bottomed bowl with flaring walls, La Venta; (c) black-brown bowl with flat rim, Miraflores, Kaminaljuyú; (d) rim-flanged bowl, Chicanel; (e) "grater bowl" with double-line break, Tlapacoya; (f) black-ware composite silhouette, Zacatenco; (g) black ware, composite silhouette, Zacatenco; (h) basal-flange grey ware, Monte Albán I; (i) thin black ware, Zacatenco; (j) deep bowl, Tlatilco; (k) deep bowl, excised decoration, Tlatilco; (l) black-brown, fine-line incised ware, Miraflores, Kaminaljuyú; (m) *tecomate*, Tehuacán Valley; (n) incised *tecomate*, Tlatilco; (o) rocker-stamped *tecomate*, Tlatilco; (p) fine red incised tripod, Miraflores, Kaminaljuyú; (q) composite silhouette tripod, Zacatenco; (r) tripod bowl, Ticomán; (s) *tecomate* tripod, Ocós, La Victoria; (t) marble tripod bowl, Miraflores, Kaminaljuyú; (u) grey-ware tripod bowl, Monte Albán I; (v) composite silhouette tripod, Ticomán; (w) grey-ware tripod bowl, Monte Albán I; (x) marble vessel, flanged tripod, Miraflores, Kaminaljuyú; (y) tetrapod, mammiform-shaped supports, incised, Holmul I; (z) shoe-shaped vessel, Monte Albán; (aa) spouted tray, Tlatilco; (bb) burner bowl with three inner horns, central vent, Chiapa de Corzo; (cc) gadrooned bottle, Tlatilco; (dd) reconstructed bottle, La Venta; (ee) grey-ware vessel with spout, Monte Albán II; (ff) black-brown grooved stirrup-spout bottle, Tlatilco; (gg) incense burner, Las Charcas type.

(From the following sources: a, b, dd, Drucker, 1952; c, t, x, Shook & Kidder, 1952; d, Smith & Gifford, 1965; e, Weaver, 1967; f, g, i, q, Vaillant, 1930; h, u, w, z, ee, Caso & Bernal, 1965; j, k, n, cc, ff, Porter, 1953; l, p, gg, Rands & Smith, 1965; m, MacNeish, 1962; o, aa, Piña Chán, 1955; r, v, Vaillant, 1931; s, M. D. Coe, 1966; y, Marquina, 1951; bb, Lowe & Mason, 1965.)

a   b   c   d

f   g   h   i   e

j   k   l   m   n   o

p   q   r   s   t

u   v   w   x

y   z   aa   bb

cc   dd   ee   ff   gg

pattern. The earliest phase at La Victoria, dating back to 1400 B.C., is called Ocós; at this time houses were being built on low platforms of earth as a flood precaution. Construction was simple: poles were covered by mud and whitewashed. It is believed that the population density was low, and there is nothing to indicate deliberate village planning. Because this coastal region was ideally suited for permanent villages owing to the food resources of its lagoon–estuary system and alluvial farming, the sheer number of villages per square kilometer in this area may well have exceeded that of the Tehuacán valley in the contemporary Ajalpan phase.

Ocós shared early vessel forms with Barra, but it offers some surprising differences. The quality of the pottery is very fine, negating any suggestion of an experimental beginning. These were skilled ceramicists who produced cord-marked pottery, a decoration rare in Mesoamerica but more common in the Old World and northern North America. This ware was decorated by wrapping a fine cord around a paddle and pressing it against the unfired clay vessel, leaving a characteristic imprint. Another most unusual find at Ocós is a pottery decorated with thin stripes of iridescent paint, which give an almost metallic luster to the finish. Identical shards of comparable age have been found in Ecuador, leading to speculation of intercontinental travel at this time, possibly by sea (M. D. Coe, 1961; Meggers, Evans, & Estrada, 1965). There is increasing evidence of early contacts between the two continents. For example, Ocós rocker-stamped pottery, both plain and dentate, has been found at many other contemporary sites in Mesoamerica, as well as in the Andean region. Rocker stamping is a particular type of incising made by "walking" a sharp edge (a shell?) back and forth over the soft clay pot before firing, which produces a curved zigzag design (see Figure 5o; Plate 4k). If the edge is notched, it then becomes a dotted zigzag or dentate rocker stamping.

Across the river at the neighboring site of Salinas La Blanca, two successive Early Preclassic phases, Cuadros and Jocotal, follow Ocós (Coe & Flannery, 1967). A definite increase in population is indicated by deep refuse deposits and extensive occupation of wide mounds. All Cuadros and Jocotal sites are located toward the backwaters of estuaries where villagers could travel by canoe but at the same time could be within walking distance of the mixed tropical forest lands. Vessel forms are essentially the same as Ocós, predominantly *tecomates* and the flat-bottomed bowl with sides slanting outward accompanied by rocker-stamped decoration, but there are important differences. Cuadros has no figurines, no iridescent painting, and no cord-marked pottery. Jocotal evolved from Cuadros and shows the same pottery types, with the addition of a white-rimmed black ware achieved by differential firing. The white rim or white area on the body of a vessel was produced simply by controlling the firing process. Although this fired white-rimmed ware was manufactured over a wide area, it was never very plentiful in Early Preclassic times.

The most widespread and important local development took place during the Middle Preclassic period (Conchas I and II phases). Population on the coast reached a peak of density not to be attained again until the Late Classic period. Villages were not necessarily larger, but simply more numerous. Clay platforms and pyramidal mounds announce the appearance of ceremonial architecture. The two Conchas phases share

Middle Preclassic pottery traits with both lowland Gulf Coast areas and highland developments in central Mexico and Guatemala. Examples of these are the composite silhouette forms, the "double-line break," "grater bowls" with interior scoring (Figure 5e, f, g), and naturalistic figurines. The double-line break is a distinctive rim decoration consisting of two incised lines, one of which is interrupted and the ends turned upward. This feature proves to be a good Middle Preclassic "marker" because it is widespread in space and narrowly restricted chronologically.

Late Preclassic times saw a great reduction in coastal population, paralleled by a shift of interest or influence away from lowland neighbors, and toward inland and highland centers such as Izapa in Chiapas and the Miraflores settlements at Kaminaljuyú. A veritable network of Late Preclassic sites covered the slopes of the Pacific, including the Crucero phase at Salinas La Blanca and Ilusiones at Bilbao (Parsons, 1967), but none has the stelae–altar complexes or bas-reliefs that characterize the great development at Kaminaljuyú of the Miraflores people (Shook & Kidder, 1952; M. D. Coe, 1966). Coastal pottery reflects strong highland influence. Crucero wares are slipped and polished, consisting of orange monochromes, red-on-orange, and streaky brown-black vessels accompanied by Usulután, an early resist-painted pottery (see Plate 4g). By the year A.D. 1, coastal Guatemala had become marginal to major developments in the highlands. We will come back to this region to continue a review of the Late Preclassic, but taking advantage of the shift of cultural leadership to the highlands, let us interrupt this sequence of events to see what was going on elsewhere at this time in the lowlands.

The chronological chart shows a long, continuous occupation of sites in the region of Chiapas, where careful and detailed excavations have been carried out for a number of years by the New World Archaeological Foundation (Dixon, 1959; Lowe, 1959; Lowe & Mason, 1965). The important site of Chiapa de Corzo is located in the great central depression of Chiapas near the modern town of Tuxtla Gutierrez, an area that has a dry tropical climate. Chiapa I (Cotorra), the lowest level of one of the longest sequences in Mesoamerica, yielded pieces of adobe plaster from some kind of early construction. In its pottery forms we again find the *tecomate* and flat-bottomed bowls with straight or flaring walls and jars with necks. There is a variety of decorative techniques: punctating, rocker stamping, filleting, and pattern incising on a white slipped ware, and red and white bichrome. Solid, hand-made figurines also form part of the first complex. The earliest Chiapa phase correlates with the Cuadros material from the Pacific Coast, and six more phases (Chiapa II–VII) follow, bringing us to the threshold of the Classic. The Chiapas sequence is an important scale for comparison of remains both west and east of the Isthmus. Stone architecture had begun by Chiapas III, as seen in stone-faced terrace platforms and foundations of small boulders. Toward the very end of the Preclassic a poor-quality lime mortar was being used. Although we believe that contacts were made with the Petén residents and that travelers may have seen corbelled arches being constructed, none are found in Chiapas.

Another Chiapas site with early architectural remains is Izapa, located on the Pacific coastal plain of Chiapas near Altamira. This site has yielded pottery affiliated with Chiapa de Corzo, as well as the Soconusco coastal sites with the exception of the very early Barra phase. The

a

b

earliest material is represented by shards from Mound 30a, a stepped pyramid faced with uncut stone, which in its final stages is estimated to have been approximately thirty feet high. Post holes indicate that it originally had supported a small temple on its summit (S. M. Ekholm, 1969). We have in this simple construction of the Middle Preclassic period, the basic elements of Mesoamerican religious architecture followed by later peoples. The way was now prepared for the extraordinary leadership and influence displayed by Izapa in late Preclassic times. These developments, however, are intimately related to events in the Gulf Coast region to which we now turn.

The Olmec Culture and Its Northern Neighbors

From the central Chiapas depression one can follow the Grijalva River eastward to the lowland region of southern Veracruz and western Tabasco where an extraordinary development was centered. So remarkable was this culture, which we know as the Olmec, that it greatly influenced contemporary groups and even later cultures. M. D. Coe goes so far as to claim that all succeeding Mexican and Mayan cultures have their roots in the Olmec civilization. The mere mention of the word Olmec is apt to excite artists and collectors; if any object can be described as Olmec, Olmec-derived, or even Olmecoid, its desirability is immediately increased. To what do Olmec artifacts owe this emotional response? To the Olmec themselves, of course, who created a culture alive with snarling jaguars, tearful babies, and Negroid and bearded figures—objects produced on both a monumental scale in basalt and a small scale in finely polished and carved articles of jade and serpentine (Plates 1, 2; Frontispiece).

c

d

e

f

Plate 1.   Olmec artifacts

a. Stone seated figure with child, Tabasco? Height: 4½ inches. Courtesy of the Museum of Primitive Art, New York.

b. Hollow figure wearing jaguar skin, Atlihuayán, Morelos. Height: 9 inches. Courtesy of the Museo Nacional de Antropología, Mexico.

c. White-slipped seated figurine, Las Bocas, Puebla. Height: 3 inches. Courtesy of the Museum of the American Indian, Heye Foundation (23/5495).

d. Black stone carving representing a kneeling Olmec figure with hollow in the top of the head. Incense burner? Height: 9¾ inches. Courtesy of the Museum of the American Indian, Heye Foundation (15/3560).

e. Hollow seated baby figure, Las Bocas, Puebla. Height: 13⅜ inches. Courtesy of the Museum of Primitive Art, New York.

f. Large stone votive axe, carved on one side. Height: 11½ inches. Courtesy of the Museum of the American Indian, Heye Foundation (16/3400).

a

b

c

d

f

e

Plate 2.   Preclassic period stone sculpture

a. Stela 2, La Venta, Tabasco. Height: 8 feet 1 inch. Courtesy of the Instituto Nacional de Antropología e Historia, Mexico.

b. Stela 21, Izapa, Chiapas. Courtesy of the Instituto Nacional de Antropología e Historia, Mexico.

c. Carved stone altar, Altar 5, La Venta, Tabasco. Courtesy of the Instituto Nacional de Antropología e Historia, Mexico.

d. Danzante relief stone slab, Monte Albán, Oaxaca. Photographed by the author.

e. Olmec god, Tlaloc, Monument 52, San Lorenzo. Height: 3 feet 3 inches. Courtesy of M. D. Coe.

f. Monument 34, San Lorenzo. Height: 2 feet 7 inches. Courtesy of M. D. Coe.

g. Colossal stone head, Monument 1, San Lorenzo. Height: 9 feet. Courtesy of M. D. Coe.

g

The name "Olmec" means "rubber people," and the south Gulf Coast region was famous in Conquest times as the best source of rubber. The ancient Preclassic Olmec should not be confused with another group also called Olmec, who once lived in highland central Mexico at Cholula and later migrated to the Gulf Coast. The latter are usually designated as "Historic Olmec" (Jiménez Moreno, 1942).

The region of southern Veracruz and western Tabasco is known as the Olmec heartland, or climax area, because it is believed that this was the main center of Olmec activity. We see no gradual elaboration of this culture in early remains, however. It is possible that the Olmecs spoke a Maya tongue, but nothing is known of the origins of their curious culture. For example, monumental stone carving appears in this region without any known precedent. Colossal heads, altars, figures, and stelae were all carved in a distinctive style. The basalt heads, found only in this climax area, are amazingly uniform (Plate 2g). They represent a huge head with infantile or Negroid-type features, wide thick lips, and a curious close-fitting cap often compared to the American football helmet. The heads are complete monuments in themselves and had no bodies, whose dimensions would have staggered the imagination. The tallest heads measure 9 feet in height and weigh up to twenty tons. Sculptures were painted in bright colors. Stelae, tall shafts of stone, were also carved in basalt. Some show figures in relief, as do the altars, large blocks with flat tops presumably used for placing offerings. A beautiful example of Olmec style is Monument 34 at San Lorenzo, representing a half-kneeling figure, now headless, which originally may have had articulated arms (Plate 2f).

Clay figurines, both hollow and solid, are amusing when compared with the huge carved figures in stone, for the same stance and heaviness of feeling have been faithfully reproduced in these small ceramic sculptures. Among them can be identified ball players wearing protective belts. They are often daubed with asphalt and are made to stand alone by means of a support at the back.

Typical Olmec pottery consists of flat-bottomed bowls with vertical or outward-slanting sides heavily carved or excised in broad gouges to form cross bands, the St. Andrew's cross, jaguar-paw-wing motifs, or flame brows. The excised areas are often roughened and filled with red hematite paint. Another characteristic design is the incised *ilhuitl*, two reversed scrolls. As we shall see, this pottery was widely traded or copied in the area stretching from La Victoria in Guatemala to the basin of Mexico (see Figure 5k; Plate 4c, d).

The Olmec heartland is too hot, too humid, and too tropical and rainy to be singled out by anyone today as a choice place to live. Yet this is a very rich agricultural area that offered an almost inexhaustible food supply: fish, aquatic birds, dogs, toads, and people were all eaten. Yes, the Olmec ate human flesh. Curiously enough, not much hunting was done, so the natural resources were never exploited to their fullest capacity. When first discovered, the abundant remains of toads caused no little interest, for what known group has a predilection for toads? It was later found that eating the flesh of this particular kind of toad (*Bufo marinus*) produces hallucinations, a very old custom indeed.

San Lorenzo, located in southern Veracruz in the Coatzacoalcos River basin, has the longest history of all Olmec sites studied (M. D. Coe, 1968a, 1970). It is, in a way, a gigantic artifact itself. Situated on a platform rising some fifty meters above the surrounding savannas, it is regularly inundated each year. The escarpment on the eastern side of the plateau is rather even, but the other three sides are sharply cut by deep ravines. These were manmade, for the ingenious Olmecs hauled up basket after basket of fill to create the artificial ridges that reach out like fingers, not haphazardly, but in a definite pattern. Atop the plateau are many mounds, the main cluster aligned along a north–south axis with rectangular courts surrounded by pyramids. The principal structure, a pyramid, is built up of earth and clay. A group of mounds in the central part of San Lorenzo may prove to be one of the earliest ball courts in Mesoamerica. Nearby house mounds are grouped around small courts.

As numerous huge stone carvings were uncovered, it became clear that they had been purposely mutilated before burial. Some represented human or animal figures; others were sculptured altars or columns. Although sometimes found deep in ravines, they had originally been ceremonially buried in a line along the tops of the artificial ridges. Untold numbers of these monuments still await discovery. The time and effort expended by the Olmecs in moving these great stone carvings is staggering. M. D. Coe estimates that to drag Monument 20 to where it was found, presumably with ropes, would have required at least 1000 men. The stone itself was quarried seventy kilometers away and was probably floated on rafts down the meandering rivers.

Another unusual feature of San Lorenzo is the location of buried drains on the slopes of the ravines, one of which is two hundred meters long. They are composed of neatly shaped sections of basalt with lids. Certainly not intended for irrigation in this area of superabundant rainfall, this engineering feat in some way controlled artificial ponds. These remains of a complicated system of water control demonstrate remarkable sophistication.

As we have seen before, the pottery serves as a barometer of change and furnishes evidence needed for establishing a chronology and correlation with other sites, for the stone monuments, with rare exceptions, are not found outside the climax area. The very earliest occupation at San Lorenzo is called the Ojochí phase (1500–1350 B.C.). It ties in with the Barra and Ocós phases of Soconusco but the pottery lacks cord marking, iridescent paint, and, with the exception of one shard, rocker stamping. The forms are comparable, however, and figurines are already present.

Even in the following Bajío phase (1350–1250 B.C.) there is still little that looks Olmec, but the San Lorenzo people were already busily hauling and dumping fill according to their planned ridge construction. Pottery featured the *tecomate*, bottles, and rocker stamping, and added the white-rimmed black ware already noted at Jocotal.

It is in the Chicharras phase (1250–1150 B.C.) at San Lorenzo that Olmec culture can first be recognized. The white–black differential firing became common, and kaolin ware, made of very fine textured clay, appeared, accompanied by various kinds of rocker stamping and some crosshatching, and hematite-slipped *tecomates*. The earliest Olmec figurines, made of fine textured white clay, are found in this phase, as are *metates* altered by the addition of two supports. Monumental stone carving was initiated, although the truly great phase at San Lorenzo is currently dated from 1150 to 900 B.C. During the latter period most of the monuments were carved and constructions raised that brought the site to its final form. The resident population on the plateau increased to an estimated 2500 persons, which clearly was not nearly enough to get the work done. San Lorenzo as well as its partial contemporary and successor, La Venta, relied on a large outlying hinterland population.

A great variety of artifacts and new materials were imported, particularly toward the end of the San Lorenzo phase. Colored obsidians, serpentines, mica, and schist, together with small sandstone slabs for lapidary working, are all signs of increased trade and contact with the outside world. Jade, so intimately associated with Olmec civilization, was apparently not worked at San Lorenzo.

In the Nacaste phase (900–700 B.C.) Olmec civilization at San Lorenzo came to an end. New pottery types, typical of Middle Preclassic settlements elsewhere, replace the old; figurines stare out of strange, large punched eyes, a style unknown to the Olmecs. The mutilation of monuments was general, and the defacement by smashing faces, knocking off heads, and marking with axes gives some indication of the effort expended in terminating the Olmec occupation. What brought about the sudden disorder is not known. New wares and figurines are indications of outside interference. The systematic destruction of monuments and their methodical concealment suggest that the Olmecs themselves chose this fate for their great stone carvings. The Nacaste invaders, whoever they were, did not share in, nor perpetuate the Olmec tradition. The succeeding phase, Palangana, introduces new pottery suggestive of contacts with La Venta, Tres Zapotes, and Mamom peoples. But activity seems to have ceased around 400 B.C., and San Lorenzo, although reoccupied in Postclassic years, never regained the prominence attained by the early Olmecs.

San Lorenzo has the longest history of any site in the Olmec heartland yet excavated, but it is only one of many to be investigated. Río Chiquito and Potrero Nuevo, minor satellites of San Lorenzo are also located on the Coatzacoalcos River and have not yet been dug, but it is known that they too have mounds around plazas, colossal heads, and carved stone monuments. Shards with fired-white rims, rocker stamping, and cord markings are hints of Early Preclassic settlements probably contemporary with San Lorenzo. Other important sites are Laguna de los Cerros, La Venta, Tres Zapotes, and El Viejón.

After the destruction of San Lorenzo, Olmec civilization lived on at La Venta (Drucker, Heizer, & Squier, 1959; Drucker, 1952). La Venta, only 18 miles from the Gulf of Mexico, is located on a small, swampy, stoneless island near the Tonalá River. At the time the Olmecs settled there, food was abundant. Tapirs, armadillos, peccaries, howler monkeys, and jaguars were common, and all sorts of reptiles and aquatic life flour-

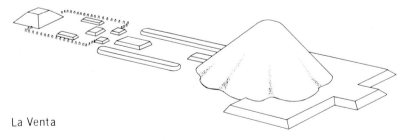

La Venta

Figure 6.
Ceremonial center of La Venta. (Adapted from M. D. Coe, 1968b.)

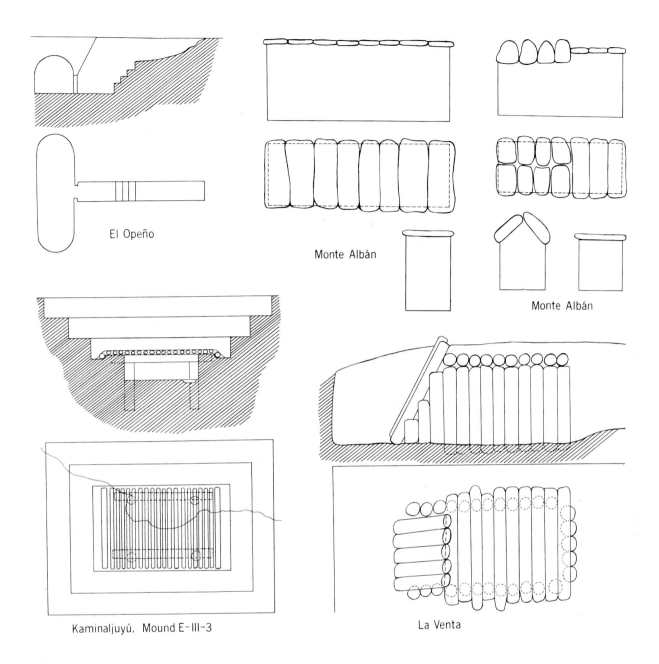

El Opeño

Monte Albán

Monte Albán

Kaminaljuyú, Mound E-III-3

La Venta

Figure 7. Preclassic tombs. (Adapted from the following sources: El Opeño, Noguera, 1942; Monte Albán, Marquina, 1951; Kaminaljuyú, Shook & Kidder, 1952; La Venta, Drucker, 1952.)

ished in the swamps and sluggish rivers. But the varied animal life also included dangerous snakes and insects, and, for a farming people, the dense vegetation was a constant opponent to be cut back again and again.

Here on this low island, on about two square miles of dry land, the Olmecs selected a north–south axis on which to erect a well-planned ceremonial center (Figure 6). The largest of the clay and earth constructions is a massive structure 110 meters in height and shaped like a fluted cone, with the exterior surface presenting an alternating series of ten ridges and ten valleys (Heizer, 1968). This is not the result of natural erosion, but was consciously constructed. It resembles a giant volcano, and was perhaps inspired by a local example. No access to the top is provided by a ramp or stairway; there is only a steep incline of about thirty degrees. The usual Mesoamerican pyramid was rectangular, an impressive platform designed to lift a temple even closer to the deities. Was the La Venta cone a pyramid in this sense? We do not yet know if it was meant to be scaled, if it supported some kind of structure, or if it might instead be a burial mound or repository of caches and offerings. North of this mound lies a great court containing two smaller mounds, bordered by two long low mounds. Beyond this area is a rectangular compound ending in another low central mound (Figure 6). The compound was once fenced in by seven-foot basalt columns set in an adobe brick wall. It has been suggested that the whole ceremonial center might have depicted a gigantic jaguar mask. Three massive mosaic pavements, each consisting of about 485 blocks of green serpentine, were laid out to form jaguar masks. Two were found on platforms to either side of the great court, and the third just north of the main pyramid. These gigantic mosaics occupy an area about fifteen by twenty feet each, some portions being filled in with colored clays. The entire pavements were carefully buried soon after they were completed. For this reason it is supposed that these identical mosaic pavements represent massive offerings. One lay under twenty jade and serpentine celts arranged in a cross-shaped design with a concave hematite mirror found at the intersection.

The entire complex, rising out of a clearing in the jungle, must have been an impressive sight with its painted constructions, colossal stone heads, and numerous stelae and altars. Like those at San Lorenzo, all these great stone monuments were hewn from enormous blocks of basalt quarried some eighty air miles to the west and floated on rafts down the rivers. La Venta is best known for its ceremonial center and stone carving (Stirling, 1943; M. D. Coe, 1965a). In view of the poor preservation, burials, as might be expected, are few. However, one famous basalt column tomb was found in Mound A-2 (Figure 7). Two youths had been wrapped separately and heavily covered with vermillion paint. The offering laid around them on the limestone floor indicates the special status of these dead, for it includes beautiful jade figurines, beads, a sting-ray spine of jade, and other jade objects. Although burials are scarce at La Venta, a number of spectacular caches or offerings have been found, usually rich in jade and serpentine objects. The jade was polished to a glossy finish with sand and water, a technique requiring tireless persistence. Of all materials available to Mesoamerican artists and craftsmen, jade was the most highly prized. And among Mesoamerican jades, none are more finely carved and polished than those of the Olmecs.

Perhaps the most extraordinary objects discovered in the offerings are concave mirrors made of magnetite and ilmenite, which are so highly polished that they can reflect images or be made to produce fire. Perforations suggest that they were suspended, and some figurines are shown with just such a concave object being worn around the neck. One supposes that these mirrors would have been used only by the most privileged, in this case, the highest-ranking priests.

The usual household remains and refuse deposits are not found at La Venta, and even pottery, so abundant at other places, is not very plentiful. The flat-bottomed bowl and *tecomate* are the most common forms, but gadrooned (modeled after bottle gourds?) or lobed bottles and deep bowls occur too. Decorative techniques include rocker stamping and the type of rim treatment known as the double-line break. The curious white-rimmed black ware is also present. Other artifacts include small, hand-modeled figurines, cylindrical clay stamps, prismatic blades and flakes of obsidian, *metates* and *manos*, and impressions of mats and baskets. The scarcity of pottery may be explained at least in part by the location of La Venta on this swampy island, certainly too small to support more than a very few elite families. The bulk of the population, estimated by Heizer (1960) at approximately 18,000, must have stretched out over the neighboring mainland, and they travelled in by water and foot for special events.

La Venta is believed to have been a thriving ceremonial center from 1000 to 600 B.C., and therefore would have slightly overlapped the Olmec occupation at San Lorenzo. Drifting sands obliterated much of the center, but later peoples visited and looted it, and some even left offerings. Although much has been excavated, many parts remain untouched. Today the island is a center for oil refineries, and the constant drilling and pumping of wells, new roads, and expanding business operations threaten the entire archaeological area with imminent obliteration.

A newly identified site, called the Stirling group, is located only a quarter of a mile southeast of La Venta's cone-shaped structure and promises further information about these people. It has not yet been excavated, but many stone sculptures have been reported, including heads, seated figures, and large stone bowls. Nothing resembling a pyramid has been located, but we already know of a large platform, court, and rows of basalt columns and two low parallel mounds, which may perhaps have been a ball court. Five stone drains are similar to those at San Lorenzo and the pottery appears to be Olmec. Let us hope that archaeologists reach the Stirling group before urbanization and progress!

The massive constructions of the Olmecs and their dexterity in moving and carving huge basalt blocks and small jade and serpentine objects are indeed notable, but their fame rests on other grounds as well. The impact of Olmec culture on a large portion of Mesoamerica was accomplished by the spread of their beliefs, portrayed in a distinctive art style (M. D. Coe, 1965b).

The central theme of Olmec art is the were-jaguar concept (Furst, 1968). There is an overwhelming emphasis on the jaguar combined with human baby features. Infantile expressions, linked with snarling mouths turned down at the corners, fangs, a prominent thick upper lip, toothless gums, a deeply notched or V-shaped cleft in the head, and perhaps a full chin, are all distinctive features of Olmec art (see Plates 1 and 2). One interpretation of this strange combination of human and jaguar elements is based on Monument 3, discovered at Potrero Nuevo. According to Stirling (1943), the remarkable carvings depict a woman copulating with a jaguar, a union that might have given rise to a mythical offspring combining jaguar and human characteristics. There are many instances of peoples who believe in complete interchangeability of form between man and animals, as well as traditions in tropical South America in which the jaguar appears as the original mother or father. The were-jaguar theme in Olmec art has been treated by Furst (1968), who based his study on worldwide ethnographic material. He sees the feline characteristics as being associated with the priest or shaman who possesses supernatural jaguar qualities and is able to achieve complete spiritual transformation. It follows that the were-jaguar should not be viewed as portraiture but as a combination of ideal and reality. There is a close correlation between the jaguar-babies and the sky or rain. The Mexican artist Covarrubias (1946) has shown that all the various rain gods of Monte Albán, Teotihuacán, Tajín, and the Maya may have been derived from this Olmec were-jaguar. There are, however, other significant animal motifs in Olmec art, of which a bird is probably next in rank to the jaguar, and a duck or duck-billed figure is not uncommon.

Of equal importance to the central motifs and themes of Olmec art is its mood or feeling. Olmec art is never cluttered; space is an important ingredient. A pottery vessel, for example, may have a single design engraved or incised on one side only, leaving the remaining portions plain. These people did not have the desire, so common in later Mayan art, to neatly fill the whole field. To the Olmecs, space, slowness of rhythm, and design were essential. Corners are gently curved or rounded. Whether small or monumental, sculptures are usually three dimensional, made to be seen from all sides. Indeed, even small objects seem large and grand, and, when measured, are smaller than anticipated.

The portable Olmec artifacts, mainly small jade and serpentine figurines, plaques, beads, and pendants, were widely traded and carried throughout Mesoamerica in Early and Middle Preclassic times (M. D. Coe, 1965b; Grove, 1968b; Flannery, 1968a). Sculptured objects turn up sporadically across the central highland area, but are particularly abundant in southern lowland Mexico, and extend in an arc from Veracruz south and west to include the state of Guerrero. Although more portable Olmec artifacts can be attributed to Guerrero than anywhere else, the center of the culture is still believed to lie in the region of the great stone monuments. Olmec stone carvings are known from coastal Chiapas around Pijijiapan and to the southeast, and the Olmec impact was felt as far away as El Salvador and Costa Rica, as evidenced by stone reliefs pecked on boulders. These figures are far simpler and cruder than those of Chalcatzingo, but are unmistakably Olmec. Curiously, Olmec objects beyond the borders of the heartland often depict warriors and military scenes unknown at home. We can only speculate that their desire for such articles as jade, serpentine, and obsidian may have led the Olmecs to establish distant colonies and trade control points, which at times might have required military force to guarantee an uninterrupted flow of materials into the heartland. From analysis of trace elements in a large number of San Lorenzo obsidian specimens it now seems evident that the Olmecs procured this material from many sources, ranging from highland Guatemala to highland Mexico (Coe & Cobean, 1970).

About one hundred miles northwest of La Venta, near the foot of the Tuxtla Mountains, is the site known as Tres Zapotes. Most of the remains there postdate La Venta, but the earliest may be partially contemporaneous with La Venta. Two colossal heads not easily moved about may well be of Middle Preclassic date and six more heads have recently been reported. What does seem certain is that Tres Zapotes became the most important center after La Venta was destroyed. Thus, at this site the Middle Preclassic blends into the Late Preclassic phase (Weiant, 1943).

The most significant find at Tres Zapotes is Stela C (see Plate 6a, Chapter 5), the oldest dated monument yet found in the New World (Stirling, 1943; M. D. Coe, 1962). Unfortunately not complete, it nevertheless has a Long Count date, the earliest known, which has been translated into our calendar as 31 B.C. Nothing at La Venta hints of bar-and-dot dates, but we can reasonably assume that some steps were being taken there toward the development of the calendar and hieroglyphs. The reverse side of Stela C depicts a rather abstract were-jaguar mask executed in an Olmec-derived style. Small Olmec jades sometimes bear hieroglyphs, and although these have no meaning for us as yet, they imply that calendrics and hieroglyphic writing were already being developed in the Middle Preclassic or even earlier.

In addition to Stela C there are other interesting aspects of the Late Preclassic period at Tres Zapotes, including a rectangular pyramid faced with cut stone, but no use of lime mortar (a later development), and the continuation of oxidized white-rim pottery and flat-bottomed dishes. In other respects the ceramics differ from La Venta and Middle Preclassic lowland sites. Bowls with wide everted rims and grooved and modeled decorations became common, a feature shared with Izapa and some Petén sites, and the composite-silhouette bowls are distinctly late in flavor. Five figurine types have been distinguished, all solid and made by hand. Some of these too are credited with Olmecoid features (Drucker, 1943a).

A few kilometers west of the ruins of Cempoala on the banks of the Chachalacas River is a site called El Trapiche, known through excavations of José García Payón. Zoned rocker-stamped and excised pottery, as well as white-rimmed black ware, are known to come from the lowest deposits, along with clay figurines similar to highland D* types (Ford, 1969).

Farther north still, early material is found on the very periphery of Mesoamerica in the Gulf Coast region known as the Huasteca. Just west of the Pánuco River and only about 100 miles southeast of the Sierra de Tamaulipas, two large stratigraphic excavations have proved most rewarding. The phases named Pavón and Ponce probably antedate 1000 B.C. and fall within the range of the Early Preclassic period (MacNeish, 1954).

Stone tools were not frequent in either phase, but fragments of *metates* and *manos*, scrapers, and flints, followed by obsidian flakes, all point to corn agriculture supplemented by hunting. The earliest pottery, that of Pavón, is some of the poorest quality found to date in Mesoamerica. It is crumbly and granular—some pots were not even fired. Forms are few and simple: *ollas* and flat-bottomed bowls. When present, decoration consists of simple cylindrical punchings. Figurines are notably lacking. After a slight gap in time, the Ponce phase continues with some Pavón traits, adding obsidian, some simple new bowl forms, and five figurine types. The quality of the pottery is not as fine as at contemporary

---

*This type of classification, often encountered in the following pages, refers to the system of figurine identification devised by George Vaillant (see page 71).

sites in the south. The Huasteca (Ekholm, 1944) conforms generally to the emerging lowland Preclassic pattern, sharing monochrome wares and the lack of vessel supports, but there is nothing specifically suggestive of the Olmecs. The greatest Olmec influence lay to the south and west, from where it spread to the highlands.

Oaxaca

An area we will return to again and again is the Valley of Oaxaca, actually a high plateau located in the Balsas depression. Blessed by a warm, temperate, semiarid climate and drained by the Atoyac River and its tributary, the Salado or Tlacolula River, the area has one of the longest cultural records in Mesoamerica. Because of the strategic location of this area between highland and lowland cultures, the history of this region is vital to an understanding of Mesoamerican development. It both received and imparted influence while producing regional cultures of its own.

The earliest Preclassic material known comes from the Valley of Etla, northwest of the city of Oaxaca, where a concentration of early sites is located in a region drained by the Atoyac River (Flannery, Kirkby, Kirkby, & Williams, 1967). Here, soon after 1500 B.C., people lived in settled communities on the high alluvium formed as a flood plain during the ancient Pleistocene age. Since the water level is only three meters below the surface, this land was not farmed by the slash-and-burn method but by "pot irrigation," a technique in which water was hauled up from wells sunk in the corn fields and then distributed around plants. This system is still in use today among modern Zapotec Indians of Oaxaca, and remains of ancient archaeological wells confirm a long tradition of the practice.

Other settlements are located up in the piedmont area, where water from tributary streams could easily have been diverted and gravity alone would channel the water into fields via small canals. Flannery (Flannery et al., 1967) has reported evidence of such canals, so there is some proof that irrigation was practiced by these early farmers at least by Late Preclassic times.

Remains of three villages atop a long promontory jutting out into the Etla Valley are the primary source of our knowledge of the San José Mogote phase, the earliest ceramic horizon in the Oaxaca area (Flannery, 1968a). The ceramics can be cross-dated in form and decoration with Chiapa I (Cotorra), the Cuadros phase of Soconusco, the San Lorenzo phase in Veracruz, Las Bocas in Puebla, and Tlatilco in the basin of Mexico. The white-rimmed black ware, excised designs, Olmec motifs, rocker stamping, and figurines of C and D types are familiar markers. The most interesting discovery was the great concentration of chips and small fragments of magnetite, ilmenite, hematite, mica, and green quartz, together with many marine mollusk shells from the Gulf Coast. These mineral deposits were lacking in the Olmec heartland, but were prized as material for luxury items such as ilmenite mirrors. It is easy to imagine workshops at San José Mogote humming at full capacity to satisfy the demands of an eager Olmec market.

Thereafter, in the Guadalupe phase, ties remained close with the Gulf Coast cultures, and many Middle Preclassic markers are shared, such as the double-line break and large hollow figurines like those found at Las Bocas, Puebla. Small solid figurines resemble A types, which have a characteristic eye with a well-defined punched pupil. The A figurine is known from the basin of Mexico and the Santa Maria phase at Tehuacán, and is generally distributed throughout lowland sites as far east as the Petén. Eventually the Guadalupe phase blends into the earliest period at Monte Albán, that magnificent site capping the long hill at the convergence of three valleys, in one of which lies the modern city of Oaxaca.

Olmec strains are still reflected in the Middle Preclassic remains of Monte Albán but have been adapted to the local style (Caso & Bernal, 1952; Bernal, 1965). The only building of this phase is a large flat-topped mound or platform flanked by a number of stone slabs each decorated in low relief with a nude male figure, either swimming or dancing, judging from the curious position of the limbs in motion, which gave rise to their name "Danzantes" (Plate 2d). The faces are Olmec in profile and the mouths droop at the corners, but the figures are not babies, since teeth are often portrayed. Perhaps rather than swimmers or dancers, these figures portray dead people, possibly captives, as suggested by the half-closed eyes and open mouths. The sexual organs are elaborately emphasized, a feature without parallel in Olmec art, where bodies were represented as nude but sexless.

Tombs were built in simple rectangular shapes roofed over with slabs of stone (Figure 7). Much of the early pottery is found in tombs and is also known from almost forty sites in the area. The fine paste grey ware, probably ceremonial, continues to dominate the many periods that follow. For daily use cream and brown wares were preferred. A variety of very small vessels with a fine polish and slip are characteristic, and bridged spouts are a prominent special form (Figure 5h, w, ee). Hand-modeled figurines are known, but not in great quantity.

The most significant contribution of Monte Albán to the Middle Preclassic horizon is the Calendar Round. Enough hieroglyphs, numerals, and calendric inscriptions have been deciphered to afford proof that the 52-year cycle was already in operation (see Figure 14c, f, Chapter 5).

To comprehend the calculation of a 52-year cycle, imagine two wheels of time rotating simultaneously. One time wheel records days, for which there were 20 names with 13 numbers. The complete name of a day must be accompanied by the appropriate number, such as 2 Rabbit or 10 House (4 Rabbit and 11 House would be different days). The other presents a somewhat parallel situation. Eighteen months of 20 days each, to which a dreaded 5-day period of bad luck was added, resulted in a 365-day cycle ($18 \times 20 + 5 = 365$), corresponding to our solar year. In order to return to the very same day and month, 52 years would have to elapse. This was the basic computation of time used in most of Mesoamerica. Known as the Calendar Round, it enables unique designation of dates within the 52-year period. Difficulties may arise when dealing with several cycles, for one needs to know to which Calendar Round the date refers. The Maya Long Count also used the 52-year cycle but avoided confusion by accurately recording lapsed time from an initial starting point, 3113 B.C. We do not know when and where the Calendar Round originated, but we are sure that it was already in use at Monte Albán in Middle Preclassic times (Caso, 1967).

Monte Albán is the best-known site of this period, but by no means is it the only one. Mitla, well known for its Postclassic occupation, was actually founded in the San José Mogote phase. Dainzú, near the village of Tlacolula, has proved to be an extensive site that perhaps reflects the final traces of Olmec flavor in the Oaxaca region. Although there is a large pyramidal platform, the fifty carved stones at the base of the structure have attracted the most interest. Two figures are humanized jaguars; others probably portray priests, perhaps dressed as deities, and ball players wearing wide pants, knee guards, and gauntlets, and holding balls in their hands. If the latter figures represent actual play, the rules at this time (600–200 B.C.) must have been different than those of Postclassic games for we know that in the latter the sport was played with "no hands." (See Chapter 6.)

Still another site, Montenegro, located west of Monte Albán in the Mixteca, was apparently occupied only during Middle Preclassic times. It is considered to be a pure Monte Albán I site, yet the material is not identical to that of Monte Albán. No Danzantes, numerals, hieroglyphs, or evidence of the Calendar Round have come to light. A very typical pottery form is a tall, simple urn decorated with an Olmec-like face on one side. Montenegro may prove to antedate Monte Albán I or it could represent just a simpler manifestation. The site was apparently abandoned by 300 B.C., and we hear nothing more of it. At Monte Albán, on the other hand, there is a gradual transition to the Late Preclassic phase.

The Late phase was initiated by the arrival of a new people, thought to have come from Chiapas or Guatemala. It is represented at Monte Albán by a curious irregular structure, Mound J, at the southern end of the great plaza. It was shaped like an arrow point, and a kind of covered gallery ran through it. A ball court also existed at this time, but its precise characteristics are not known. The Maya or Olmec area may have provided the inspiration for erecting stelae carved with hieroglyphics, and ties with highland Guatemala can be inferred from the presence of numerals. Tombs became more elaborate with the addition of antechambers and vaulted roofs. The earlier well-modeled pottery was replaced by geometric designs and a more impersonal trend. Many deities have been identified, and the elaborate headdresses and complicated decorations so typical of Classic styles were already initiated during this phase.

Although sites like Monte Albán and Mitla have been known for a very long time, the Preclassic peoples of the Oaxaca region have been little understood and their remains were largely untouched until recently. Now we know that some were farmers who practiced irrigation while others specialized in working in exotic raw materials much in demand by the cultural leaders on the Gulf Coast. Although Olmec influence is strongly reflected in the early manifestations in Oaxaca, it became subordinate to the emerging Zapotec culture by Middle Preclassic times.

Puebla and Morelos

If, as we suspect, the Olmecs were avid traders and eagerly sought out and maintained commercial contacts with the highlands, one route would logically lead from Oaxaca northwest to Puebla, a source of the coveted serpentine. Both hollow and solid clay figurines from the Late Ajalpan phase at Tehuacán indicate possible contact between these peoples. Tehuacán was located in a very advantageous position to deal with the people of Oaxaca and the lowlands as well as with central Mexicans. Indeed, there is evidence, through numerous ceramic affiliations, that the Preclassic peoples of Tehuacán maintained a close cultural relationship with the inhabitants of the Oaxaca valley (MacNeish, Peterson, & Flannery, 1970).

Bearing westward across southern Puebla, the traveler finds a natural opening in the hills leading to Las Bocas, an Olmec site located at the base of a large hill or cliff at the eastern edge of the Izúcar de Matamoros Valley. Las Bocas is known largely from the spoils of looting parties, which have brought out large hollow baby-faced figures, white-rimmed black ware, spouted trays, and black-excised pottery with the jaguar-paw-hand motif (Plate 1c, e; Plate 4c). Across the valley, one of the few passes in the mountains affords access to the central Morelos plains. At the Morelos end of the pass is Chalcatzingo, perhaps the most important Olmec highland site and unique for having the only Olmec-carved bas-reliefs in the highlands (Grove, 1968a). It could have served both as a religious center and as a traffic or trade control point. There are several groups of carvings, which seem to deal with agriculture, fertility, and rain. Some convey a suggestion of militarism. The human figures, scrolls and volutes, clouds, rain, and flame eyebrows are in purest Olmec style.

The location of Chalcatzingo parallels that of Las Bocas. Both are situated at the base of a tall cliff and both would have been well situated to check on travelers arriving from or leaving for Gulf Coast regions. Chalcatzingo could have controlled three-way traffic: south to Guerrero, north to the basin of Mexico, and southeast to the Olmec heartland on the Gulf Coast. We believe this site to have been active from 1200 to 900 B.C., making it contemporary with San Lorenzo and the beginnings of La Venta (Grove, 1968b).

At an altitude of 4500 feet, Morelos enjoys a temperate year-round climate that today attracts thousands of visitors to the city of Cuernavaca to bask in the continual sunshine and escape the more rigorous highlands. Open forests of pine and oak, numerous streams, and abundant summer rainfall would have made the Morelos valleys favorable habitation sites in ancient times as well.

There are other Preclassic sites in Morelos, and several of them may also be considered Olmec. Gualupita was one, but it has now been absorbed by the city of Cuernavaca and we know it largely from George Vaillant's published accounts (Vaillant & Vaillant, 1934). While making a road cut at Atlihuayán on the Yautepec River, workers came across a magnificent hollow Olmec ceramic figure, seated and wearing a jaguar skin (Plate 1b). Morelos looks more and more like an area with Olmec connections, although its remains present elements from other sources. Rubbish and graves of ancient settlers along the Cuautla River are giving some perspective to Olmec influence in the highlands. Two sites are being excavated, La Juana and San Pablo. La Juana is dated at perhaps 1250–1000 B.C. and is followed by San Pablo, a short phase lasting until 900 B.C. Styles and types of wares are mixed at La Juana, but it seems to be a contemporary Olmec site yielding the flat-bottomed cylindrical bowls, spouted trays and white-rimmed black wares, and D and C-9 figurines. Unexpectedly, *tecomates* are rare.

San Pablo material clarifies some earlier confusions and discredits once again an old belief that burial mounds do not exist in Mesoamerica. The San Pablo site is located on the Cuautla River some thirty kilometers below the town of Cuautla. On a river terrace, a low, roughly circular mound reinforced by a stone wall proved to be a true burial mound, probably originally containing 150–250 graves, some accompanied by offerings. The ceramics are those of the so-called Río Cuautla style, consisting of bottles with stirrup spouts, composite bottles, bottles with long tubular necks, negative or resist painting, hollow figurines of a mixture of D and K types, and small solid K figurines. What do these things mean and from where did they come? How do they relate to Olmec remains? At La Juana, these vessels appear with the familiar Olmec traits of excising, zone and panel decoration, rocker stamping, spouted trays, kaolin ware, and Olmec figurines. In the basin of Mexico at the Tlatilco cemetery, Olmec and Río Cuautla styles are also found. The answer seems to lie in the continued use of certain areas like La Juana and Tlatilco over a considerable period of time that represents at least two phases of occupation, the earlier one having purer Olmec remains (Grove, 1970a, c).

Although the cultural composition of these Morelos sites, as we will see shortly, is paralleled at Tlatilco, at the latter site this chronological distinction is not clear as elements of the Río Cuautla style (also called Tlatilco style) pottery seem to occur from the earliest time (Tolstoy & Paradis, 1971). The inspiration for this ceramic style may have come from an entirely different direction, western Mexico, a region lying outside Mesoamerica at this time (Grove, 1971; Tolstoy & Paradis, 1971). There is further evidence, discussed in Chapter 9, to show that the ultimate source of this influence could have been northwestern South America.

The quantity of Olmec pottery in Morelos leads us to believe that Olmec people were important in this valley following 1300 B.C. Thereafter their influence waned or was diluted, and their pottery was replaced by Río Cuautla ceramics. Nor did this strain endure, for Morelos soon fell under the influence of the basin of Mexico, where people were constructing their first religious centers and creating their own ceramic tradition.

Guerrero

As mentioned already, Morelos was at the hub of three choice routes of communication. One of these, of course, connected via Puebla with Oaxaca and Gulf Coast points. The basin of Mexico was easily accessible if one ascended another 3000 feet through the mountains north of Chalcatzingo to enter the valley from its southeastern corner. The third route, perhaps the most exciting and challenging of all, followed the Cuautla–Amacuzac River south and west to the great Balsas River, which traverses Guerrero and offers a natural thoroughfare to the Pacific Ocean. Why, one may ask, would anyone leave the temperate climate and pleasant life in Morelos or Oaxaca to penetrate the difficult, rough, and often forbidding terrain of the Balsas depression? The answer is simple—Guerrero was the land of tin, copper, silver, gold, and semiprecious stones. But more important than the rich deposits of metals and minerals, some of which were not appreciated this early, Guerrero was a probable source of jade, the most prized of exotic materials.

We also suspect that even in early times the immense delta of the Balsas River was an exciting port, offering shelter to ocean-going crafts as well as being the terminal of the vast interior communication line to the highlands. Another logical corridor for movement of peoples lay along the coastal strip that stretches south from the delta to Oaxaca. There is ample archaeological evidence that Preclassic peoples looked beyond the grubby cactus- and mezquite-covered hills and found their way to the rich river valleys and to the coast itself.

At Puerto Marqués near Acapulco, pottery and figurines are clearly related to the Preclassic Mesoamerican tradition (C. Brush, 1969; E. Brush, 1968). A very early pitted pottery like that of Purrón Tehuacán has already been mentioned, and this is followed by a long sequence of remains. Olmec-type baby-faced figurines had a wide distribution on this coast during Middle Preclassic times, only to fade out completely in the late phase.

Preclassic material is also known from the Balsas delta itself, but even richer remains have come from inland areas around Iguala and Chilpancingo; some of these areas relate to the basin of Mexico through red-on-brown wares, the double-line break, and D-1 figurines.

No other region can rival Guerrero's production of portable Olmec art treasures such as green stone plaques, masks, figures, and celts. Olmec merchants not only exploited the natural resources but also lived and worshipped around Chilpancingo, where two caves are decorated with remarkable paintings executed in pure Olmec style. Just east of Chilpancingo and only twenty miles apart are the caves of Juxtlahuaca and Oxtotitlán, each high above the river valley. The Juxtlahuaca paintings, some of the oldest known in the New World, date from perhaps 3000 years ago. Lying nearly a mile inside the mountain, they are painted in black, green, red, and yellow. A great bearded (?) figure with a *quetzal*-plumed headdress, tunic, and cape wears gauntlets and leggings of jaguar skin. He holds out a rope-like object toward a smaller, crouching figure. In the next chamber a bright red serpent on a slab of rock faces a smaller feline creature (Gay, 1967).

Oxtotitlán, about twenty miles to the north, is located high up a hillside, and some paintings decorate the very mouth of the entrance. Although not all the details are well preserved, one painting depicts a human figure seated on a jaguar-monster head. Themes include water or fertility and possibly mythical origins. A similar association of the jaguar-monster-mouth cave is seen in the relief carvings at Chalcatzingo and probably can be symbolically associated with the jaguar stone altars of the Olmec Gulf Coast sites. The interior cave paintings, in polychrome black or red, portray jaguars, baby faces, and the earliest known occurrence of the speech scroll, so common in later Mesoamerican art. Grove (1970b), who has interpreted this art, believes that the paintings more closely resemble the art of La Venta than that of the earlier site of San Lorenzo. Thus, he dates the two Guerrero cave paintings around 900–700 B.C., which correlates with other archaeological evidence of the Olmec presence in central Mexico.

One must be impressed by the distances these Olmecs traveled from their Gulf Coast heartland to record their favorite themes of human figures, jaguars, and serpents on the walls of Guerrero caves. Surely these represent some kind of shrine, and the large bearded Olmec is certainly a figure to be respected.

A further indication of Olmec presence in Guerrero was the discovery in 1967 of an Olmec stela at San Miguel Amuco near Coyuca in the Middle Balsas area—a full standing figure wearing a cape and holding in his arm a bundle of reeds (?) much resembling the later Aztec year symbol, the *xiuhmolpilli* (Grove & Paradis, 1971). This is a rare example of an Olmec monument of this nature in a setting outside the Gulf Coast heartland. There is no longer any doubt that the Olmecs themselves lived in Guerrero. They even may have irrigated the river valleys in order to stay on. The Preclassic remains already reported, together with abundant sites awaiting excavation, indicate that this region formed part of the mainstream of Mesoamerican culture at this early period.

The Basin of Mexico

We now come to the basin of Mexico, where archaeology of the Preclassic horizon has been extremely difficult to interpret for several reasons. First, in addition to nourishing its own local cultures, the Basin of Mexico received influences from many other directions. Thus, there are many different features from many different peoples who met, mingled, and competed. Some cultural traits lost out, others survived, and some were altered almost beyond recognition. Into this veritable stew of cultural remains the unsuspecting archaeologists dug their first trenches, which, as it turned out, produced selected slices of Middle and Late Preclassic material. Only now, after twenty-five years of probing, erring, and revising, do we have a chronological sequence for this complex region that promises reasonable cross correlations with the lowlands and Maya area. The presentation that follows is a much simplified version of events based on recent studies by Tolstoy and Paradis (1970, 1971), Heizer and Bennyhoff (1958b), Grove (1968b), and M. D. Coe (1965c).

The Olmecs Again

The adventurous Olmecs entered the basin of Mexico, perhaps after stopping to visit Las Bocas, Puebla, or the religious shrine at Chalcatzingo, and settled at various points along the shores of Lake Texcoco. We are not certain just who they found in residence, because their remains are the earliest found. The earlier residents may have been farmers who inhabited the southwestern lake shore around the area of Cuicuilco, where their refuse eventually was used as fill for later platforms and plazas. Tentatively identified as the Tlalpan phase (2100–1800 B.C.), the radiocarbon samples await conclusive association with the pottery that bears some resemblance to the Ajalpan red ware from the Tehuacán Valley. Meanwhile, we can say only that the first known settlers in the valley were the Olmecs, who we believe were present around 1200 B.C. (Tolstoy & Paradis, 1970). Their rubbish has been found at Ayotla, near the modern settlement of Tlapacoya, and they buried some dead across the lake at Tlatilco. This early Preclassic horizon is known as the Ixtapaluca phase (see Chart 1). A rapid inventory reveals traits already familiar from Puebla, Morelos, and the southern lowlands: flat-bottomed cylindrical bowls, excising, plain rocker stamping and zoning or designs, the St. Andrew's cross motif, the fired-white rimmed ware, red-on-buff pottery, and the use of specular hematite, red pigment, and small hand-modeled figurines (types D-2 and K). Large hollow figures often called dolls, typically with spread, chubby legs and a baby-like face, are associated with this complex; one was found by Tolstoy in his Ayotla subphase. Of the same complex is the seated figure, sucking its finger, from Las Bocas, a truly remarkable ceramic sculpture (Plate 1e). Of the tools, small pointed-stem projectile points and *metates* without supports are typical of all related sites. That these early Olmec residents were farmers is indicated by the presence of *metates, manos,* and even tiny maize cobs recovered at Ayotla, but their diet was supplemented by deer, rabbits, gophers, domesticated dogs, and even people. Mud turtles and waterfowl were also eaten, but curiously enough no fish remains have been found in the rubbish. Although this Early Preclassic occupation is still very imperfectly known, there are as yet no indications of ceremonial structures at this time.

Were the Olmecs an elite group that dominated other peoples, as envisioned by Covarrubias? The spread of Olmec culture has been variously attributed to imperialism, economic or social factors, and "missionary" activity. These need not be mutually exclusive, of course, and multiple factors are undoubtedly involved. Whatever else was going on, archaeological evidence suggests that commercial relationships were maintained for several hundred years, accompanied by some religious activity, as seen in the bas-reliefs of Chalcatzingo and the cave paintings of Guerrero.

Evidence of exchange or procurement of commodities is easily recognized archaeologically when sources of raw materials can be traced and objects are found outside the resource area. In the case of the Olmecs there is ample proof of their taste for fine products, which were themselves intimately associated with ritual and ceremonialism. Wherever the Olmecs went, their ideology accompanied them, but in the basin of Mexico their impact was tempered by other cultural strains, and was of relatively short duration.

Tlatilco

Around the year 900 B.C. changes took place. For one thing, we know that more land was occupied and farmed around the lake. New villages appeared to the southwest of the lake at Cuicuilco ·and on the northwestern shores at Zacatenco and El Arbolillo, while Tlatilco continued to be used as both a cemetery and residential area (Vaillant, 1930, 1931, 1935; Porter, 1953; Piña Chán, 1958). Residents of Tlatilco dug deep triangular or bottle-shaped pits into the earth. These may have been used originally for food storage, but when found by archaeologists they were filled with general household debris: pottery and figurine fragments, burned pieces of walls from wattle and daub huts, animal bones, ash, and charcoal.

Tlatilco today is a brickyard where clay is removed from vast areas and molded into sun-dried brick for building. In the process, untold remains of the Tlatilco inhabitants have been destroyed or redistributed. Several hundred burials and some refuse debris have been excavated, revealing a very long occupation of the site if the carbon-14 dates are accurate (Photo 6). Some burials have few or no offerings, but others were lavishly supplied with pottery vessels, figurines, masks (see Plate 5d), tools, and jewelry. To judge from the pottery (rocker stamping, Olmec designs, differential firing), certain graves may be Olmec of the Ixtapaluca phase (Figure 5k, o, aa) but an entire range of other traits is not part of the Olmec tradition and may be slightly later in time. In-

Plate 3. Preclassic period figures and figurines

a. D-1 figurine, Tlatilco. Height: 4½ inches. Courtesy of the Museum of the American Indian, Heye Foundation (22/4692).

b. D-2 figurine, Tlatilco. Height: 5½ inches. Courtesy of the Museum of the American Indian, Heye Foundation (22/710).

c. Chupícuaro figurine of local style. Height: 3 inches. Courtesy of the UCLA Museum of Cultural History collections, gift of Miss Natalie Wood.

d. Shaman (?) wearing animal skin, wig, and mask, Tlatilco. Height: 4 inches. Courtesy of the Museo Nacional de Antropología, Mexico.

e. H-4 figurine, Chupícuaro. Height: 3 inches. Courtesy of the UCLA Museum of Cultural History collections, gift of Miss Natalie Wood.

f. Figurine with slab base, Cuitzeo, Michoacán. Height: 5½ inches. Courtesy of the Museum of the American Indian, Heye Foundation (23/9352).

g. Effigy vessel, warrior (?) with sling, Colima. Height: 14 inches. Courtesy of the Museum of Primitive Art, New York.

h. Polychrome figure of a woman holding jar, Nayarit, Mexico. Height: 10½ inches. Courtesy of the Museum of the American Indian, Heye Foundation (23/2275).

i. Hollow figure, Gualupita, Morelos. Height: 13⅜ inches. Courtesy of the Museum of the American Indian, Heye Foundation (22/1351).

cluded are many of the Río Cuautla-style vessels as known from the San Pablo Pantheon mound in Morelos. Possibly associated with these long-necked bottle forms and stirrup spouts (Figure 5cc, ff) is a great variety of effigy and whistling vessels portraying both human and animal forms. Consider the range of fauna represented: peccaries (Plate 4k), ducks, fish (Plate 4d), birds, opossums, frogs, bears, armadillos, rabbits, and turtles, along with some purely imaginary grotesque forms. In the hand-modeled figurines we see mothers holding babies or dogs, while men are depicted as ballplayers, shamans, musicians, or acrobats. The dwarfs, hunchbacks, and monstrosities with two heads or one head with three eyes are curiosities the meaning of which eludes us. Styles of clothing, coiffures, and body adornment of the figurines suggest uses of some of the minor artifacts. For example, pyrite mirrors are shown hanging from the neck, and elaborate clay stamps produce designs similar to those painted on the bodies of the figurines. Since clothing was minimal, often limited to a saucy skirt or fancy bloomers, an animal skin, or even just a turban or necklace, exposed portions of the body were decorated by stamped colored designs. For humor, imagination, and mimicry (?), and certainly for sheer perfection of execution, the Tlatilco figurines are superb (Plate 3a, b, d). The site is famous for the beauty of its figurines and the exotic pottery shapes and decorations, many of which, especially those found in graves, are probably the result of Río Cuautla influence. The rest, some from graves but mostly from household rubbish, is recognized as the emerging local tradition known as El Arbolillo-Zacatenco, also a Middle Preclassic manifestation. These pottery forms are dominated by tripod vessels and composite silhouettes, banded geometric, incised decorations, and white-on-red painted wares (Figure 5f, g, i, r).

The only architecture positively identified at these western shore sites are fragments of wattle-and-daub house walls. El Arbolillo and Zacatenco were, to all appearances, simple farming communities. But the people at Cuicuilco went a step further. In deciding to construct an oval truncated cone, they initiated religious architecture in the basin of Mexico and started Cuicuilco on its long road to domination of the highlands (Photo 7). At the same time, perhaps under the leadership of Cuicuilco, people began to look away from were-jaguars and baby faces, nourishing their own tradition of banded geometric designs, composite silhouettes, and tripods. Perhaps they felt less apprehensive of the jaguar than of Xiuhtecuhtli (or Huehuéteotl), the Old Fire God, who controlled the restless volcanoes close by.

The small, hand-modeled figurines, a popular product of Preclassic peoples, are particularly abundant in central highland Mexico and to the west and merit some commentary. Although some types are identified as belonging to the Early Preclassic, the greatest proliferation is seen in the Middle and Late phases (Plate 3). Thereafter, though produced by molds, some kind of small solid figurine was in vogue until the Conquest and even after, into Colonial times. Why, one asks, were they made? Although some represent males, the great majority are females. Some exhibit exaggerated sexual characteristics or are obviously pregnant. Other variations are women in childbirth and mother and child groups. Figurines are most commonly found in household refuse and therefore are usually broken. Burial of figurines, as practiced at Tlatilco, where as many as sixty were found in a single grave, preserves complete specimens, but this is unusual. A number of functional interpretations have

Photo 6. Graves at Tlatilco cemetery, Valley of Mexico.
Courtesy of Arturo Romano P.

Photo 7. Pyramid at Cuicuilco, Valley of Mexico. Courtesy
of the Instituto Nacional de Antropología e Historia, Mexico.

a

b

c

d

e

f

Plate 4.   Preclassic period pottery

a. Grey-black incised bowl, Chanchopa tomb, Colima. Rim diameter: 6⅛ inches. Courtesy of Isabel T. Kelly. Col. Instituto Nacional de Antropología e Historia, Mexico.

b. Black incised composite silhouette bowl, rifled tomb, Chanchopa, Colima. Rim diameter: 4¾ inches. Courtesy of Isabel T. Kelly. Col. Instituto Nacional de Antropología e Historia, Mexico.

c. Black excised *tecomate*, cinnabar paint in roughened areas, Las Boca, Puebla. Height: 3¾ inches. Courtesy of the Museum of the American Indian, Heye Foundation (23/7832).

d. Black, excised fish effigy from Tlatilco grave. Height: 5½ inches. Courtesy of the Museo Nacional de Antropología, Mexico.

e. White-on-red cylindrical tripod, Valley of Mexico. Height: 7 inches. Courtesy of the Museo Nacional de Antropología, Mexico.

f. Goblet or vessel with pedestal base, decorated in *al fresco* technique, polychrome, Tomb 2, Tlapacoya, Valley of Mexico. Height: 7½ inches. Courtesy of the Museo Nacional de Antropología, Mexico.

g. Jar decorated in Usulután resist technique, Cobán, Guatemala. Height: 3½ inches. Courtesy of the Museum of the American Indian, Heye Foundation (9/9473).

h. Large red-ware hollow dog, Colima. Height: 5⅛ inches. Courtesy of the Museum of the American Indian, Heye Foundation (23/8366).

i. Red-on-buff spider-leg tripod, Chupícuaro, Guanajuato. Height: 6¼ inches. Courtesy of the Museum of the American Indian, Heye Foundation (22/5691).

j. Hollow jaguar figure with Zapotec style claws and mouth, Monte Albán II (?). Height: 15 inches. Courtesy of the Museo Nacional de Antropología, Mexico.

k. Hollow effigy vessel in form of peccary, with rocker-stamped decoration, Tlatilco. Height: 7 inches (figure is enlarged to show decoration). Courtesy of the Museum of the American Indian, Heye Foundation (23/6193).

been suggested, for the making of clay figurines is shared with other parts of the world, notably the Near East, where a parallel is seen in the mother goddess figures. Among some contemporary Indians of Mexico and Colombia a figurine may have special curing powers bestowed on it by a shaman. After it has performed its function it is kept around the house or thrown out. Among other groups figurines are used as protective fetishes during pregnancy. In primitive magic and religion miniatures often play a vital role. Figurines in Mesoamerica are too plentiful to have been luxury objects. This fact, together with their appearance in household refuse, suggests that they were part of a popular household cult and perhaps served as talismans or charms.

So abundant were figurines at El Arbolillo, Zacatenco, and Ticomán that George Vaillant based his Preclassic chronology, the first ever devised, on an intricate figurine typology (Vaillant, 1930, 1931, 1935). Indeed, his classification by letters and numbers is still the best we have, though it has since been modified. Difficulties and confusions have arisen from attempts to apply this classification to Mesoamerica as a whole. Then the classification loses its usefulness, for the figurines of each region are sensitive to local tastes and styles, and only in a general way can some correlations be made. The finest Middle Preclassic figurines are the D-1, D-3, and D-4 types, well represented in Tlatilco graves. Other Middle phase markers are C-1, C-2, C-3, C-5, A, B, and F.

Around 400 B.C. innovations in ceramics and architecture mark the beginning of the Late Preclassic phase in the basin of Mexico. Pottery began to be enthusiastically polychromed in combinations of red, white, yellow, black, and white. The technique of resist, or negative painting, became very popular (see Plate 11d, Chapter 7). This rather laborious method of decorating a pot consisted of protecting a field, perhaps with wax, before painting the vessel, and thereafter removing the protective covering to reveal a portion left in the base color. It is similar to using a stencil except that the design or the background may be painted. Resist-painted white ware shards were found by Tolstoy in his Ayotla phase, but are scarcely represented elsewhere in the valley at such an early date. In Morelos the technique is associated with Río Cuautla-style vessels (Grove, 1970c, 1971). Although it undoubtedly has early roots, it did not become common in the basin of Mexico until the Late Preclassic horizon.

Resist painting and polychroming of pottery are two outstanding changes that took place in ceramic decoration, but the basic El Arbolillo–Zacatenco tradition of composite silhouettes and tripod supports continued. Figurines too reflect the innovations; new types were added and old ones modified. Characteristic Late Preclassic figurines are the H, E, and G types.

I fully appreciate the difficulties encountered by anyone attempting to understand the myriad Preclassic phase names that occur in the literature dealing with the archaeology of the basin of Mexico. In the simplest of terms, the early Vaillant scheme of El Arbolillo–Zacatenco–Ticomán with its overlapping subphases eventually could stand no further modification, and a new classification was worked out by Tolstoy and Paradis (1970) based on stratigraphic work at Tlapacoya. This scheme, which is designed to apply to the general basin of Mexico, is presented in Chart 1. The former El Arbolillo–Zacatenco phases are now combined (Middle Preclassic) and a new earlier phase never encountered by Vaillant, called Ixtapaluca (Early Preclassic), has been added. Most of the Tlatilco material from stratigraphic cuts and grave lots belongs in the Zacatenco period, but some burials date from the earlier Ixtapaluca phase.

Cuicuilco

The Late Preclassic phase in the basin of Mexico has long been known as Ticomán, named for the north-shore village where it was first identified by Vaillant (1931). We now realize that the most important center must have been Cuicuilco, which was experiencing a tremendous growth and building boom (Heizer & Bennyhoff, 1958b). The earlier cone structure was altered and enlarged, resulting in a round temple platform faced with stone having two ramps leading up to the double altars at the summit, ninety feet above the ground. Less than half a mile to the west, eleven additional mound structures have recently been cleared. Cuicuilco emerges as a bustling hub of activity dominating the basin of Mexico in Late Preclassic times. Cuicuilco III–V on Chart 1 replaces the Ticomán period of Vaillant's chronology.(Photo 7).

It is likely that by this time the lake shore was peppered with settlements. Recent studies of settlement patterns in the Texcocan region suggest a far greater exploitation of lacustrine resources than during previous years. At the same time other towns were established away from the lake, along barrancas or rivers. Population estimates for some centers range from 1800 to 3500. Toward the southern end of the lake the first platform was raised at Tlapacoya, an island village rich in pottery that

Photo 8.   Pyramid at Tlapacoya, Valley of Mexico. Courtesy of
the Instituto Nacional de Antropología e Historia, Mexico.

resembles not only that of its valley neighbors Ticomán, Zacatenco,
Copilco, and Cuicuilco but also that of Monte Albán, Teotihuacán, and
Chupícuaro (Photo 8).

A Protoclassic phase is convenient and appropriately applied to the
very terminal Preclassic development in this region. Between the years
200 B.C. and A.D. 300, these valley peoples were subjected to various
pressures or influences from the east and northwest that resulted in
cultural diversification. Population continued to increase and, if the
Texcocan region reflects the prevailing settlement pattern, the great
majority of people lived in large concentrated centers characterized by
ceremonial or public works. The remains at Cuicuilco reflect the dis-
ruption of the times in the eventual destruction of its temples. Tlapacoya may have inherited its function of serving as a religious center.
Temesco, also on the eastern lake shore, is another contemporary settlement, and the remains at Cerro del Tepalcate (literally "potsherd hill")
high above Tlatilco, probably relate to this period, which basically
continue the Cuicuilco tradition (see inset, Map 2).

One source of new influence was Chupícuaro, a late Preclassic site
on the Lerma River, some eighty miles northwest of the valley. From this
center, elaborate polychrome vessels and H-4 figurines, a kind of mouse-
faced flat type with slanted eyes, were traded into the basin of Mexico
and also Morelos (Plate 3e). Bennyhoff (1967) feels that other features
were introduced into the valley from the area of Puebla. These include
flat-based bowls, more resist-painted decorations, *comales,* and perhaps
the idea of modeling figurines to represent deities.

Why some features are discarded and others selected to survive in
history is often a mystery. Of the competing styles and forms at this time,
Chupícuaro was the loser, and it is the southern or eastern influence that
blends with the older Cuicuilco–Ticomán tradition to emerge as Classic
Teotihuacán ceramics.

Teotihuacán

Teotihuacán, the one name in Mexican archaeology that everyone can pronounce, is known popularly as "the pyramids." It well merits the many thousands of visitors who come each year to see one of the most impressive ancient centers of the New World. Stretched out over nine miles in a green and once-forested valley (an offshoot of the main Valley of Mexico), Teotihuacán emerged slowly around 200 B.C. and picked up momentum at the expense of Cuicuilco, which it totally eclipsed by A.D. 150. The violent eruption of the nearby volcano of Xitli, which probably occurred later, around A.D. 400, buried the southeastern edge of the valley in molten ash and lava. But some 150 years earlier, the settlers of Cuicuilco and Copilco had already moved away, perhaps eager to participate in the growing excitement generated by Teotihuacán. The latter was destined to become the leading cultural, religious, and political force in all Mesoamerica and to maintain this unprecedented power for six centuries. The culmination of Teotihuacán culture is a story of the great Classic period, but about the time the southern lake builders were basking in their accomplishments at Cuicuilco and beginning another temple-pyramid at Tlapacoya, some astute theologians at Teotihuacán, studying the stars and planets, conceived a plan. Not just one temple aloft a pyramid would they build, but groups of temple-pyramids, to be neatly arranged in relation to a central axis, a great "avenue," oriented along a straight, north–south line just seventeen degees east of magnetic north. Were they inspired by a legacy from the more ancient Olmecs in their planning and orientation? All we can say is that this may well have been the case. It is difficult to know when the decisions were made and precisely when each structure was added, for many forms of construction were constantly in progress—building, rebuilding, remodeling, and enlarging.

Photo 9.   Pyramid of the Sun with associated structures along the Avenue of the Dead, Teotihuacán. Courtesy of Compañia Mexicana Aerofoto, S. A.

Although archaeological research has been almost constantly in progress at Teotihuacán since the 1930's, a burst of financial enthusiasm gave impetus, in 1964, to a concentrated program of joint studies composed of Mexicans directed by Jorge Acosta and a team from the University of Rochester headed by René Millon. The resulting studies have greatly expanded our knowledge of the site (Sanders, 1967; Bennyhoff, 1967; C. Millon, 1966; R. Millon, 1967; Spence, 1967; Wallwrath, 1967).

Between the years 100 B.C. and A.D. 1, known as the Patlachique phase or Proto-Teotihuacán I, we are told that there were two settlements at Teotihuacán, located just north of what was to become the main ceremonial center. Some sacred structures were probably in existence, possibly grouped in complexes of threes. The population is estimated at 5000 (Millon, 1967). To the valley farmers and part-time artisans, this tremendous religious effort offered the opportunity to "do something" about crop increases, to lure the game closer, to make it rain more frequently, or perhaps to have another son. Unified by common desires and problems and ably directed by religious leaders, the people rallied behind the preconceived plan: the time was ripe. During the next 150 years (Tzacualli or Teotihuacán I), news of the religious Mecca spread and people poured in (or perhaps were brought in), swelling the local population to 30,000. During this time groups of Oaxaca people may have moved into the area, for about three kilometers west of the Ciudadela typical Monte Albán II and IIa pottery, including an effigy urn, was found. Was Teotihuacán already so strong a center in these early days that groups were attracted from as far away as Oaxaca? These people could have been technicians or specialists in some field, and one wonders if the transfer to the city was voluntary or involuntary and if perhaps colonies from other areas of Mesoamerica will not be found. The city center now extended over seventeen square kilometers. Workers toiled as never before, and under pressure of gods and priests, most of the Pyramid of the Sun was completed, and perhaps the first structures that were to become the Pyramid of the Moon and the Temple of Quetzalcóatl.

Even legends current at the time of the Conquest refer to the Pyramids of the Sun and Moon, and unlike most labels given to ancient structures, these probably correctly relate to the gods honored at each temple. The Pyramid of the Moon guards the northern end of the central axis, the Avenue of the Dead. The Sun, located just east of the great avenue, faces west (Photo 9). A hasty and faulty reconstruction done many years ago completely destroyed the exterior facing, and although it is mammoth in size at present (two hundred feet high by seven hundred feet base length), the Pyramid of the Sun was once even larger. We believe the original was built up with the typical *talud* and *tablero* facing, in four tiers (see Figure 21, Chapter 6). The *talud–tablero* is an architectural feature that typifies Teotihuacán, and many other groups who saw it carried the idea home with them, and copied or modified it to suit their special tastes. It consists of a rectangular body (*tablero*) with recessed inset, which rests on an outward sloping basal element (*talud*). Elsewhere, the relative proportions varied, but at Teotihuacán the *tablero* always was larger than the *talud*. In the case of the Pyramid of the Sun, the interior was built up of adobe bricks. These were faced with volcanic stones set in clay and plastered over with a smooth coating of lime. The staircase located on the west side was divided at the base, then merged in the final ascent to the thatched hut on top, the sacred temple. Construction was basically of this type throughout the city, interiors consisting of adobe or rubble faced with stone set in clay and finally covered with a lime plaster.

The center of the religious complex lay nearly two miles further south where the Avenue of the Dead met another great group of structures, the Ciudadela. The Temple of Quetzalcóatl, begun at this time, was part of this group. Probably the East Avenue was also laid out as part of an east–west axis that, together with the Avenue of the Dead, divided the ceremonial center into quarters. The intricate drainage system whose web-like pattern eventually covered the whole city was also initiated. Nothing approaching the magnitude of such planning had ever been attempted before, and by A.D. 150 Teotihuacán had achieved total domination of the Valley of Mexico and perhaps even the entire highland area (see Figure 20, Chapter 6).

The next hundred years (A.D. 150–250), known as the Miccaotli or Teotihuacán II phase, marks the maximum expansion of the center, which came to occupy 22½ square kilometers. A corresponding increase in population brought the total number of people to 45,000. In this final Preclassic phase, Teotihuacán was on the threshold of its great Classic florescence. The city was now carefully laid out in quarters, containing public religious structures, palaces, and multifamily dwellings. Teotihuacán will be described and discussed in the chapter dealing with the Classic period, and we now turn to developments further west.

Western Mexico

Preclassic remains west of the basin of Mexico are still sporadically known, but considerable work in recent years is rapidly increasing our knowledge of this vast region. Western Mexico is composed of the modern states of Michoacán, Jalisco, Colima, Nayarit, and Sinaloa. Zacatecas and Durango are sometimes considered separately as the northwest frontier, and the state of Guanajuato lies directly between these two groups. With the exception of Guanajuato, the remaining areas can probably be considered as lying outside the Mesoamerican boundary at this time (see Map 2).

A long-known site that exerted considerable influence on central Mexico is Chupícuaro, to which reference has already been made. This village community lay on the banks of the Lerma River in the southern part of the state of Guanajuato. Thousands of complete pottery vessels from this site stock museums and private collections around the world, but the site itself is now covered by an artificial lake created by the Solís Dam, completed in 1949. Prior to the inundation, extensive excavations undertaken by the Instituto Nacional de Antropología e Historia of Mexico uncovered nearly four hundred richly stocked graves, a veritable cemetery located along the top of a hill at the confluence of the Lerma and a small tributary. The only remains of construction were stone alignments somewhat similar to those on the Cerro del Tepalcate and burned clay fragments presumably from floors (Porter, 1956).

Chupícuaro was the scene of great Late Preclassic activity. The people showed no interest in ceremonial architecture but lavished pottery figurines and small artifacts on the dead, so great was their preoccupation with events after death. Scattered throughout the cemetery were rectangular mud-packed basins filled with fine ash, around which were strewn burials. We imagine that interment took place while fires burned in the sunken basins.

Pottery can be divided into two distinct lots: (1) the black-brown unpainted wares, typical of Ticomán types as seen in composite silhouette, mammiform or plain tripod shapes and (2) elaborate polychrome wares decorated in combinations of red and black, brown-on-buff, and red-on-buff bichrome. Designs are geometric without exception. Variety lies in form: elongated and kidney shapes, shallow bowls with great long "spider leg" supports (Plate 4i), effigy vessels, and the stirrup spout again. The H-4 figurine was produced with great enthusiasm and traded into the basin of Mexico and Morelos, while several other related styles were limited to the locality (Plate 3c, e). Musical instruments—clay *ocarinas*, flutes, whistles, and rattles—were interred with children at death. Dogs were carefully buried, and sometimes they too were given offerings. Decapitated skeletons remind us, however, that life was not all music and gaiety. Horizontally cut skulls, painted red and perforated for suspension, were stacked on the knees of some bodies.

There are probably two successive phases represented in the graves, both falling within the Late Preclassic horizon (Porter, 1956; Weaver, 1969). The elaborate polychromes and H-4 figurines are amply represented in the central highland region. West of Chupícuaro closely related material is known from several sites around Lake Cuitzeo in Michoacán. Northwest of Chupícuaro and slightly later in time, the Canutillo phase of the Chalchihuites cultures in Zacatecas and Durango have pottery designs, motifs, and red-on-buff styles very reminiscent of Chupícuaro (Kelley, 1966). Kelley points particularly to quadrant interior decoration and nested triangles along with the red-on-buff combination as significant ingredients of these cultures. These features, along with some figurine traits, may have been introduced into the Mogollon and Hohokam cultures in the American Southwest from this northern area of Mesoamerica (J. C. Kelley, 1960, 1966).

By Classic times, all activity at Chupícuaro had ceased; these people must have either moved off or been absorbed by others, as this period is not represented in the region. Although the end of the Preclassic spells the end of Chupícuaro, its red-on-buff pottery tradition was kept alive, perhaps by the northern cultures, and we will see it reassert itself many years later in the Postclassic Matlazinca culture of the Toluca Valley and in the Coyotlatelco tradition (Weaver, 1969).

Noteworthy Preclassic material from Michoacán comes from several tombs excavated many years ago near Zamora at El Opeño (Noguera, 1942) (Figure 7). These tombs, surprisingly well made, were cut into the *tepetate* to a depth of 1.1 meters. Entrance was gained by steps leading down to an underground antechamber connected to the stone-lined tomb. In one of these tombs, the dead, stretched out on the floor, had been buried with notched and stemmed arrow points, a green stone reclining figure, jade ear plugs, and pottery figurines and vessels. The assemblage resembles that of the Ticomán–Cuicuilco horizon. Recently the Mexican archaeologist, Arturo Olivares, had the long-awaited opportunity to open another unlooted tomb. The ceramics contained therein provide one more link between the Río Cuautla-style pottery of Tlatilco and Morelos and the west, specifically with the Capacha pottery from

Colima (Grove, 1971). The carbon-14 date for this tomb is 1300 B.C., which is considerably earlier than the dates for other western Mexican tombs (see below). The chronological range of this tomb complex is still undefined but falls within the Preclassic period. The tombs may prove to be earlier than I have indicated in Chart 1.

New information from the Pacific coastal states is presently contributing much to our knowledge of early settlements in western Mexico. Although the record is still spotty and very incomplete, this area was occupied perhaps as long and densely as any other. The earliest material is that from coastal Nayarit near San Blas, where some nine feet of shell-mound refuse were excavated. The topmost stratum contained pottery, but below were found crude cobble hammers and some worked obsidian flakes. This nonceramic complex, called Matanchén, is dated at 2000 B.C. It was followed by the San Blas complex (around 500 B.C.). The latter is known from two sites located at the southernmost point of the Sinaloa–Nayarit coastal plain, just north of where the Sierra Madre Occidental mountains descend to the ocean. Its economy was oriented toward the sea and estuaries. The monochrome wares and a life based on marine exploitation form a complex reminiscent of the earlier Ocós, on the Guatemalan coast. Some of the ceramic traits (forms of jars, clay figurines, and some stone ornaments) are vaguely suggestive of Pioneer Hohokam features in the southwestern United States (Mountjoy, 1970).

To the south, in Colima, Kelly has recently uncovered a monochrome complex called Capacha, which looks unlike any other known material from western Mexico. Composite vessels, bottle forms including a stirrup spout, and figurine types resemble early Preclassic Morelos and basin of Mexico material. The pottery is heavy and poorly made, and is decorated by gouging, punching, and incising. Work in stone is of better quality. As of now, this material is known only from graves and is dated tentatively at 1450 B.C. (Kelly, 1970).

Other Preclassic manifestations are the long-known Tuxcacuesco, Jalisco, and Ortices phases of Colima. Lack or near lack of vessel supports, decoration by incision on monochrome pottery, and hand-modeled figurines are characteristic. Additional related material comes from the boundary between the two states, on coastal Colima at the Morett site. A good midden some ten feet in depth has yielded a fine stratigraphic sequence that may reach back to 500 B.C. Large jars with grooved and punched ornamentation and jars with tall necks and flaring rims decorated by incising and grooving are the ingredients of some sites in the Armeria drainage. A great variety of decorations are found including white-on-red, negative, and polychrome painting. Most interesting because of similarities with the Conchas phase of Guatemala and early material from Ecuador is zoning in red and white. Chanchopa, related to the Ortices phase, ties in with eastern Colima (Kelly, 1945–1949) (Plate 4a, b).

The general region of Colima, Jalisco, and Nayarit has produced a great variety of hollow figurines or effigy vessels as well as small solid figurines. The large Colima figures (Plate 3g), often of highly polished red or brown clay, portray adults and children in a variety of activities such as grinding corn and carrying jars; some are abstract figures that may well have a symbolic meaning as yet unidentified. Nayarit figures likewise portray a variety of human activities in a somewhat different style (Plate 3h). Particularly charming are small figures forming scenes of people grouped around a house or temple. Musicians beat drums, shake rattles, and play flutes while others dance and do acrobatics. This gaiety and frivolity is in marked contrast to the later macabre sobriety of altiplano art. The Colima modeled pottery flutes are among Mesoamerica's finest. The red pottery dogs (Plate 4h) of Colima (Ortices phase), found in graves, are avidly collected by art dealers. They are usually believed to have been made for interment, to carry the soul of the deceased across a river, one of the obstacles to be overcome before reaching paradise. Much could be learned from the dress, ornamentation, and polychrome designs of these ceramic sculptures, but no definitive study has been attempted. One imaginative effort has been made by Furst (1965b), who has dealt with figures from shaft-and-chamber tombs. He believes that the many figures bearing arms do not represent warriors, but rather indicate a strongly developed shamanistic complex. Thus, the single or paired horns on many Colima and Nayarit figures may be the insignia of supernatural power worn by priests or shamans, an idea derived from ethnographic studies among contemporary Indians of western Mexico and groups in northern Asia. The implication is that of survival of an extremely ancient substratum common to these groups.

Shaft-and-chamber tombs are abundant in the region around Guadalajara in Jalisco and in Colima and Nayarit, but they have usually been thoroughly ransacked before the arrival of an archaeologist. The tombs, generally boot shaped in form, consist of a vertical shaft usually four to six meters deep that leads to one or more horizontal chambers. The deepest tombs are frequently located in high places overlooking the surrounding country. The shaft-tomb complex is known to extend from north of Ixtlán del Río, Nayarit, to south of Guadalajara, Jalisco, and is tentatively dated around the beginning of the Christian era, which is to say, in Late Preclassic times (Taylor, Berger, Meighan, & Nicholson, 1969).

What is believed to be the total contents of one tomb near Etzatlán, Jalisco, came to rest in the Los Angeles County Museum. It consists of nine articulated skeletons and jumbled bones of three others without skulls. The nine deceased were accompanied by seventeen hollow polychrome figurines ranging in height from 27.5 to 51.5 centimeters, forty polychrome dishes and bowls, several rectangular ceramic boxes with lids, shell and obsidian ornaments, and conch shell trumpets. Of the conch shell trumpets, one proved to be of Caribbean and one of Pacific Coast origin. It is not uncommon to find Caribbean trumpets in the shaft tombs. This one yielded a carbon-14 date of 266 B.C.; the west coast shell from this tomb is dated at A.D. 254. These dates refer, of course, to the death of the mollusks, not to their placement in the tomb. Opinions differ as to whether this particular tomb represents one occupation or two, but the reuse or continued use of tombs is a common practice (Furst, 1965b).

Another shaft tomb, from Tequilita in the southern temperate highlands of Nayarit, yields a date around A.D. 100, and a Chanchopa tomb near coastal Colima is slightly earlier. Thus, in western Mexico during Late Preclassic times, people were greatly preoccupied with burial of the dead and dug these curious tombs, which in themselves are far more characteristic of northwestern South America than Mesoamerica and may be the result of direct contact by sea (see Chapter 9). And because a number of the hollow ceramic sculptures come from the Etzatlán tomb, we can now place them on the Preclassic horizon.

These western cultures were apparently very active during Pre-classic years, and their potential role in Mesoamerican affairs has here-tofore been greatly underestimated. It is hard to imagine the delta of the Balsas River as other than an intersection, transfer point, or redistribu-tion center, for here people could converge from three routes of communi-cation: the overland route to highland central Mexico following the great Balsas River, the low Pacific coastal plain and the sea itself, for sea-going craft must have been attracted by the excellent port with its unusual opportunities for communication. Early archaeological remains are difficult to locate and probably lie beneath deep accumulations of silt and modern settlements, but pressure is mounting to search for them as cultural resemblances between far-flung areas of Mesoamerica and Central and South America increase.

Passing eastward along the Pacific Coast to the Isthmus of Tehuan-tepec, we return to events in the Maya area, where early peoples of coastal Chiapas and Guatemala lived much like the estuary inhabitants of San Blas. However, as maize became more important to their sub-sistence, the populations of these areas were able to increase steadily throughout the Middle Preclassic period, and more and more time was devoted to building religious structures. About the time the inhabitants of Nayarit, Jalisco, and Colima were preoccupied with constructing deep shaft tombs, Soconusco peoples began to move inland, as if they felt drawn by the dynamic forces that were to propel their highland con-temporaries toward a great Late Preclassic climax.

Eastern Mesoamerica

The Pacific Coast and Highland Guatemala

Not so many years ago it was thought that the story of the Maya began in the central region, the lowlands of the Petén, but we now know that although there were Preclassic settlements in the lowlands, even north to the tip of the peninsula of Yucatán, the most extraordinary advances were being made in the highlands of Guatemala at Kaminaljuyú, the outskirts of the modern capital.

Bordered by lofty volcanoes jutting above the surrounding hills, the broad green plateau at 4897 feet above sea level, where Guatemala City sprawls today, has always been favored as a living site for man. Offering a temperate climate that varies little throughout the year, with rainfall often adequate for two planting seasons, the area possesses rich volcanic soil, small game in the pine and oak forests in the surrounding higher country, and abundant resources of minerals and plants. Few areas could offer more advantages to the farmer, the builder, and the artisan. Of more than thirty-five prominent archaeological sites in the valley, by far the largest settlement was on the western edge. Known as Kaminaljuyú, it was the scene of great activity throughout Preclassic and Classic times (Borhegyi, 1965; Kidder, Jennings, & Shook, 1946; Shook & Kidder, 1952; Sanders & Michels, 1969).

No habitation mounds have actually been excavated of the earliest phase (Arévalo), but again many burned adobe fragments show impres-sions of poles and vegetal material. Living sites were scattered, open, and undefended. The quality of the pottery is outstanding, even superior to some of later periods. The variety in form and decoration shows that potters were in complete command of their craft. Monochrome wares are red, black, buff, white, or gray-brown; bichromes are largely combinations of red and white or buff. Small hand-modeled figurines, clay stamps, and hollow effigy whistles all conform to similar developments elsewhere.

The earliest phase, Arévalo, was followed by Las Charcas A; two Middle Preclassic phases, Las Charcas B and Providencia–Majadas; and a Late phase known as Miraflores–Arenal (Borhegyi, 1965). Las Charcas is best remembered for its bottle-shaped rubbish pits like those of Tlatilco and beautiful white kaolin pottery handsomely painted with abstract designs, dragon masks, or realistic portrayals of monkeys. Clay temple-pyramids were probably already being constructed by these people.

During the Middle and Late Preclassic years (600 B.C. to A.D. 300), religious architecture got off to a good start. Temple-pyramids, which in some cases served also as burial mounds, were arranged along both sides of a long rectangular plaza or avenue. Religion was the driving motivation, and all nearby peoples must have contributed heavily, in time and muscle, to the necessary labor force. Apparently there was no fear of outsiders since the sacred or civic centers were located on open valley floors without visible means of protection. Sanders and Michels (1969) suggest that these centers may have been utilized largely for ritual burials of chiefs.

A brief look at the Miraflores phase may serve to exemplify the peak of Preclassic development in the highland area (Shook & Kidder, 1952). Huge earthen mounds were brightly painted, and two to eight staircases led to a hut-like temple on top. But these mounds were not built to their final height of sixty feet all at once. One such mound may contain as many as seven interior structures. The custom of enlarging a pyramid periodically is a common feature of Mesoamerican builders. Thus, the oldest structure will be the smallest and form the initial interior core of a mound, with successive pyramids superimposed upon it. All this was done at Miraflores, but just prior to one of these periodic enlargements the builders dug through the top of an existing pyramid and excavated a rectangular-stepped opening to be used as a tomb (Figure 7). The corners were carefully braced by wooden uprights, and then the privileged deceased, covered with red paint, was carefully extended on a litter in the center. In the case of Tomb 2 in Mound E-III-3, both adults and children were offered in sacrifice, along with more than 300 objects, to accompany the distinguished corpse in afterlife. These objects were items of great luxury, such as jade beads, mosaics, and masks; beautifully carved vessels of soapstone, fuchsite, and chlorite schist (see Figure 5t, x); sting-ray spines, symbols of self-sacrifice; stuccoed gourds; sheets of mica; fine implements of obsidian and basalt; bone; quartz crystals; fish teeth; and quantities of fine pottery vessels. The contents complete, the tomb was then roofed over with crossbeams and rush mats, the flooring restored, and construction of a new, grander pyramid accomplished by covering the entire mound according to plan. Two such tombs were found, both occupying prominent positions in pyramidal structures. Mound E-III-3 is the largest and best-known structure of the Miraflores people. Actually it forms part of a small compact group of nine mounds which were arranged around a plaza. Two other such groups of public buildings have also been identified which contain similar though smaller constructions. Each of these has a high terraced temple platform and a low sprawling platform presumed to be the sub-structure of an elite residence. Nearby trenches yielded remains of refuse, hearth, and earth floors, abundant pottery and obsidian tools, indicating that there was a small but dense resident population (Sanders & Michels, 1969).

A very distinctive pottery, called Usulután ware, was much in style in Late Preclassic times (Plate 4g). Usulután refers to a decoration in resist or negative painting technique that produced groups of wave-like yellowish lines on a dark orange or brown background. The uniform spacing of the lines on a given vessel indicates the use of some kind of applicator. Usulután vessels have a continuous range in western Honduras, Salvador, and Guatemala but are not known from Mexico, except for stray examples in neighboring Chiapas. Chronologically Usulután ware is of Late Preclassic manufacture, but it persisted into Classic times in the extreme southern regions of Mesoamerica (Rands & Smith, 1965).

Although clay figurines, stamps, and whistles were made in abundance by the Miraflores people, none was found among the numerous articles in the tombs. One suspects, therefore, that these were not prestigious goods and were destined only for daily usage among the general populace.

The possible significance of toads as a hallucinogenic medium was mentioned earlier in relation to the San Lorenzo inhabitants. We again encounter the toad or frog represented on stone mortars and pottery bowls among the contents of Tomb 1 at Miraflores. A "mushroom" stone was also found in the same tomb. These stones are curious objects not yet explained to anyone's complete satisfaction. They are cylindrical shafts of stone set on annular or tripod bases with mushroom-shaped caps. Some are plain, while others are decorated by human figures or animals (jaguars, toads or frogs, rabbits, deer, or birds), which may replace the shaft. They may represent some kind of mushroom cult with hallucinogenic connotations, or they may symbolize a totem of some kind. Mushroom stones are distributed throughout the Guatemalan highlands and Pacific slopes, and more rarely in the lowlands, Chiapas, and El Salvador. They were made during Preclassic and Classic times, but apparently their manufacture ceased thereafter (see Plate 10i, Chapter 6) (Borhegyi, 1965).

The larger stone sculpture at Kaminaljuyú reflects the result of a long history of Preclassic monumental carving shared by the Pacific slopes and the region of the Isthmus of Tehuantepec. As elsewhere this sculpture seems to be primarily religious in nature, and at Kaminaljuyú uncarved plain stelae are often associated with mounds. Possibly dating from this time are a series of curious boulder sculptures of human heads and figures (Shook, 1965; Miles, 1965). The sexless figure commonly represented is fat, heavy shouldered, and usually clasps his flexed knees. With a flat nose, thick lips, fat cheeks, and long ears adorned with spools, he is a distinctive personality. A vague resemblance is noted by some to the colossal heads found in the southern Veracruz and Tabasco areas. The boulder sculptures found at Kaminaljuyú were deliberately smashed and suffered heavy damage, which recalls the treatment given to the San Lorenzo and La Venta monuments. Sculptures of similar style were scattered about the slopes of the Pacific, in particular at a site called Monte Alto. To a slightly later time belong the pedestal sculptures that depict jaguars, *pisotes*, monkeys, and some human figures capping a long square shaft. Although most numerous at Kaminaljuyú, they have also been found throughout the highlands, on the Pacific slopes, and in Honduras. The peak of Preclassic sculpture is exemplified by two great sculptured stelae from the Miraflores phase of Kaminaljuyú, both of which exhibit a style related to that of Izapa (Stirling, 1943; M. D. Coe, 1966). Stela 11 shows a single standing human figure, attired in a cape and bearing four different varieties of the dragon mask. Standing on an Izapa-type platform and observed from above by the sky god, he carries in his left hand a kind of ceremonial hatchet and an "eccentric" flint like one found in the Miraflores tombs. The most important sculpture is Stela 10, made of black basalt, which unfortunately was deliberately smashed and mutilated before being buried with Stela 11. It depicts an anthropomorphous jaguar, a human figure, and probably a god. Below a pair of outstretched arms is a long hieroglyphic text—the earliest known —that is considered to be unquestionably Maya, although it does not bear a date (Miles, 1965).

There are also some sculptures in the round, such as a handsome frog altar presently in the Guatemala Museum, toad mortars, and three large monuments closely related to the much-discussed masks flanking the staircases of the E-VII-sub pyramid at Uaxactún. These exhibit elements of the serpent, Chac the rain god, and perhaps a tinge of Olmec flavor. The Kaminaljuyú monuments are executed in Miraflores style although they were found in association with an Arenal structure. Other sculptures attributed to the Late phase are tenoned or "silhouette" figures. These stones have a projection at the back which permits them to be embedded in walls or floors.

The glory and luxury evident at Kaminaljuyú can only signify a high degree of social stratification with wealth, power, and prestige in the hands of an elite few. The trend toward standardization of ritual material and the exclusion of certain artifacts such as figurines from the rich tombs suggests that religion was becoming formalized and rigidly patterned. The Protoclassic phase, Santa Clara, shows clearly that decline had set in, for the building boom ended, population declined, and people fell upon hard times.

Izapa and the Late Preclassic Period

While the people of Miraflores were actively building religious structures and honoring their dead with their finest treasures, strange new religious ideas in the west were rapidly capturing the souls of men. In Chiapas, about twenty miles from the Pacific Coast near Tapachula, the inhabitants of Izapa created a flurry of interest by narrating scenes and recording mythological episodes in a vivacious new style of stone carving (Plate 2b) (Miles, 1965). Izapa was an enormous center of activity and boasted eighty temple-pyramids arranged around courts and plazas, but its most outstanding remains are the stelae, altars, and huge stones covered with elaborate carved compositions. One figure, perhaps a deity, is shown with a greatly extended upper lip. Those who have made comparative studies of Olmec, Izapa, and Maya monuments believe this long-lipped god to be derived from the more ancient Olmec were-jaguar that later became the Maya rain god, Chac (M. D. Coe, 1966).

Several Izapa stelae are executed in Miraflores style, and there is little question that considerable exchange of ideas took place between the people of Chiapas and those of the eastern highlands of Guatemala. Although Izapa has a long cultural history, it was a site of particular importance during Late Preclassic and Protoclassic times. Its influence is reflected in Pacific Coast sites as well as at Kaminaljuyú and sites to the east in the Maya lowlands. Perhaps the marked decline in coastal settlements is partly attributable to Izapa's success. La Victoria and Salinas la Blanca, so attractive to people during the Early and Middle Preclassic days, seem to have been forsaken for living sites on the western slope such as El Baúl, Bilbao, El Jobo, and Abaj Takalik, all of which clearly reflect Izapa influence in the Late period.

It is in this region that the first calendrical inscriptions from the Maya area are found. Stela 2 at Abaj Takalik shows two figures facing each other over a vertical column of hieroglyphs (Miles, 1965; Proskouriakoff, 1950). The glyphs identifying period and cycle are missing, but those present clearly depict position numerals. This remarkable stela shows a large bearded head surrounded by dragon masks and scrolls. It was executed in a style clearly derived from Izapa yet with unmistakable links to the Early Classic sculptures in the lowlands.

At El Baúl, halfway between Kaminaljuyú and the Pacific, another stela with glyphs, some of which are numerals, was associated with Arenal (Late Preclassic) pottery. In this case also, the hieroglyphs are badly eroded, but these two stelae show that Long Count dates were being recorded. M. D. Coe (1957, 1966) reconstructs both stones as having a baktun 7 coefficient; thus, Stela 1 at El Baúl (see Plate 6d, Chapter 5) would be read as 7.19.15.7.12, or A.D. 36 in our calendar (see Chapter 5). This interpretation credits El Baúl with the earliest dated monument in the Maya area, but it postdates Stela C of Tres Zapotes (Plate 6a) and antedates by some 260 years the first known dated monument in the eastern lowlands (Plate 6b).

The Lowland Maya: Central and Northern Regions

In a way, the lowland areas of the Petén and the peninsula of Yucatán occupy a cultural position similar to that of central highland Mexico in that both regions were peripheral to the greater development taking place in the region from Tres Zapotes extending south through the Isthmus to the area of Soconusco and the Guatemalan highlands (see Map 2).

As we have seen, Preclassic remains are strongly represented all through the regions of Chiapas, the coastal and Pacific slopes of Guatemala, and the southern highlands around Kaminaljuyú. Remains of Preclassic people in the northern highlands are few in comparison and little is known from the Alta Verapaz region and the Motagua Valley, a logical route from the southern highlands to the Petén region. The earliest Preclassic settlements we know of lay in Soconusco, and they in turn could have inspired the southern highlands. The Petén region to the east and north, to which we now turn, seems to have been more heavily influenced by adjacent Gulf Coast lowlands than by their closer neighbors, the highlanders.

We now descend to the dense tropical jungle, a rather unlikely place for a civilization to develop, where the rain forest growth of Spanish cedars, mahogany, and sapodilla trees join overhead, only occasionally letting through the dazzling sunlight, while underneath, young trees, vines, and palms thrive in the hot, humid shade. Today this area holds little interest for the outside world, except perhaps as the home of chewing gum, made from chicle, the thick, milky sap of the sapodilla tree, but its importance in Mesoamerican history is great, for it was also the chosen home of the Maya Indians, who found here the inspiration to achieve one of the greatest civilizations of the western hemisphere.

The very earliest Preclassic remains belong to the Xe complex, a ceramic sphere of influence centering in southern and southwestern Guatemala. This material (early Middle Preclassic) comes from the sites of Seibal and Altar de Sacrificios on the Pasión River. At Seibal, a site located on a one hundred-meter-high bluff overlooking a great bend of the Pasión River, rubbish left by Preclassic peoples underlies later constructions—floors, buildings, and patios. Their remains are also known from a few pits. The pottery is known as the Real Xe complex, which is closely affiliated with the Xe pottery at Altar de Sacrificios. The *tecomate* form, monochrome wares, and double-line break are all familiar, but the Real Xe also has a white ware with thick slip and a large bolstered *tecomate* form. As far as we know, this Xe complex, the earliest Maya lowland pottery, is limited to this region. Of outside areas, it is most closely related to the Late Dili–Early Escalera phases at Chiapa de Corzo, but ties can also be found with the Guatemalan Pacific coast (Conchas) and the Gulf Coast cultures as far north as the Huasteca (Willey, 1970).

Other pre-Mamom pottery has been found at Dzibilchaltún, that extraordinary site in Yucatán with abundant remains spanning Middle Preclassic and Conquest times (Andrews, 1960, 1965). The earliest Preclassic remains there (the Zacnicte complex) show little similarity to other lowland sites and represent rather a local development of black-on-tan and black-and-red-on-tan polychrome decoration of simple forms. The Maní Cenote narrow-mouthed and pointed-bottomed jars found by George Brainerd in Yucatán may also be this early, but they are quite unlike any other material except for their pattern-burnished decoration.

About 600 B.C. remains of the Mamom horizon are reported from central and eastern Maya lowland sites. It was first identified as a complex at Uaxactún and Tikal, sites located in the dense tropical jungle of northeastern Petén (Kidder, 1947). Mamom remains consist largely of pottery and figurines. The monochrome pottery—red, orange, black, grey, brown, or cream—may be decorated by daubs of red in bands. The ware has a characteristic waxy feel owing to a glossy slip that makes up the bulk of any Mamom pottery sample. Common shapes are flat-bottomed bowls and cuspidors. The figurines are not unlike some from Chiapas and the highlands, being fashioned by punching and filleting. However, they are all monotonously alike, presenting none of the vigor, imagination, and sophistication displayed by their contemporaries in the basin of Mexico. The horizon includes a few artifacts of stone and obsidian, but no evidence of construction. Despite these generalities, there is considerable diversity between sites and relationships between complexes are not always clear.

A pure Mamom cache was found in a *chultun* at Tikal, only a few miles south of Uaxactún. A *chultun* is a pit hollowed out of limestone bedrock; it is composed of one or more inner chambers and is closed with a stone lid. These *chultunes* are found both at Tikal and Uaxactún, and various suggestions have been offered to explain their possible use. They could have been used as water cisterns, burial chambers, sweat baths, food storage pits, or some kind of subterranean shrine. In recent excavations at Tikal however, *chultunes* were most commonly found in the area of living quarters and are located on high ground. The most logical explanation now seems to be that they were food storage pits, for at least one is associated with each household group (Puleston, 1965). More recently Haviland (1970) states that by 200 B.C. these were used specifically for storing the breadnut.

Mamom must have been a simple village culture, and as such it forms part of a general complex found at other Petén sites such as Seibal and Altar de Sacrificios along the Pasión River. It is also found at British Honduras sites, at Dzibilchaltún in Yucatán, and in the Chenes area of Campeche, but it is lacking in the Motagua Valley and at Copán in the south.

In Yucatán the Middle Preclassic ceramics of Dzibilchaltún are simple but far from primitive. The relationships of this pottery to Petén wares are vague, but it occupies an equivalent stratigraphic position. The people built mud-walled houses and low platforms, but nothing at this time is distinctly Maya in appearance (Andrews, 1960, 1965).

Late Preclassic remains, called Chicanel, are both more extensive and more uniform than Mamom. The complex includes virtually all the southern Maya lowlands and extends throughout the peninsula of Yucatán. All indications lead us to suppose that it represents a long period of intense occupation of the Maya lowland. The contrast with Mamom is enormous. Complexes now show a great degree of similarity. Chicanel people left behind them a variety of pottery forms, mostly legless, but they did add wide-everted rims and flange protuberances. Usulután and some waxy wares are diagnostic. Figurines, which in Mamom faithfully conformed to the prevailing trend, now virtually disappeared. The most exciting innovations were architectural. A variety of structures were suddenly erected, including rich tombs, temple-pyramids, great plazas, terraces, and primitive corbelled vaults decorated with painted murals. Many of these changes did not occur until Late Chicanel, around A.D. 1, and about this time rapid strides were made toward full Classic status. At this time there were distinct signs of the emergent Maya civilization (Thompson, 1965a).

The beautiful white stuccoed pyramid known as E-VII-sub of Uaxactún is a Chicanel structure (Photo 10). Preserved intact by later superimposed buildings, this squat little pyramid, measuring only twenty-seven feet in height, is famous for its eighteen grotesque monster masks that flank the staircases, which lead up all four sides. Some masks have elements of the jaguar, such as curled tusks and flat snouts, but others suggest the rain god or the serpent. Even such a carefully stuccoed and adorned structure, set off by its own plaza, was crowned by a simple, perishable temple (Thompson, 1943).

A somewhat similar pyramid with painted stucco masks, also of Chicanel date, has been uncovered at Tikal (W. R. Coe, 1967). Some Chicanel temples were built with masonry walls, and recent excavations have shown that the great plaza and much of the planning of Tikal was done at this time. Temples and tombs were adorned with mural paintings, the earliest of the Maya area. As might be guessed, the theme is religious. The style is Izapan. The presence of obsidian is good evidence of contact with the highlands. Tombs equal in splendor to those of their highland contemporaries at Miraflores have the unique distinction of being roofed over by a primitive corbelled arch.

Much is made of this corbelled or "false" arch for several reasons. It was the most sophisticated arch known in New World architecture,

Photo 10.   Pyramid E-VII-sub at Uaxactún, Petén region of Guatemala. Courtesy of the Peabody Museum, Harvard University.

and we believe it was developed by the Maya for roofing their tombs and was later used to support roofs of temples, palaces, stairways, and passageways (see Figure 23, Chapter 6). It is called a "false" arch because it lacks the central keystone that can support an enormous weight and permits wide doorways and graceful curves. The corbelled arch results in narrow, dark rooms and necessitates thick, massive walls. It is built up from the top of a column or wall, each successive stone jutting slightly out over the one below, eventually closing the gap with a capstone. The corbelled arch is always associated with fine Classic Maya architecture, and its primitive beginnings in Late Chicanel tombs at Tikal and Altar de Sacrificios are of considerable interest (Thompson, 1954; W. R. Coe, 1967).

Chicanel structures are also known from Dzibilchaltún, where great massive aggregations were attempted; at Yaxuná, just south of Chichén Itzá, is a single great pyramidal mound. But neither these nor other sites in Yucatán have produced any corbelled vaulting of Preclassic date.

The lowland Maya were rapidly catching up with their highland counterparts and now had the corbelled arch to their credit, but what about monumental stone carving, writing, and dates? The only known Preclassic lowland sculpture is a rock carving near the entrance to Loltun Cave, Yucatán, which also boasts of a hieroglyphic inscription, but few other hieroglyphics have come to light. There was excellent raw material at hand, but apparently interests and efforts were devoted to other fields of religious activity. Or it may be that monuments were battered and defaced, and have been more effectively hidden by the jungle than were those at Kaminaljuyú. If so, they still await discovery.

Sometimes a Protoclassic (Holmul I or Matzanel) phase is included here. It is represented at a group of sites south of the Petén, notably Holmul, Mountain Cow, Barton Ramie, and Douglas in British Honduras.

Corbelled vaulting of tombs is present at these southern sites together with unusual ceramic features. The tetrapod bowls, pot stands, great breast-shaped or mammiform supports (see Figure 5y), and polychrome decoration at these sites are scarcely represented in the Petén and yet are much in evidence in Late Preclassic material at Monte Albán in Oaxaca. The distribution in this case is so broken that not until more work is done in intervening areas can we hope to clarify the history of these types (Thompson, 1943, 1965a).

The Southern Periphery

On the southern periphery of Mesoamerica, some truly primitive-looking pottery has been found at Lake Yojoa in northwestern Honduras, but we do not know how early this really is (Strong *et al.*, 1938). It was found in the lowest levels of two pits beneath Maya polychrome horizons, sealed by a three-foot sterile layer. The complex includes plain wares, very little paint, some tetrapod supports, and simple hand-modeled figurines. Some crude stone tools complete the inventory.

In the same general area on the Ulua River, the sites called Playa de los Muertos and Santa Rita yield Preclassic material. The presence of zoned and excised decorations, rocker stamping, bottle forms, a stirrup-spouted effigy pot, and hand-modeled figurines seem to relate this material to Middle Preclassic remains elsewhere. Another site is Yarumela in the Comayagua Valley. From deep stratigraphic tests, the pottery recovered is not crude but very simple, having monochrome plates and jars without decoration or slip, handles, feet, or spouts. This pottery lay beneath other ceramics decorated by pattern burnishing, which in turn was followed by a level with Usulután resist ware accompanied by mound building. The most recent level contains remains of a full Classic horizon (Canby, 1951; Strong *et al.*, 1938). Some shards from central Honduras resemble Valdivia pottery from coastal Ecuador (Stone, 1957; see Chapter 9), while M. D. Coe (1961) relates other wares to Ocós and Chiapa I and II material. The entire area of Honduras is badly in need of more extensive excavations before its role in Nuclear American relationships can be fully appreciated.

Preclassic material has also been found in El Salvador at Quelepa and Cerro Zapote, buried under layers of volcanic ash. We need additional information for accurate relation of all these southern sites to their northern contemporaries, but there is little question that this southern frontier of Mesoamerica was settled by Preclassic peoples. It is a region of considerable interest because of its geographical location on Meso-america's southern frontier (Longyear, 1966).

Cultural Diversity and Unity by A.D. 300

Considering the many gaps in our knowledge of Preclassic peoples, it is remarkable that we know so much about life at this time. Village farming communities were widespread, and sedentary life became increasingly dependent on cultivation of maize, beans, and other cultigens, together with a continuing exploitation of other food resources in varied microenvironmental situations. Other general characteristics that were to continue as traditions are: the planned ceremonial center, clay figurines, the *tecomate* and flat-based vessel form, the striking of parallel-sided blades from prepared cores, and the *mano* and *metate*. The trough *metate* seems to be earliest, followed by the addition of supports and finally a flat form used with a *mano* that projected over either side.

Nevertheless, the period is marked by considerable differences among regions and development is far from homogeneous. Slash-and-burn agriculture, "pot" irrigation, *tlacolol* farming, and canal irrigation were all practiced according to local conditions. Other areas relied entirely on dry farming without attempting to control the water supply. Material from the earliest Pacific coastal settlements of the Soconusco region suggests possible contacts with early contemporaries in South America. Pottery styles and techniques of decoration provide increasing evidence that certain groups in both areas of Nuclear America were aware of one another. There are many signs of special local developments, which makes for dissatisfaction with the inclusion of all these cultures under the aegis of "Preclassic." For example, the Olmec culture is of sufficient complexity and sophistication to be considered a civilization.

The early leadership of the Olmecs is manifested in the remains at San Lorenzo and La Venta, where the inhabitants hauled great stones over long distances to be carved into monuments and excavated great amounts of earth for tremendous building ventures—all for the glorification of religious beliefs closely associated with the were-jaguar theme. The formal planned ceremonial center at La Venta set a precedent followed throughout Mesoamerica until the Conquest. From their lowland heartland, the Olmecs traveled extensively, to highland Mexico (possibly via Oaxaca), west to Guerrero, and south to El Salvador, in search of the stones they prized for making celts, plaques, beads, and figurines. They may well have initiated calendric calculations, but it is at Monte Albán that we see the first glyphs and evidence of the Calendar Round, and at Tres Zapotes the earliest Long Count date.

The Olmecs came early to the basin of Mexico (competing with people from the west?), but a distinctive local tradition gradually replaced the influence of the jaguar people. By Late Preclassic times, people erected temple-pyramids and traded extensively with their neighbors, and the great ceremonial center of Teotihuacán was laid out with construction well under way. Its leadership became firmly established and the population increased daily, resulting in the eclipse of Cuicuilco and other valley centers.

In 500 B.C. the littoral peoples of western Mexico may have lived much as did the residents of Soconusco a thousand years earlier. Indeed, the latter may have had contemporaries in Colima, if the one early date for Capacha is confirmed. The Pacific Coast is studded with Preclassic remains, and the ecological conditions of the coastal flood plains could have supported a dense population. These western groups kept up with trends and advances in pottery and agriculture, but as yet their settlements have yielded no indication of ceremonial centers, water works, or calendrics. In Colima and Nayarit, deep shaft-and-chamber tombs were specialties, along with remarkable ceramic sculptures of large figurines. The archaeology of this enormous area is so distinctive that the region should be considered outside of the mainstream of development in Mesoamerica during this horizon. There are suggestions of overland contact with the present southwestern area of the United States (Mountjoy, 1970) and maritime contact with northwestern South America (C. Brush,

a

**Plate 5.   Various   Preclassic   period
artifacts**

a. Stone sculpture with mask of
the Long-Nosed God. Height: 57¾
inches, weight: 117 pounds. Courtesy of
the Museum of the American Indian,
Heye Foundation (9/6718).

b. Cylindrical clay stamp or seal,
Las Bocas, Puebla. Height: 3½ inches.
Courtesy of the Museum of Primitive Art,
New York.

c. Jade mosaic mask representing
Bat God, Monte Albán II grave. Height:
6⅞ inches. Courtesy of the Museo Nacional de Antropología, Mexico.

d. Small clay mask with two perforations for suspension, Tlatilco. Diameter:
4¾ inches. Courtesy of the Museum of
the American Indian, Heye Foundation
(23/5589).

b

c

d

1969; West, 1961; Oviedo y Valdés, 1851–1855; Edwards, 1969; Willey, 1971a). The result is seen in special art styles and tomb construction, the inference being that we are dealing here with an independent cultural strain.

Turning again to eastern Mesoamerica, we find some rather remarkable achievements. Soconusco ceded its early leadership to Izapa and related sites, which in turn influenced the lowland Maya cultures, and the Pacific piedmont of Guatemala and may have played a role in the extraordinary sequence of events leading to the Preclassic climax at Miraflores, Kaminaljuyú. To the east and north, the Petén cultures were more closely allied to adjacent lowland developments than to their highland neighbors, and by late Preclassic times they were set on a course already recognizable as Maya, having the corbelled arch, elaborate tombs, and ceremonial architecture. Preclassic lowland development had been remarkable in the Gulf Coast region, but by A.D. 300, the threshold of the great Classic period, it was already apparent that Teotihuacán had wrested leadership from the lowland cultures. East of the Isthmus, just the reverse took place; the center to watch there is the Petén.

T HE SELECTION OF A.D. 300 FOR THE INITIATION OF the Classic period is based largely on the appearance of the Long Count or Initial Series inscriptions in the lowland Maya area. This recording of dates and other hieroglyphic inscriptions may be the most important contributions of the Maya Indians to Mesoamerican civilization. Before examining the events of the Classic period, let us first look in some detail at the unusual scientific achievements of the Mesoamerican peoples: their counting systems, calendrical recordings, and methods of writing. I have relied on the following general sources for the material in this chapter: Caso (1967), Kelley (1962a, b, c), Knorozov (1958, 1967), Morley (1915, 1956), Satterthwaite (1965), and Thompson (1950, 1962, 1965b).

The Mesoamerican peoples in general were fascinated by the passage of time. The entire written record, their calendar, commemorative dates, and books, shows an obsession with permutating cycles, the recording of elapsed time, and predictions for the future. At first glance, one might imagine that these Indians were dedicated to the advancement of astronomy. Upon careful scrutiny, however, other reasons for this preoccupation seem more likely. Whether one is considering the Maya Indians of the Petén region of Guatemala, the Zapotecs of Oaxaca, the Mixtecs of Puebla, the Nahua of the basin of Mexico, or the Tarascans of Michoacán, the predominating reason for such an exact record of passing time and the attendant writing systems seems to have been intimately related to astrology and prognostication of the future. Only by being able to accurately predict, or be forewarned of future events; eclipses; seasonal changes; movements of the sun, moon, and other planets; forthcoming period endings and cyclical concurrences, could these men prepare themselves to deal with the gods, the forces of good and evil, by making the necessary offerings and sacrifices to insure their continued support. The chronological events of a ruler's personal life, his major victories, and proud achievements—his past—were recorded in stone to stand in public places of honor. Such a recording of the past may have served at the same time as a kind of religious insurance against an uncertain future.

We know from the Spanish accounts of the sixteenth century that only a small fraction of Maya society could read and interpret the inscriptions. Indeed, only an even smaller group, probably made up of nobles and religious leaders, had a working knowledge of all the scientific details. Undoubtedly traders and merchants had a rudimentary knowledge of the inscriptions, enough to handle their own accounts and identify place-name glyphs of towns on maps. The general populace, however, relied on its leaders, first religious and later secular, to tell them when it was time for a new year festival, or whether a certain day would be auspicious for a wedding ceremony or the baptism of a child. It is easy to understand the respect and awe granted a priest if, after his prediction

5

The Written Record

a

b

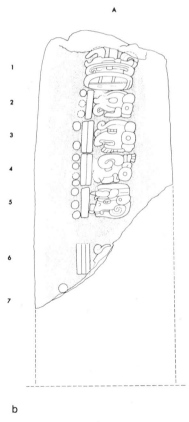

A

1
2
3
4
5
6
7

Plate 6.   Stone stelae with hieroglyphic texts

a. Stela C from Tres Zapotes, Veracruz. This is the earliest dated monument from the New World, 31 B.C. Courtesy of the Museo Nacional de Antropología, Mexico.

b. Stela 29, Tikal, Guatemala, with a drawing of the inscription. This is the earliest known lowland Maya inscribed monument, dated at A.D. 292. Courtesy of the University Museum, University of Pennsylvania.

c. Part of finely carved hieroglyphic text of Stela 26, Tikal. Courtesy of the University Museum, University of Pennsylvania.

d. Stela 1, El Baúl, Guatemala, which bears a partially eroded hieroglyphic text. Assuming a 7 baktun, the date corresponds to A.D. 36 in our calendar. Courtesy of the Peabody Museum, Harvard University.

e. Stela C, Copán, with double figures and lateral hieroglyphic texts. The figures are bearded and entire monument was painted red. The Long Count date (9.17.12.0.0) corresponds to A.D. 782. Photographed by the author.

c

d

e

of an eclipse of the sun on a certain day, the event took place as scheduled. There would be no reason, then, to doubt his advice on far simpler matters. The scholarly priests undoubtedly controlled the people for many years, at least for several centuries following A.D. 300.

Sources of Mesoamerican Hieroglyphs, Inscriptions, and Writing

Maya hieroglyphs were carved on vertically set shafts of stone called stelae (Plate 6c, e), on stone altars, and on stairways and lintels. Others were worked in stucco or painted on pottery, on the walls of temples and tombs, and in the books (Photo 11). Occasionally some inscriptions are found carved in shell, bone, or semiprecious stones. We already have seen that hieroglyphics were in use by Late Preclassic peoples in highland Guatemala, the Isthmus of Tehuantepec, and Veracruz. The Zapotecs, Teotihuacanos, and later central Mexican peoples all recorded dates.

Mesoamerican books, called *códices*, were a kind of picture album, made by gluing together pieces of paper to form a long strip ten or more meters in length, which was then folded like an accordion. The Maya made the paper for these *códices* from the inner bark of a variety of trees. The bark was pounded, the fibers were separated by soaking in lime water, and they were beaten to form a smooth surface. Once dry, the paper was covered with a thin coat of calcium carbonate, at which point the page was ready to be painted. Some central Mexican groups wrote on deer skin, but demand often exceeded supply, and the bark of the *amatle* tree was often substituted. Paper also was in constant demand for decoration and making offerings, and for this reason was frequently listed in tribute payments.

Only three pre-Conquest Maya *códices* and fragments of another have survived (Villacorta & Villacorta, 1930). Their subject matter involves astronomy, chronology, disease, hunting and agricultural ceremonies, and deities. By far the most useful, the Codex Dresden, which is preserved in its entirety in Dresden, Germany, resembles an almanac in that it is filled with tabulations for consultation (Photo 11). It also includes material copied from an earlier manuscript. The Codex Tro-Cortesiano, now in Madrid, is not complete, nor is it as finely executed as the Codex Dresden. It contains much that is not understood, probably some errors and confusion of glyphs. The Codex Peresiano in Paris dates from the period of Mayapán's supremacy and deals with predictions and prophecies as well as the 52-year cycles. However, two pages are missing and it is in a poor state of preservation; hence its value, archaeologically speaking, is minimal. In 1971 a fragmentary *codex* of bark cloth was on temporary exhibit in New York City. The authenticity of this document has not been verified as yet, nor has its history been disclosed. However, if this *codex* proves to be genuine, it will supply us with a considerable amount of new information regarding the cycles of the planet Venus with which it deals.

Despite the scarcity of pre-Conquest Maya documents, other valuable sources of information on ancient Maya life are preserved in the Books of the Chilam Balam, which were compiled in the Colonial period after the Indians had learned to write with the Spanish alphabet. The word "Chilam" is derived from the name of a famous prophet, *chilan*, known as jaguar (*balam*). The so-called Books of Chilam Balam are in

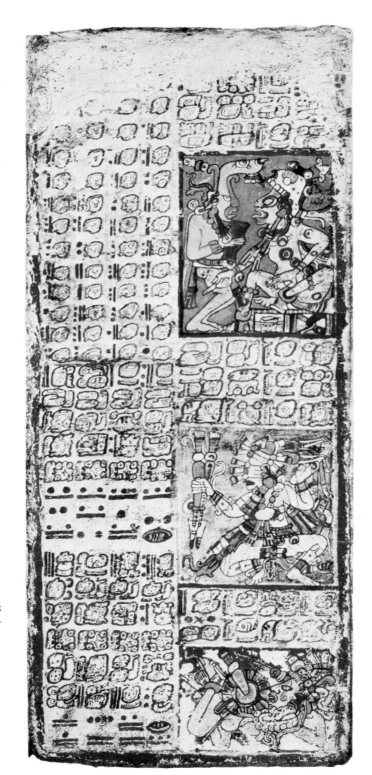

Photo 11. Page from the Codex Dresden. Courtesy of Arturo Romano P.

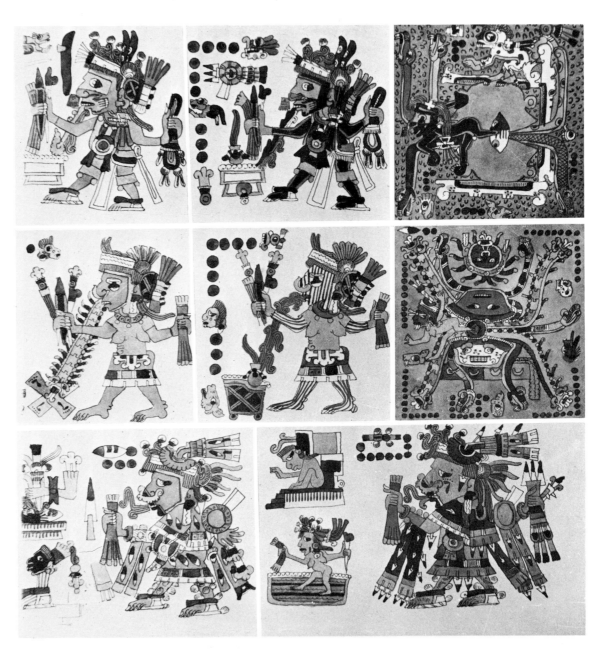

Photo 12. Page from the Codex Borgia. Courtesy of the Instituto Nacional de Antropología e Historia.

fact documents which bear the name of the towns in which they were kept: Chumayel, Tizimin, Maní, and Kaua. Information found in these ancient records other than the usual calendrical material includes songs, recitations, magical formulas, medicinal knowledge, and notations on prominent families. The Popul Vuh, literally "Book of the Community," of the highland Maya is an invaluable collection of documents on mythology, astronomy, history, religion, and the legends of the Quiché and Cakchiquel people. The original Quiché manuscripts have never been found, but are believed to have consisted of pictorial writings or paintings. An anonymous transcription was made into the Quiché language about 1554, and modern versions are based on this document (Recinos, 1950).

Many more *códices* are known from northwestern Mesoamerica than from the Maya area, and the subject matter differs according to region. Pre-Columbian *códices* from the Valley of Mexico deal largely with the Tonalpohualli, or 260-day cycle. As the gods regulated the lives of men, events were not left to chance, as it was deemed important to know which deity would be presiding over particular days and scheduled ceremonies. Accordingly, the Tonalpohualli could be consulted if one needed to know whether a day would be lucky or unlucky, if one wanted to select an auspicious date for a marriage or trading expedition, or which days were propitious to plant and harvest. The Mixtec *códices* are particularly valuable, for they provide historical and genealogical information about Oaxaca and probably the region of Puebla as well. The Borgia group includes those Mixtec *códices* known as the Borgia, Vaticanus B, Laud, Fejéváry-Mayer, and Culto del Sol, all of which deal predominantly with the luck of the days, directions, sacred numbers, and ritual (Photo 12). These books may have been written in the Puebla–Tlaxcala region as the style resembles that of the mural paintings of Tizatlán, Tlaxcala. The Vidobonensis, Nuttall, Bodley, Selden, and Becker *códices* give unique historical information about the ruling dynasties in the region of Oaxaca; all are beautifully drawn in great detail. There are various ways in which Aztec *códices* might be read: from bottom to top, top to bottom or even right to left, or left to right. Once the manner of reading was established, consistency was maintained. Many of the hieroglyphs were pictographic, that is, the message was portrayed by pictures, while in others ideographs were used to register both concrete and abstract ideas.

Other *códices* were written by the Indians just after the Conquest. Best known are the *Tira de la Peregrinación*, which relates the migrations of the Aztecs (Mexica) until they settled in the Valley of Mexico; the Tonalamatl of Aubin, with the calendrical cycles; and the Codex Mendoza or Mendocino. The latter was drawn up upon orders from the Viceroy Antonio de Mendoza and deals with Aztec conquests, the tribute they exacted from various towns, and an account of Aztec daily life.

Mesoamerican Numeral Systems

The Maya "Zero," Numbers, and Counting

The Maya had several ways of representing numbers (Figure 8). The most common was a dot for 1 and a bar for 5. Thus, three bars placed side by side represent 15; two bars with three dots equals 13. As this system was quite cumbersome if one wanted to write a larger number, such as

843 or even 45, the Maya devised a vigesimal system of position numerals based on the unit of 20, comparable to our decimal system using the unit 10. Instead of progressing from right to left as we do, they proceeded from bottom to top. The value of each unit was determined by its position, which progressed by twenties. That is, the first position included numbers from 0 through 19; in the second position, each unit had the value of 20; in the third position each unit was worth 400; and so on. However, in order to represent 20 by a single dot in the second position, the first position had to be occupied by a "zero" or, more accurately, a symbol for completion.

The invention of the zero, or symbol for completion, is a basic necessity to higher mathematics and calculation. Kroeber (1948) attributed the failure of the Romans to develop higher mathematics as resulting from their lack of the concept of zero. For example, even the simplest of mathematical problems became unwieldy because they could only express 1888 as MDCCCLXXXVIII. Anderson (1971) has shown that arithmetic can be carried out using Maya numerals, but these procedures were probably not utilized by the Maya. How they actually performed their calculations is not known. Very simple additions and subtractions may have been scratched in the soil, with the possible aid of some kind of counter.

To our knowledge, the zero was invented only twice in the Old World. The best known is its formulation by the ancient Hindus, who eventually passed it on to the Arabs from where the zero made its way to the Western world. The other Old World invention was by the ancient Babylonians, who in all likelihood developed it to assist them with their weights and measures but used it only a short time. The Mesoamerican zero may have been in use as long ago as the Hindu one, whose estimated origin is around 500 B.C., for although we have no recorded dates of that age, the fully developed calendrical system was probably known by 36 B.C., and the zero was a necessary prerequisite for its evolution.

Once the concept of zero was understood, the result of the scholarly studies of Ernst Förstemann, the door was open for him to work out the position numeral systems and subsequent calendrical calculations. Whether the Maya themselves or some of their neighbors invented the concept of the zero is not yet clear, but certainly it was the Maya who took the early invention of the 260-day cycle and the vague year of 365 days and elaborated upon them, eventually evolving the very complex calendrical system known as the Long Count (see below).

The number glyphs used for carving in stone were different from those used for painting on the *códices*, due undoubtedly to differences in medium and technique. Although the bar-and-dot numbers are most common, numerals sometimes had head variants when carved in stone. For example, 4 could be represented by the head of the sun god with a very square eye, 6 by a head with a cross in the eye, and 8 by a representation of the young corn god. The number 10 was a death's head, and the glyphs for larger numbers were composed of a death's head (10) plus the attributes of the lower number. For example, 14 equals 10 plus 4, or a death's head (10) plus the attributes of the sun god (4); 18 is formed by a death's head (10) plus the attributes of the young corn god (8) (see Figure 8). Not all the numerals from 0 to 19 are as easily deciphered as this may sound, for variations are great and the glyphs are often badly weathered.

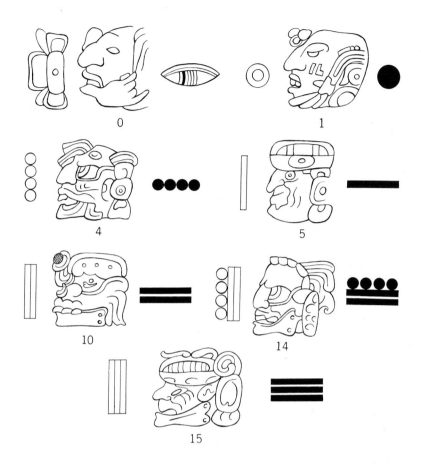

Figure 8. Maya numerals. (From Thompson, 1942.)

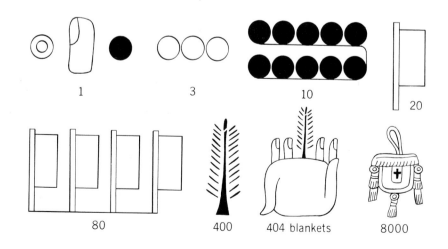

Figure 9. Mexica or Aztec numerals. A dot was used for each unit through 19; a flag represented 20; a feather (?) 400; a bag of copal incense 8000. (From Codex Mendoza, 1830–1848.)

Mexica or Aztec Numerals

Among the Mexica, who also used a vigesimal system, numbers from 1 to 19 were made up of the corresponding numbers of dots or circles (Figure 9). Symbols were arbitrarily selected to represent greater quantities. A flag equaled 20, strands of hair or a feather 400, and a bag of copal incense 8000. Only rarely was a bar used to signify 5 as was done among the Maya and in some Mixtec and Zapotec regions. The bar seems to have been in early use at Teotihuacán, Xochicalco, and Tenango, but it was later replaced by dots (Caso, 1967). There is no sign for zero among the Mexica, for they did not make use of position numerals. These numerals were essential for recording Long Count dates, but such dates are not found among the central Mexicans.

Mesoamerican Calendars

Origins of the Maya Calendar

We have already seen that glyphs were being carved in relief as far back as the sixth century B.C. at Monte Albán. Among them day signs with numerical coefficients have been identified (see Figure 14f), which is the earliest known evidence of the 260-day cycle. Other early inscriptions are those on Stela C from Tres Zapotes, dated at 31 B.C. (Plate 6a), and Stela 2 from Chiapa de Corzo, which, if the reading is correct, gives a date of 36 B.C. These are the earliest known Long Count dates in Mesoamerica. Unfortunately, in each of these monuments the initial coefficients are missing, leaving some doubt as to the reliability of these estimates. Other possible Preclassic dates come from El Baúl and Abaj Takalik on the Pacific slopes of Guatemala. Stela 1 from El Baúl shows two vertical columns of glyphs before a standing figure carrying a spear in one hand (Plate 6d). Again the vital baktun glyph (see page 94) denoting with which period of 144,000 days the inscription deals, is missing, but reconstruction of the Initial Series date, assuming a baktun 7, leads to a Calendar Round day of 12 Eb, which seems to be correct. In our calendar this Long Count date, reconstructed as 7.19.15.7.12, would be read as A.D. 36 (M. D. Coe, 1966). There is a growing list of monuments of possible Preclassic date from the area of southern Veracruz, the Isthmus region, Oaxaca, and the Pacific slopes of Guatemala. Not all may be correctly interpreted at the present time, but in view of the fact that the earliest known Long Count date from the lowland Maya region is that of Stela 29 from Tikal, currently dated as A.D. 292 (Plate 6b), evidence is mounting in favor of an origin of the calendar outside the Maya region, probably in the southern lowlands of Mexico. An examination of the fauna represented in the day glyphs reinforces this assumption because crocodiles, monkeys, and jaguars, jungle animals, would not have been likely selections of a highland people.

At present, nothing indicates an evolution of the calendar in the Petén. Stela 29, mentioned above, bears a Long Count date of 8.12.14. 8.15, which demonstrates that full knowledge of the solar year and the systems of permutating time cycles were already in operation. The Maya may well have acquired the basic knowledge of the 260-day cycle from their lowland neighbors since a single origin seems probable. With the Calendar Round as a base, it is believed that they developed the idea further and carried it to the complex culmination exemplified by the Long Count.

The Calendar Round

The basic unit of time was the day. Neither the Maya nor any other Mesoamerican groups broke time down further into hours, minutes, and seconds. The 260-day cycle, already in use during Preclassic times, formed a basic part of all Mesoamerican calculations. Among the Mexica, this cycle was known as the Tonalpohualli, as mentioned earlier; the Maya called it the Tzolkin. This cycle was composed of 20 day signs, which ran consecutively, combined with a number from 1 to 13 as a prefix. A day would be designated, for example, as 5 Atl (water) or 8 Tochtli (rabbit) in the Tonalpohualli. In order for the exact day 5 Atl to come around again, 260 days would have to elapse (or 20×13, since there is no common denominator). This 260-day cycle is not based on any natural phenomenon and we do not know how to account for its invention (Figures 10 and 11).

In addition to the Tonalpohualli or Tzolkin, another cycle ran concurrently, resembling our solar year of 365 days. This was made up of 18 months of 20 days each ($18 \times 20 = 360$), plus 5 additional days of apprehension and bad luck at the end of the year. Days were numbered from 0 to 19. The Mexica called the 360-day year the Xihuitl, and the 5-day period of bad luck the Nemontemi. The equivalent Maya periods were named the Haab (360 days) and Uayeb (5 days) (Figures 12 and 13).

In the rotation of days, only four could occupy the first position in any month. In 365 days the 20 day names would revolve constantly, but at the end of the year there would always be a remainder of 5 days ($365 \div 20 = 18$ cycles $+ 5$ days). Dividing these 5 days into the 20 day names shows that only 4 of them will constantly turn up to begin the new year, or any month. The Maya called these 4 days the Year Bearers because one of the four days, Ik, Manik, Eb, or Caban, always started the new year. At a later date, a shift took place and Ben, Eznab, Akbal, and Lamat became the Year Bearers. At the time of the Conquest, the Year Bearers were Muluc, Ik, Cauac, and Kan, indicating still another slip forward. In the same manner the central Mexicans recognized 4 days as rotating Year Bearers. The system was exactly the same; only the names varied. The Mexica Year Bearers were Acatl (reed), Técpatl (flint), Calli (house), and Tochtli (rabbit).

The Tzolkin and the Haab ran concurrently, like intermeshed cogwheels, and to return to any given date, 52 years, or 18,980 days, would have to elapse (because both 365×52 and $260 \times 73 = 18,980$). In other words, the Tzolkin would make 73 revolutions and the Haab 52, so that every 52 calendar years of 365 days one would return to the same date. A complete date in this 52-year cycle might be, for example, 2 Ik 0 Pop (2 Ik being the position of the day in the Tzolkin, 0 Pop the position in the Haab). Fifty-two years would pass before another 2 Ik 0 Pop date returned.

One cannot overemphasize the significance of this 52-year cycle for Mesoamerican peoples. It is called the Calendar Round or Sacred Round. Aside from the Maya and Mexica we know it was in use by the Mixtecs, Otomís, Huastecs, Totonacs, Matlazinca, Tarascans, and many other groups (Figure 14). The cycles of time are believed to have been primarily divinatory in purpose. When these coincided, it was an event of great importance, marked by special ceremonies and perhaps by the enlargement of architectural structures.

It was expected that the world would end at the completion of a 52-year cycle. At this time, among the Mexica in the Valley of Mexico, all

Figure 10. The twenty Maya day signs represented in stone (left) and painted in *códices* (right). (From Codex Dresden, 1830–1848; Thompson, 1942.)

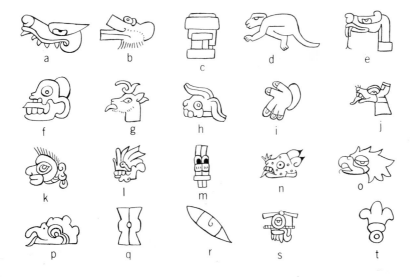

Figure 11. The twenty Mexica day signs.
(a) Cipactli—crocodile; (b) Ehécatl—wind; (c) Calli—house; (d) Cuetzpallin—lizard; (e) coatl—serpent; (f) Miquiztli—death; (g) Mazatl—deer; (h) Tochtli—rabbit; (i) Atl—water; (j) Itzcuintli—dog; (k) Ozomatli—monkey; (l) Malinalli—herb; (m) Acatl—reed; (n) Ocelotl—jaguar; (o) Quauhtli—eagle; (p) Cozcaquauhtli—vulture; (q) Ollin—movement or earthquake; (r) Técpatl—flint knife; (s) Quiauitl—rain; (t) Xóchitl—flower. (From Codex Laud, 1830–1848.)

Figure 12. The eighteen Maya months with five remaining days (Uayeb). (From Morley, 1915.)

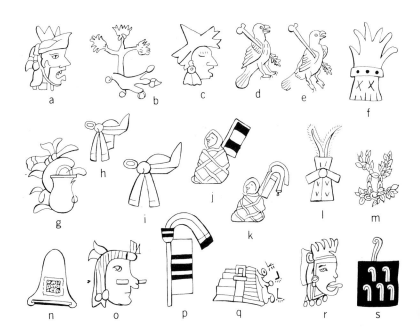

Figure 13. The eighteen Mexica months with five remaining days (Nemontemi).
(a) Izcalli; (b) Atecahuallo; (c) Tlacaxipehualiztli; (d) Tozoztontli; (e) Hueytozoztli; (f) Tozcatl; (g) Etzalcualiztli; (h) Tecuilhuitontli; (i) Huey tecuilhueitl; (j) Miccail-huitontli; (k) Huey micaeilhuitl, (l) Ochpaniztli; (m) Pachtli; (n) Huey pachtli; (o) Quecholli; (p) Panquetzaliztli; (q) Atemoxtli; (r) Tititl; (s) Nemontemi. (From Caso, 1967.)

fires were extinguished, pregnant women were locked up lest they be turned into wild animals, children were pinched to keep them awake so that they would not turn into mice, and all pottery was broken in preparation for the end of the world. In the event the gods decided to grant man another 52 years of life on earth, however, a nighttime ceremony was held in which the populace followed the priests through the darkness over a causeway to the top of an old extinct volcano that rises abruptly from the floor of the basin of Mexico, known today as the Hill of the Star, the hill above Ixtapalapa. There, with all eyes on the stars, they awaited the passage of the Pleiades across the center of the heavens, which would announce the continuation of the world for another 52 years. When the precise moment came, a victim was quickly sacrificed by making a single gash in his chest and extracting the still palpitating heart. In the gory cavity the priests, with a fire drill, kindled a new flame that was quickly carried by torches across the lake to the temple in Tenochititlán, and from there to all temples and villages around the lake. This was known as the New Fire Ceremony among the Mexica, and in some way this same completion and renewal of each 52-year cycle was recognized by all Mesoamericans (Figure 14d). It was probably rare for a person to witness more than one of these celebrations in his lifetime, so undoubtedly it was an event approached with great anticipation and relived many times after its passing.

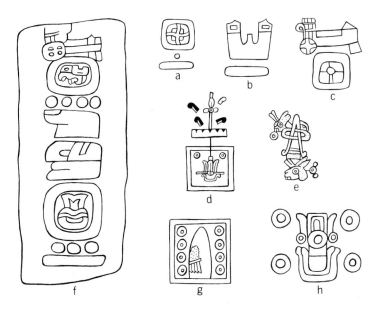

Figure 14. Various glyphs from Zapotec, Mixtec, Toltec, and Mexica calendars.
(a) day sign, Zapotec; (b) month sign, Zapotec; (c) year glyph, Monte Albán II; (d) fire drilling glyph over Ome Acatl or 2 Cane (1351), completion of the 52-year cycle; (e) year glyph, Mixtec *códices;* (f) early glyphs and numbers, Stela 12, Monte Albán I; (g) Mexica day sign, 8 Técpatl; (h) Toltec year sign, 4 Acatl. (From the following sources: a, b, c, f, Caso 1965b; d, Codex Mendoza, 1830–1848; e, Caso, 1965c; g, h, Acosta, 1956–1957.)

Calendrical and Astronomical Calculations: The Maya Long Count

Most Mesoamerican peoples were satisfied with calculating this 52-year cycle and being able to place a date accurately within that span of time. The Maya, however, were more demanding of their calculations. In addition to situating a date within the 52-year cycle, they wanted each cycle itself to be related to the beginning of time. Thus, they elaborated the system further and developed the Long Count or Initial Series dating, so that they could tell how many days had passed since the beginning of their calendar, their starting point in time. This is exactly what we do when writing any complete date such as March 10, 1955. What we are saying is that 1955 years, 2 months, and 10 days have passed since the beginning of our record of time, which is the birth of Christ in A.D. 1. In like manner the Maya recorded Long Count dates, for example, 9.14.8.0.0, which means that 9 baktuns, 14 katuns, 8 tuns, 0 uinals, and 0 kins had passed since the beginning of their record of time (Figure 15). Each position represents a period of lapsed time as follows:

$$
\begin{aligned}
1 \text{ baktun} &= 144{,}000 \text{ days} \\
1 \text{ katun} &= 7{,}200 \text{ days} \\
1 \text{ tun} &= 360 \text{ days} \\
1 \text{ uinal} &= 20 \text{ days} \\
1 \text{ kin} &= 1 \text{ day}
\end{aligned}
$$

It will be seen that a uinal is 20 kins, a tun is 18 uinals, a katun is 20 tuns, and a baktun is 20 katuns. There are even larger units, such as the pictun, which equals 20 baktuns. To be consistently vigesimal, the tun should logically be 20 uinals or 400 days, but when recording calendrical time, the Maya made the tun equal to 18 uinals or 360 days, more closely approximating the solar year.

The Maya starting date of 13.0.0.0.0, 4 Ahau 8 Cumkú, is 3113 B.C. according to Goodman–Martínez–Thompson correlation, which is followed here. This is the Maya "zero" date because after 13.0.0.0.0 baktuns had passed, the Maya began to count again with 0 baktun. The date 4 Ahau 8 Cumkú is the beginning day and month of the new baktun cycle. This was probably just a mythological event in the past, since no recorded contemporary Long Count dates are known to be that old. Remember that the oldest contemporary Long Count date from the lowland Maya is from Stela 29 at Tikal, which reads 8.12.14.8.15 or A.D. 292, and the most recent is A.D. 909 from Quintana Roo. These dates mark off the Classic period of the Maya (see Plate 6b).

We find Long Count dates carved on altars, stairways, stelae, and lintels (Plate 6b, e). The usual stela inscription shows a large introductory glyph heading two vertical rows of hieroglyphs (Figure 16). Beginning at the top and proceeding from left to right are the baktun, katun, tun, uinal, and kin glyphs, each prefixed by the proper numeral in either the bar-and-dot or head variant. Immediately following is a glyph that represents the day in the 260-day cycle reached by the recorded Long Count date, and after approximately eight more glyphs, the corresponding month glyph is found. The intervening glyphs tell which of the Nine Lords of the Night presides over the specified day involved and give information on the day-by-day moon age count of the current lunar month on this particular Long Count date.

(Introductory)   Baktun

Katun   Tun

Uinal   Kin

Figure 15.   Maya calendrical hieroglyphs. (From Thompson, 1942.)

The so-called lunar series might include up to eight glyphs. The
lunar calendar consisted of 29 and a fraction days between two successive
new moons. In addition to keeping track of a vague year of 360 days, a
solar year of 365 days, the 260-day cycle, and the phases of the moon,
the Maya also displayed great interest in the movements of the planet
Venus. All Mesoamericans considered this planet to be sinister and a
threat to man's affairs on earth. The Maya divided the Venus cycle of
584 days into four periods of 236, 90, 250, and 8 days, corresponding to
the appearances and disappearances of Venus as the morning and evening star. The Dresden Codex has lengthy tabulations of the Venus cycles,
and it is with this planet that the newly discovered codex deals.

In addition to the Maya region, observation points for the planet
Venus were located in Tehuacán, Puebla, and Teotitlán del Camino,
Oaxaca. The central Mexicans also took into account the Venus cycle of
584 days, which was apparently of considerable significance, and they,
as the Maya, were aware that eight solar years exactly equaled five
Venus periods. More spectacular still was the completion of 104 years,
at which time several cycles coincided: the 584-day Venus period, the
365-day solar year, the 52-year cycle, and the Tonalpohualli. This event
was the cause of great rejoicing and special ceremonies.

Aside from these calculations, there are Maya glyphs recording the
dates of katun period endings or fractions thereof. There also are dedica-
tory or commemorative dates, which serve as base dates for further calculations. These may reach back several katuns or more. Recording of
future dates was rare.

By the sixteenth century, the Maya of Yucatán had replaced the Long
Count by a shorter system known as the *"U kahlay katunob"* or Short
Count. Rather than a time-distance count such as the Long Count, this
abbreviated system started from the end of katun 13 Ahau, and used tuns
and katuns. Tuns were numbered; katuns were named. The katun was
the time span of greatest concern. In this system, the cycle always

ended on a day Ahau; thus, katun 13 Ahau was followed by katun 11 Ahau, and katuns 9, 7, 5, 3, 1, 12, 10, 8, 6, 2, and 13; after 260 years, katun 13 Ahau was repeated. Prophecies, most of which were unlucky, were associated with each katun. Therefore, certain events were expected to repeat themselves accordingly, thus compounding the problems of the historians.

Noncalendrical Inscriptions and Writing

Can any hieroglyphs be "read" then, aside from dates and numbers? Yes, indeed, they can, and there are still avenues of research yet to be exploited. The *códices* contain approximately 287 different signs, which were published in 1956 by G. Zimmermann. Since then Thompson (1962) has published the first comprehensive catalog of glyphs in which the preceding and following glyphs in each context are included. There is a need for analyzing whole Maya texts and for publishing complete photographs and drawings of monuments to facilitate hieroglyphic studies (Kelley, 1962c).

Perhaps the greatest contributions to understanding the structure of ancient Maya writing have been made by Thompson, who has supplemented archaeological evidence with that from early colonial documents and studied traces of the ancient calendars among present-day Indian groups. In his studies of Maya hieroglyphic writing (Thompson, 1950, 1959), he identified dozens of glyphs and outlined many basic concepts that have been accepted by Maya scholars. There are many isolated glyphs such as those for sun, moon, colors, directions, death, and eclipse for which the meaning is clear. But it is possible to go beyond simple identification of certain glyphs. Thompson does not see good evidence for syllabic writing, and his approach to decipherment lies an attempt to connect affixes with sounds. He believes that grammatical particles were expressed as affixes, for example, *al*, *il*, and *ti*, while some affixes made use of the rebus principle (in which a picture stands for an abstract idea that is a homophone).

Rebus Writing

An examination of glyph writing during the historic period of contact with the Spanish in central Mexico gives us some idea of the processes involved in reading earlier hieroglyphs. Using the mid-sixteenth century Codex Xólotl, as an example, we can see clearly that these glyphs are ideographic, representing a kind of play on homonyms or

INITIAL SERIES
Stela E, Quiriguá

Figure 16. The Long Count or Initial Series. The date is read from top to bottom and left to right. Under the introductory glyph it begins with the baktun glyph with the bar-and-dot coefficient for 9. To the right of the baktun glyph is the katun glyph with its coefficient for 17. Continuing below in order, the reading is 0 tuns, 0 uinals, 0 kins. The following glyph is 13 Ahau, the day in the 260-day cycle reached by this Long Count date. The corresponding month glyph is not found until the very end, 18 Cumkú. Between the 13 Ahau and 18 Cumkú glyphs are the glyphs of the nineth deity, Lord of the Night, who presides over this particular day, and those dealing with the position of the moon and its age. Redrawn from *The Ancient Maya*, Third Edition, by Sylvanus G. Morley, revised by George W. Brainerd, with the permission of the publishers, Stanford University Press. Copyright © 1946, 1947, 1956 by the Board of Trustees of the Leland Stanford Junior University.

rebus writing. The central Mexicans had no real alphabet, but combined pictures of objects to give a meaning (Figure 17). For example, to represent Tenochtitlán they would combine a picture of a stone (*tena*) with a picture of nopal cactus (*nochtli*); similarly Chapultepec was represented by a grasshopper (*chapullin*) sitting atop the glyph for hill (*tepec*) (Figure 17d). A path was indicated by a row of footprints, while footprints plus water signified a bridge. The figures are characteristically shown in profile; no perspective was attempted, and depth of field was indicated by placing an object higher on the page. Speech was simply represented by volutes in front of the mouth, and song, therefore, consisted of speech scrolls decorated with flowers (Figure 17c). Charles Dibble (1940), who has made thorough studies of Náhuatl documents, points out that there is no evidence of any use of an alphabet, but as Spanish influence increased, so did the rebus-type writing. Eventually the glyphs were read from left to right in a line instead of from bottom to top as in pre-Conquest examples. This principle of rebus writing was easily applied to the Maya language, which was largely monosyllabic. Thompson (1965b) gives several examples that use representations of animals. A dog glyph might be used to symbolize drought in the Books of Chilam Balam, or be associated with disease in other texts. *Pek* means dog and "worthless rains"; it is also the name of a skin infection in Yucatec. The reader would be expected to choose which meaning best suited the text.

Phoneticism

Attempts at deciphering Maya hieroglyphs have gone through various stages of study and each step has had a profound effect on contemporary and succeeding work. Thus, in 1904 when Cyrus Thomas became discouraged and repudiated his own attempts at discovering phoneticism in Maya hieroglyphs, studies in this field were abandoned for many years. When Landa's Yucatec day and month names were published, it was hard to see that these corresponded in any way with the hieroglyphs of the monuments. As a result, scholars were discouraged from looking for any phonetic approach and decided that the Maya hieroglyphs were largely ideographs and required no knowledge of the ancient Maya language. Ideograms or any recognizable representation could be dealt with on a very mechanical basis in much the same way

Figure 17.   Mexica picture writing.
(a) warrior receiving insignia for having taken three prisoners of war; (b) priest playing *teponaztli* drum; (c) symbol for song (speech scroll adorned with a flower); (d) glyph for Chapultepec, from Náhuatl *chapulin* (grasshopper) and *tepec* (hill); (e) glyph for Coatepec, from *coatl* (serpent) and *tepec* (hill); (f) glyph for Cuernavaca (near a tree); (g) goldsmith at work; (h) priest observing the stars; (i) boy fishing; (j) temples of Huitzilopochtli and Tlaloc in Tenochtitlán; (k) King Huitzilíhuitl—glyph is a hummingbird's head and 5 white down feathers; (l) the conquest of Azcapotzalco—*azcatl* means ant, and *putzalli*, sand heap; thus, Azcaputzalli signifies ant heap. *Co* means in. Thus, the translation of Azcapotzalco is "in the ant heap" or the place of dense population. The temple toppled by flames, is a sign of conquest.
(From the following sources: a, b, d, e, f, g, h, i, j, k, l, Codex Mendoza, 1830–1848; c, Codex Borbónico, 1899.)

a

b

c

d

e

f

g

h

i

j

k

l

that one can work with mathematics using Arabic numerals, without needing to know the English language.

Therefore, throughout the 1930's and 1940's studies centered around the deciphering of dates and calendrical information, while the remaining inscriptions were largely ignored. Now, due in part to some controversial articles of a Russian epigrapher, Yuri Knorozov, the existence of phonetic glyphs is being examined once more, and this entire field of research is being revitalized by serious studies.

Knorozov began publishing articles in 1952. As his early work was filled with errors of interpretation, and as he also had antagonized Western scholars by suggesting a general lack of competence, his New World counterparts were very unfavorably disposed toward him and his work. However, despite exaggerated claims of success and poor presentation and style, his scientific work is now regarded by some to be a major contribution to the decipherment of Maya script. D. H. Kelley and M. D. Coe are among those who feel he has demonstrated the existence of some phonetic glyphs. Thompson has been Knorozov's severest critic, yet he does not deny some phonetic element in Maya writing. It was Thompson who initially pointed out that the fish glyph could mean "count." (The Maya word *xoc* can be interpreted as meaning either "large fish" or "count.") One fundamental difficulty hampering this research is our ignorance of the language in which the hieroglyphs were written. We are faced with hieroglyphic texts of an ancient Maya language nearly two thousand years old. The closest related language Knorozov calls Old Yucatec, used in the Colonial sources of Yucatán in the sixteenth century such as the Books of Chilam Balam. Old Yucatec has been subjected to many changes as a result of the influx of Toltec, Putún Itzá, and Xiu groups. Nevertheless, Landa's information was recorded in this language and it forms a basis for study. About one hundred years ago Landa published about twenty-seven signs which he called a Maya alphabet. Landa's glyphs are genuine Maya glyphs, but he was mistaken in believing they were simple consonant and vowel signs. They seem to be Maya sound symbols for Spanish names of the alphabet and probably were recorded incorrectly by the native informant. Knorozov thinks that these signs can be better understood when viewed as a syllabary rather than an alphabet.

If Maya texts were simply composed of pictographs, then one would expect to find that these glyphs occurred with the same frequency throughout. In the Maya texts, however, the number of newly appearing signs diminishes as one progresses, which is a hint that one is dealing with recurring speech sounds. Knorozov believes that the Maya alphabet is a mixed morphosyllabic system. Some of the signs represent phonemes, forming parts of morphemes, while others represent morphemes. His best work is a monograph published in 1963, of which three chapters have been translated into English by Sophie Coe (Knorozov, 1967). This very scholarly work includes many illustrations of hieroglyphs and provides a base for the testing of this theory. Probably Knorozov's most important point is that single morphemes with a consonant–vowel–consonant pattern may be written by two phonetic glyphs of the consonant–vowel pattern, thus creating syllabic signs, which have no semantic connection with the word. All phonetic glyphs consist of an initial consonant and vowel, and when paired, the final vowel is not pronounced. Conflicting views at present deal with the nature and extent of phoneticism and the frequency of true ideographs. The hieroglyphic texts include historical, astronomical, and ritualistic information. There are probably many logographic glyphs, that is, glyphs with one or more morphemic referents, and a knowledge of the language is a necessary prerequisite for deciphering both logographic and phonetic glyphs.

In comparing Maya hieroglyphic writing with Old Yucatec, the word order was basically the same, and there were several structural similarities. Ancient Maya was considered sacred and carefully preserved by the priests for generations. There is some evidence that the *códices* sometimes were buried with the priests. The spoken language changed greatly, owing to outside influences. Thompson has been able to demonstrate that the affix *te* in the Dresden Codex shifted to the sound *che* in Yucatec; in other cases *ch* changed to *c*. These problems must be considered in any study of phonetics.

To prove any theory, of course, one must put it to the test. In this case, the correctness of a phonetic reading of a syllabic sign is found when the sign is read the same way in different words. Once the sound is established, the semantics must be worked out. This is where our ignorance of the ancient Maya language is keenly felt. Though a great deal of work lies ahead before anyone can "read" Maya script, the nature of the system has probably been identified and scholars are once more hopeful of deciphering a real writing system.

Personal Histories

Other kinds of decipherments have been made without using linguistic analysis. I refer to the recent knowledge of some hieroglyphs relating to historical events, which through still a different method of interpretation may provide us with the means to read firsthand the records of the Maya about themselves and their lives.

Tatiana Proskouriakoff, well known for her beautiful drawings and reconstructions of Maya sculptures and architecture, has also been analyzing and studying the hieroglyphs. In observing the carved stone stelae at Piedras Negras, her attention was caught by the repetition of certain glyphs on groups of monuments related to a particular temple. Investigation of the dates revealed that these stelae were erected at five-year intervals, and that all the dates of a single group fell easily into the life span of a single individual. Her curiosity thoroughly aroused, she embarked on a complete study of thirty-five monuments at Piedras Negras and others at Yaxchilán and Naranjo, with astounding results (Proskouriakoff, 1960, 1961). She now believes that each group of monuments represents the reign of a single individual or lord. The figures carved in relief are not gods and priests, as formerly assumed, but the current ruler. For example, the first monument erected typically depicts a young man seated in a niche accompanied by two glyphs. One of these, the "up-ended frog" glyph (Figure 18), probably records the birth date of the ruler and may be repeated on later monuments. The other glyph, dubbed the "toothache," or "accession," glyph, is believed to mark the ascension of the young man to power (Figure 18). In one case, a later monument shows a woman and child. Personal names and some titles are believed to have been identified, so that a set of monuments is interpreted as dealing with the life of one ruler and recording his birthday, the events of his reign, his marriage, birth of offspring, and perhaps military victories. Since it is known that

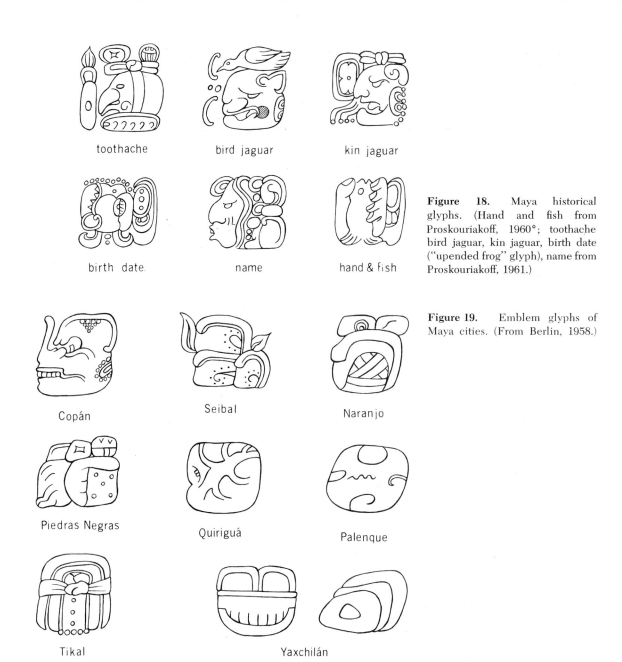

toothache　　bird jaguar　　kin jaguar

birth date　　name　　hand & fish

Figure 18. Maya historical glyphs. (Hand and fish from Proskouriakoff, 1960°; toothache bird jaguar, kin jaguar, birth date ("upended frog" glyph), name from Proskouriakoff, 1961.)

Figure 19. Emblem glyphs of Maya cities. (From Berlin, 1958.)

Copán　　Seibal　　Naranjo

Piedras Negras　　Quiriguá　　Palenque

Tikal　　Yaxchilán

the Maya were astrologers rather than astronomers, one can assume that these dates were not simply historical records, but provided a basis for predictions of good and evil events in the reign. Confirmation of these interpretations lay in the examination of the next set of monuments associated with the erection of another temple. Once again, a young man seated in a niche accompanied by "up-ended frog" and "accession" glyphs unfolded the subsequent story of a new reign.

Kelley (1962a) has attempted similar studies of the glyphic contexts at Quiriguá. He believes that over a period of seventy-five years a single ruler reigned for forty years, after succeeding his father (?), a ruler at Copán, and that certain family relationships are also recorded.

°Reproduced by permission of the Society for American Archaeology from *American Antiquity*, Vol. 25, No. 3, 1960.

At Yaxchilán there is evidence of some kind of a jaguar dynasty, but the record is far from clear at present. There seems to be a relationship between the ruler and the jaguar as his protector. It is hoped that the Yaxchilán hieroglyphs will some day tell us something about prevailing politics and local conflicts, as no other Maya site portrays so many militant battle scenes.

Other promising studies are being made by Berlin (1958), who has been able to identify what he calls "emblem glyphs" (Figure 19), that is, glyphs that appear in a single center and rarely at other sites. These may stand for the name of the center or region, or possibly the dynasty. Thus far, emblem glyphs have been identified for Copán, Quiriguá, Tikal, Naranjo, Piedras Negras, Palenque, and Seibal.

Current Studies

The study of Maya hieroglyphs was for many years confined almost entirely to the decipherment of dates, in the belief that these were recorded solely for their astronomical and calendrical significance. Now not only are other explanations feasible but we are beginning to see a variety and originality in approaches to the decipherment of all Maya script. Proskouriakoff's observations and research at Piedras Negras and Berlin's study of emblem glyphs have opened up exciting possibilities in the realm of historical interpretation of ancient Maya life. These are nonlinguistic studies. A true phonetic writing system would be very good news indeed, but no one, including Knorozov, expects to be able to read all texts in the near future. If his system proves to be essentially correct, a determination of values for all signs will have to be worked out, a Herculean task. If Thompson is correct about the nonsyllabic character of the hieroglyphs, then we can expect progress to be even slower, for the solution to the meaning of one glyph would not necessarily reflect on others. Advancement in any case will be greatly accelerated by a more comprehensive recording and publishing of complete texts. To this end, Ian Graham is currently working under the auspices of the Guttman Foundation to compile a record of ancient Maya glyphic material, which at present is widely scattered, inaccessible, and incomplete.

Nearly one hundred years have passed since Alfred Maudslay struggled into Copán, his team of mules hauling four tons of plaster of Paris, with the determination to make molds from the stelae. Eventually the molds reached England, casts were made, and from them the drawings that set Ernst Förstmann on his way to calculate the first Long Count dates. Equally dedicated to the study of the ancient Maya was Sylvanus G. Morley, who combed the jungles in his search for new inscriptions. His enthusiasm kindled the interest of the Carnegie Institution of Washington and led to the extensive program of excavation and restoration at Chichén Itzá and Copán. All studies of Maya glyphs are based on the early works of pioneer scholars in this field such as Paul Schelhas, Teobert Maler, Herbert J. Spinden, John E. Teeple, Herman Beyer, and Thomas Barthel, each of whom has made some significant contribution. Following good Maya tradition, I prognosticate very rewarding years ahead for those very special people who are currently devoting their talents to the decipherment of Maya hieroglyphs.

T HE CULTURAL ACHIEVEMENTS IN MESOAMERICA IN
the six hundred years between A.D. 300 and 900 were so remarkable
that this span of time is called the Classic period. A long gradual
development from groundwork laid in previous Preclassic cultures, its
beginning is marked by the earliest recorded Long Count dates from the
Petén, and it ends with their cessation. During these years we see an increase of population, true urban development or the rise of cities, more
elaborate ceremonial centers, and increased socioeconomic differentiation of the population.

The terms "urban" and "city" are so familiar to us today that they
would seem to require no explanation, but not all archaeologists agree on
their application to early population clusters. If any settlement with
residents engaged in nonfarming activities were to be called a city, then
very small communities would be included. Agreement is general that
urbanism and cities involve nucleation or a large concentration of population. Are urbanism and cities synonymous terms? They are often used
interchangeably as I have done here. Sanders and Price (1968) use
"urbanism" in the sociological sense and restrict application of the word
to populations numbering in the thousands, reserving "city" for larger
nucleations. I have not made this distinction, and consider any concentration of population in the tens of thousands as a city or an urban development. The head count is not, of course, the only criterion. With
urbanism or city life we may also expect to find nonfarming residents,
occupational specialization, a class-structured society, and the concentration of capital wealth. This broader, more flexible definition of a city
or urban development permits the inclusion of great contrasts in Mesoamerica as urbanism in highland Mexico is very different from a special
kind of urbanism among the lowland Maya.

Throughout Mesoamerica skilled architects directed the erection of
pyramids, temples, buildings with many rooms, and ball courts. Each
region developed its own basic architectural style, but the vaulted or
corbelled arch was a distinctive feature of the lowland Maya, where
sculptors were in particular demand for executing full-round stone
carvings, decorating facades, and carving altars, stelae, tablets, and inscriptions. Mural painting was an important medium of liturgical expression at Teotihuacán and perhaps also at Tikal, Uaxactún, and Bonampak. Ceramicists specialized in elaborate decorative techniques, and
distinctive regional wares were traded between important centers,
which indicates extensive trade and travel. Advanced knowledge of
calendrics and astronomical calculations permitted the priests to predict
cosmic events with accuracy. Among the lowland Maya, Long Count
dates were carefully and methodically recorded. No physical effort
was spared in erecting huge ceremonial centers; no task was too great
or required too much patience if a stucco sculpture, a carved mirror, or
a champ-levé vessel was needed for an approaching ritual. Activity was

6

Cities and Ceremonial Centers: The Classic Period

117

Chart 2.   Classic Chronology

| | WEST MEXICO | | | | | NORTH CENTRAL MEXICO | BASIN OF MEXICO | PUEBLA | |
	Michoacán	Jalisco	Colima	Nayarit	Sinaloa			W	SE
A.D. 900									
LATE	Apatzingán	Cojumatlán		Los Cocos / Amapa	Chametla	Ayala	Xometla–Coyotlatelco	Cholula	Venta Salada
		El Arenal					Oxtoticpac–Proto-Coyotlatelco		
A.D. 600			Ortices						
EARLY		Ameca				Alta Vista	Teotihuacán IV (Metepec)		Palo Blanco
							Teotihuacán IIIa (Xolalpan)		
							Teotihuacán III (Tlamimilolpa)		
A.D. 300									

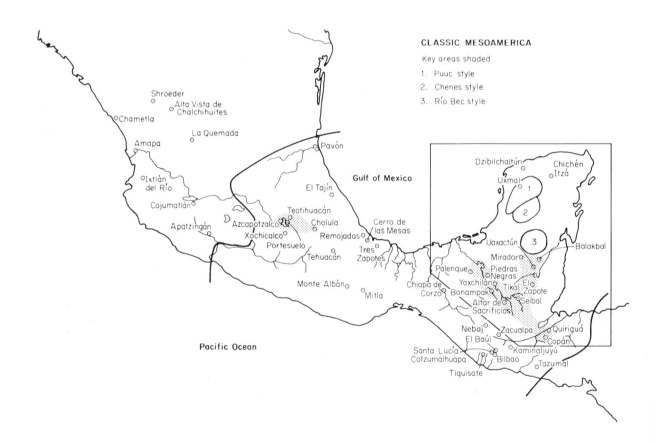

CLASSIC MESOAMERICA

Key areas shaded

1. Puuc style
2. Chenes style
3. Río Bec style

Shroeder
Alta Vista de Chalchihuites
Chametla
La Quemada
Amapa
Ixtlán del Río
Cojumatlán
Apatzingán
Azcapotzalco
Xochicalco
Portesuelo
Tehuacán
Monte Albán
Mitla
Teotihuacán
Cholula
Pavón
El Tajín
Gulf of Mexico
Remojadas
Cerro de las Mesas
Tres Zapotes
Palenque
Chiapa de Corzo
Bonampak
Yaxchilán
Altar de Sacrificios
Nebaj
El Baúl
Santa Lucía Cotzumalhuapa
Tiquisate
Bilbao
Kaminaljuyú
Tazumal
Zacualpa
Quiriguá
Copán
Seibal
Tikal
El Zapote
Piedras Negras
Mirador
Uaxactún
Balakbal
Dzibilchaltún
Uxmal
Chichén Itzá

Pacific Ocean

Map 3

HUASTECA		VERACRUZ	OAXACA	CHIAPAS	PACIFIC SLOPES Guatemala	HIGHLAND MAYA	LOWLAND MAYA	
Inland	Coast						South	North
La Salta	Zaquil	El Tajin — Remojadas — Cerro de las Mesas — Upper Tres Zapotes	Monte Albán III b	Chiapa XI (Paredón) Chiapa X (Maravilla)	Santa Lucía Cotzumalhuapa	Pamplona Amatle	Tepeu	Puuc– Chenes– Río Bec
Palmillas Eslabones	Pithaya		Monte Albán III a	Chiapa IX (Laguna) Chiapa VIII (Jiquilipas)	Laguneta		Tzakol	
								Early Petén

Inset

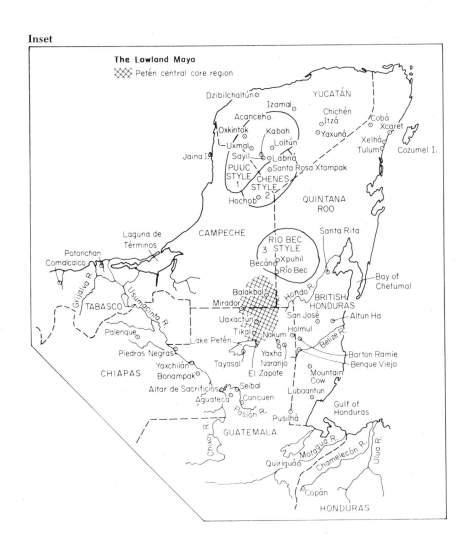

The Lowland Maya

XXX Petén central core region

constant. Whether one walks down the Avenue of the Dead at Teotihuacán or looks out at Palenque's temples banked against the jungle-covered hills, one is awed by the magnitude of the undertaking, the depth of inspiration that made it possible, and the painstaking physical labor that was expended upon its materialization. In short, the Classic period signifies what we traditionally think of as the cultural peak of Mesoamerican culture. It was unquestionably the apogee of the lowland Maya. Other areas present greater variation. Central highland Mexico likewise attained an extraordinary civilization at this time centered at Teotihuacán, but it was succeeded by two more cultural climaxes in the "Postclassic," a misnomer for this region. Once again the reader is reminded to think in terms of periods rather than stages.

We know when events took place in the Classic period. However, the questions of how and why they came to pass are not so easily answered. One wonders what motivated these people to achieve such creative heights and how, with their simple neolithic culture, they were able to build majestic cities, which, even lying in ruins as we see them today, are stunningly impressive. Two areas stand out as key centers of development: the Petén region of the lowland Maya and central highland Mexico at Teotihuacán. Monte Albán of the Zapotecs was another great center of activity, as was El Tajín in Veracruz. Events at all these centers are reflected in important regional developments throughout Oaxaca, the Gulf Coast, and highland Guatemala. Other areas of Mesoamerica developed distinctive cultures reflecting regional tastes and styles from their Preclassic base.

In our treatment of this period, let us take up once again the events in the basin of Mexico, first examining Teotihuacán and her neighbors. We will then turn to the Classic Maya.

Highland Mexico: Urbanism at Teotihuacán

Throughout the Preclassic period knowledge had been accumulating: trials and errors led to perfecting of techniques and selection of styles, and gods such as Huehuéteotl, having proved worthy of man's constant reverence, survived into the new period. The two hundred years just prior to and after the start of the Christian era was a time of basic reorientation when, if pots and figurines are correctly interpreted, the Valley of Mexico received the impact of two different influences. One, which came from the northwest and had its origins in the Lerma River region of Chupícuaro, brought in a profusion of curious slant-eye figurines together with an elaborate polychrome pottery decorated with repetitious geometric designs. The second influence, of more lasting significance, came from the east and included flat-based bowls, more negative painting, Thin Orange ware, nubbin supports, *comales*, and perhaps the idea of modeling figurines after deities (Bennyhoff, 1967). Despite exposure to these new tastes and styles, popular preference rallied around the old Cuicuilco–Ticomán tradition, which, with a few progressive local changes, led to the emergence of Classic Teotihuacán by A.D. 300. By this date Teotihuacán had become the most powerful force in all northern Mesoamerica, and for the next four hundred years its religious and political dominance remained unchallenged. The Classic years at Teotihuacán saw the culmination of the architects' dreams. A true city embracing an estimated population of 85,000, Teotihuacán contained special residences for its aristocracy and large apartment-type com-

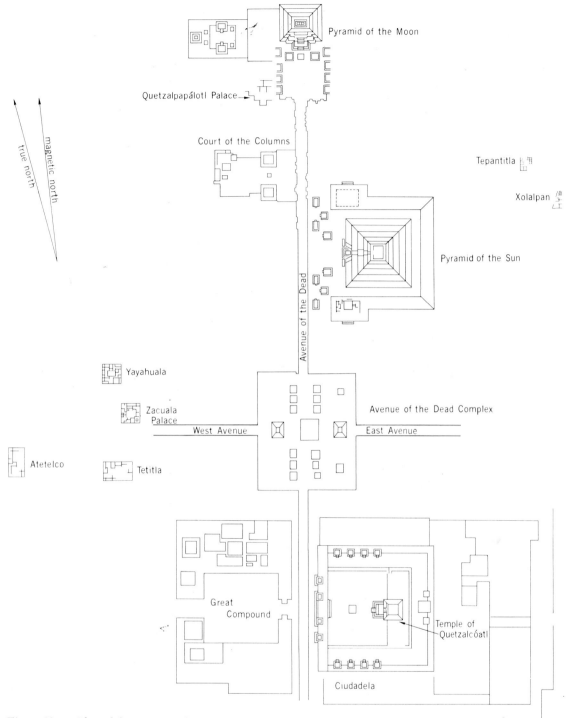

Figure 20. Plan of the ceremonial city of
Teotihuacán. (Adapted from Millón, 1967;
Wallwrath, 1967.)

Photo 13. (*Above*) Aerial view, northern sector of Teotihuacán. Pyramid of the Moon at upper left, Pyramid of Sun at right center. Courtesy of Compañia Mexicana de Aerofoto, S. A.

Photo 14. (*Right*) Interior patio with columns carved in relief, painted cornice. Quetzal-Butterfly Palace, Teotihuacán. Courtesy of the Instituto Nacional de Antropología e Historia, Mexico.

munal dwellings believed to have housed farmers, craftsmen, and specialists of all kinds (Millon, 1967).

The Archaeological Site

Having been started during the Preclassic period, the Avenue of the Dead was already constructed, the Pyramid of the Sun was nearing completion, and the original Pyramid of the Moon and the Ciudadela were initiated. Upon laying out the East Avenue, which roughly bisects the Avenue of the Dead just north of the Ciudadela, the fundamental planning was completed (Figure 20). Climbing to the heights of the Pyramid of the Moon and marking the northern end of the great Avenue of the Dead, one can look straight down the great central axis of the city and marvel at this urban planning (Photo 13). Directly in front of the pyramid is a great plaza flanked by three pyramids on either side. On the right, behind Structure 5, is the sumptuous Palace of Quetzalpapálotl, the

Butterfly-Quetzal Palace, with its inner patio lined with sculptured columns of polychromed bas-reliefs (Photo 14) and murals in surrounding rooms painted with motifs all associated with water and Tlaloc, all of which has been completely restored. Perhaps this building was a priestly residence, for were not the priests the terrestial manifestation of the gods (Acosta, 1964)?

Looking once more down the Avenue of the Dead past the Pyramid of the Sun, the eye will finally reach the city's center, the Calle de los Muertos complex, located at the intersection where the Avenue of the Dead is crossed by the east–west streets. This intersection is located about half way between the Ciudadela and the Pyramid of the Sun. The Calle de los Muertos complex consisted of a cluster of tiered temple-mounds, platforms, stairways, patios, and possibly some residential quarters, arranged around a central court. Its prominent location in the very center of the main axis suggests that it played an important, but as yet undefined, role in the ceremonial life of the city (Wallrath, 1967). Beyond this lies the huge Ciudadela, facing the Great Compound which may have served as a marketplace. So great is the distance that these structures are barely discernable from the Pyramid of the Moon. Both sides of the main avenue are lined with civic and religious buildings. Narrow, alley-like streets lead off into residential areas, which are crowded in between the more important religious edifices (Linné, 1934, 1942).

By the time one has trudged down the Avenue of the Dead, ascended and descended countless staircases, and crossed seemingly endless sunken courts, one may be tempted to agree with the opinion of the visitor who said that Teotihuacán presents the dullest architectural form since the sand castle. The *talud–tablero* combination is repeated throughout on every platform, shrine, and altar (Figure 21). The repetition of this terraced profile emphasizes its privileged form, which is restricted to religious structures. The *tablero* often served as a frame for painted or sculptured motifs, much of which has deteriorated so completely that one can see only the stone base. Architects did not continually erect *talud–tablero* forms for lack of imagination, but in order to communicate a religious symbolism (Kubler, 1970) (see Photo 15 and Figures 21 and 25).

During the Tlamimilolpa (or Teotihuacán III) phase, the population of the city grew, attaining an estimated 65,000 inhabitants. The Ciudadela was completed, and in the name of progress the old Temple of Quetzalcóatl was partially buried by a larger plain, tiered platform-pyramid of *talud–tablero* style.

The Ciudadela is not only an excellent example of the size, precision, and long-range planning that marked the culmination of Teotihuacán architecture but also provides a hint of how the structures really looked in their days of glory. The Ciudadela is actually a gigantic square, approximately four hundred meters long, which is limited by a wide platform on the north, east, and south sides. Each supports four smaller pyramids on top with the exception of the eastern side, which has three. A wide staircase on the west affords access to the entire compound. The platforms enclose a huge patio, toward the back of which is the famous Temple of Quetzalcóatl, a six-tiered structure of typical *talud–tablero* construction that was partially covered over by a plain structure, probably soon after A.D. 300 in the Tlamimilolpa phase. The facade of this spectacular temple is elaborately carved with undulating feathered serpents, which are bordered by shells and marine motifs (Photo 15). Serpent heads protrude from a kind of flower with eleven petals. These alternate with Tlaloc or rain god heads with large circular eyes and straight bar moustaches, from which hang two fangs. These tenoned heads, which have an extension that is imbedded in the wall, represent some of the finest stone carving in the city, for unlike the Maya and Gulf Coast cultures, the Teotihuacanos rarely carved stone on a monumental scale. Remains of red and white paint are still preserved. Imagine the dramatic sight this must have been in the fourth century, when the six-tiered pyramid was complete, its carved and tenoned heads protruding from a stuccoed and brightly painted facade and capped by a proud temple lit by sacrificial fires and torches. The monotony of the repetitious architectural scheme is relieved if one imagines the entire city ablaze with color, for as we shall see, Teotihuacán was indeed a painted city.

Figure 21. (*Right*) The architecture of Teotihuacán (a) reconstruction of a Teotihuacán pyramid and temple, based on an excavated stone model; (b) profile of *talud–tablero* architecture; (c) *talud–tablero* construction. (From the following sources: a, Salazar, 1966; b, c, Acosta, 1964.)

Photo 15. (*Below*) Carved facade of the Temple of Quetzalcóatl, Teotihuacán. Courtesy of the Instituto Nacional de Antropología e Historia, Mexico.

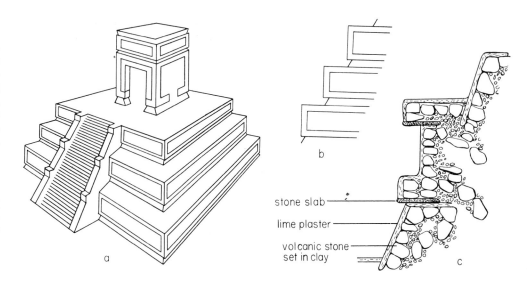

a

b

stone slab
lime plaster
volcanic stone
set in clay

c

Contrary to what one might expect, no elaborate tombs and few cemeteries have been found at the great city. Simple slab-lined graves were sometimes placed under floors of the residences, but the deceased were usually carefully wrapped and then cremated. Offerings such as finely painted vessels, utilitarian artifacts, textiles, and food were then placed with the remains.

The city's peak of power and influence was reached about A.D. 500 in the Xolalpan (Teotihuacán IIIa) phase. Most of the structures visible today, with the exception of the early ones already mentioned, were erected at this time.

The Housing Problem

The city of Teotihuacán had to house not only craftsmen and skilled workmen but also a considerable number of religious leaders, some of whom, if not all, must have been full-time practitioners, to judge from the size and number of temples under their supervision. The palace structures of Tetitla, Tepantitla, Zacuala, and Xolalpan are believed to have served as their residences. They are composed of clusters of rooms arranged around small open patios with central altars. Rain water drained into a kind of cistern in the patio and was conducted from there to the

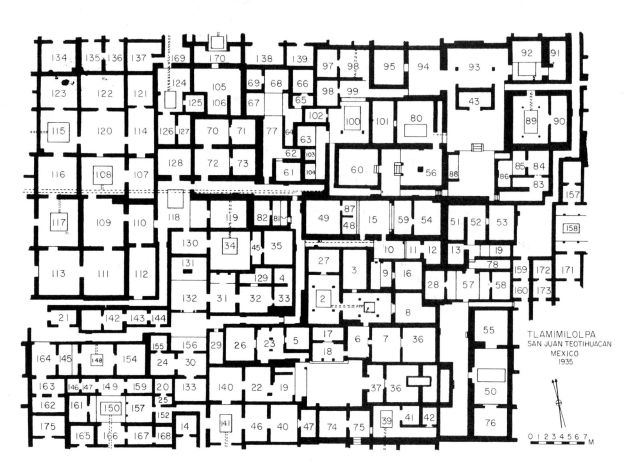

Photo 16.   Plan of Tlamimilolpa building, Teotihuacán. Courtesy of the Instituto Nacional de Antropología e Historia, Mexico.

outside by an interior drainage system. There were no windows, but the small patios and courts admitted additional light and air (Linné, 1934, 1942).

Larger apartment-type dwellings for the less privileged have been uncovered, as for example, that of Tlamimilolpa, partially excavated many years ago by Linné (1942) (Photo 16). This is the largest compound known. Its 3500-square-meter area contained an estimated 176 rooms, 21 patios, and 5 larger courts, plus numerous alleys. Although the sunlight at Teotihuacán is dazzling today, one must bear in mind that the city was so solidly filled in with structures during Classic times that interior rooms must have been gloomy. Tlamimilolpa would not have been a luxurious, or even comfortable residence, but it looks as if it were constructed as a multifamily dwelling to ease the housing demand. Conditions must have been crowded, and there was the constant threat of a violent storm that might damage the drainage system or a sudden fire that could leave a resident hopelessly trapped in the narrow alleys or cramped quarters. Yet the urban advantages of a bustling city's daily activities—living close to work and the market, the excitement of frequent arrivals of foreign traders and pilgrims, the desire to see, to hear, and to participate freely in every new event—must have more than offset the inconveniences of dark, damp, crowded living quarters. Indeed, where else was one to live? Even most of the farmers or part-time farmers were city dwellers. The urban leaders supposedly controlled the agricultural lands and even resettled local populations, so that if one were to move away to a planned rural community, living conditions were much the same.

Some rural villages of perhaps six hundred people were located nearby, but these too are believed to have been controlled directly by the city authorities. In one housing complex excavated by Sanders (1967), some residences were designed for the privileged few, administrative officials perhaps. Their construction was good and offered special features such as benches and light wells. The ordinary dwelling was similar to that of Tlamimilolpa, only on a smaller scale. These rural communities were expertly planned, very compact, and not scattered about at random.

Curiously enough, although people moved into the city in increasing numbers (the population is estimated to have been 85,000 at this time), the actual area of occupation contracted slightly in the Xolalpan phase (Millon, 1967). The reason for this is not clear but it may be related in some way to defense or to an unwillingness to allow the city to encroach further on agricultural land. Nothing seems to have been left to chance, and one wonders what measures would have been taken to deal with squatters who inadvertently homesteaded a new suburban area.

Earning a Living

The subsistence economy was based on the cultivation of maize, squash, and beans, supplemented by a variety of other cultigens. Hunting does not seem to have been very important, and the daily food supply depended heavily on local crop production. For a flourishing urban center, with commercial interests and a complex sociopolitical structure, an agricultural surplus was a prime necessity. Members of the religious hierarchy were surely not expected to till the soil in addition to attending to the temples and daily demands of the populace. Likewise, specialized artisans must have devoted the greater portion of their time to their trades.

Could a large urban center like Teotihuacán have been supported by agricultural activities based on natural rainfall alone, or did its inhabitants practice irrigation? A valley survey shows that during the Tzacualli phase people moved down from the string of hills north and south of Teotihuacán to the piedmont and alluvial plains, where they reestablished their agricultural pattern. Sanders and Price (1968) believe that many terrace systems were provided with flood-water irrigation canals as long ago as the early part of the Classic period. Traces of such terraces and canals have been found, but there is no way as yet to place them chronologically. The Teotihuacanos were certainly a sophisticated people, and it is reasonable to assume that they utilized springs for daily use and stored water. Irrigation practices have already been documented for Late Preclassic peoples in the Etla Valley of Oaxaca (Neely, 1967) and for the Tehuacanos in Puebla (MacNeish, 1962) so it can be assumed that at least by this time Teotihuacán farmers were in step with such advances, although no direct evidence has been uncovered to date. The existence of irrigation is of fundamental importance in this instance because it bears on the whole question of the evolution of civilization in central highland Mexico (Millon, 1957; Wolf, 1959; Wolf & Palerm, 1957; Sanders & Price, 1968). In order to control enough water to maintain such an urban development as Teotihuacán we are dealing not with simple canals but with a very sophisticated system necessitating the cooperation of a great number of people. In the geographical setting of central Mexico there is much land that cannot be irrigated, creating an extremely competitive social environment. The hydraulic zone of the Teotihuacán Valley would have placed it in a very advantageous position and would have stimulated the development of highly organized and complex political systems.

Combined with the resulting increase in food and population, we find a great diversity of activity which involved both residents and outsiders. A city of this magnitude must have required a constant work force of masons, painters, stone cutters, jewelers, architects and engineers, and craftsmen skilled in the arts of pottery making, feather working, flint and tool manufacture, and weaving. There may even have been entertainers in the fields of music and literature, but the oral arts have left no traces. However, specialized workshops have been found within the city limits. An extraordinary concentration of obsidian chips and flakes found in certain areas has led us to believe that these areas were actual workshops where tools were manufactured for export in addition to satisfying local demand. The source of the green-gold obsidian used has been identified as the Cerro de las Navajas near Pachuca. Grey and other types of obsidian could have been obtained on the eastern edge of the Teotihuacán Valley or from Guadalupe Victoria near Orizaba, Puebla, though these are not the only deposits known. Trace element analyses now can be made to identify the specific source (Coe & Cobean, 1970). Green Pachuca obsidian has been identified in Classic sites in the Maya area both in the Petén and at Kaminaljuyú, Guatemala (Spence, 1967). It is entirely possible that some tools produced in the Teotihuacán workshops were obtained by foreign traders in the huge marketplace at the city center.

A group of structures directly west of the Ciudadela, across the Avenue of the Dead, has been named the Great Compound. It is believed to have been utilized as a secular rather than a religious center, and perhaps it was here that a large daily market was held (Millon, 1967). The huge complex is surrounded by wide streets and plazas, providing more air space than anywhere else in this busy city. A market complex such as the Great Compound would have been vital to the proper functioning of the city. Since all members of the society—farmers, craftsmen, builders, and even religious leaders—had interdependent functions, a well-organized market must have served as a necessary and perfect vehicle for the distribution and exchange of goods as well as an instrument of social control (Figure 20).

This constant movement of raw materials and finished products is further evidence of the interaction and interdependence of peoples living in correspondingly different environmental zones. Sanders (1956, 1962) has applied the term "symbiotic regions" to these areas with diverse needs and resources. The central Mexican symbiotic region in which Teotihuacán is found comprises the central highlands and adjacent southern escarpment (modern states of Michoacán, Mexico, Puebla, Tlaxcala, Morelos, and northern Guerrero), which embraces an extraordinary number of varied environmental zones differing from each other in altitude, climate, and rainfall patterns. Accordingly they vary as to what plants are produced and in local resources, such as firewood or obsidian. A population increase, combined with more intensive agriculture, would accordingly stimulate interaction between peoples with different products to offer, thus promoting specialization and the importance of the market system. All of these factors contributed to the spectacular urban development of Teotihuacán.

Religion and Art

Religion was seemingly the key factor in the integration of Teotihuacán society. One has only to see the clusters of temple-pyramids, shrines, altars, and quantities of smaller temple mounds to realize how religion dominated the lives of these people. We have no direct knowledge of politics at this time, but the clearly theocratic nature of Teotihuacán leads us to believe that the religious leaders had little competition for control of the mind, spirit, or body. These leaders at the same time may have been the supreme rulers, combining the powers of church and state. As an intellectual elite, the priest-scholars were able to interpret the Tonalpohualli, calculate the ever-recurring cycles, recite the procession of days and months, and issue instructions for forthcoming events (Caso, 1967). The prominence of religion in the everyday life of the outlying communities is reflected in the ubiquitous household altar. In addition, abundant household rubbish there has yielded religious artifacts such as figurine fragments, censers, ritual vessels, and a few representations of Huehuéteotl, the Old Fire God, or Hearth God among the later Mexica, carved in *tepetate* or basalt. The lack of pottery molds or obsidian cores and chips suggests that finished products were acquired from the city market in return for agricultural surplus.

Teotihuacán artisans turned out beautiful pottery in great variety but preferred polished monochromes to the multicolored vessels of their ancestors and Maya contemporaries. Having developed from the local Preclassic tradition, many ceramic features continued to be used, but it

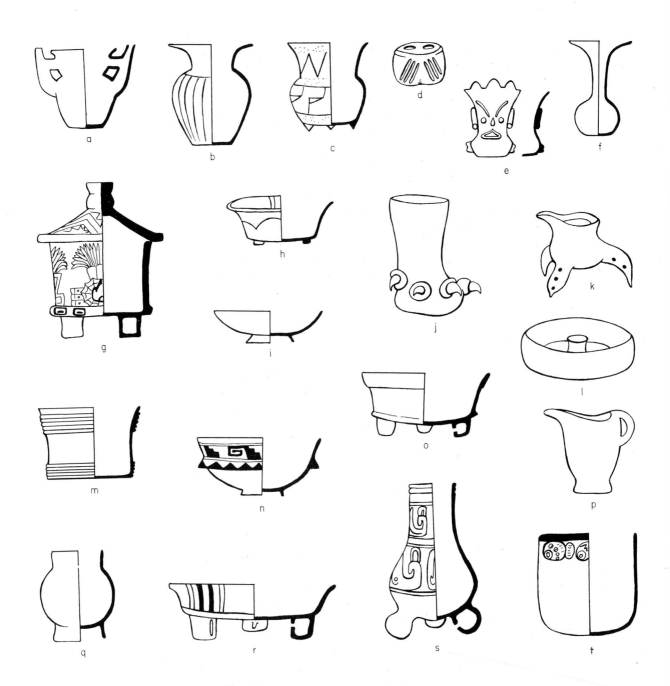

Figure 22. Classic period pottery.

(a) black-ware jar with two spouts, Teotihuacán III; (b) black incised jar, Teotihuacán III; (c) polychrome vessel with three tiny solid supports, Teotihuacán III; (d) *candelero* (incense burner); (e) so-called "Tlaloc" vase, Teotihuacán II; (f) *florero* form, Teotihuacán II; (g) painted cylindrical tripod with lid, Teotihuacán III; (h) incised brown tripod bowl, Teotihuacán III; (i) Thin Orange bowl, annular ring base, Teotihuacán II; (j) gray-ware vessel in the form of a jaguar foot, Monte Albán IIIa; (k) gray-ware spouted tripod cup, Monte Albán IIIa; (l) bowl with interior cup, incense burner (?), Monte Albán IIIa; (m) cylindrical vessel with moldings, Cerro de las Mesas II; (n) polychrome basal-flanged bowl, Early Classic, Copán; (o) negative-painted black tripod bowl, basal molding, hollow cylindrical feet with a square vent on the inner side, Early Classic, Nebaj, Guatemala; (p) brown-ware Tzakol pitcher, Kaminaljuyú; (q) vessel with ring stand, Uxmal; (r) polychrome Tepeu tripod, Uaxactún; (s) Fine Orange Tepeu tripod, Chichén Itzá; (t) Polychrome Tepeu vessel banded by glyphs, Zaculeu.

(From the following sources: a, b, c, g, Piña Chán, 1960; d, e, f, h, i, Séjourné, 1966; j, l, Caso & Bernal, 1952; k, Caso & Bernal, 1965; m, Drucker, 1943b; n, Longyear, 1952; o, Smith & Kidder, 1951; p, Kidder, Jennings, & Shook, 1946; q, Ruz, 1963; r, s, Smith & Gifford, 1965; t, Rands & Smith, 1965.)

is the changes and innovations that help identify a particular period of development. The four phases of Classic Teotihuacán are more easily distinguished in the ceramics than architecturally or in settlement patterns.

Figurines continued in popularity but were made in distinctive Teotihuacán styles, and after the Late Tlamimilolpa phase, about A.D. 400, they were turned out by molds (see Plate 8a). The "portrait" figurine is a very standardized, easily recognized type. In addition to a triangular-shaped face, there is usually a depression in the top of the head. Articulated figurines with movable limbs were another innovation (see Plate 8b). Although many fragments have been recovered, complete figures are rare. Through the study of figurines and vessel decorations, two more deities have been identified: the Fat God, a deity represented with his eyes closed, who may have been associated with a second god, Xipe Totec, God of Springtime. The latter is also called the Masked God, and was honored by a priest wearing a flayed human skin, symbolizing the new vegetation covering the old. The cult of Xipe is believed to have had its origin in the Guerrero or Oaxaca region (Plate 7e) (Caso & Bernal, 1952).

During the Tlamimilolpa phase (Teotihuacán III), contact was close with Gulf Coast cultures, and toward A.D. 450 Maya influence can be recognized. These contacts are evident in both form and style of ceramics as well as in the mural paintings. The Tajín-style scroll, appliqué ornamentation, and the first plano-relief decoration appear on vases, and these elements are continued and more fully elaborated in the great phase that followed. The lidded cylindrical tripod, Teotihuacán's single most distinguished pot, became popular at this time. It was decorated by painting, plano relief, fresco, incising, or was simply burnished. This pottery form has been called the hallmark of Teotihuacán, and was produced in quantity and traded widely. In the great Xolalpan phase (Teotihuacán IIIa), potters took this form and carved intricate designs in plano relief that were set off by combinations of colors and textures (Figure 22g). Symbolism and life-figure styles replaced the Tajín scroll, and resist painting became more popular.

Thin Orange pottery was also distinctive; this ware probably originated in the Valley of Puebla and had been introduced in the final days of the Preclassic period (Figure 22i, Plate 7c). Its descriptive name is derived from the fine orange-colored paste that was used to form the vessel. Dishes, bowls, pedestal and ring bases, a thin-necked jar called a "florero," small nubbin feet, three-pronged burners, and censers (*candeleros*) were all common (Figure 22a–i).

Numerous masks of green stone, serpentine, onyx, and obsidian, sometimes encrusted with turquoise mosaic or having inlaid eyes of cut shell and obsidian, are attributed to Classic Teotihuacán (see Plate 9e). Oddly enough, not one of these masks has been found *in situ*, and it is therefore impossible to date them with any accuracy, or in some cases to be certain of their authenticity. Thin clay masks found in the household rubbish of Yayahuala and Tetitla are believed by Séjourné (1966) to have been tied to the wrapped and bundled deceased before cremation.

The art of Teotihuacán, which is profoundly religious, is manifested in new forms and media. When compared with the much earlier Olmec

a

b

c

d

Plate 7.   Classic period pottery

a. Large orange jar with stamped decoration, Teotihuacán IV (Metepec). Height: 8 inches. Courtesy of the Museo Nacional de Antropología, Mexico.

b. Black-brown vessel with excised and incised decoration, Teotihuacán II–III (Late Tlamimilolpa). Height: 8 inches. Courtesy of the Museo Nacional de Antropología, Mexico.

c. Thin Orange effigy vessel: Early Classic Teotihuacán type. Toluca, State of Mexico. Height: 12¼ inches. Courtesy of the Museum of the American Indian, Heye Foundation (16/6067).

d. Cylindrical tripod vessel with incised panel decoration. Lid has modeled parrot at apex, Kaminaljuyú, Guatemala: Esperanza phase. Height: 13¾ inches. Courtesy of the Museum of the American Indian, Heye Foundation (16/6235).

e. Life-size ceramic sculpture representing Xipe Totec, who holds a jaguar paw vessel of Monte Albán type in his right hand; Teotihuacán culture. Courtesy of the Museo Nacional de Antropología, Mexico.

f. Funerary urn representing goddess "13 Serpent," Monte Albán III. Height: 19¾ inches. Courtesy of the Museo Nacional de Antropología, Mexico.

g. Grey ware funerary urn representing the god Cocijo, who wears a mouth mask with forked serpent tongue, Monte Albán IIIA. Height: 19 inches. Courtesy of the Museum of the American Indian, Heye Foundation (23/5554).

h. Maya cylindrical vessel of Tepeu Phase. Polychrome figure and band of hieroglyphs. Height: 6⅝ inches. Courtesy of the Museum of Primitive Art, New York.

i. Black incised bowl with basal flange, jaguar lid, Holmul, Guatemala: Early Classic Maya. Height: 9½ inches. Courtesy of the Peabody Museum, Harvard University.

f

e

g

h

i

civilization, one is surprised that Teotihuacán has produced so little stone carving. It has been suggested by way of explanation that decoration of buildings and temples may have been in such demand that the more rapid technique of painting was substituted for the slower and more painstaking one of stone sculpting and carving. Murals are found in temples, palaces, public buildings, shrines, and even private dwellings. The art style is very austere (Kubler, 1967) and almost monotonous in its overwhelming liturgic character, with the notable exception of the Tlalocan murals at Tepantitla, which depict the Rain Gods' paradise with little figures dancing, singing, and frolicking about (Photo 17) (Caso, 1942). With few exceptions, whether the painted object is a mural or a pottery vessel, the theme is religious ritual or prayer (Photo 18). The common motifs of flowers, butterflies, fish, and *quetzal* birds are always related in some way to a god or religious cult. The lively Tepantitla mural just mentioned shows a ball game in progress, which is of some interest since no ball courts as such have been found. In the painting, the limits of the court are marked by some kind of end marker or post, which may represent an earlier form of the later stone-faced courts with large rings. A composite stela interpreted by Aveleyra (1963) as being such a ball game marker furnishes supporting evidence of this sport among the Teotihuacanos (Plate 9i). Among the later Aztecs we know that it was a religious event as well as a game. A match might be

Photo 17.   Wall painting from Tepantitla, Teotihuacán, depicting Tlalocan, the Rain Gods' paradise. Courtesy of the Instituto Nacional de Antropología e Historia, Mexico.

scheduled to prognosticate future events, and would thus function as a means of divination. The fact that the game at Teotihuacán is played in the Rain Gods' paradise may indicate an early religious association.

Teotihuacán paintings have been the subject of considerable study by Clara Millon (1966), who points out that the earlier murals depict plumed serpents, jaguars, fish, and other creatures and may represent some mythological allegory. The truly great paintings are those from Tepantitla, Tetitla, the Zacuala Palace, and Teopancaxco. They not only help us identify the prominent gods of the Teotihuacán pantheon, such as Tlaloc, Itztlacoliuhqui (the God of the Curved Knife) and his associate the God of Dart, Shield, and Owl, but also provide information about distant contacts.

In the murals we see evidence of relationships with Oaxaca, the Gulf Coast, and both highland and lowland Maya areas. The "Pinturas Realistas" show a "long-nosed deity," certainly a stranger to Teotihuacán. These paintings portray foreigners such as Mayoid peoples with distinctive slanted eyes, body paint, masks, and dress. The bands of glyphs placed in a row are clearly Maya inspired. Gradually a trend toward painting in tones of red became widespread all over the city, along with a great predilection for detail. Finally, in the Late Classic period, armed deities and priests appear for the first time along with warriors, shields, spears, and *atlatls*. Style changes occurred, and motifs varied according to period, but one figure is recurrent, Quetzalcóatl, the feathered-serpent deity who adjusted to each new phase and survived the catastrophe that finally engulfed Teotihuacán.

Photo 18.   Wall painting from Atetelco palace building, Teotihuacán. Courtesy of the Instituto Nacional de Antropología e Historia, Mexico.

Warfare and Expansion

For a long time the Classic period was envisioned as a time of complete peace and harmony. Now this conception of Classic life is gradually eroding as a result of the analysis of murals and the careful study of household rubbish. After A.D. 500 a trend away from purely religious symbolism toward individual glorification and warfare can be seen in the carved reliefs and Metepec figurines as well as in pottery, murals, and sculpture (Kubler, 1967; Millon, 1966; Sanders, 1967). For example, the household rubbish of the rural community gives some indication of militarism. Few animal bones were found but obsidian projectile points were common. Since they were not used for hunting, one supposes that they must have been used as lance points against an enemy. Human bone was quite common in the form of mandibles and fragments of worked human skulls. Cannibalism may even have been practiced, since cooking pots contain some human bone.

Weapons that might have been used against either man or beast include clubs, knives edged with obsidian, axes, large knives, *atlatls*, slings, harpoons, and, after A.D. 500, bows and arrows. A red Tlaloc warrior-priest in the Tepantitla fresco holds a bunch of arrows in one hand and a tiger claw in the other. The drops of liquid often associated with drawings of weapons or knives could represent water, but blood is a more likely possibility. A figure on one pottery lid clearly represents a warrior with a shield and *atlatl*. Among the clay figurines we find helmets to protect the head and both round and rectangular shields. Some figurines wear a garment that suggests the padded cotton shirts worn by later Mexica warriors.

Although no battle scenes, sacrificial victims, or prisoners are represented in the murals, the finds mentioned above indicate that the Classic years were not spent exclusively in pious devotion to theocratic pursuits. The constant warfare so characteristic of later Mesoamerican history may have been founded on a very long, deep-rooted tradition.

Thus far, we have been concerned with the site of Teotihuacán itself, and have only indirectly referred to trade and other far-reaching relationships. We must now consider the extent of Teotihuacán's influence and power. Millon (1967) describes Teotihuacán as a "pilgrim–shrine–temple–market complex," emphasizing the interaction between the religious and economic aspects of the city's life. A city of this magnitude would have needed a constant flow of food for its sustenance, and raw materials and other products for its artisans to fashion into marketable objects for local and foreign consumption. Once communications were established and trade initiated, the system would tend to perpetuate itself, demanding greater political expansion to assure a continual market for exports as well as a source of foreign products. We suspect that early in its history Teotihuacán won the support of valley centers such as Cuicuilco and sought out relationships with other neighbors such as Cholula in the Puebla Valley, Xochicalco in Morelos, and thereafter Oaxaca and other areas to the south. In the last few pages we have seen how commerce throve and contact with other regions and other peoples can be found in household and ceremonial goods as well as in the paintings.

We do not know if Teotihuacán's influence spread by conquest or trade. Nor is there any indication of the existence of institutionalized traders such as the Mexica's *pochteca*, but traveling merchants of some kind were definitely operating for the benefit of Teotihuacán. Teotihuacán-style stone carving, vessel shapes, and Thin Orange pottery are found sporadically in the western states of Michoacán, Jalisco, Nayarit, and Colima. There is no evidence of migration or colonization, but simple commercial transactions probably resulted in the spread of some Teotihuacán wares to the west.

Teotihuacán influence was more strongly felt on the coast of Guerrero, where Ekholm (1948) and the Brushes (1968, 1969) have reported Teotihuacán-type pottery and mold-made figurines. Even the unspectacular but highly characteristic *candelero* (Figure 22d) found its way down to the Pacific Coast. The relationship seems to have been broken off abruptly, however, and replaced in coastal Guerrero by a more Maya-type flavor.

Many objects showing Teotihuacán influence are known to come from the upper Balsas River basin near Mezcala, again exposed by looters rather than scientific explorations. Because of their style, these Mezcala stone artifacts have been tentatively placed in an Early Classic context, but some may prove to be earlier. Stone vessels; masks; human and animal figures; tools such as axes, chisels, and punches; and curious models of columned temples in a severe and rectilinear style are typical (Plate 9a, b). Strangely enough, more Teotihuacán masks come from Guerrero and Puebla than from Teotihuacán itself, and the Guerrero examples are too numerous to be explained by trade alone. Preferred stones were serpentine, jadeite, andesite, white nephrite, quartz turquoise, chalcedony, amethyst, garnet, alabaster, soapstone, and diorite. Having these natural resources at hand, Guerrero became a major production center. Pottery of Teotihuacán style is also reported, but it did not figure as prominently as stone.

We also know that Teotihuacán influenced and in turn was influenced by the Gulf Coast cultures, in particular that of El Tajín, by the great Zapotec culture of Monte Albán, and by the Maya civilization. So strong is the central Mexican influence seen in the *talud–tablero* construction, grave goods, and possible traded articles at Kaminaljuyú, Guatemala, that Kidder felt that the Esperanza phase at that site might well represent actual conquest by Teotihuacanos (Kidder *et al.*, 1946). This idea has been reinforced by more recent excavations (Sanders & Michels, 1969). Although not as strong as in the highlands, Teotihuacán influence is also evident in the Classic cities of the Petén (W. R. Coe, 1965) as we shall see shortly.

The Collapse of the City

By A.D. 650, cracks and strains are detected in the civilization of Teotihuacán, and during the next hundred years there was a rapid decline in population, a reduction in area of habitation, and a degeneration in artistic quality. For some unexplained reason, many people decided to move east of the city.

This last phase at Teotihuacán itself we call Metepec or Teotihuacán IV. Bowls with annular rings were left unpainted, and stamped pottery decoration appeared for the first time (Plate 7a), only to become more prominent in the next phase, Oxtoticpac. Prominent in the waning Classic days were elaborate mold-made figurines with complex headdresses and very ornate incense burners, but no artistic elaboration was sufficient to

Plate 8. **Classic period figures and figurines**

a. Pottery mold for producing figurine head (photo enlarged to show detail): Gulf Coast cultures. Height: 4 inches. Courtesy of the Museum of the American Indian, Heye Foundation (22/9145).

b. Mold-made figurine made for articulation: Teotihuacán culture. Height: 10 inches. Courtesy of the Museum of the American Indian, Heye Foundation (24/6664).

c. Solid clay figurine with asphalt paint on legs, Pánuco, Veracruz. Height: 7½ inches. Courtesy of the Museum of the American Indian, Heye Foundation (23/8592).

d. Hollow figurine representing ball player wearing yoke about the waist; knee and arm guards, Santa Cruz, Quiché, Guatemala. Length: 14½ inches. Courtesy of the Museum of the American Indian, Heye Foundation (12/3347).

e. Hand-modeled figure in a pod, Jaina, Campeche: Late Classic Maya. Height: 8⅛ inches. Courtesy of the Museum of Primitive Art, New York.

f. Remojadas standing figure decorated with asphalt paint, Central Veracruz. Height: 12½ inches. Courtesy of the Museum of Primitive Art, New York.

g. Hollow "laughing face" figure, central Veracruz: Remojadas culture. Height: 14 inches. Courtesy of the Museum of the American Indian, Heye Foundation (23/3925).

h. Hand-modeled pottery figurine representing a warrior-priest, Jaina, Campeche: Late Classic Maya. Height: 11¼ inches. Courtesy of the Museum of the American Indian, Heye Foundation (22/6348).

i. Clay red-ware effigy rattle, mold-made, Jaina, Campeche: Late Classic Maya. Height: 7 inches. Courtesy of the Museum of the American Indian, Heye Foundation (21/4632).

j. Bearded male figurine, Jaina, Campeche: Late Classic Maya. Height: 14½ inches. Courtesy of the Museum of the American Indian, Heye Foundation (23/2573).

f

g

h

i

save the city or postpone its collapse. The Metepec phase is clearly decadent, although many ceramic details carry over into the last horizon of Mesoamerican pre-Conquest culture (Bennyhoff, 1967).

The Teotihuacanos had managed to establish a prestige and influence unsurpassed in the history of Mesoamerica. Why, just when their art and architecture were being copied, their pottery popular and much prized, and even their religion was spreading — why at the seeming peak of their power did the great city suddenly and completely collapse? For some great catastrophe did bring about a rapid shrinking of the population and a burning of the city about A.D. 700.

j

Recent studies show that the population fell off to 70,000 and that the residents moved east of the main ceremonial center. This was not a good region for defense, and in spite of the interest in warfare noted above, there is no direct evidence of foreign invasion or pitched battles. Power and prestige diminished for some reason not yet apparent. The collapse was sudden, catastrophic, and complete. The city was burned and purposely destroyed. By the year A.D. 750, Teotihuacán was a ghost of its former self; only a few people lived in villages occupying no more than one square kilometer (Millon, 1967). The fame and fable of Teotihuacán was not extinguished so easily, however. Eight centuries later it was still known as a sacred city, home of the gods, and the scene of frequent pilgrimages.

The collapse of Teotihuacán as a great urban center does not mark the end of the Classic period in central Mexico. To see this great city destroyed before their eyes must have had a formidable impact on the residents, and through archaeological research we know that many refugee groups moved closer to Lake Texcoco in the central valley, settling at Cerro Portesuelo and Azcapotzalco. The Teotihuacán tradition

a

b

c

e

f

d

g

h

Plate 9. Various Classic period objects

a. Stone figure, Mezcala style, Guerrero. Height: 13¾ inches. Courtesy of the Museum of Primitive Art, New York.

b. Stone model of a temple, Mezcala style, Guerrero. Height: 7⅛ inches. Courtesy of the Museum of Primitive Art, New York.

c. Hematite mirror back with perforations for suspension, El Tajín, Veracruz. Diameter: 3⅜ inches. Courtesy of the Museum of the American Indian, Heye Foundation (22/6252).

d. Wheeled pottery cart in form of an alligator, Veracruz, Mexico. Length: 10 inches. Courtesy of the Museum of the American Indian, Heye Foundation (22/5562).

e. Green-stone mask, Teotihuacán type, Santiago Tlaltelolco. Height: 10½ inches. Courtesy of the Museum of the American Indian, Heye Foundation (2/6607).

f. Stone figure, with incisions and cavities for inlays, Teotihuacán. Height: 11¾ inches. Courtesy of the Museum of the American Indian, Heye Foundation (10/7462).

g. *Hacha* or thin stone head with projecting tenon. Height: 11⅜ inches. Courtesy of the Museum of the American Indian, Heye Foundation (16/3474).

h. *Palma* or palmate stone, Veracruz. Height: 8 inches. Courtesy of the Museum of the American Indian, Heye Foundation (16/3473).

i. Composite stela used as ballcourt marker (?), volute carving in Tajín style, La Ventilla: Teotihuacán culture. Height: 6 feet 11 inches. Courtesy of the Instituto Nacional de Antropología e Historia, Mexico.

j. Stone representation of Tlaloc with a serpent tongue, subterranean structures, Teotihuacán. Height: approximately 2¾ feet. Courtesy of the Museo Nacional de Antropología, Mexico.

k. Stone yoke carved with Tajín style volute, El Tajín, Veracruz. Length: 17⅜ inches. Courtesy of the Museum of Primitive Art, New York.

i

j

k

was carried on, but it lacked the earlier cultural unity. Ceramic studies reveal that the end of its Classic period was a gradual phenomenon.

The final Classic phase is Oxtoticpac (Proto-Coyotlatelco), in which the surviving Teotihuacán tradition blended with some new ceramic styles, contributed perhaps by Xochicalco or the giant center of Cholula, located beyond the volcanoes to the east. Although these two centers were more prominent in the Postclassic period, Cholula is a very old site, having been occupied continually since Preclassic times. Some of the structures at Cholula are built in the *talud–tablero* style of Teotihuacán. Of Classic date too are some recently discovered murals, already dubbed "the Drunkards." In fifty meters of beautifully polychromed frescoes, life-sized figures are shown serving one another and drinking. More than a dozen illustrated vessels can be duplicated in the archaeological collections (F. Muller, personal communication). When Teotihuacán fell, Cholula not only withstood the shock, but probably gained and profited from her neighbor's misfortunes.

The Classic period in central Mexico reached a drab conclusion around the year A.D. 850 with a fragmentation of the earlier cultural conformity. During the days of Teotihuacán's greatness, at least three other regions north of the Isthmus had shared in the prevailing prosperity. The Classic Veracruz cultures remained very much abreast of developments at Teotihuacán by maintaining close contact. Although heavily influenced by Teotihuacán, the Gulf Coast cultures contributed perhaps even more than they received. The art style associated with the site of El Tajín is proving to have had an impact felt by every major Classic center with the exception of the Yucatán peninsula.

Veracruz Cultures

The impact of Teotihuacán civilization was greatest to the east and south. In Preclassic days the Gulf Coast cultures had enjoyed distant trading relationships with both highland and lowland regions but were most closely allied to lowland developments in the Isthmus and Maya Petén. Now the attraction of Teotihuacán civilization was so great that all eyes turned to the central highlands, and who could resist the opportunity to associate with success? Certainly not the Classic cultures of central and southern Veracruz.

One very important development was centered at El Tajín, five miles southwest of the town of Papantla in the humid, heavy tropical rain forest where the present-day Totonac Indians make their home (García Payón, 1955, 1957). The ruins of El Tajín are deceptively small, as the exposed buildings are tightly clustered, but untouched mounds extend for several hundred acres into the lush tropical growth that covers the surrounding small hills. The Pyramid of the Niches, a six-tiered structure enveloping a similar earlier one, is unique in its variation of the *talud– tablero* form by the incorporation of 365 niches into its facing. Their

Photo 19.   (*Opposite, top*) Pyramid of the Niches, El Tajín, Veracruz. Courtesy of the Instituto Nacional de Antropología e Historia, Mexico.

Photo 20.   (*Opposite, bottom*) Relief carving of a ball court showing sacrificial scene. El Tajín, Veracruz. Courtesy of the Instituto Nacional de Antropología e Historia, Mexico.

purpose might have been symbolic, but perhaps was only decorative (Photo 19). Nearby are two of the seven ball courts. The vertical walls of one are elaborately carved bas-reliefs in the interlaced outlined scrolls and volute patterns for which the site is famous. The relief represents a scene in which a ball player, chest thrust forward, is about to receive the sacrificial knife and lose his heart (Photo 20).

The ball game may well have its ancient origin in the lowland Veracruz area not only because it is the homeland of rubber trees but also because archaeology shows that the game was extraordinarily important to these people. Three curious stone sculptures are associated with the ball game: yokes, *palmas*, and *hachas* (Plate 9g, h, k). We believe that the U-shaped stones called yokes, often elaborately carved on the outer surfaces and weighing from forty to sixty pounds, were imitations of protective belts worn by ball players. Clay figurines and sculptured reliefs, such as the ball-court scene mentioned above, show such belts being worn (Plate 8d). The *palmas*, or palmate stones, are tall stones, fifteen to eighty centimeters in height, and are usually fan shaped, notched at the top, and have a concave surface at the base as if meant to be supported by a curved edge. The back is smooth and left plain. The front may be decorated with such motifs as birds, iguanas, human figures, or inanimate objects. Pictorial representations suggest that the *palmas* rested on the yokes. Certainly they were designed to be viewed from the front. The *hachas*, or thin stone heads, were somehow associated with the yokes and the ball game. Their use is not known. *Hachas* often have a deep cut or notch at the back, or an undecorated projecting tenon. Like *palmas* and yokes, they are beautifully carved to represent human, bird, or animal forms. Neither *hachas* nor *palmas* can stand without support. Proskouriakoff (1954) feels that Veracruz was without doubt the center of manufacture of these stones, although they were widely traded throughout central Mexico, Guatemala, and El Salvador. They were made during the Classic period but cannot be chronologically placed more precisely at the present time. On stylistic grounds, the thicker *hachas* may be Early Classic, the thinner ones later, and the *palmas* later than both *hachas* and yokes. Artistically, these are some of Mesoamerica's finest stone sculptures.

Beyond El Tajín's ball courts and the Pyramid of the Niches and at a slightly higher level are a series of palace-like structures with roof combs and corbelled-vaulted rooms with great colonnaded doorways, all reminiscent of the Maya area. Particularly interesting is the massive masonry, constructed of a concrete mixture of sand, seashells, and wood, laid in sections using wooden molds. Numerous relief carvings reveal a predilection for toads, jaguars, serpents, and human beings. Bar-and-dot numerals associated with day glyphs are also found, and we know that the people of El Tajín followed their own Tonalpohualli (260-day) and Xihuitl (365-day) cycles.

The influence of Teotihuacán is so marked throughout that Wolf (1959) suggests that El Tajín may have been an actual colony of the great highland center. But though El Tajín shows many flavors, some Olmec-derived, some Maya, and some Teotihuacán, she in turn contributed a major art style of ornamental spirals and interlaced outlined ribbons found on yokes, *palmas*, *hachas*, pyrite mosaic mirrors, and bas-relief carving. This style, remarkably comparable to motifs on Chou period bronzes of China (Ekholm, 1964), was widely copied from central highland Mexico to Honduras. It is found in paintings at Teotihuacán, on monolithic stone stela-altars at Cholula, on the back of carved stone mirrors in Guatemala, and on marble vases along the Ulua River Valley of Honduras (Plate 9c, i, k; Plate 10k). El Tajín itself probably dates from around A.D. 600 and survived the major upheaval that devastated many Classic sites. Wolf (1959) believes that its final destruction by fire and subsequent abandonment could have taken place as a result of Chichimec invasions around A.D. 1200. But in those 600 intervening years, the artists of El Tajín left us a legacy of exquisite stone carving.

Not far from the port city of Veracruz the potters of Remojadas busied themselves producing molds from which masses of hollow figurines flowed. Mostly of Late Classic date, these figurines are quite distinctive, although they may have some affinities with those of the Classic Maya. Their jolly, laughing faces often expose filed teeth through great smiles (Plate 8g). Men and women as well as infants are represented, along with some ball players and warriors. Black asphalt paint, from natural outcroppings in the area, was used to highlight the features and ornamentation (Medellin, 1960) (Plate 8c, f). This is also the region where small wheeled animals have been found, which look at first glance like children's pull toys. Several interpretations of their possible significance have been offered; one explanation even sees them as imitations of ancient Chinese bronze carts in miniature (Ekholm, 1964) (Plate 9d). They are of considerable interest because their wheels are the only ones known in the New World; apparently the principle was never put to any practical use. These wheeled animals have a wide but not abundant distribution in the Gulf Coast region. Some belong to the Late Classic period of the Remojadas culture. They have also been reported from central Mexico, and one from Nayarit in western Mexico shows a man sitting on a wheeled platform. Five curious examples from Cihuatán, El Salvador, came from a very late (probably Postclassic) horizon heavily influenced by Mexico. The El Salvador examples also functioned as whistles.

South of the Remojadas culture in Veracruz, the people of Tres Zapotes and Cerro de las Mesas, who inherited much of the Olmec tradition, contributed heavily to the Classic period (Drucker, 1943a, b). Not satisfied with their own local wares, they fell under the spell of Teotihuacán, as evidenced by the presence of cylindrical tripods, *candeleros,* and mold-made figurines. Cerro de las Mesas is an extremely important site where a great deal of activity was taking place and where we have yet much to learn. Among the stone monuments, carved stelae with bar-and-dot numerals bear Long Count dates of A.D. 468 and 533. Here Maya and Teotihuacán influences met and both prospered.

The Zapotecs

The Classic period in Oaxaca is represented by hundreds of sites, but the one we know most about is Monte Albán, for phases IIIa and IIIb at this site represent its greatest climax (Bernal, 1965; Acosta, 1965). Whereas in the earlier Pre- and Protoclassic periods Oaxaca was most closely related to the lowland cultures of Chiapas and the Maya, by Classic times the attention of the Zapotec culture was drawn to central Mexico. Ties with the Valley of Mexico were stronger during the Early Classic period than at any other time in history, but never to the extent seen at El Tajín or Kaminaljuyú. Monte Albán always remained staunchly Zapotec.

The main buildings constructed during Monte Albán IIIa (the Early Classic period) were plastered and painted, most frequently in red. Facades form a series of rectangular *tableros* in two planes that alternate with recessed spaces. Also, rather than standing out as separate additions, many staircases are set into the structures (Photo 21). The large, handsome, I-shaped ball court is located at one corner of a huge central plaza. Here, as elsewhere in the Oaxaca area, the ball game was played without rings. As if to compensate, two niches were placed in opposite diagonal corners, though we do not know if they were involved in scoring or if they were perhaps designed to hold idols of the game's patron deities.

The typical gray ceremonial ware of Monte Albán persists, so it is the form or ornamentation of the vessel rather than the color of the ware itself that signals change. Some of the earlier types survived, including spout handles, spider-foot vessels, perforated incense burners, and bird-shaped bowls, but new forms reflecting Teotihuacán tastes were added, such as *floreros* (Figure 22f) and *candeleros* (Figure 22d), stucco coating, cylindrical tripods, so-called Tlaloc jars (Figure 22e), ring bases, and some Thin Orange ware and resist painting. These all make their appearance in the transition to the full Classic period and are well represented during Monte Albán IIIa in twenty-two tombs, twelve graves, and fifty-one offerings at Monte Albán itself, as well as at many sites in the valley below. Distinctive local developments are a serpentine motif and the urn, in particular the funerary urn, a Zapotec specialty (Plate 7f, g). Made of gray, unpolished clay, it is composed of a very elaborate deity usually but not always seated cross-legged against a cylindrical receptacle. It will be recalled that in terminal Preclassic times a Zapotec habitation site was identified at Teotihuacán. In fact, two urns typical of Monte Albán were found three kilometers west of the Ciudadela, the only examples to date of these objects outside their local habitat (Paddock, 1968). Whether these Zapotec residents eventually returned home or were absorbed by the Teotihuacanos we do not know. Nor can we know for certain that the Zapotecs did not in turn host foreign resident

Photo 21. Building complex at Monte Albán, Oaxaca. Photographed by the author.

groups until further investigation is made of habitation sites in Oaxaca. At present, archaeological remains suggest that a strong local development, centered in Oaxaca, was influenced by the Valley of Mexico during the Monte Albán IIIa phase.

In addition to ceramics, Teotihuacán influence is present in the beautiful *tecali* plaque known as the Lápida de Bazán, which was found in the debris of Temple X. On it, a figure believed to represent a priest named Eight Turquoise stands beside a Monte Albán god. The priest is depicted in the style of Teotihuacán's Tepantitla frescoes. Stelae belong to this great period also, but are known largely from areas outside Monte Albán. Hieroglyphs are numerous and are found everywhere — carved in stone, incised on pottery, and even painted on the walls of tombs. The essential elements of the Mesoamerican calendar had been present since Preclassic times. Glyphs of the Tonalpohualli, the 365-day year, and the four Year Bearers are found in the Zapotec inscriptions through Period IV, but never with evidence of position numerals. A trend seems to lead away from the earlier custom of carving stelae toward the use of slabs (*lápidas*), sometimes small. The center of this slab-carving style may have been Zaachila (Bernal, 1965).

Mural paintings are largely confined to tombs, where mineral colors were applied *al fresco* to a white base color. The theme is always religious and symbolic. People and animals are shown in profile without shading. The best preserved of all painted tombs is Tomb 104, where the urn of a god wearing a Cocijo head (the Zapotecan rain deity) as a headdress gazes down from his niche over the entrance. The people in the murals, probably priests, are toothless old men with protruding chins. They bear a close resemblance to figures in Teotihuacán's Tepantitla. Tomb 105 shows a scene of nine gods and nine goddesses paired in a procession.

Toward the Late Classic period, Monte Albán seems to have terminated its relationship with the Valley of Mexico, reflecting the collapse and abandonment of Teotihuacán. Now, free of outside distractions, the Zapotecs looked inward, reexamined their own culture, and with renewed pride in their tradition rebuilt Monte Albán, leaving it as we see it today. Nearly all architecture, inscriptions, and tombs now visible date from Period IIIb, the Late Classic phase.

In order to build Monte Albán, hundreds of acres of mountaintop were altered. Some areas were cut and leveled; in other places existing features served as cores for new structures. Painstakingly a gigantic religious center was formed, oriented along a north–south axis. The tremendous central plaza measures 700 meters long by 250 meters wide and is completely surrounded by great pyramidal structures. Tomb facades became more complex and murals reached their peak. Deities such as the Bat God, Rain God, Feathered Serpent, and Old Fire God are represented both in the frescoed wall paintings and on urns.

Having withdrawn from foreign influence, the great Zapotec center might have been expected to thrive in cultural isolation and not succumb to the ills that beset major centers at the close of the Classic period. Some settlements in the valley, such as Yagul and Lambityeco, did survive, but Monte Albán fell into disrepair by A.D. 1000. No new buildings were erected and the ceremonial structures were abandoned. Some people continued to inhabit the area, but the great enthusiasm had passed.

Could Monte Albán, at any time in its history, be considered a city, an urban center like Teotihuacán? It is probably too early to say, as little attention has been given to the habitation sites that dot the hillsides.* The religious center must have required constant support from a large resident population, part of which could have lived on the terraced slopes, but many more people could have resided in the valleys below. The water supply would certainly have always been a problem; there are no springs on the mountaintop. Nevertheless, Bernal (1965) believes that Monte Albán was more than strictly a ceremonial center because of the great abundance of everyday pottery found there, along with ordinary tools, figurines, and nonceremonial objects. Although the lavish tombs have received the greatest attention, humble burials exist alongside them. There is still much to learn from Monte Albán.

As we look farther south and east, the influence of Teotihuacán is notable in central Chiapas at Mirador and Miramar, both upper La Venta River sites. But at the better-known site of Chiapa de Corzo, Teotihuacán culture had little impact. The area of Chiapas was probably given only a passing glance by the central Mexicans once they established a connection with the residents of highland Guatemala.

The Highland Maya

The events surrounding the rise of Teotihuacán caused repercussions over most of Mesoamerica, but nowhere were these more directly felt than at Kaminaljuyú, Guatemala. This highland settlement had already seen a period of extraordinary development during Middle and Late Preclassic times, and by the year A.D. 300 was in somewhat of a slump. Here, in the Guatemalan highlands, the term "Classic" and all it implies pertains equally well to the great Miraflores phase of Late Preclassic development. The term "Classic" is used for the years between A.D. 300 and 900 largely to conform to Maya lowland chronology, where achievements at this time merit the label "Classic." The highland cultures were drab by comparison at the beginning of the Classic period. Construction works had slowed down, the pottery was far less elegant and less well made than formerly, and all carving of stelae had ceased. The great Classic boom in the Guatemalan highlands that did take place was instigated by outsiders.

The first Classic phase at Kaminaljuyú, a rather undistinguished brief period called Aurora, was followed by the Esperanza phase (A.D. 400–700) (Kidder et al., 1946). The latter provided a setting for some enormously exciting events sparked by non-Maya intruders. Around A.D. 400 the quiet village life of these peasants was abruptly interrupted by the arrival of foreigners from central Mexico. It is not known whether this was a welcome or forced intrusion, but apparently the new authority went unchallenged. So striking is the scope of Teotihuacán influence that Sanders and Michels (1969) feel the occupation was due to outright conquest and political intervention.

In the Esperanza phase, a great massive complex of buildings was raised in the north central area, called the Palangana. In this acropolis-

*As a result of field work currently in progress at Monte Albán, we now know that this great site became a huge urban center in Late Preclassic times (Monte Albán II). Living quarters have been discovered tightly clustered on small terraces clinging to the hillside. Rain water was carefully channeled to these terraces and to the agricultural fields below. Two dams as well as defensive walls have been identified. The peak of population density was reached in Monte Albán IIIb (Richard Blanton, personal communication).

like construction high buildings towered over an interior court, presumed to be a ball court ("palangana" means ball court). The building activity is estimated to have taken place in several stages over a period of two hundred years, corresponding to the Xolalpan or Teotihuacán III period in central Mexico. The buildings are in pure Teotihuacán style with *talud–tablero* architecture. At times they were faced with neatly cut volcanic pumice blocks, covered with clay, and plastered in white.

The tombs were still constructed according to the old Preclassic practice of building rectangular burial chambers roofed with logs, on the floor of which the honored dead were laid in an extended position, accompanied by retainers—men, women, and children—and lavish offerings of pottery, jade, obsidian, and pyrite mirrors. Instead of placing the tomb in a prominent position in the mound as the Miraflores people did, the Esperanza builders located the graves in front of the structure or in the subsoil beneath. These tombs are plain rectangular pits, very different from the elaborately constructed tombs of their predecessors. However, the rich contents of these tombs, all of which contained objects of pottery, shell, jade, obsidian, and a *metate*, confirm strong Teotihuacán influencé. The familiar lidded, slab-leg, cylindrical pot, Tlaloc vases, *candeleros*, *floreros*, and Thin Orange ware are definite proof of central Mexican influence or even domination, for surely these well-stocked tombs belonged to an elite, the highest ranking and most powerful members of society (Borhegyi, 1965; Kidder *et al.*, 1946). Although Teotihuacán in form and decoration, wares were largely produced locally, as shown by ceramic analysis. The central Mexicans seem to have brought along the cults of Tlaloc and Xipe Totec, Xólotl, and Ehécatl (variants of Quetzalcóatl—see Chapter 8), whose presence is manifested in both ceramic painting and modeling. It has been suggested that these early Teotihuacán migrants to the Guatemalan highlands were Náhuat-speaking Pipils. "Pipil," a term found frequently in the literature, refers to Mexicans with Náhuat speech and culture. There is great confusion regarding their various migrations, but archaeological research is helping to identify their movements at various times. We think that some of these Teotihuacán Pipils settled along the Gulf Coast areas of Veracruz, Tabasco, and Campeche; others lived in the states of Morelos, Puebla, and Oaxaca. Because Teotihuacán influence is limited largely to ceremonial and ritual objects, it has been postulated (Borhegyi, 1965) that these intruders were not migrating families but rather for the most part religious leaders or merchants. There seems little doubt now that whatever the makeup of the outsiders, strong political administrators were among them (Sanders & Michels, 1969). If, when household refuse is examined, the daily utensils prove to be purely local in inspiration, it will support the idea that women were left behind and took no part in the foreign occupation. However, with or without their families, the control of the Guatemalan highlands would have assured Teotihuacán a continuing supply of cotton and *cacao* since the important productive centers lay close by on the warm Pacific slopes and could be conveniently controlled from a base at Kaminaljuyú.

No residences comparable to Tlamimilolpa or Zacuala are known, and knowledge of the Esperanza phase is limited almost entirely to tombs and ceremonial structures. As a result we have little information about everyday life and utensils. Perhaps populations were also resettled and strictly controlled on the Teotihuacán model. We might therefore expect a planned nucleation of settlements around the Palangana as well as outlying hamlets. In any event, we have as yet a very unbalanced view of Esperanza life, but one that does serve to separate the ceremonial from the common everyday paraphernalia. For example, clay figurines, mushroom stones, and three-pronged incense burners are conspicuously absent. These may have been common household artifacts that will be found when studies of habitation sites are completed, or they may prove to be lacking entirely, as though thoroughly discredited and unsanctioned by the new order. Current research by Sanders on settlement patterns in the Guatemala Valley will undoubtedly answer part of these questions.

The Esperanza phase represents a highland blending of Teotihuacán styles with many features of the lowland Petén Maya. Close trade relationships were maintained with lowland Maya cities, for some products, such as lime were considered indispensable and others, such as pelts, feathers, eccentric flints, and fine polychrome wares, were highly prestigious. Thus, basal-flanged Tzakol vessels, a lowland Maya style, are found at Kaminaljuyú side by side with the cylindrical tripods inspired by Teotihuacán. Commerce was mutually beneficial, for lowlanders were eager for highland jade, obsidian, volcanic ash (used for tempering pottery), cinnabar (often used to cover jades and graves), specular and crystalline hematite (used for painting pottery), and the feathers of the *quetzal* bird, which could only be found at altitudes above 5000 feet.

On the Pacific Coast at Tiquisate, the Esperanza phase is also represented. Here too Teotihuacán and Petén influences are found side by side in pottery, but architectural remains bear a close resemblance to Kaminaljuyú.

In the highland of Chiapas, a new population influx is seen in the central plateau around San Cristobal las Casas toward the end of this early Classic phase, designated locally as Kan. These new sites are not related to the Grijalva Valley settlements as they were during the Preclassic horizon. Adams suggests that the Mayan Tzeltal and Tzotzil people, historic populations of the Chiapas plateau, may have come in at this time. They built their ceremonial-residence centers on higher land in preference to the valleys, a change that might suggest a need for defensive positions (R. M. Adams, 1961).

Chiapa de Corzo in the Grijalva depression relates to the Petén through imported polychrome wares and to Teotihuacán through imports such as its cylindrical, lidded tripod, but all this changes at the end of the Early Classic period when the site was seemingly deserted. Thereafter settlements moved upland, following trends in living patterns characteristic of areas to the east.

The Late Classic phase (Tsah) shows the most widespread occupation of the Chiapas region. At this time the ceremonial centers and public structures were located on the highest promontories or hilltops, while the population lived on lower terraces farther down the slopes and worked their farm lands in the valleys beneath them. R. M. Adams (1961) feels that there was no organization of communities into a coordinated political structure but that instead settlements were politically independent and self-defended. There are few direct evidences of defensive construction, but Cerro Chavín seems to present an exception. It is one of the earliest sites with military installations, positioned atop a high promontory surrounded by cliffs on three sides, where only a narrow strip of land connected it to the main mountain. This access was broken by two parallel stone walls with offset entrances. In other respects the area of highland Chiapas in the late Classic period seems to have occupied a rather marginal position to more active centers to the west and east. Mexican influences are not prevalent in the central highlands of Chiapas, and the new Plumbate wares that begin to appear in the highlands of Guatemala are rare.

In highland Guatemala the Late Classic phases are known as Pamplona and Amatle and are well represented both in the highlands and on the Pacific Coast (Borhegyi, 1965). The prominent Mexican influence, so strong during the Early Classic phase at Kaminaljuyú, is no longer in evidence, a reflection, no doubt, of the collapse of the great city of Teotihuacán itself. At best the Teotihuacán occupation seems to have been only partial, perhaps largely of a religious and commercial nature. Although we know little of the common people's life and activities, it is easy to imagine that they participated only vicariously in the foreign occupation and that their simple folk beliefs continued without serious interruption. Whether or not the Teotihuacán takeover was only a thin cultural veneer, it cracked and crumbled easily enough. Lacking stimulation and leadership from the west, these highland Maya communities now looked only to themselves. Apparently without the ability or interest to perpetuate the foreign cults, they reverted back to their earlier, less complicated patterns.

At the beginning ceremonial centers continued to be constructed in tightly knit, compact groups in open country such as valley floors, where stone and *talpetate* masonry platforms were built. One architectural innovation was the huge basin-shaped or *palangana* ball court. Cotío is a typical Amatle site located just a few kilometers west of Kaminaljuyú; its constructions made use of boulders, clay, earth fill, adobe, and lime mortar. Toward the end of the Amatle phase, the valley sites were abandoned for more favorable defensive positions along hilltops. In the western highlands, circular subterranean structures of cut stone have been identified as sweat houses. This widespread trait was shared by the lowland Maya.

Unfortunately, as most of the remains come from ceremonial centers, we have little information about daily life. The pottery, however, is degenerate when compared to the finer quality and taste of Esperanza wares. Pots were rarely painted, but some ceramic ties with the lowlands can be traced through the presence of Tepeu-like polychrome wares. Although the pottery as a whole is drab, new types appear, such as the Fine Orange and San Juan Plumbate wares. The latter (Shepard, 1948), thought to have originated in the Pacific slopes of Guatemala, is a distinctive, fine-textured ware with a high percentage of iron compounds. Upon firing, the surface acquired a hard metallic luster. In this respect it resembles the Postclassic Tohil Plumbate, but differs from the latter in paste, shape, and decoration. San Juan Plumbate was made into tall cylindrical vessels that contrast sharply with later effigy forms.

Late Classic sites are more numerous than Early Classic ones in the Guatemalan highlands. A particular style of stone sculpture, often called Cotzumalhuapa, is represented at a cluster of sites on the Pacific slopes which looks very Mexican without having specific parallels with other areas. Stones are carved in full round or relief and depict scenes of deities, skulls, serpent heads, and human sacrifice. Carved hieroglyphs were enclosed in circles like a medallion, but have no resemblance to

Maya glyphs and are stylistically more Mexican. A subject of considerable controversy, the Cotzumalhuapa stone carvings are now generally recognized as a Late Classic manifestation largely because of their associations with San Juan Plumbate pottery (Thompson, 1948; Parsons, 1967). The Mexican influence probably reflects movements of peoples and ideas from Teotihuacán. Recent work in the area suggests that several periods may be represented and that some of the sculptures may even be Late Preclassic or Early Classic in date. The typical site for this art style is actually Bilbao, a short distance northeast of the town of Santa Lucía Cotzumalhuapa (Parsons, 1967), which is located on the sloping piedmont area in a natural rain forest. The ceremonial center is made up of four main groups that include seventeen pyramids, plazas, and courts faced with stone rubble or adobe plaster along with some finely dressed stone-block stairways. A number of large ball-player stelae may once have marked off a ball court, but these were moved to Berlin many years ago. There are six stone monuments still *in situ*, and many more have been illustrated in publications, through which the Cotzumalhuapa style has become well known.

Borhegyhi (1965) suggested that a second Pipil migration could have taken place at this time, which would clarify certain highland events. If some of the Teotihuacán Pipil colonizers settled around the area of El Tajín, Tabasco, and Campeche during the Classic period, they may have absorbed many Gulf Coast traits. Certainly El Tajín, with its specialized art style, exerted considerable influence on this group, and Stirling (1943) believes that they adopted a decapitation sacrifice and trophy-head cult associated with the ball game from these coastal people. Eventually the Pipils may have formed a second migratory wave to the highland Maya area just about at the end of the Classic period, between A.D. 700 and 900. One wonders if they contributed to the end of this great period, although after A.D. 700 a gradual decline was already in progress. An intrusion of these Pipils would coincide with the general abandonment of the valley sites as ceremonial centers and the beginnings of hilltop defensive sites. Artifacts attributed to this second wave of influence from central Mexico and the Gulf Coast lowlands include the earliest variants of Fine Orange ware (Z and Y), stone yokes, *hachas*, and stone ball-court markers. The Pipil migrations may not have affected the lowland Maya to any great extent, but they could have contributed to the changes seen in highland Classic cultures.

The Lowland Maya

In Protoclassic times, the flavor of Maya civilization had begun to emerge. Remember that among the lowland Maya, the corbelled vault had already appeared and ceremonial centers, polychrome pottery, and the beginnings of dated monuments all demonstrate a gradual movement toward a distinctively Maya, as well as Classic, civilization. Though certain roots may well stem from an Olmec-Izapan tradition, Maya culture certainly experienced vigorous development on its own in the lowland jungle area of the Petén, exemplified by such sites as Uaxactún and Tikal. To see how all this came about, let us return now to the archaeological record in the lowlands and follow the development that took place after the Mamom and Chicanel periods.

Prior to A.D. 300, during the Protoclassic phase, new people and influences moved into the region of northern British Honduras in the

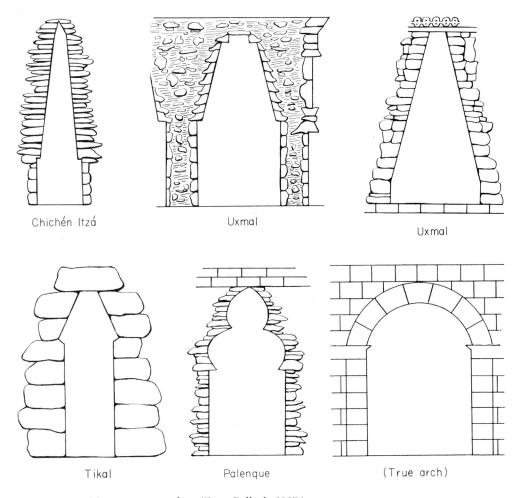

Chichén Itzá

Uxmal

Uxmal

Tikal

Palenque

(True arch)

Figure 23.   Mesoamerican arches. (From Pollock, 1965.)

Belize Valley at Barton Ramie, and the same impact is also manifested in northeastern Petén at Holmul and at Altar de Sacrificios on the Pasión River. Evidence of this intrusion is known as the Floral Park phase (Willey, Culbert, & Adams, 1967). True polychrome pottery using combinations of orange paint and both geometrical and conventionalized designs is characteristic. A distinctive new shape is a Z-angled bowl with four mammiform supports. These innovations most likely were brought in by intrusive groups from El Salvador and Honduras. They did not interrupt the cultural processes at Tikal and Uaxactún, however, where the Chicanel phase continued until the full Classic period.

Even so, an astute prognosticator could have detected a change in the air in Floral Park. The true Classic manifestations initiated by A.D. 300 are very different from the simplicity of the older Chicanel pattern. Three unmistakable events signal the attainment of true Classic status:

1. Polychrome pottery.
2. Carved stelae with hieroglyphic inscriptions and Initial Series dates.
3. The spread of stone temples and buildings with corbelled vaulting (Figure 23).

The time must have been ripe, culturally speaking, for the changes spread rapidly and were adhered to tenaciously for about three hundred years.

Rise to Civilization: The Case of Tikal

Lowland Classic Maya centers probably number in the hundreds (Graham, 1967). Unlike central highland Mexico where Teotihuacán had no rival in power and influence, the lowland Maya had many centers of varying degrees of importance. Among them I have singled out Tikal to discuss in detail because our knowledge of this site far exceeds that of any other Classic Maya city at the present time. It may not have been more influential or powerful than Copán or Palenque, for example, but undoubtedly ranked high among the leaders. In order to understand Classic Maya civilization, which is unique in many ways among pristine cultures, it is necessary to have some background regarding settlement and socioeconomic patterns. It is here where we will begin.

Population and Settlements. Classic Maya ceremonial centers typically included centrally located temples, multiroomed structures called "palaces," and public buildings. The general populace is commonly believed to have lived in small hamlets in the surrounding area, which in turn consisted of clusters of houses situated on low rectangular mounds. These occur singly and in groups; in the latter case, the mounds are also arranged around small courts. Aggregates of mounds have been classified progressively from small to large as (1) clusters, (2) zones with minor ceremonial centers, and (3) major ceremonial centers (Willey & Bullard, 1965; Willey, Bullard, Glass, & Gifford, 1965). A cluster typically includes from five to twelve scattered households occupying a small area two hundred to three hundred meters in diameter without displaying any particular sign of planning. The zones consist of several clusters, the whole occupying perhaps three or four square kilometers and boasting a modest ceremonial center with small temples and palace mounds, but no stelae, altars, or ball courts. The major ceremonial centers contain all these features. Serving a district of perhaps one hundred square kilometers that included several zones, these great centers were the setting for impressive ceremonies and public events, to which pilgrimages were made.

Although the vast majority of Maya settlements belong to one of these types, another may be added, that of the large urban center, which was characterized by all the elements of the major ceremonial center and, further, supported a permanent, resident population numbering in the tens of thousands. Combine these features with socioeconomic diversity and do we not have the very ingredients of a city? We do indeed, yet somehow the Maya city manages to retain the flavor of an oversized ceremonial center. Such a center emerged at Tikal in the northeastern Petén and there may have been others. It is only in recent years that researchers have devoted great energy to the investigation of settlement patterns, and the excavation of Tikal has been the most thorough of these studies.

Let us consider Tikal as an example of a Classic Maya city. The most extensive of all Maya sites, Tikal has been the object of a sixteen-year program of excavations sponsored by the government of Guatemala in conjunction with the University of Pennsylvania (W. R. Coe, 1962, 1965, 1967). We do not know how many of the Petén centers were of equal importance, but Tikal probably was not unique. Its setting is a rain forest in northeastern Petén. Rivers are rare in this area and the most reliable sources of water were water holes called *aguadas*. These were favorite habitation sites, as were the level ridges of natural or artificial elevations, the edges of lakes, and *bajos*, low areas that become swampy in the rainy season. The rains fall mostly between June and December, contributing an average of 135 centimeters annually. Tikal was settled in this hilly, tropical terrain, which was obviously unsuited for a grid plan of settlement. The choice of location was apparently dictated by the local topography, and such requirements as water resources and drainage. The large natural supply of flint, valuable for tools, is another advantage which may have played a part in the selection of the site.

At the peak of its development, following A.D. 550, Tikal was occupied by an estimated 45,000 people and covered an area of 123 square kilometers (Haviland, 1970). Central Tikal alone can boast of five great pyramid-temples as well as "palaces," shrines, terraces, ball courts, ceremonial platforms, sweat baths, and thousands of structures considered to be housing units. Individual houses were constructed of wood, mud, and thatch, of which nothing remains. A large number of walls, temples, and "palaces" still stand because they were built of limestone and mortar and faced with stucco. The walls of these structures typically were very thick and solid, and the windowless rooms, which today are usually damp and clammy, very small in proportion to the walls. We would not consider such quarters to be habitable, but the ancient Maya might have used some "palaces" as prestigious residences for the elite. Imagine the city at its prime, with the vegetation cut back and the plaster pavements kept in repair—measures which alone would go far toward preventing humid, moldy conditions. Adams (1970) visualizes these rooms as dry and cool, furnished with benches, skins, mats, and textiles. Benches seem to be a particular feature of residential "palaces." Other such multiroomed structures were probably used for storage or administrative functions. A "palace" may often be identified as residential by its general arrangement and appearance, which is but a larger all-masonry version of the smaller perishable house. Other evidence of habitation would be the presence of household rubbish, ordinary burials, and the absence of traces of ceremonial activity (Haviland, 1970).

House mounds and residential units have been studied in the same way to determine their function. The presence of utilitarian artifacts denotes living quarters as opposed to workshops or rooms designated for ceremony or ritual. With this in mind, the structures on strips of land five hundred meters wide by twelve kilometers long that radiate in the four cardinal directions from the Great Plaza have been carefully mapped and studied. In contrast to the typical ceremonial center with a small resident population, Tikal reveals a concentration of ruin mounds close to the core that falls off in density farther from the center, where the structures are distributed around plazas, but these groupings in turn are scattered at random. Nevertheless, the general pattern is a dense central core which is surrounded by a less densely populated periphery. Haviland's latest population estimates are 39,000 for the central zone of 63 square kilometers and 6000 more people in the surrounding 60 square kilometers (Haviland, 1970).

Estimating population of Maya settlements is a very complex task. Some of the difficulties involved in using the "house-mound count" methodology can be appreciated when one realizes that the Maya often had the disconcerting habit of moving out of their huts after burying a dead person therein. Thompson (1971) cites various examples of this practice from Postclassic sources, but believes the custom very probably was followed in Classic times as well. Other than a death in the family, house mounds could have been abandoned for a number of reasons, such as the exhaustion of the soil, epidemics, fear of an enemy, or even to avoid oppression or some other undesirable social situation. The physical move would involve only a small expenditure of time and labor, for the Maya did not accumulate household goods on the scale that is done today. To make matters more confusing, houses might be rebuilt at a later time and mounds reoccupied. How then can the archaeologist cope with such deranging factors? Any meaningful population estimate would have to be based on the number of houses inhabited simultaneously. If excavations showed that pottery styles remained unchanged while remodeling of the house took place, this would be one clue favoring continual occupation. If abandonment and reoccupation at a later time had taken place, some observable accumulation of debris would result. The fact that the great majority of burials in the structure platforms of Tikal remained undisturbed is viewed by Haviland (1970) as additional proof of continuous occupation. Archaeologists at Tikal have been aware of these problems and have attempted to control the necessary variables in making their calculations. Other sites may present different kinds of problems, but one way or another, these factors must be taken into account.

Haviland reconstructs the population of Tikal as attaining its peak by A.D. 550 and maintaining this level until roughly A.D. 770. A decline is noticeable by A.D. 870, and by A.D. 1000 all the mapped structures had been abandoned. Both the dates and figures are tentative estimates and subject to change; but the large concentration of population is supported by archaeological evidence. Now we want to know how the population reached these proportions and how this extraordinary nucleation was maintained, that is, what was the economic base and social structure of these people, and how did they maintain order and authority?

Economy.   The economy of Tikal was probably based on slash-and-burn agriculture of maize, squash, and beans. Just how Maya civilization developed in the tropical lowland forest in which it was found has been the subject of much controversy over the years. Speculation abounds, but opinions are roughly divided into two opposing camps. One vigorously supports, as do I, the idea of the *in situ* development of Maya civilization while the other argues equally strongly that this could never have been. The latter school of thought states that such an environment, instead of stimulating the growth of civilization, would have imposed drastic limitations on a slash-and-burn economy, which would have been incapable of providing sufficient food for a large, dense population. Slash-and-burn agriculture is considered by this group to be ruthless and wasteful, destructive of much forest, and a primary cause of rapid soil erosion through the exposure of the land to the heavy tropical rains and sunlight. Sanders and Price (1968) believe that slash-and-burn agriculture required little or no cooperation of labor, and of necessity the population density had to be kept low. According to this theory, a settlement pattern of small dispersed hamlets would be the natural pattern for a population that periodically exhausted the soil and was forced to move off and clear new areas, thus effectively preventing any real concentration of population, theocratic control, and centralized government. Some exponents of this school of thought feel that the basic ingredients of Maya civilization evolved elsewhere, perhaps in the highlands, arrived full-blown in the lowlands, and slowly declined thereafter as the demands of the economy gradually wore away the structure of society. The ultimate downfall of the great Maya culture would be predictable and could be explained as a kind of "running out" or depletion of cultural potential or reserve. In addition, the homogeneous ecological setting would have deprived the population of any real motivation for interaction or the formation of nucleated settlements (Sanders & Price, 1968).

Other researchers disagree with these views of the beginnings of lowland Maya civilization. A good case has been made to show that slash-and-burn agriculture could have supported a large sedentary population. The combination of maize, squash, and beans makes optimum use of the natural resources: the vines of the squash protect the soil from erosion, the corn grows tall, breaking the force of the rain, and beans grow up the corn stalks, increasing the foliage. With erosion thus prevented, one could obtain the maximum yield per surface unit. The evidence from Tikal shows that some house platforms were in continuous use from Preclassic to Classic times, indicating that a slash-and-burn economic base need not always require nomadic farming. Numerous recent studies comparing yields of slash-and-burn agriculture among the modern Maya and other peasant societies have shown that a crop surplus is sometimes produced (Carneiro, 1960; Cowgill, 1962; W. R. Coe, 1957; Dumond, 1961; Drucker & Heizer, 1960).

Furthermore, food production would have been substantially increased if the Maya did indeed practice root-crop agriculture in addition to the cultivation of maize. Mention is made of root crops in the early Spanish histories, and a variety is farmed by the modern Maya. Cultivation of manioc has been postulated at Altamira, Chiapas in Early Preclassic times. For a people inhabiting a large dense rain forest, root crops offer greater subsistence potential than maize (Bronson, 1966). Still another source of dependable food was the breadnut or *ramon* tree (*Brosimum alicastrum*) that yields a fruit of high nutritional value. These were grown in the central zone of Tikal by each household separately and required little time or effort (Haviland, 1970). The Pulestons (1971) believe that the breadnut constituted the primary subsistence base. Certainly food resources were varied and the economic potential probably never fully exploited.

Although most of Tikal's population was probably engaged in agriculture, there must have been many who were dedicated to other economic pursuits. For example, the abundant supply of flint not only provided local material for tools, but could have been exported either raw or as a finished product. Such exchange of goods and commodities is found over and over again to be an important process in the emergence of both New and Old World civilizations, and Tikal is no exception. Despite a relatively homogeneous environment which basically offered the same products and resources, the Classic Maya centers of the lowland Petén shared many features such as architecture, religious symbolism, a system of dating and inscriptions, and ceramic styles. But as we shall see, it may not have been local but long-distance trading relationships that were the major integrating force in the young civilization. Three essential household commodities have been singled out by Rathje (1971) for analysis, all of which were lacking in the Petén. Mineral salt had to be imported from the Guatemalan highlands or from northern Yucatán (Thompson, 1970). The only sources of obsidian, so necessary for making sharp knives, are found in the highlands. The third Petén import is the *metate*, the standard grinding quern in every household. Although the Petén has ample limestone deposits, this is too soft a stone for a *metate* as it leaves particles of grit in the corn during the grinding process. Of the 2000 *metates* found at Tikal, eighty-five percent are of imported hard stone (Culbert, 1970). In addition hematite, jade, slate, pyrite, and marine materials were brought into Tikal (Haviland, 1970). The presence of Petén polychrome ceramics in both the Guatemalan highlands and northern Yucatán is evidence that the long-distance trade was reciprocal. We will see that the procurement of commodities from outside areas had far-reaching implications for the whole development of the northeastern Petén region (see pages 167–168).

Archaeological Remains. In the following description of the ruins of Tikal and a few of the outstanding tombs and caches, the skills that were prerequisite must be kept in mind: knowledge of architecture and engineering, astronomy, and craftsmanship in all the arts. Full-time craft specialization has been amply documented; flint and obsidian workshops have been identified in central Tikal. After the description of the city itself, current ideas about the structure of Classic Maya society will be reviewed.

The very core of Tikal consisted of the East, West, and Great Plazas, and the huge complexes of the North and Central Acropolis. Two temples of Late Classic date—Temple I, also known as the Temple of the Giant Jaguar, and Temple II (the Temple of the Masks)—are located on the Great Plaza. These giant temple-pyramids with their high roof combs soar to a height of 528 feet; together with lower buildings, courts, and plazas, they make up the central ceremonial cluster (Photo 22) (Carr & Hazard, 1961). From this nucleus, three causeways, in Late Classic times flanked by parapets and separated by two ravines, lead to other structures and groups of buildings, all of which have vaulted ceilings. The exteriors, which once had elegant flying façades, are very simple, with relatively little stone carving, while the combs were elaborately decorated with stucco masks. The Temple of the Inscriptions marks the end of the southeastern or Mendez Causeway, while the Maler Causeway originates behind Temple I and runs north to three twin-pyramid complexes known as Q, R, and O. The pyramids are accompanied by stelae and altars, some of which are magnificently carved and bear Initial Series dates. Continuing north, this causeway terminates at a large plaza bordered by two temples, another twin-pyramid complex, and acres of other structures, many of which are still untouched by the archaeologists. This entire area is now called the North Zone. The third or Tozzer Causeway leads northwest from the central area to Temple IV, the tallest (212 feet) of all standing New World structures, which is connected by the Maudslay Causeway to the North Zone and the Maler Causeway, thus completing a huge triangular thoroughfare. From the height of Temple IV, or from the base of the enormous roof comb, if one is bold enough for the climb, the view of all Tikal is superb. Imagine this magnificent jungle city in its Late Classic splendor, a bustling wealthy center where priests, merchants, artisans, and administrators circulated through the paved courts and causeways, temples, "palaces,"

Photo 22. Temple of the Giant Jaguar
(Temple I) at Tikal, Guatemala. Height:
145 feet. Courtesy of the University Museum,
University of Pennsylvania.

and accessory buildings—all stuccoed and painted, roof combs and
stelae erect—and the luxuriant jungle cropped back to the city limits.

The Great Plaza, dating from the Late Preclassic period and re-
plastered four times, was the heart of ancient Tikal. Temples I and II,
built about A.D. 700, face each other across the plaza, while between
them on the north side is Tikal's single most complex structure, the
Northern Acropolis. Occupying two and one-half acres, it alone supports
sixteen temples and conceals nearly one hundred buildings underneath.
As we have already seen, much of the known Preclassic material under-

lies the Northern Acropolis, and two of the finest Early Classic structures, Temples 33-1 and 33-2, are found within this structure and today can only be reached by tunnel. These temple facades are flanked by masks, also found on the underlying platform, some of which measure over ten feet in height and represent long-nosed gods (Coe & McGinn, 1963).

Numerous stelae have been found at Tikal, many uncarved, others bearing Initial Series dates (see Plate 6b, c, Chapter 5). Stelae are found most frequently in prominent positions in courts or plazas before stairways and buildings, and are usually paired with altars. It was once believed that stelae were erected to stand throughout eternity to commemorate important calendrical events, but at Tikal the stelae often were deliberately broken and smashed, some were placed in tombs, while others were reused and even reassembled upside down. Perhaps these stelae, like some from Piedras Negras, were dedicated to a particular ruler or important dignitary and, after his death, were fragmented to accompany him to his grave. Thus, rather than being public monuments designed to last an eternity, such stelae may have been personal tributes honored only during one individual's lifetime.

The history of Stela 26, known as the Red Stela (see Plate 6c, Chapter 5), serves as one example of the treatment given to a carved monument (Shook, 1958). When clearing away accumulated debris in the back room of one of the temples (Structure 34) of the Northern Acropolis, investigators found this spectacular stela ruthlessly smashed and broken. Apparently it originally had stood at the back of the room facing the doorway in a position of prominence. The front of the stela was carved with an elaborate figure—double rows of beautifully made glyphs adorn the lateral sides—and the entire stone was painted bright red. One fatal day, however, the monument was tumbled, the face was smashed, and chunks were broken off, chips flying. All these fragments were gathered and heaped into pits dug into the floor, other rich offerings were added, and the floor was sealed over. To conceal the base of the stela, a stone altar was raised above it, upon which ceremonial fires were kindled. Eventually the altar too was defaced and partially destroyed. What curious furor possessed these Tikal Maya to vent such destruction upon the Red Stela? Certainly it was not a rage of disrespect, for the cache offerings accompanying the stela fragments are some of the finest and most exotic objects known. A great variety of marine material was included, including fish vertebrae, sponges, coral, shells, and sting-ray spines, as were fragments of jade and obsidian and a mosaic plaque of jade and crystalline hematite mounted on mother-of-pearl that could only have been traded down from the highlands of Guatemala. The eccentric obsidians and small incised obsidians in this cache represent some of the finest and rarest objects uncovered to date (Plate 10a).

The oldest dated Maya stela known is Tikal's Stela 29 (see Plate 6b, Chapter 5). This stela was found neither in a tomb, in temple debris, nor in a plaza or court, but had been cast aside about two hundred yards west of the Great Plaza, where it lay for centuries, buried in the forest under soil and leaf mold (Shook, 1960). It too had been fragmented, and one part was recovered on the slopes of a nearby mound. This remarkable stela, carved in bas-relief, bears a Long Count date of 8.12.14.8.15 (July 6, A.D. 292), antedating Uaxactún's famed Stela 9 by thirty-six years. Stela 29 is fairly representative of Early Classic stelae. Although this one was not recovered *in situ*, other stelae of this period often are accompanied by a small, round altar. The large limestone slabs usually have a single male figure, typically represented with the shoulders in full-front view and the head and lower limbs in profile, on one side and hieroglyphs on the other.

A distinctive Late Classic feature is the twin-pyramid and stela room complex. These pyramids are relatively low and have stairways on all four sides. They are associated with a long, narrow room across a court to the north, which presumably was roofed over with thatch and contained a stela. In the Late Classic period, Tikal stelae were fashioned wider and taller than previously, with figures carved in high relief, and the appearance of women for the first time. A general change notable in Late Classic stelae is that of presenting the body in full front view with feet pointing outward. The altars of this phase, like the stelae, also were heavier and larger than earlier ones. Wall paintings and elaborate burials of important personages emphasized class distinctions and social rank.

A good example of this was the interment of a prestigious adult male (known to archaeologists as Burial 48) who was given a very special burial in a tomb tunneled into bedrock under a succession of temples in the Northern Acropolis. Prior to interment, both head and hands were removed. He was buried in a seated position but his bones eventually collapsed into a heap. There is no question that his rank was high; not only was he accompanied by the bodies of two teen-agers, but the walls of the tomb itself had been stuccoed and painted with an Initial Series date of 9.1.1.10.10 (A.D. 457). Among the rich offerings were elegantly decorated pots, a particularly fine Teotihuacán-type cylindrical tripod covered with painted stucco, and a fine alabaster bowl also stuccoed in pale green and decorated with a band of incised glyphs. Jade, a highly prized possession that had to be brought from the Motagua River where boulders and small stones of apple-green color are found, was represented here by hundreds of beads and two pairs of ear-plug flares. Marine products, food offerings, and greenish obsidian, a possible central Mexican import, gave the deceased ample supplies for any eventuality in afterlife. Such treatment was only given to very privileged people of the highest rank. The commoners were usually interred under the floors of their houses, so nothing resembling a cemetery has been found.

After A.D. 600 Late Classic additions and changes were made that altered the profile of the city. The Temple of the Giant Jaguar was built at this time, undergoing many stages of construction to bring it to its present form. Prior to the initial construction, however, a large vaulted tomb was dug deep into the Great Plaza. Its main occupant was lavishly buried with the finest offerings available: 180 pieces of worked jade, pearls, pottery, alabaster, and shells. Quite remarkable is a pile of ninety bone slivers, located in one corner off the dais on which the deceased had been extended. Thirty seven of these bones were delicately carved depicting deities in naturalistic scenes such as traveling by canoe, and some of these have hieroglyphic texts. The richly stocked tomb of Burial 116 is admittedly one of the finest, but apparently important interments were frequently made prior to starting construction of a temple-pyramid. Archaeologists conducting a dig can usually tell when they are approaching an underground tomb because quantities of chips of obsidian and flint appear in the fill (W. R. Coe, 1967).

Above this tomb, the Temple of the Giant Jaguar rises to imposing heights, its nine sloping terraces supporting a temple of three rooms at

a

b

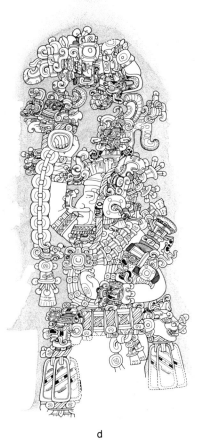

d

c

Plate 10. Various objects from the Maya area

a. Late Classic incised obsidian flakes and blades, often found in caches, Tikal, Guatemala. See scale for dimensions in centimeters. Courtesy of the University Museum, University of Pennsylvania.

b. Shell carving of seated Mayan man with a pearl inlaid in ear spool (greatly enlarged), Palenque, Chiapas. Height: 2⅞ inches. Courtesy of the Museum of the American Indian, Heye Foundation (22/4955).

c. "Eccentric" flint of ceremonial use, considered of great value and widely traded, Río Hondo, Orange Walk, British Honduras. Length: 14 inches. Courtesy of the Museum of the American Indian, Heye Foundation (13/5547).

d. Drawing of front and lateral faces of Stela 31, Tikal, Guatemala. Figures on sides carry *atlatls* and appear to be from central Mexico. Early Classic Maya. Courtesy of the University Museum, University of Pennsylvania.

e. Stela 5, Piedras Negras. Height: 8 feet. Courtesy of the Museum of Primitive Art, New York.

f. Beautifully modeled life-size stucco head, placed on floor of funerary crypt, Temple of the Inscriptions, Palenque, Chiapas. Courtesy of the Museo Nacional de Antropología, Mexico.

g. Jade mosaic mask with eyes of inlaid shell and obsidian. Placed as death mask in sarcophagus of funerary crypt, Temple of the Inscriptions, Palenque, Chiapas. Courtesy of the Museo Nacional de Antropología, Mexico.

h. Carved wooden figure, Tabasco. Height: 14 inches. Courtesy of the Museum of Primitive Art, New York.

i. Human effigy mushroom stone, Momostenango, Guatemala. Height: 13 inches. Courtesy of the Museum of the American Indian, Heye Foundation (9/8304).

j. Carved jadeite figure, Copán, Honduras. Height: 8 inches. Courtesy of the Museum of the American Indian, Heye Foundation (10/9827).

k. Marble vase carved in Tajín style, Ulua River Valley, Honduras. Height: 5 inches. Courtesy of the Museum of the American Indian, Heye Foundation (4/3956).

e

f

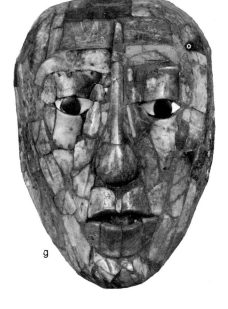

g

h

i

j

k

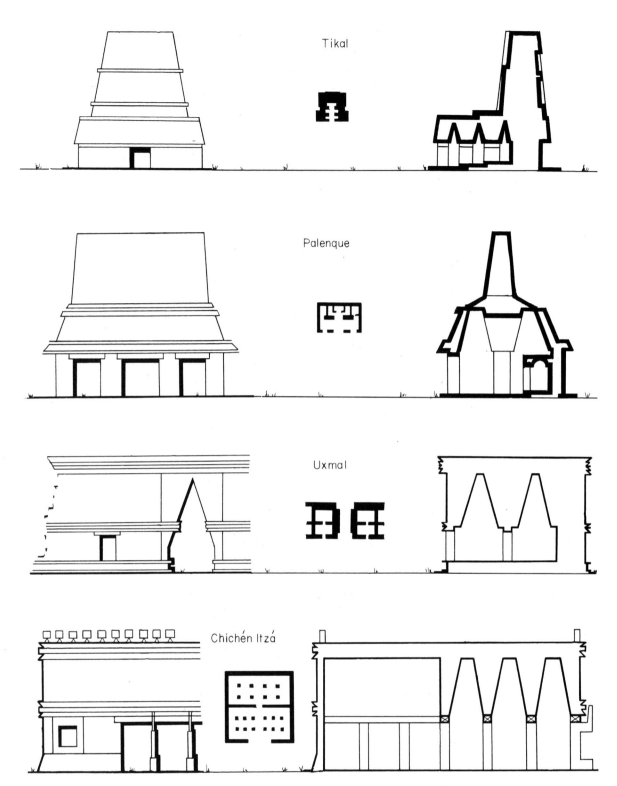

Figure 24. Lowland Maya temples, floor plans, and profiles. (Adapted from Marquina, 1951.)

the summit. These rooms, recessed one above the other, are small and dark—typical of the period, for not until later times were doorways wider and more plentiful, and walls thinner. Each vault was supported by *sapote* wood, the exceedingly hard wood of the sapodilla tree, which fortunately has resisted the decomposition characteristic of the tropical forest, preserving some magnificent carving. The exquisitely carved lintels of Tikal are well known, as some have found their way to foreign museums. Fortunately, others still perform their intended function. Not all the beams and lintels were carved, and as a rule, outer doorways have plain lintels. Over the wall of the last of the three temple rooms rises a tall, two-leveled roof comb, the face of which was decorated with stone blocks representing an individual seated between scrolls and serpents that are now badly weathered. The entire limestone temple once was painted red, with a roof comb of red, cream, and perhaps blue or green (Photo 22; Figure 24).

The Late Classic period at Tikal has also revealed sweat houses consisting of a single room with a low doorway from which a channel leads to a firepit at the rear. Sweat baths, or *temescales*, which probably were of ritual significance and may have been associated with the ball game, are known from both lowland and highland regions.

Tikal was also not without its ball courts. A small one, with low sloping benches much like that of Copán, was located in the Great Plaza. A second was found in the East Plaza, and another, in the Plaza of the Seven Temples, contained a triple court. None had markers, and all are open ended, as is typical of lowland Maya ball courts.

Another unique feature of Tikal deserves comment. Two and a half miles north of the Great Plaza of Tikal, archaeologists came upon the remains of a Classic period wall and ditch that continued six miles in an east–west direction before disappearing into the swamp. This may have been a defensive mechanism to guard Tikal from neighboring Uaxactún (Puleston & Callender, 1967). Another earthwork of similar nature was located to the south, about eight kilometers from the main center.

Maya Society. From the partial results of diggings at Tikal, which are rapidly appearing in reports and articles, one cannot but marvel at the complexity of construction and the extent of accumulated material wealth. Using archaeological evidence, Haviland (1966) and more recently Adams (1970) have attempted a reconstruction of Classic Maya society. The latter visualizes the existence of four main social classes, each with its ascribed status. The top ranking hierarchical class was probably semidivine. Occupations associated with this group would logically have been administrative posts, religious activities, warfare, and trading. In representations painted on pottery or in murals figures engaged in these pursuits are always decked out in elegant attire, indicating that these would surely have been prestigious positions. Next in line might be scribes, accountants, and skilled sculptors, followed by specialized artisans like potters, tool makers, weavers, and feather workers. The fourth and lowest strata belonged to the peasants who could offer nothing more than their manual labor in the fields. The relationships among these groups would tell us much about the functioning of Maya society.

How flexible was the class structure? Any social mobility was probably confined to permanent urban residents of the top ranking class.

Rathje (1970) has hypothesized that the accretion and redistribution of wealth became a circular movement limited to a few families. Perhaps warfare eventually became an activity in which one could gain prestige and improve one's social status. These are the kinds of inferences drawn from the archaeological record that support the existence of a strong centralized authority, with an aristocratic ruling elite. This view of ancient Maya society is that held by A. Ruz, J. E. S. Thompson, R. E. W. Adams, W. R. Coe, T. Proskouriakoff, and D. H. Kelley.

Another stimulating hypothesis about the functioning of ancient Maya society has been advanced by E. Z. Vogt who studied the modern Tzotzil *municipio* of Zinacantan in highland Chiapas. He suggests that this contemporary modern community may be used as a model for the interpretation of Classic Maya society (Vogt, 1968). Zinacantan can be described as a ceremonial center sustained by a population living in scattered small communities known as *parajes*, each numbering from 50 to 1000 persons. Only about six percent of the total population lives in the center itself. The *parajes* in turn are divided into smaller groups, which would correspond to the Petén clusters (Willey *et al.*, 1965). Vogt calls these "water-hole groups." The smallest unit in Zinacantan is the *sitio*, or the extended patrilocal family. The outlying population sustains the town or center through religious, political, and commercial participation. Vogt points out a correspondence not only in the physical settlement pattern but also in subsistence and social and ceremonial life.

The Zinacantan center is supported by a kind of *cargo* system, in which a rotation of offices take place among farmers coming in to occupy specific positions in the religious hierarchy. Upon completion of a one-year term during which time he enjoys a special prestige, the farmer returns to his *paraje* to accumulate resources to enable him to apply for the next position up the social or political ladder. Such a system of graded ranks would have permitted considerable mobility and would have been a strong integrating force in Maya society. Thus, the building and maintenance of public works would be easily explained. In addition, the sacred mountains around Zinacantan, where rituals are performed, are seen as fulfilling the role of the ancient pyramids.

This model, when applied to clusters, zones, and ceremonial centers, makes a great deal of sense. Recently, it has been postulated that this could have led to the highly structured, wealth-conscious, less flexible social pattern that becomes evident in the Late Classic period in such centers as Tikal. Rathje (1970) reexamined the entire problem by studying well-documented Maya burials interred in house platforms, palaces, and temple structures. Lacking sufficient material from a single site, he utilized house mound burials from British Honduras and temple and palace burials from Uaxactún, assuming that both areas shared common patterns of sociopolitical organization. The comparison of data suggests that a change took place in Maya society—a shift of emphasis from one of social mobility between rural populations and the ceremonial center to a pattern of strict concentration of wealth and power in the hands of an elite few.

How was this shift reflected in the burials? During the Early Classic period the wealthy were mature adults in the temple areas, as well as young adults among the rural population. By Late Classic times as more "palaces" were erected (probably as residences), the wealthy burials were confined to the adult population of the ceremonial centers. The *cargo* system as outlined by Vogt would be compatible with the social pattern of the Early Classic period in which the accumulation of wealth could have been the key to achieving power and participation in ceremonial life. By Late Classic times, the carefully structured society depicted by R. E. W. Adams would have been attained by the largest centers.

Conformity and the Spread of Knowledge

Every Maya center had distinctive features and specialties, but in general the Early Classic in the lowland Maya area can be characterized as one of homogeneity (Thompson, 1943, 1954, 1965a; Willey *et al.*, 1967). These years between A.D. 300 and 600 were marked by the rapid spread of religious symbolism and technology seen in architecture, the stelae cult, hieroglyphic writing and astronomical knowledge. This homogeneity is clearly reflected in Tzakol ceramics, a term used for Early Classic pottery of this area. Monochrome and polychrome wares predominated. Vessels often were decorated with conventionalized designs of animals and humans, and perhaps the most common Tzakol form is the polychrome vessel with a ring base and basal flange (Figure 22n), although Teotihuacán-flavored slab-footed, cylindrical tripods and pitchers are also diagnostic (Plate 7d; Figure 22p). For the first time a widespread ceramic complex can be discerned. Its uniformity is so consistent as to be almost monotonous, in great contrast to the earlier variety of Preclassic ceramics.

The earliest important centers were located in northeastern Petén; they are known to us through extensive excavations such as those at Uaxactún and more recently at Tikal. Balakbal, Mirador, and El Zapote are less well-known sites in the same region. From this central core area, Classic Maya culture spread westward to the Usumacinta Valley sites of Yaxchilán, Piedras Negras, and Palenque; south to Altar de Sacrificios on the Pasión River; farther south to Copán; and as far north as the Yucatán peninsula. There are hundreds of recorded sites. This was a period of enthusiastic activity that accelerated toward a cultural culmination realized only a few generations later.

This widespread cultural uniformity in the Early Classic period is of considerable interest since it is in precisely this region where the great Maya civilization reached its peak. We have seen that adaptation to diverse ecosystems resulting in economic symbiosis and hydraulic agriculture are thought to have been important stimuli toward the evolution of urban civilization in highland central Mexico (see pages 128–129). In the rather redundant environment of the Petén region where the main subsistence technique was slash-and-burn agriculture, where irrigation was not a factor, and transportation of goods was difficult, the same model cannot be applied. Here there were different processes at work although the procurement and distribution of essential resources were still of major importance; trade was vital to the emergent civilization. A reasonable explanation has been suggested by Rathje (1971) who points out that the beginning of complex sociopolitical organization among the Maya seems to have taken place precisely in that area most remote from the desired resources, that is, the northeastern Petén. It was this landlocked region that apparently developed the organization to mount large trading expeditions and maintain lines of communication. A complex and efficient organization was an absolute necessity which at the same time stimulated bustling ceremonial activity between communities and increased the production of luxury goods. The sophisticated commercial ties required specialists, skilled craftsmen, and astute businessmen. Whereas the market system was a perfect vehicle for the movement of goods in an area of great regional diversity such as the highlands, here there was little motivation to exchange products that were easily available to everyone. However, certain essential resources were lacking for the proper functioning of every Mesoamerican household. These deficiencies, Rathje believes, forced the central area into a sociopolitical complexity of which Maya civilization was the result.

Altar de Sacrificios, located on river junctions, could have served as an important station between the northeastern Petén and the Guatemalan highlands, affording access to salt and obsidian. Another salt-procuring route lay to northern Yucatán, perhaps by way of Tulum. Likewise Copán may have been drawn into the commercial scheme because of nearby obsidian. Petén centers are commonly strewn with obsidian flaked blades from the highlands. Cores were probably traded in and blades flaked off on location as demand required. In turn the Petén could provide the highlanders with excellent limestone, which was always in demand for making stucco and lye for steeping maize, as well as skins of jaguars and alligators, and bright feathers of parrots, toucans and humming birds. Other exports included fine polychrome pottery and worked flint (Andrews, 1965; W. R. Coe, 1959, 1967; Thompson, 1970). The communication network reached not only throughout the peninsula of Yucatán and highland Guatemala but as far as central highland Mexico. We have already seen that the Esperanza phase at Kaminaljuyú was dominated by the Teotihuacanos. There is also increasing evidence of Teotihuacán influence in Classic Petén centers. Does this represent a second-hand transmission from the Guatemalan highlands? Possibly, but it seems more likely that ties existed directly between the Petén itself and central Mexico (Plate 10d). At Tikal some platform architecture, tomb offerings, and stone sculpture can be identified with the highland Mexican center around A.D. 500. Petén centers have yielded characteristic Teotihuacán slab-leg cylindrical tripods, and Teotihuacán styles of incising, stucco painting, and stone carving. There are representations of Mexican deities such as Tlaloc and Xipe Totec, while far to the west at Teotihuacán itself we find Petén jades, ceramic wares, and mural paintings of Maya-like peoples.

However, in spite of the dependence on trade and communication with distant regions, which seems to have been a prime force in the extraordinary emergence of Maya civilization, the Early Classic or Tzakol period remained thoroughly Maya in conception and orientation. There follows a period of forty to sixty years between the Long Count dates of 9.5.0.0.0 and 9.8.0.0.0, corresponding to the interval between Early and Late Classic phases, when construction work seems to have paused and few stelae were erected. This lack of activity is noted throughout the southern lowlands (Willey *et al.*, 1967). After A.D. 600, however, Maya culture underwent further cultural changes in which central Mexican influences played little part and Maya civilization rededicated itself to its own artistic achievements. Through the widespread use of the calendar and hieroglyphic inscriptions, hierarchical integration was achieved.

Cultural Climax

The three hundred years between A.D. 600 and 900, known ceramically as Tepeu, witnessed the culmination of Maya civilization. During this time no one center can be singled out as the dominating or coordinating political or religious nucleus. In sharp contrast to central Mexico, we instead must think in terms of many independent but interrelated nuclei. As showcases of Maya civilization, their combined culture constitutes an integrated whole. Late Classic or Tepeu pottery is much less monotonous than that of Tzakol and varies greatly in styles of painted decorations. Most striking of all is a flat-based cylindrical vessel painted with handsome polychromed figures and bands of glyphs (Plate 7h, Figure 22t). Figurines, now made in molds, once more became popular, and sometimes these small representations of animals or human beings were made to be used as whistles. Toward the end of the great Classic period, regionalism became very pronounced. The ceramics never hint of decadence or the impending cultural breakdown, although motifs in the final occupation at Altar de Sacrificios and Seibal show the presence of intruders, probably the Putún from the mouth of the Grijalva River. This period can only be understood by studying and comparing many sites, for they provide the details necessary to a functional comprehension of the phenomenon we call Maya civilization.

During these remarkable three hundred years, Maya civilization spread from the core region in the Petén westward to the lower Usumacinta River in Tabasco and far south to include Copán and the Ulua River in Honduras. Yucatán too underwent a remarkable Late Classic development that is displayed in three flamboyant architectural styles known as Río Bec, Chenes, and Puuc. A listing of the most important lowland sites includes the following (see Inset, Map 3):

Central area: Uaxactún, Tikal, Nakum, Naranjo, Yaxhá, Holmul, Benque Viejo, San José, Lubaantun, Pusilhá, Altun Ha
Southern area: Copán, Quiriguá
Usumacinta–Pasión river drainage: Piedras Negras, Yaxchilán, Palenque, Bonampak, Altar de Sacrificios, Seibal, Cancuen
Northern area: Jaina, Chichén Itzá, Yaxuná, Dzibilchaltún, Cobá
Puuc area: Oxkintok, Uxmal, Kabah, Labná, Sayil, Acanceh
Chenes area: Santa Rosa Xtampak, Hochob
Río Bec area: Becán, Río Bec, Xpuhil

Uaxactún has long been known as one of the earliest Petén sites because it was the scene of intensive excavations by the Carnegie Institution for a period of twelve years beginning in 1926 (Morley, 1937–1938; Smith, 1950). The resulting ceramic studies laid the basis for the whole lowland Maya chronology (Kidder, 1947). The site itself is centered around a large platform supporting three temples that face one another across a central court. Stela 9 was for many years the earliest Petén Initial Series date (dated at A.D. 328), but, as mentioned previously, this distinction has now been replaced by Stela 29 at Tikal, carved thirty-six years earlier. Uaxactún also boasted a beautiful wall painting depicting a religious ceremony. However, the site is now in ruins and once more enveloped by the jungle (Smith, 1950). Uaxactún was never considered to be a city of the first magnitude, but it will always be remembered as an early precursor to Maya civilization (Photo 10, Chapter 4; Figure 25).

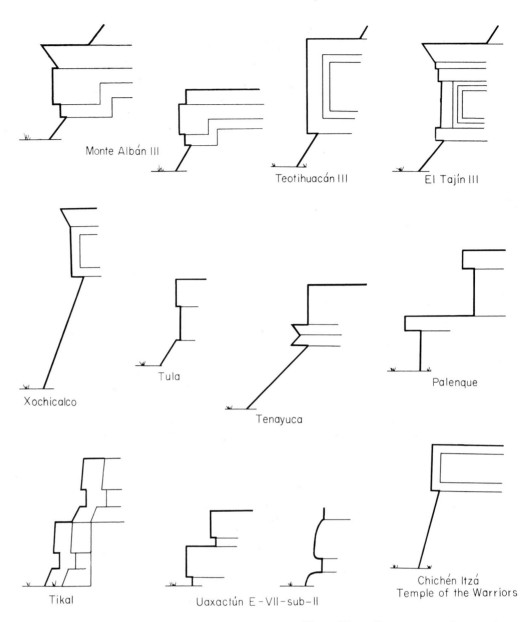

Figure 25. Comparative architectural profiles of Mesoamerican pyramids. (Adapted from Marquina, 1951.)

Copán. Slightly removed from the mainstream of the Petén nuclear region and representing the most important and spectacular of the southern Maya sites is the main group of ruins at Copán in western Honduras (Morley, 1920, 1956; Stromsvik, 1947; Longyear, 1952; Thompson, 1965a). Located in a valley surrounded by forested hills, Copán occupied an enviable natural setting. At 2000 feet above sea level, its climate was temperate and forest game, fish, and bird life abundant. Excellent building stone was available close by in the form of a greenish volcanic trachyite that was easy to cut and work when freshly quarried but hardened upon constant exposure to air. The light green cast of Copán buildings and sculptures is both distinctive and pleasing. The main group of ruins consists of a massive cluster of constructions known as the Acropolis, which is composed of repeated constructions overlying earlier buildings.

The principal multiroomed structures and temples are ornately decorated with roof combs and flying facades. The top of the Acropolis may be reached by the famous monumental hieroglyphic staircase, which is ninety feet high and thirty feet wide. The riser of each of the sixty-three steps is intricately carved with hieroglyphs, 2000 in all, constituting the longest Maya text in existence. Spaced at intervals up the steep flight of steps are five seated figures of stone, each six feet high.

From the top of the Acropolis one commands an impressive view of the Copán River far below, in addition to the main courts and their surrounding buildings and stepped terraces. One is also struck by the imposing view of the great plaza, which is over seven hundred feet long and studded with handsome stelae and altars elaborately carved with personages and hieroglyphs in high relief. It is at Copán where figures most closely approximate true sculpture in the round. Altars are intricately carved in heavy relief, and hieroglyphs are particularly ornate and imaginative (see Plate 6e, Chapter 5). The individuals depicted on stelae are characteristically stiff and sedate in posture, but richly attired and gigantic in size. Mention is often made of the oriental cast of the Copán style of stone carving with its curious bearded individuals. There is no doubt but that Copán represents something special in regional development. Perhaps, in its southern isolation, it was freer to embellish stelae and altars with its own artistic taste.

Copán is outstanding not only for the beauty but also for the abundance of its stone carving. Facades are lavishly decorated with human, bird, and animal figures; altars, stelae, stairways, and temples provide a wealth of hieroglyphic inscriptions, many of which still await scholarly interpretation.

The buildings are of massive proportions and combine simplicity with intricate relief sculpture in stone and stucco. The Temple of Meditation (Temple 22) is an example of such cyclopean masonry. One mounts the enormous stairway and enters the temple through a doorway carved in the form of a gigantic serpent's mouth, a feature usually associated with Río Bec architecture. The facade was originally decorated with rain gods, huge grotesque masks, gargoyles, and seated human figures. The inner doorway to the temple is carved with naturalistic human figures seated on skulls and accompanied by elaborately intertwined motifs of grotesque monsters. The temple has been accurately restored by the Carnegie Institution, following a careful description by Maudslay, even to such details as holes near the doorways for inserting poles, probably to support a curtain or mat.

On the northern side of the court of the Hieroglyphic Stairway lies one of the most beautiful ball courts known (Photo 23). Following the typical plan of an elongated H, the long playing alley had crosswise rectangular end zones and floor markers. Wide sloping benches on either side border the playing area and are studded with three pairs of large parrot heads set into the upper edges. Rings were still unknown during the Classic period.

The Mesoamerican ball game was played as early as Preclassic times, to judge from representations of ball players among clay figurines, stone reliefs at Dainzú, and possibly a very early court at San Lorenzo. Not until the Classic period, however, are stone masonry courts found. These are an important element of each major ceremonial center of the Classic and subsequent periods. The game itself has been described for us by the early Spanish chroniclers who witnessed these competitions (Sahagún, 1946). They tell us that the game was very rough and that it was played by two opposing teams, each numbering from two to eleven men, with a solid rubber ball that might measure nearly a foot in diameter and weigh as much as five pounds. According to the rules of the game, the ball had to be kept in motion by using only the torso of the body and possibly the head, but no hands or feet! The players often were seriously injured or even killed, but the dangers in no way diminished the enthusiasm for this sport. Accounts from central Mexico at the time of the Conquest describe the elegant spectators who arrived in their jewels and fine clothes to watch and root for their team from the reviewing stands on the sides. If perchance the ball passed through the stone ring, a difficult and not too common feat, the game was immediately won, and to the winners belonged the right to claim any wearing apparel of the spectators. As a consequence, upon seeing the ball pass through the ring, the audience fled with the winning team in hot pursuit. These games had religious significance, and matches sometimes were scheduled as a form of divination to determine the outcome of future events or to make decisions. At Copán, the remains of two earlier courts lie beneath the well-preserved one with parrot-head markers. The game clearly had a long tradition by this time (Krickeberg, 1961; Blom, 1932). In Classic times the rules and significance of the game may have differed somewhat, but the ball court is a prominent feature of each major ceremonial center.

Quiriguá. A short distance to the north in today's banana land of the Motagua River Valley, Guatemala, some of the tallest sandstone stelae known were carved by the inhabitants of Quiriguá. The few structures here in no way compare to those at Copán or in the Petén, but hieroglyphic inscriptions representing fantastic mythical monsters were masterfully carved on stelae and gigantic flat boulders. As were other cities, Quiriguá was abandoned before Cycle 9 came to a close, the last recorded date being that found on the hieroglyphic bands on the doorways and exterior molding of Structure 1, which read 9.19.0.0.0. Undoubtedly the most handsome building at Quiriguá, this structure was entered by three doorways leading to seven chambers. A tall roof comb once rested on the massive rear wall (Morley, 1935).

Altar de Sacrificios. Turning to the west we come to Altar de Sacrificios (Willey & Smith, 1969) strategically located in the relatively flat plain of the Pasión River where it is joined by the Chixoy River, thus providing a trade route to Alta Verapaz. Below this juncture the river is known as the Usumacinta, a main thoroughfare of communication from the western regions of Tabasco to the Petén during the Classic period. By making a short portage to the Sarstoon River from Altar de Sacrificios, canoes could reach the Bay of Honduras on the east coast of Yucatán. Thus, Altar de Sacrificios occupied a prime location for commercial transactions, an advantage not overlooked by the aggressive Putún (Thompson, 1970). A leading ceremonial center in its own right, Altar de Sacrificios flourished throughout Classic times. Here in the southwestern Petén the Maya erected a pyramid of nine or ten terraces with almost vertical walls. An elaborate staircase led up to the summit, once crowned by a perishable temple. A curious feature is the placement of stelae and altars on the stairways of platforms and buildings rather than in the courts and plazas. Consistent with prevailing trends, the buildings were arranged around courts and plazas. A ball court at the site resembles that of Copán but lacks the masonry superstructures. Toward the end of the great Classic period, one sees in Altar art faces and motifs that reflect a new strain. This outside influence is markedly apparent in the pottery and figurines from what has been called the Ximba phase at this site. Fine Orange, particularly the variety known as the Y type, and Fine Gray wares predominate. Fine Orange paste was also used for the figurines that present non-Maya features.

Thompson, after a thorough study of linguistic and historical source material and archaeological data, believes that the Chontal Maya people, whom he identifies as Putún, were responsible for these outside influences noticed first at Altar de Sacrificios (about A.D. 800) and later (about A.D. 850) at Seibal (Thompson, 1970). The Putún Maya lived in the large delta lands of the Grijalva and Usumacinta rivers in southern Campeche and Tabasco, an area culturally marginal to the great Classic Maya centers. These people are known to have been aggressive traders and merchant seamen who eventually controlled the sea routes around the peninsula of Yucatán to the Bay of Honduras on the east. Their center of operations was Chakanputún, a province of Putún in Tabasco and possibly the name given to their capital. Possessing Mexican, Náhuat-speaking neighbors, they naturally intermarried and absorbed some Mexican tastes and habits. In late Classic years, these Putún had already made incursions by canoe up the Usumacinta River, and the blend of Maya and Náhuat elements that makes its appearance at this time is attributed to them. The Putún may also be the producers of Y-Fine Orange, a ware prominent in the Petén and the area drained by the Usumacinta River.

Seibal. As Altar de Sacrificios declined in power and influence around A.D. 751, its neighbor, Seibal, located one hundred kilometers

Photo 23.   Ball court at Copán, Honduras.
Photographed by the author.

Photo 24. (*Above*) Wall painting showing a procession of musicians, Bonampak, Chiapas. Courtesy of the Instituto Nacional de Antropología e Historia, Mexico.

Photo 25. (*Right*) Wall painting showing torture of prisoners, Bonampak, Chiapas. Courtesy of the Instituto Nacional de Antropología e Historia, Mexico.

upstream, gradually rose to take its place. Like Altar, Seibal's roots date back to Preclassic times, particularly Late Preclassic, but Seibal has few remains from the Early Classic period. It became important during the Late Classic period but was never one of the large Petén cities (Tourtellot, 1970).

The three groups of ruins are located on a range of limestone bluffs precisely at a bend of the Pasión River. They are connected by causeways, the entire building area occupying about one square kilometer. Their high location would have been advantageous for defense, which was becoming a factor to consider in Late Classic times. The structures themselves were of the ceremonial type typical of the organized religious hierarchy believed to have been in existence. At Seibal most of the populace lived outside the main nucleus in small peripheral clusters grouped around central courts. The highest elevations available were selected for building, undoubtedly for better drainage but possibly also for purposes of communication. More than forty-three structures have been excavated, revealing corbelled vaults and open-ended ball courts, as

well as a round three-terraced structure with a large jaguar altar located at the end of a causeway.

There was a steady growth in population and public construction, with maximum activity in the sixty years prior to A.D. 890. In the first half of the fifth century, Seibal art shows a mixture of Mexican and Maya influences, as seen in the serpent motif, Tlaloc faces, and speech scrolls. The Putún seem not to have maintained control over Seibal for long, and were not the cause of its collapse. Indeed, these intruders joined in the erection of dated stelae (Thompson, 1970). Around A.D. 930, however, Seibal too was overcome by the same forces that caused the decline of the great Classic Petén centers.

Bonampak. Further along the Usumacinta drainage, western centers of Maya civilization were also constructing temple-pyramids, erecting stelae, and recording dates and events in hieroglyphic carvings. Bonampak in Chiapas, a contemporary of Altar de Sacrificios, is a site renown for its unique mural paintings of the ancient Maya, which provide us with infinite detail of dress, processional scenes, musicians, sacrifices, sacred rites, and warfare (Ruppert, Thompson, & Proskouriakoff, 1955). Bonampak lies deep in the jungle home of the modern Lacandon Indians, who bear such great resemblance to their Maya ancestors that they appear to have just stepped down from a stela. The ruins of Bonampak lie on the banks of the Lacanjá River and are so completely covered by the dense vegetation that one is close upon them before they are seen. Around a great rectangular plaza, groups of platforms support temples at varying levels. The temples are small, but all are built with vaulted roofs. The Temple of the Paintings contains three rooms, each with a stone lintel carved in relief, and fresco paintings that cover the entire wall from floor to ceiling. The walls were first prepared with a lime coating three to five centimeters thick, and while they were still damp the paintings were executed in orange, yellow, green, dark red, and turquoise blue. The processional figures are shown in fancy headdresses and elaborate attire, carrying children, using umbrellas for shade, wearing animal disguises and fantastic masks, dancing, and conversing. Musicians rattle turtle shells, beat drums, and shake clay (or gourd?) rattles (Photo 24) (Thompson, 1954; Villagra, 1949). On the walls of another room a battle scene and its consequences is depicted — the trial and punishment of prisoners (Photo 25) and a group of warriors and their leader, who wears a jaguar skin thrown over his back and holds a staff of authority in his right hand, perhaps in a gesture of intervention on behalf of the prisoners. Other scenes include bound victims whose fingers drip blood, some of whom are seminude and have disheveled hair. This sequence is completed by a painting of a decapitated skull resting on a step; in the murals of the next room victory is being celebrated (Villagra, 1949). Bonampak is Late Classic in date (A.D. 450–750), and we can only speculate about whether the conflicts represented are simply local raids or whether they indicate warfare on a larger scale. Certainly the murals provide us with invaluable, seldom preserved ethnographic data.

Yaxchilán. Yaxchilán, a huge site that sprawls across the Usumacinta River in the modern Mexican state of Chiapas, shares the mansard-type roof with the more westerly Palenque. Despite the fact that the site has yielded more than 125 inscriptions on carved lintels and stelae, no major work has ever been done at this site. We do know, however, that buildings of the palace type with three entrances, rather than the pyramid-temple, prevail. The upper facades slope like those of Palenque, and the perforated roof combs are centrally located. Two ball courts have been identified. This center may have been controlled by some Putún groups for a short time prior to A.D. 750. Influence from the Campeche region is seen in a particular method of recording dates, and Yaxchilán provides a hint of the unrest and change soon to come (Proskouriakoff, 1960, 1961; Thompson, 1970). Prominent themes in art are group compositions of conflict and strife. In the later paintings, warriors had become a favorite subject.

Piedras Negras. Nearby Piedras Negras, a settlement with no Pre-classic background, is located in very steep terrain and rises from a high hill. It is typical of Usumacinta sites where height was achieved by leveling and terracing natural elevations. The ruins consist of tightly grouped courts, structures with wide stairways, two ball courts, and eight sweat houses (W. R. Coe, 1959). It became a thriving Classic center where stelae were superbly carved, exhibiting great detail in styles of clothing and unusual care in the execution of hieroglyphs (Plate 10e). Both wall panels and stelae distinguish Piedras Negras from other sites, and it was these groups of stelae that led Proskouriakoff (1960) to her remarkable study of the personal histories of important leaders (see Chapter 5). Artisans at Piedras Negras were slow to take up the corbelled arch, but eventually ceilings were vaulted in pure Maya style. Widespread trade is much in evidence and was clearly important, as shells from both coasts, obsidian, and jade are common in caches. However, the lack of deep middens and a Preclassic horizon at this site argues against a long occupation. As at Yaxchilán, themes in art eventually depict military scenes. Although few weapons are included in caches and burials, a warrior group may have been important here as well.

Palenque. Palenque, special in many ways, has long been a favorite of visitors (Maudslay, 1889–1902; Ruz, 1960). Nestled in the foothills of the great Chiapas mountains, which are covered with forests of mahogany, cedar, and *sapote,* Palenque excels in stucco bas-reliefs and the sheer beauty and grace of its scattered temples. From each temple one looks far out over the low coastal plain that extends to the Gulf of Mexico some eighty miles away. Unique features of Palenque include a curious palace with a square four-story masonry tower supported not by corbelled arches but by horizontal beams of wood (Photo 26). Such a tower might well have served both as an observatory and a watchtower. T-shaped windows, trefoiled niches in vaulted roofs, courtyards, galleries beneath corbelled passages, and sculptured panels combine to make the palace unique among Maya structures. The entire complex is situated on an artificial platform some 300 feet long by 240 feet wide. Its pillars were lavishly decorated and covered with stucco reliefs; walls were decorated with stucco masks and figures. Traces of the hieroglyphs and scenes that once adorned the walls may still be seen.

A vaulted aqueduct runs beneath this central complex to the great platform to the east. Here three temples perch at varying heights atop grass-covered pyramids on three sides of a court—the Temples of the Sun, the Cross, and the Foliated Cross, the latter two being very deteriorated. The Temple of the Sun, now restored, contains three doorways leading to two rooms that have far more light than the dark, massive-walled structures of Tikal. In contrast, the temple walls are thinner at Palenque, the doors wider and more numerous, and the roof combs are centered over the middle of the temple roof, instead of over the rear. The back room has a typical "sanctuary" at the rear, against which stands a superb bas-relief panel bearing a hieroglyphic text and some human figures. These interior shrines with their own roofs are characteristic of Palenque temples (see Figures 24 and 25) (Marquina, 1951).

The ball court is small at Palenque and lacks rings or markers of any kind. Today it looks only like two long parallel platforms, but it can be recognized as a ball court, the playing alley lying between the platforms.

Of the other structures, the Temple of the Inscriptions is most noteworthy, for it was the scene of one of the most spectacular funerary rites in Mesoamerica (Photo 27) (Ruz, 1952, 1960).

About the year A.D. 692, Palenque was saddened by the death of a most important dignitary. He may have been both high priest and ruler, and his final resting place had been carefully prepared years in advance. Now, upon his death, he was given the most sumptuous funeral Palenque had ever witnessed. The form of the rite is unknown to us, we but can imagine that it was accompanied by audible wailing and much music. At last, however, the deceased was carried up the steep staircase to the Temple of the Inscriptions, where the floor of the sanctuary revealed a vaulted interior stairway by way of which he was lowered to his sacred crypt. Here he was carefully laid out in a great stone sarcophagus with a jade in his mouth and one in each hand, wearing a jade ring on every finger, bracelets, a diadem of jade disks and ear plugs, his favorite necklace, and, finally, his face was covered by a mosaic mask with eyes of shell and obsidian (Plate 10g). Having left with his body the finest gifts they had to offer, his subjects carefully fitted the lid over the U-shaped box, and the removable stoppers were dropped into place for the last time. Over this lid, another gigantic lid, twelve and one-half feet long and exquisitely carved, was slowly lowered into place (Photo 28). The crypt containing these sacred remains was located five feet below the plaza floor; its walls had been entirely covered with stucco reliefs perhaps representing the nine Lords of the Night and the Nether World, the Bolon-ti-Ku. Two stucco heads and pottery vessels containing food were left on the floor (Plate 10f). The final sealing of the crypt was accomplished by fitting a triangular slab into one of the vaults, whereupon five or six youths were promptly sacrificed and left to accompany (or guard?) the privileged deceased among offerings of jade beads, ear plugs, shells with red pigment, and a pearl. A solid masonry wall in turn sealed in this macabre scene, after which all attention was turned to careful concealment of the crypt.

In preparation for these funeral rites, the Temple of the Inscriptions had been constructed above the prepared secret chamber long before, and, as the pyramid was built, so was the interior staircase with its neatly vaulted roof. The stairs turned at a landing and, keeping pace with the exterior construction, finally reached the summit. A temple then was raised, discretely in keeping with the times. Thus, the Temple of the Inscriptions resembles others at Palenque in its mansard roof and central roof comb. The five entrances are framed by stuccoed human figures representing children wearing masks of the rain deity. Great stone panels carved with hieroglyphs and the Initial Series date of A.D. 692 adorn the back room. Almost unnoticeable among the neatly cut and fitted stones that form the paving of the floor is one with a double row of stone stoppers, the only clue to the interior staircase leading to the sealed crypt some seventy-five feet below. When the Mexican archaeologist Alberto Ruz lifted this stone in 1949, the vaulted stairway was found entirely filled with rubble. Four field seasons later, on June 15, 1952, the crypt and its secrets were revealed. Now both Tikal and Palenque have proved to have pyramids that contain tombs rather than serve exclusively as temple platforms, as previously thought.

Palenque has contributed enormously to our knowledge of the Classic Maya. Artistically it portrays perhaps the very ideal of Maya figures, an "aristocratic beauty," says Tatiana Proskouriakoff (1946, 1950), that does not emphasize sexual or muscular features. The carved bas-reliefs and modeling in stucco are some of the finest the Maya ever produced. Toward the end of Cycle 9, the stela cult was reaching its

Photo 26.   Palace complex at Palenque, Chiapas, showing the square tower. Photographed by the author.

Photo 27.   Temple of the Inscriptions, Palenque, Chiapas. Courtesy of the Instituto Nacional de Antropología e Historia. Mexico.

peak in all Maya centers. At the same time, artists showed a greater freedom in composition, and Palenque artists were leaders in this new trend. In addition to contact with other Usumacinta drainage sites, Palenque extended its influence to the alluvial plains of Tabasco, where the large site of Comalcalco (Blom & La Farge, 1926–1927) shows similarities in art and architecture. Here are systems of courts and plazas and a huge artificial platform that supported a number of buildings. A report on this site is eagerly awaited. Situated in the homeland of the Putún or Chontal Maya, these people mingled with their Mexican neighbors. In effect, some of the stucco reliefs reflect both Maya and non-Maya features.

One day, however, without any warning, work stopped at all these centers. One by one, the Usumacinta Valley sites of Palenque, Piedras Negras, and Yaxchilán halted all work, joining other major centers in signaling the end of the great Classic period in the Petén and adjacent regions. Meanwhile, what was happening in the northern regions?

Jaina. Following the Gulf Coast north and east, one comes first to the extraordinary island of Jaina, thirty-two kilometers north of Campeche. This site boasts two ceremonial centers, Zayosal and El Zacpool, accompanied by a small ball court. The buildings were all constructed of an earth nucleus faced with irregular stones, which were stuccoed and painted. However, had these Maya not produced beautiful figurines, probably the most spectacular of such objects in the New World, the name Jaina would scarcely be known. The life-like figurines are truly portraits in clay recording the gestures, dress, and ornamentation of the day (Plate 8e, h, j). Animals and abstract objects are also known. The finest figures are solid and were hand modeled, while more standardized, hollow examples were produced by molds. Both techniques might even be combined in one figurine—a mold-made body and a hand-modeled head. Some examples are whistles and others rattles (Plate 8i), but we believe that all were manufactured primarily as grave offerings (Piña Chán, 1968).

Jaina was unquestionably one of the few great cemeteries of the Late Classic period, and it may have served other nearby localities as well, because ground burial is not possible in parts of Yucatán where bedrock lies close to the surface. The most common type of burial at Jaina was that in which the body of deceased was flexed, a figurine placed in the flexed arm, and wrapped in a cloak or *petate*, and the head was covered with a tripod vessel after a jade bead was placed in the mouth. The entire grave then was sprinkled with cinnabar paint. Other offerings might include any kind of adornment, musical instrument, or utensil of bone, pottery, shell, or other form of marine life. The skulls are usually found to be artificially deformed frontooccipitally, and the teeth may be mutilated and have incrustations of jade or pyrite. Children were interred in large urns and covered by a tripod vessel or fragment of a large pot.

We know that the Maya usually buried their dead under house floors or in the ground as at Jaina. Sometimes, however, they cremated the remains or buried them in caves, *chultunes*, or urns; in the case of the privileged classes, elaborate tombs were even constructed. The practice of retainer burial, in which an important person was accompanied by others, often wives or servants, the presence of red pigment or cinnabar

Photo 28. Funerary crypt, Temple of the
Inscriptions, Palenque, Chiapas. The carved
slab covers the sarcophagus. Courtesy of the
Instituto Nacional de Antropología e Historia,
Mexico.

paint and the placement of a jade bead in the mouth as currency for the next world are all widespread burial customs in Mesoamerica.

Northern Yucatán. We come now to Classic development on the peninsula of Yucatán, where we find conformity to the southern sites in the presence of the corbelled vault, Maya-styled monumental sculpture, and some similarities in hieroglyphics and calendrical inscriptions, although these were never as well developed as those in the Petén region. The late Preclassic sites of Yaxuná and Acanceh were rebuilt. Oxkintok rose to prominence as an Early Classic center, and near Mérida, Dzibilchaltún witnessed a very large population boom. Three curious local styles of architecture, Río Bec, Puuc, and Chenes, are known. The centers for these styles are known largely from their structures since burials are not plentiful and hieroglyphic inscriptions, although present in all these areas, are scarce. The old idea of a sparsely settled Yucatán that remained static if not backward until the year A.D. 900, when suddenly vast Maya migrations poured out of the Petén region to settle and create a "New Empire," has long been discarded.

George Cowgill's theory of forced depopulation of the southern Maya lowlands represents a return to this early idea, but with some modification (Cowgill, 1964). He does not see depopulation as necessarily being a cause of the collapse but rather as the result of invasion, warfare, and subsequent famine. He postulates that people were moved closer to Chichén Itzá to facilitate political and economic control. Although indications of late Classic conflict and intruders are growing, this may have been only one of several factors contributing to internal disorders within the social structure. There is good reason to believe however, that the Putún Maya settled at Chichén Itzá and from there controlled a sizable "empire" following A.D. 918. Thus, after all, "New Empire" may prove to be a valid description of northern Yucatán in the tenth century (Thompson, 1970). We do not believe that the southern lowlands were as deserted as Cowgill seems to imply but we do know that the northern lowlands enjoyed a long period of development and apparent prosperity that paralleled the Tzakol and Tepeu phases in the south. The short, unexplained, abrupt break in the six hundred year span noted in the southern lowlands was not reflected in the north (Andrews, 1965).

There is some question of just when the Río Bec–Chenes–Puuc sites flourished. Andrews (1965), whose viewpoint is based on his work at Dzibilchaltún, which favors the Spinden correlation (see Introduction), is inclined to place them in the Early Postclassic period, but Thompson (1954) and Willey (1966) consider them to be a Late Classic manifestation and it is as such that they are included here. The structures at these sites no longer follow the older traditional grouping around courts, and are scattered at random.

Río Bec, the southernmost area of the three, borders on Quintana Roo. No ceramic study has been made, nor have any dated stelae been found, so Río Bec is known largely from its architecture, which is based on stucco and fine uncut masonry, vertical facades, and elaborate decoration that is largely ostentatious, since the stairways are too steep to use and lead only to models of temples on top (Photo 29). So-called palace structures are more frequent than temple-pyramids, and ball courts are present as expected. Two-story structures are known in which the second story rests on solid fill.

Photo 29. Example of Río Bec architectural style: reconstruction of structure at Xpuhil, Campeche. From drawing by Tatiana Proskouriakoff. Courtesy of the Peabody Museum, Harvard University.

Hochob (Photo 30) is a good example of Chenes-style architecture. At this site, a long platform once supported three buildings. The doorway to the palace-type structure forms the mouth of a monster and the entire facade is elaborately decorated in deep relief. Chenes architecture presents a kind of transition from the Río Bec style to that of Puuc.

The word "Puuc" refers to a series of hills in northern Yucatán where a large number of rather well-preserved remains have been found. Veneer masonry walls are highly characteristic of this style. Quantities of presculptured stone elements were assembled and then combined as needed into masks and geometric designs. The mosaic veneer was mounted on walls of rubble and concrete, producing repetitious motifs characterized by excellent craftsmenship. There is no particular monumental style associated with the Puuc sites (Proskouriakoff, 1946). A few simple stelae with illegible inscriptions have been found. Some sculptured columns could represent a precursor for the later ones at Chichén Itzá, although there is no apparent connection between the sites. But, as we shall see, neither is there any tradition in central Mexico that could account for the sculptured columns found at Tula.

Photo 30. (*Above*) Example of Chenes style architecture: model of temple at Hochob, Yucatán. Museo Nacional de Antropología, Mexico. Courtesy of Victoria Bach.

Photo 31. (*Right*) The Nunnery, Uxmal, Yucatán. The facade is composed of cut stone to form mosaics. Courtesy of the Instituto Nacional de Antropología e Historia, Mexico.

A good example of Puuc architecture is Uxmal, a well-known center about seventy-eight kilometers south of Mérida (Andrews, 1965; Morley, 1956; Thompson, 1954). The Monjas, or Nunnery, is a huge quadrangle surrounding a great patio entered through a corbelled arch on the south side (Photo 31). The long buildings contain numerous chambers, each with its own doorway. The facades are all intricately decorated by small cut stones set in masonry. Motifs in the friezes are huts among latticed panels; Chac, the Rain God; masks; small columns; and serpent heads.

The Pyramid of the Magician, also called El Adivino, rises sharply just east of the Nunnery. It has a roughly elliptical base and was rebuilt at five different times. Although considered to be purely Maya in flavor, a bit of Teotihuacán influence can be seen in year signs and masks of Tlaloc, the rain deity of the central Mexicans.

Impressive for its tremendous size, the so-called Governor's Palace consists of a central building and two lateral structures containing a series of chambers. The facade is decorated in the same Puuc style with rain god masks, stepped frets, and lattice panels (Photo 32). The entire structure rests on a stepped terrace some four hundred feet long by ninety feet wide, which in turn is supported by a natural elevation. A small ball court and several other structures, some badly eroded, complete the ruins. The distribution of buildings at Uxmal does not conform to any particular plan. The site is impressive for its massive structures and mosaic facades in soft shades of pink and yellow stone.

Only a short distance away are Kabah (Photos 33 and 34) and Labná, both Puuc sites, the former renowned for a building completely faced with stone mosaic masks with long hooked noses. At Labná one can walk

Photo 32. Detail of Governor's Palace, Uxmal, Yucatán. Courtesy of the Instituto Nacional de Antropología e Historia, Mexico.

Photo 33. Puuc style architecture, Kabah, Yucatán. Courtesy of the Instituto Nacional de Antropología e Historia, Mexico.

Photo 34. Arch at Kabah, Yucatán. Courtesy of the Instituto Nacional de Antropología e Historia, Mexico.

through an amazing arch decorated by stone mosaics that spans a short *sacbé*, a Maya causeway, built with considerable energy and imagination. Huge blocks of stone were laid, subsequently leveled with gravel, and finally paved smooth with plaster. The *sacbé* at Labná links only the temple-pyramid and palace, but at Cobá in northern Quintana Roo such causeways connect many scattered ruins, and one extends some sixty-two miles to Yaxuná near Chichén Itzá. The main axis of Dzibilchaltún is just such a *sacbé*. These are often called roads and were probably constructed for religious processions. Although the flat peninsula of Yucatán and the well-constructed *sacbés* seem to us to be a combination well suited for wheeled vehicles, there is no indication that the wheel was ever utilized in a practical sense. The only wheel in Mesoamerica, or in the New World for that matter, as mentioned previously, is that found on miniature pottery animals in the Gulf Coast and central Mexican regions (see page 145).

The latter part of the Classic period in Yucatán was marked by a general continuation of development and refinement. Chichén Itzá, which rose to prominence in the Postclassic history of Yucatán, was an insignificant settlement in Late Classic times, but it was nonetheless influenced by Puuc architectural style. Several buildings, such as the so-called Nunnery, the Church, and the Akab Dzib, have definite affinities with their Puuc neighbors (Photo 35). These buildings are grouped apart from the later Toltec ones and are often called "Old Chichén." Dzibilchaltún (Andrews, 1960, 1965) (Photo 36) was undoubtedly the largest city; indeed, evidence indicates that it must have had a population far greater than could be maintained by outlying agricultural settlements. Trade undoubtedly flourished, and the fine salt deposits nearby provided an exchangeable commodity. Even so, how such a heavily urbanized settlement was supported has not yet been satisfactorily explained.

Stone sculpture was used widely for ornamentation of buildings, as, for example, in the stone mosaic veneer architecture of the Puuc sites. Unfortunately, work in stucco has seldom survived. The carving of stelae, altars, and lintels is not as characteristic of this northern section as it is of the southern Maya region, but Initial Series dates found at

Photo 35. (*Opposite, top*) Late Classic Puuc architecture at Chichén Itzá, Yucatán: the Church and the Nunnery. Courtesy of the Instituto Nacional de Antropología e Historia, Mexico.

Photo 36. (*Above*) The Temple of the Seven Dolls, Dzibilchaltún, Yucatán. Courtesy of the Instituto Nacional de Antropología e Historia, Mexico.

Tulum, Cobá, Chichén Itzá, Dzibilchaltún, Oxkintok, and a few other sites fall within the years A.D. 475–879. The characteristic Yucatán slateware pottery, which probably originated in Preclassic times, continues throughout until the Spanish Conquest. Of great aid chronologically is the presence of Petén trade wares, a variety of Tepeu polychromes, which permits cross dating with the central and southern areas. We think that for each Petén polychrome pot, its equivalent in salt made the return trip to the central core region (see pages 158, 168).

The Close of the Classic Period

By the year A.D. 900 the Maya ceased to record Long Count dates. Copán seems to have been suddenly abandoned after the carving of its final date, A.D. 800. Stelae were smashed and some construction was halted in the very building process, as at Uaxactún. No more palaces or temples were built. At Quiriguá and Piedras Negras, A.D. 810 is the last recorded date. Altar de Sacrificios recorded one of the last dates of all—A.D. 889. One by one throughout the ninth century, city after city ceased all construction and sculpting. Some of the last stelae carved are but sad imitations of an earlier grandeur.

Becán, a Late Classic site in Campeche, is considered to be an early fortified site in Mesoamerica because of a surrounding ditch that may have served as a moat. More convincing evidence of warfare is that reported from highland Chiapas, where Late Classic settlements were regularly located on hilltop sites or ridges bordered by easily defended ravines or cliffs (Adams, 1961). Cerro Chavín, it will be recalled, had actual defensive works. Although highland Chiapas was apparently outside the main lines of communication and trade, it is interesting that this region manifests such early preoccupation with fortifications. In line with this development, it may be significant that the first indications of conflict are found in the Usumacinta drainage sites. Scenes of raids, sacrifice, and conflict manifest themselves in wall paintings at Bonampak and in stone sculptures at Piedras Negras and Yaxchilán. On the Pasión River both Seibal and Altar de Sacrificios show evidence not of warfare but of non-Maya intruders. Aguateca, a small site south of Lake Petexbatun, is located on the edge of a chasm spanned by natural bridges. All but one of these bridges were found to be blocked by stone walls, perhaps the remains of a gallant defense.

Classic manifestations continued longest in the most remote areas— Tikal, Uaxactún, Flores, and San Lorenzo—the farthest removed from western unrest. Even at Tikal, however, there is a wall that has been interpreted as a defensive earthwork (Puleston & Callender, 1967). The last Initial Series date known, A.D. 909, was carved on a jade ornament from Quintana Roo, which was located about as far as possible from the strife and trouble radiating from central Mexico.

The decline and collapse of the Classic Petén sites around A.D. 900 must be viewed in terms of Mesoamerica as a whole. Attempts to explain this crisis purely as a local event have been disproved one by one. The theory that slash-and-burn agriculture eventually exhausted the land is refuted by recent studies showing that it was possible to maintain a dense population. In addition, sites such as Copán and Quiriguá, which were located in fertile valleys where the soil was constantly revitalized by flooding, were among the first centers to be abandoned. There are no indications of sudden climatic changes such as those that might be caused by earthquakes. Malaria was a European contribution. Why, then, just when all was going so well, did Maya civilization fall apart?

Obviously, all was not going well. Although the gaps in our knowledge are abysmal, we do know that the very basic foundations of the structure of society were dealt a severe blow. Here we find ourselves once again confronting not only the collapse of the Classic Maya but also a major upheaval in all major Mesoamerican centers. Although local ecological conditions may well have contributed in various ways in diverse settings, some common flaw existed throughout, so that as the waves of dissension rolled from region to region, the centers collapsed. The greater the center, the more susceptible it was and the faster it succumbed.

A brief overview of Mesoamerica about A.D. 900 reveals some significant similarities and differences. At this time, the site of Teotihauacán lay in ashes and for all practical purposes had been abandoned for some 250 years. Stratigraphy and carbon-14 dating support this chronology in central Mexico, although a problem of correlation with the Maya area as well as with the Oaxaca region remains. The Goodman–Martínez–Thompson correlation is the one generally followed here, but it is not without difficulties. (See the Introduction for a discussion of the two correlation systems.) The Spinden, or 12.9, correlation favored by Andrews, would allow more time for his Florescent, usually called Postclassic, period in Yucatán. It would also have the advantage of agreeing more closely with the early carbon-14 dates from Oaxaca. On the other hand, the Tikal sequence supports the 11.16, or Goodman–Martínez–Thompson, correlation. Absolute dating aside, the firmest archaeological cross ties are those of Teotihuacán's Xolalpan phase with Tzakol 2–3 in the Petén. If the Spinden correlation were applied, moving Tzakol 2–3 back some two hundred years, the Teotihuacán phases would have to be adjusted accordingly, which would place the crisis at Teotihuacán far too early. The correlation problem thus remains unsolved, and any eventual solution will have to accommodate certain cultural relationships such as those between Teotihuacán's Xolalpan and the Maya Tzakol.

Why was Teotihuacán so abruptly destroyed? If this was a secular revolt of some kind, where are the results of its success? The decadent remains of Portesuelo and Azcapotzalco are poor manifestations of success or victory. Rather, it would seem to have been a revolt without winners, only survivors, who moved away from the tragic scene of their giant error.

Xochicalco, settled in Late Classic times possibly by Mixtec speakers, was a fortified site, an early sign of the coming new militarism. As a harbinger of the secular future, it survived and prospered. Cholula, badly neglected by archaeologists until recently, fared very well in the wake of the Classic crisis. Cholula was never destroyed and may have become the beneficiary of Teotihuacán's disasters. It emerges as a cultural giant of Postclassic periods beginning with the rise to prominence of the Mixteca Puebla people.

West Mexico, engrossed with its own local activities, had no large urban centers and suffered no major upheaval. Logically it was least affected because it lay outside Mesoamerica. As power was fractured in central Mexico, one begins to see a sharp increase in communication and interaction with the peoples of west Mexico. The introduction of metallurgy around A.D. 900 could have served as one stimulus.

The Gulf Coast cultures also survived the end of the Classic period. El Tajín was not destroyed, and, as far as we can tell, continued with little change until its final abandonment around A.D. 1200.

On the other hand, Monte Albán in Oaxaca was apparently severely affected; this great Zapotec center was unable to survive the waves of catastrophe that engulfed major centers of Mexico and the Maya region. The site was probably abandoned and reoccupied later by the Mixtecs.

The collapse of the Classic Petén Maya is dramatic for the abandonment of many major sites and the cessation of construction and recording of Long Count dates. However, the area was not deserted. Barton Ramie and San José in Belize seem to have retained a substantial population after the close of the Classic period, as did Tikal, which supported a rural population devoid of its former grandeur. This would argue against a forced depopulation of the southern Maya lowlands as proposed by Cowgill (1964), but many of his ideas regarding the role of Chichén Itzá in Postclassic Yucatán may prove to be prophetic. As one rereads his article, the newly identified Putún Itzá fit his description of aggressive intruders who controlled a vast region of the lowlands from their strong base established at Chichén Itzá.

In Yucatán, Cobá was not destroyed and Dzibilchaltún moved along without interruption. Changes in art and architecture are not noticeable, and Teotihuacán influence, although perhaps remotely inspired, is nonetheless apparent. The cultural sequence here in no sense suggests collapse, abandonment, or disintegration. Maya civilization did not end, but underwent the most radical upheavel ever experienced prior to the Conquest. By A.D. 600 the highland Maya had already retreated into a simple village life, and by A.D. 900 they were forsaking their valley dwellings and moving up to the hilltops in search of strategic sites to fortify against new-found enemies.

It will be some years yet before we have clearer indications of exactly what happened to the lowland Maya at this time. Current studies in progress from Tikal, the Pasión River sites, Comalcalco, and Dzibilchaltún will all provide new perspectives and are awaited with understandable anticipation. But if some centers continued with their daily affairs and in some areas these were uninterrupted, what is meant by the decline or collapse of the Classic period? It refers to events in the major centers: Teotihuacán, Monte Albán, and the lowland Maya Petén sites. Other areas with less centralized authority, less political and economic influence, survived relatively unscathed and merely reflected the current changes in new styles and tastes in material goods.

As to what could have caused this upheaval or cultural crisis, the best explanation seems to lie in some social conflict inherent in the structure of society as it was conceived. If we try to imagine or speculate on the ostentation of the cities and the advantages and privileges granted to an elite class of leaders, we can understand that sooner or later their wisdom, power, and authority might be challenged. Prosperity eventually spilled over to the populace, and, as trade led to increased contacts with other peoples and greater circulation of new opinions and ideas, craftsmen gained confidence in their ability and potential. In a stimulating atmosphere that vibrated with hope and eagerly sought new channels for expression, is it any wonder that secular thoughts arose to challenge the power of the priests? The old system may not have been as singularly theocratic as is often depicted, yet the strength of religious authority is hard to deny as one contemplates center after center of temple-pyramid complexes. The decadence manifested around the shores of Lake Texcoco and in the simple villages of the Petén forest reflects once again the crushed hopes of a popular movement. Instead of new-found glory, prosperity, and freedom from oppression, the populace found itself freed from any centralized authority, without which the centers could not exist. With no demand for luxury articles, crafts declined and ceased, and trade routes broke down, along with faith in the religious doctrine and the spirit of the people.

As insufficient as this may seem as an explanation for the tremendous upheaval that wrenched the powerful centers, so painstakingly and patiently created by so many for so long, it is nevertheless the one that seems to me to be most consistent with the information at hand. A forced evacuation of parts of the southern lowlands still remains a possibility (Cowgill, 1964). Although much remains to be explained about decline of the Classic Maya, the emergence of Chichén Itzá as a new power in the Postclassic is becoming clearer. But before we turn to Yucatán, it is necessary to understand the events that took place in central Mexico.

As we approach the beginnings of legendary history, where names of people are known for the first time, it is indeed curious that this brief period should be so confusing and so poorly known archaeologically. In these three hundred years Mesoamerica had to readjust to many changes that resulted from the crises suffered by the major centers at the close of the Classic period. Tula rose to assume the role of leadership formerly held by Teotihuacán, a geographical shift of less than one hundred miles in central highland Mexico, but one that placed the new capital closer to the northern limits of agriculture. In the Maya region, the key area from now on is Yucatán. However, despite many years of archaeological work and the advantage of the first legendary-historical records, there are great gaps, conflicting views, and many unsolved problems relating to the events of this unsettled period.

By A.D. 900 the highland Maya were moving out of the valleys to occupy defensive positions on the hilltops. The old Petén region was never totally abandoned. Ceramic remains there show occupation by people who manufactured a very inferior pottery, largely monochrome and unslipped. The former elegant polychrome painted wares have disappeared. Among students of Maya ceramics this period is known as the New Town horizon; it is well represented at Barton Ramie in British Honduras but only meagerly at Tikal. This new material, bearing no resemblance to earlier traditions, could be explained by a reoccupation of the area by strangers (Willey *et al.*, 1967).

As already mentioned, the peninsula of Yucatán was less drastically affected by the events around A.D. 900. Dzibilchaltún provides a continuous record since it was never abandoned (Andrews, 1960). Buildings were erected with stone mosaic facades and art became largely geometric. The interest displayed in public buildings emphasizes a secular rather than religious trend. Glyphs look more Mexican than Maya and cannot be translated. Teotihuacán influence can still be identified in the early years, but it faded out shortly thereafter. The great Puuc sites like Uxmal were soon abandoned. This vaguely known period in Yucatán is now more readily understandable if we examine the history of the Putún Maya as outlined by Thompson (1970). The hundred years following A.D. 850 saw Putún domination of northern Tabasco, southern Campeche, and the east coast of Yucatán including Cozumel, Bakhalal, and Chetumal. Accordingly, it was precisely during these early Postclassic years that a Yucatecan branch of the Putún called the Itzá established themselves at Chichén Itzá in A.D. 918. These Putún of Tabasco and Campeche were noted for being aggressive militarists, seamen, and merchants. The traditional account of Chilam Balam of Chumayel (Roys, 1933), written after the Conquest, tells of the Itzá invasion from Polé on the northeast coast, the mainland port for Cozumel. This island, originally reached by sea from their homeland in Tabasco, is presumed to be the

7

_____

The Toltec Period: Early Postclassic Developments

195

Chart 3.   Postclassic Chronology

	WEST MEXICO	NORTH CENTRAL Chalchihuites	CENTRAL HIGHLAND MEXICO
A.D. 1521			
AZTEC PERIOD (Late)	Tarascan Apatzingán, Michoacán Culiacán, Sinaloa	Calera phase	Aztec Phases II–IV Cholulteca Phases I–III
A.D. 1200	Santa Cruz, Nayarit		
TOLTEC PERIOD (Early)	Aztatlán complex	Río Tunel phase	Aztec I Tula– Mazapan
		Las Joyas phase	Cholula Xochicalco
A.D. 900			

point of departure for their journey into northern Yucatán. After considerable wandering in Yucatán, they settled at Chichén Itzá in A.D. 918. These early Itzá settlers are credited with erecting the inner temple-pyramid of the Castillo, and their presence accounts for many elements of Pre-Toltec Mexican influence in Yucatán. According to this new interpretation, the result of a meticulous reexamination by Thompson of ethnohistorical sources, the Toltec invasion of Yucatán was accompanied by a second group of Putún Itzá. To better understand the so-called Toltec period in Yucatán, we must logically begin with the events that took place in central Mexico after the destruction of Teotihuacán (see Map 4 and Chart 3).

One of the outstanding centers during these uncertain years was Cholula, which probably served as a haven for survivors of Teotihuacán. The foundations of Cholula had been laid hundreds of years earlier when a Preclassic population constructed a small pyramid only 55 feet in height and decorated it with creatures resembling mythical insects painted in red, black and yellow. This pyramid was enlarged four times until it finally covered 40 acres and reached a height of 181 feet, the largest single structure ever erected in the New World. Today it is easily

| GULF COAST | | | OAXACA | MAYA | |
| HUASTECA | | VERACRUZ | | HIGHLAND | LOWLAND |
Inland	Coast				
San Antonio los Angeles	Pánuco	Soncautla Teayo Cempoala	Monte Albán V (Mixtec)	Chinautla Mixco Viejo Tohil	Independent states Mayapán
San Lorenzo	Las Flores	Upper Cerro de las Mesas	Monte Albán IV	Ayampuc	Toltec–Maya

mistaken for a hill, as the pyramid is covered with grass and soil and crowned by a Catholic church, an effort by the Spaniards to substitute their religion for the old (Photo 37). Much of the construction at Cholula dates from Classic days, and includes two large stelae-altars bordered by Tajín-like stone carving and Teotihuacán-type architecture, indicating close connections with both the Gulf Coast cultures and Teotihuacán. At this time the *altiplano* (high plateau) of Puebla–Tlaxcala was under the domination of Teotihuacán, but in early Postclassic years a group called the Olmeca-Xicalanca, the "Historic Olmecs," controlled this important region from their base at Cholula. Jiménez Moreno (1942, 1955) believes that these people subjugated the Puebla–Tlaxcala region as well as the eastern portions of the basin of Mexico. The fortifications at Xochicalco may have been thrown up as a defensive measure against the increasing strength of these Olmecs.

At Cholula itself there is no evidence of defensive works or the rising militarism. It must be kept in mind, however, that we are just now beginning to learn about this highly important site. If we see no evidence of defensive mechanisms, we also know little about geographical extension, ball courts, marketplaces, or settlement patterns. A modern map

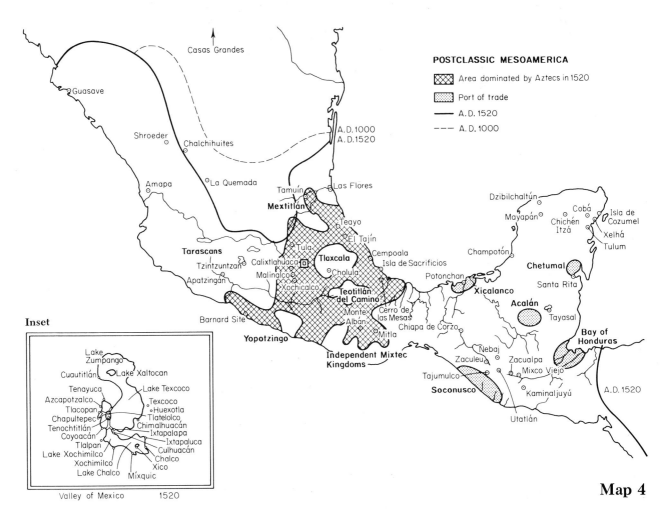

POSTCLASSIC MESOAMERICA

▨ Area dominated by Aztecs in 1520
▦ Port of trade
—— A.D. 1520
--- A.D. 1000

Casas Grandes

Guasave

Shroeder

Chalchihuites

A.D.1000
A.D.1520

Amapa

La Quemada

Tamuín · Las Flores

Mextitlán

Teayo

Dzibilchaltún

Mayapán · Cobá · Isla de Cozumel
Chichén Itzá
Xelhá
Tulum

Tarascans

Tzintzuntzan

Apatzingán

Tula

Calixtlahuaca
Malinalco
Xochicalco

El Tajín

Tlaxcala
Cholula

Cempoala
Isla de Sacrificios

Champotón

Chetumal

Santa Rita

**Teotitlán
del Camino**

Potonchan

Xicalanco

Acalán

Tayasal

Barnard Site

Monte
Albán

Cerro de
las Mesas

Chiapa de Corzo

Yopotzingo

Mitla

**Bay of
Honduras**

**Independent Mixtec
Kingdoms**

Nebaj

Zaculeu

Zacualpa
Mixco Viejo

Tajumulco

Soconusco

Kaminaljuyú

A.D. 1520

Utatlán

Inset

Lake
Zumpango

Cuautitlán · ◯ Lake Xaltocan

Tenayuca

Azcapotzalco
Tlacopan
Chapultepec
Tenochtitlán
Coyoacán
Tlalpan
Lake Xochimilco
Xochimilco
Lake Chalco

Lake Texcoco

Texcoco
Huexotla
Tlatelolco
Chimalhuacán
Ixtapalapa
Ixtapaluca
Culhuacán
Chalco
Xico
Míxquic

Valley of Mexico   1520

Map 4

of Mexico shows highways radiating from the Valley of Puebla in east, south, and west directions. The valley has always been strategically situated to attract travelers, merchants, and warriors from the earliest pre-Conquest days to the present. The history of Cholula is linked to that of the neighboring basin of Mexico, and the control of both regions seems to have been necessary to maintain major stability in the central highlands. Only in Classic times was complete unity achieved under Teotihuacán. The Toltecs were initially thrown back by Cholula's Olmeca-Xicalanca, and the later Mexica were only partially successful in their military endeavors there. The control of the Puebla–Tlaxcala region and the role of Cholula as a giant mercantile and religious center were key factors throughout Mesoamerican history.

Current excavations are revealing a veritable maze of superimposed platforms, walls, patios, and open and covered stone drains, an indication that our present knowledge of Cholula is still fragmentary. Its chronology is based largely on ceramic correlations with other areas (Noguera, 1954, 1965). The early Postclassic phases known as Cholulteca I and II are characterized by *molcajetes,* negative painting, handled censors, griddles with high walls, and a special ware known as Coyotlatelco. This ware features a red-on-buff decoration and is a forerunner of Mazapan ware, which is decorated with parallel wavy red lines on buff (Plate 11e) and is also found at this site. Plumbate and Culhuacán wares, the latter from the neighboring basin of Mexico, are also found at Cholula. Fine Orange vessels from the Isla de Sacrificios are proof of continuing ties with Veracruz. These ceramics are the new wares and styles that we will also see at Tula.

An elaborate polychrome style of ceramics known as Mixteca-Puebla (Nicolson, 1961) is believed to have centered in the area of Cholula in early Postclassic years. In fact, one can properly speak of a Mixteca-Puebla culture in this horizon in terms of the style that emerged in these years. This style gradually dominated central Mexico, and it can best be understood as a synthesis of the styles of Teotihuacán, Veracruz, and Xochicalco. Excellent examples are found in *códices* such as the Borgia and in the polychromed ceramics and three-dimensional sculpture. The influence of this distinctive pottery reached the far western cultures of Mexico and forms part of the Aztatlán complex in Sinaloa. So strongly represented are these central Mexican traits that Ekholm (1942) believes that an actual migration west must have taken place around A.D. 900.

From Cholula one can pass south of the great volcanoes of Popo-catépetl and Ixtaccíhuatl and proceed west into the state of Morelos where, only twenty-five miles from the modern town of Cuernavaca, one comes upon a major fortified site of Postclassic times, Xochicalco, "place of the house of flowers." Xochicalco was probably constructed at the end of the Classic period, perhaps by Mixtec-speaking people. Certainly many features at the site suggest southern as well as Toltec ties. The buildings were constructed on a steep, terraced hill where they could be defended by a series of moats and walls (Sanders, 1956; Sáenz, 1962).

The most important structure is a pyramid supporting remains of long walls on top. The profile is still basically the *talud* and *tablero*, but in proportions different from those at Teotihuacán. Here the *talud* is tall and the *tablero* short. The latter contains no niches or recessed panels but is surmounted by an upper molding (Marquina, 1951). The *talud* is faced with slabs of andesite carved in reliefs depicting feathered serpents. Their undulating bodies enclose human figures wearing elaborate headdresses seated in typical Maya postures (Photos 38 and 39). Some glyphs have been identified as day and year signs. The upper gallery has a carved frieze of warriors armed with darts and shields.

A small building complex called Structure A is located about ninety feet south of the main pyramid that houses the Temple of the Stelae, named for three finely carved shafts of stone found in the debris of the sanctuary (Photo 40). These magnificent monuments had been intentionally defaced and broken and were only completely assembled after archaeologists broke through the stucco floor to uncover the remaining fragments, which were found with Teotihuacán figurines, eccentric obsidians, and shell, jade, and turquoise beads, as well as late Classic pottery of Teotihuacán, Toltec, Mixtec, and Fine Orange types (Sáenz, 1961). Nearby is Structure B, known as the Palace, a great building complex with a series of rooms, passageways, interior courts, staircases, and the *temescal,* or sweat bath. These quarters most likely were used as residences by the ranking authorities. A street twenty by fifty meters leads down the hill from these constructions to the ball court, which originally had rings and was built much in the style of Tula (Photo 41). The people who lived at Xochicalco also made use of numerous

Photo 37. (*Above*) Excavations on the south side of the large pyramid at Cholula on which the church is built. Photographed by the author.

Photo 38. (*Opposite, top*) Main pyramid at Xochicalco, Morelos. Feathered serpents carved in low relief adorn the *talud*. Courtesy of the Instituto Nacional de Antropología e Historia, Mexico.

Photo 39. (*Opposite, bottom*) Detail of sculptured relief of main pyramid at Xochicalco, Morelos. The seated figure shows Maya influence. Courtesy of the Instituto Nacional de Antropología e Historia, Mexico.

natural caves and passages in the hill itself. Some of these were enlarged, the floors stuccoed, pillars raised, and ventilation shafts installed. Their excavation has not yet been completed.

Since modern settlements have not encroached on Xochicalco, its ancient setting and defensive situation can be readily appreciated. It is outstanding as one of the earliest fortified sites. The hieroglyphs on the stelae as well as those on other carved slabs (Caso, 1967), the reliefs on the main pyramid, and pottery and stone yokes indicate that in Late Classic and Early Toltec times various influences converged on this region, including Náhua, Zapotec, Teotihuacán, Toltec, Mixtec, and Maya. Its prominence, however, was short-lived.

Tula

The most important site is that of Tula, the legendary Tollan, which has been identified with the modern town of Tula in the state of Hidalgo (Jiménez Moreno, 1941). Its geographical location is vitally important in that it was situated very close to the northern boundary of Mesoamerica, which from A.D. 1000–1300 was pushed to its northernmost limits.

Legends of the Toltecs tell us that they were a most extraordinary people, taller than any people known today, and that they excelled in sports and in all arts and sciences. Their proud descendants attribute to them all major achievements. It is said that they could grow cotton in colors and raise gigantic ears of corn. Above all, hunger and misery were unknown, everything was plentiful, and all were rich and happy. Is it any wonder that at the time of the Spanish Conquest groups all over Mesoamerica claimed descent from the ancient Toltecs? By then the Toltecs were mythical heroes, and to identify oneself with them was to claim a superior birthright (Armillas, 1950; Dutton, 1955).

The history of the Toltecs as reconstructed by the archaeological record is in sharp disagreement with the foregoing (Acosta, 1956–1957). It portrays them as constantly engaged in strife and conflict, a people who were rather poor builders and who owed past generations far more than they liked to admit. Although the basic pattern of Mesoamerican culture continued, new features are indicative of changing times and thought. Specific innovations under the Toltecs include full-scale warfare emphasizing human sacrifice, alterations in religious architecture, and new art styles in stone carving and ceramic production. Change, however, is not necessarily synonymous with improvement, and Toltec pottery and figurines, with their characteristic stiffness and monotony, are a far cry from the imaginative elegance achieved by their Preclassic and Classic ancestors (Plate 11). Indeed, the remains at the site of Tula itself give the impression of having been put together in haste, skilled and unskilled alike having had a hand in the carving and modeling.

We say that the historical record begins with Tula, but fact and fiction are so confused and distorted that interpretation is not easy. The Toltecs do seem to have been Nahua and Chichimec peoples who, according to tradition, came down from the northwestern frontier. Some roots can be seen in the archaeology of the Classic period Ayala phase of the Chalchihuites culture, which occupied a vast area from Zape in Durango to San Miguel de Allende on the present boundary between the states of Guanajuato and Querétaro (Kelley, 1966). Eventually the

Photo 40.   Three stelae with calendrical hieroglyphs from Xochicalco, Morelos. Height:
5 feet 10 inches. Courtesy of the Instituto Nacional de Antropología e Historia, Mexico.

Photo 41.   Ball court with stone rings in lateral walls. Xochicalco, Morelos. Courtesy
of the Instituto Nacional de Antropología e Historia, Mexico.

Toltecs incorporated many other groups into their ranks. One of these additional elements was probably the Nonoalca, people from southern Veracruz who spoke a Nahua dialect. Thus, in Toltec culture we can find remote Teotihuacán influence combined with that of the northwestern Tolteca-Chichimeca peoples and probably the Nonoalca, along with people from Xochicalco and maybe even Monte Albán, El Tajín, and the Huasteca. One is confronted, however, with two alternative explanations of Toltec history based on partially conflicting sources. If one follows the accounts given in the *Anales de Cuauhtitlán* and *Relación de Genealogía*, then the events took place as follows, as interpreted by the Mexican historian Jiménez Moreno (1941, 1955).

This version begins with the figure of Ce Técpatl Mixcóatl, the leader of a great northern horde of Tolteca-Chichimecas and founder of the Toltec dynasty. Armillas (1969) believes that the first Toltec thrust from the north was probably due to aggressive warlords eager to challenge and harass their southern neighbors; in sharp contrast, the general movement of people in the same direction three hundred years later was due to drought and famine. Mixcóatl is supposed to have settled in the Valley of Mexico near the Cerro de la Estrella at Culhuacán and from there conquered Otomí peoples to the north and south. A Nahua woman bore him a son, who was born after his assassination. The son, Ce Acatl Topiltzin, born in Tepoztlán, avenged his father's death and eventually moved the capital to Tula, Hidalgo in the year A.D. 968. There he became a religious reformer, assuming the title of high priest of the plumed serpent, Quetzalcóatl. Under his leadership the arts were stimulated and metallurgists, feather workers, sculptors, and craftsmen of every type were assembled from other regions and encouraged to produce their finest work. All was not smooth sailing, however, because Quetzalcóatl's rival, Tezcatlipoca, God of the Night and the North, attempted to lead the people down the road of revolution. Adherents of the cult of Tezcatlipoca were enthusiastic supporters of the rising new order of militarism, championing human sacrifice as opposed to the traditional theocratic views of Quetzalcóatl, whose gods were satisfied with symbolic offerings of butterflies, snakes, and jades. In a final act of treachery, the followers of Tezcatlipoca succeeded in humiliating Quetzalcóatl by intoxicating him and consequently causing him to neglect his religious obligations. In total disgrace, he sadly left Tula in A.D. 987 and with a band of faithful followers crossed the Valley of Mexico, passing between the two volcanoes, and proceeded to the Gulf of Mexico where, according to one source, he set fire to himself and rose to the heavens to become the Morning Star. In a different version, he set sail eastward on a raft of serpents, prophesying that in another year Ce Acatl, the anniversary year of his birth, he would return to conquer his people. If one were to sail east from the southern part of Veracruz, for example, where would one arrive but at Tabasco or Campeche, home of the Putún? And as we shall see, precisely in the year A.D. 987 some Yucatecan sources report the arrival from the west of a personage called Kukulcán, a name meaning "feathered serpent," or Quetzalcóatl in the Maya tongue.

Meanwhile, back at Tula, a series of new rulers carried on until Huémac, the final sovereign, took over for a very long reign. But fresh barbaric attacks from the north resulted in the violent destruction of Tula, and Huémac abandoned the city, fleeing to Chapultepec in A.D.

1156 or 1168, where he finally committed suicide. At Tula a few Toltecs struggled on for another fifteen years.

A second interpretation of Toltec history is that based on another source, the _Memoria Breve de Chimalpahin._ According to Kirchhoff (1955), who has also made a thorough study of the early documents, Quetzalcóatl and Huémac were contemporaries and ruled simultaneously at Tula, Quetzalcóatl as religious leader or priest and Huémac as king or secular authority. The former was bound by strict rules of continence and was forbidden to pass his authority on to a member of his family. Conflict broke out between the two as a result of Quetzalcóatl's desire to place his natural son in his place. This friction resulted in the abandonment of Tula in A.D. 1168, first by Quetzalcóatl and later in the same year by Huémac. According to this interpretation, our Toltec history would be greatly shortened because all events would occur during the joint reign of Quetzalcóatl and Huémac instead of extending over 169 years. At the other end of the line, the Kukulcán who appears in Maya traditions could not have led the Mexican intruders of A.D. 987, but would have to be a later Kukulcán, Ah Naxcit Kukulcán, who arrived in A.D. 1184 or 1204, depending on which chronology is being followed.

Whichever account more closely approximates the truth—and both are undoubtedly a combination of myth and allegory—there does seem to have been a leader symbolizing the concept of Quetzalcóatl. The personalities may be seen as representing a struggle for control between secular and religious powers. The bloodthirsty Tezcatlipoca, Huémac's forces, were clearly the victors. From this time forward wholesale human sacrifice and militarism are dominant themes reinforced by religious beliefs. The famous Legend of the Sun, in which the gods sacrifice themselves to create a new sun so that man may not be forced to live in darkness, is probably a political myth explaining the Toltec rise to power.

All ancient Mexicans had heard of this Legend of the Sun (Caso, 1958), which relates how the world formerly had been illuminated by four previous suns, but each time all living creatures had died when the suns were destroyed in turn by jaguars, fire, wind, and water. In order to create the fifth sun, which lights our present world, Quetzalcóatl himself gave his own life and blood. The Mexica believed that this sun too would one day be destroyed by another evil force—earthquake. Although man's fate was sealed, the day of doom could be delayed by providing the gods with sacred nourishment: human blood and hearts.

By the sixteenth century some sources identify Quetzalcóatl as a god while others refer to him as a priest-king. Among the Aztecs, Quetzalcóatl was known as a dignitary or the holder of a titled position in the priesthood. In one aspect he is Ehécatl, the wind god, at other times he is associated with Tlaloc, the God of Rain (Caso, 1958).

The concept of Quetzalcóatl as a plumed serpent dates back at least to Teotihuacán, where he is represented in stone carvings in the Ciudadela and also in pottery. His image is found in the mural paintings of Zacuala as well as in the _códices_ of the Maya, Mixtecs, and central Mexicans. Representations of feathered serpents are found sculptured and painted in many Maya sites of the Classic and Postclassic periods. It is not clear whether feathered serpents of all periods were related to this later concept of Quetzalcóatl, but their association with rain or water dates back to the Preclassic horizon.

Photo 42. (*Top*) Aerial view of central Tula, Hidalgo. The ball court is at upper left, Pyramid B center, and Building C lower right. (The photo was taken before the Atlantean figures were returned to their original location as in Photo 43.) Courtesy of Compañia Mexicana Aerofoto, S. A.

Photo 43. (*Bottom*) Pyramid B, dedicated to Quetzalcóatl. Tula, Hidalgo. Photographed by the author.

Photo 44. (*Opposite, top*) Colossal Atlantean figures that supported the temple roof, Pyramid B, Tula, Hidalgo. The figures represent warriors with an *atlatl* and a bag of incense. Height: 15 feet. Photographed by the author.

In late years the legend of Quetzalcóatl was kept alive by such believers as Ayocuan of Tecamachalco, Tecayehuatzin of Huexotzinco, and Nezahuacóyotl of Texcoco. These men fought against the rising tide of enthusiasm for the new order of warrior mysticism under the Aztecs and strove to perpetuate faith in the old doctrine. Despite all efforts by Tlacaétel, the famous Aztec lawyer, to stamp out every trace of the Quetzalcóatl beliefs, they persisted in the hearts and minds of many until finally recorded for history by the Spanish.

How much of Toltec legendary history is supported by archaeology? What can be seen today at Tula? The ruins, destroyed in A.D. 1156 and ravaged by every succeeding group, are a poor testimony to the greatness once achieved by the people of Quetzalcóatl. Only sixty kilometers north of Mexico City and easily reached today by either automobile or train, the ruins overlook the modern town of Tula and are perched on a high promontory that may have been chosen for defensive advantages (Photo 42). There is a large central plaza faced on two sides by pyramids; to the east is Building C, a pyramid almost completely destroyed when the original stone facings were removed, probably by the Aztecs. The smaller but more impressive structure is Building B, the pyramid to the north of the plaza (Photo 43). It was built to support a temple to Quetzalcóatl in his aspect as Venus or the Morning Star, hence its official designation as the Pyramid of Tlahuizcalpantecuhtli. In the willful destruction of Tula, the temple was defaced and the great warrior Atlantean figures that supported the roof with their flat-topped heads were disjointed and hurled into a deep trench cut into the heart of the pyramid, along with dismembered feathered-serpent columns and carved pillars.

Now, after many seasons of excavation and reconstruction, these great stone Atlantean figures have been reassembled and returned to

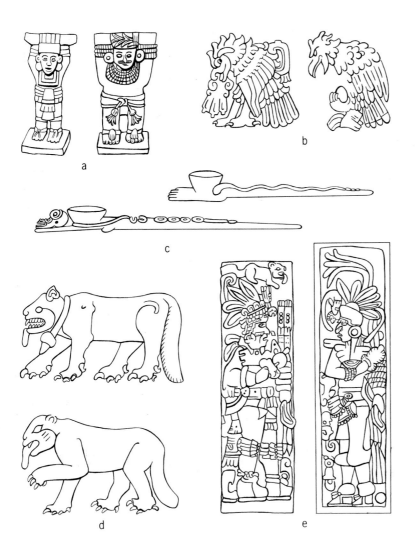

Figure 26. (*Left*) Comparative features: Tula and Chichén Itzá.
(a) Atlantean figures (Bacabs?) (left, Tula; right, Chichén Itzá); (b) eagles with human heart from sculptured panels (left, Tula; right, Chichén Itzá); (c) pottery pipes (upper, Tula; lower, Chichén Itzá); (d) jaguars in relief (top, Tula; bottom Chichén Itzá); (e) figures from sculptured columns (left, Tula; right, Chichén Itzá). (From the following sources: a(left, right), d(bottom), Tozzer, 1957, Courtesy of the Peabody Museum, Harvard University; b(left), Marquina, 1951; b(right), c(bottom), Morris, Charlot, & Morris, 1931; c(top), Acosta, 1945; d(top), e(left, right), Acosta, 1941.)

Figure 27. (*Opposite*) A comparison of benches carved in relief from Tula and Chichén Itzá. Each shows a procession of richly attired figures. Rattlesnakes adorn the cornice above. (Top, from Marquina, 1951; bottom, from Acosta, 1945.)

their original places on top of the pyramid (Photo 44). Each one is made in four sections, which are doweled together. A complete figure measures over twelve feet high and represents a warrior richly attired, wearing rectangular ear pieces, a butterfly breastplate, a belt that clasps in the rear with a great disk, necklace, bracelets, anklets, and sandals decorated with plumed serpents. The smooth elliptical mouth and eye sockets were probably inlaid with shell or obsidian. One hand holds an *atlatl*, the other a curved sword and a bag of incense. Even today one sees traces of the red and white pigment with which they were painted. Similar warriors adorn pillars of the same height that supported the roof beams in the rear chamber of the temple, where small Atlantean figures with raised arms held up an altar or shrine (Figure 26a). The lintel of the temple doorway rested on serpent columns, which, although incomplete, are believed to have been positioned with their heads on the ground while their tails supported the lintel itself. The five tiers of the pyramid originally were completely faced with sculptured panels of walking jaguars (Figure 26d, top), coyotes, eagles devouring human hearts (Figure 26b, left), and fantastic heads composed of human, bird, and serpent elements. Of these, only the panels on the east and north sides have survived. An enormous colonnaded court or gallery spanned the front and west side of the pyramid. Around the walls of both colon-

Chichén Itzá

Tula

naded halls are low benches carved with processions of richly attired figures, wearing great plumed headdresses, jewelry, and short skirts, that carry darts and shields. The red, blue, yellow, white, and black colors in which they were originally painted are still remarkably well preserved. Rattlesnakes adorn the cornice above the processional figures in the frieze (Figure 27).

The so-called Burnt Palace west of Building B has two large colonnaded halls with similarly decorated benches around the walls as well as altars, fire pits, and sunken central patios. Adjoining Building B on the east, a number of structures believed to have been residences, perhaps for Quetzalcóatl himself, were erected against the pyramid. Much of this construction has been destroyed, but the walls were originally of adobe faced with stone and stuccoed.

A new architectural feature makes its appearance at Tula and thereafter continues as an integral part of the Mesoamerican pattern. This is the serpent wall, or *coatepantli*, which does not surround the Pyramid of Quetzalcóatl at Tula as is the custom in many of the later Aztec complexes, but simply extends along its northern side. This too was toppled during Tula's destruction but has now been carefully restored. Between two friezes of geometric design on the *coatepantli*, a gruesome scene repeated on every two slabs shows a serpent that has swallowed a dead

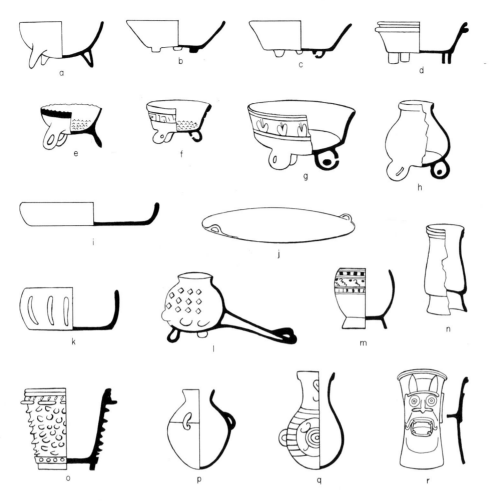

Figure 28. Ceramics of the Toltec period.
(a), (b), (c) tripods, Tula; (d) coarse brown tripod, Tula; (e), (f) *molcajetes*, Tula; (g), (h) Z Fine Orange ware, Chichén Itzá; (i) brown ware bowl, Tula; (j) *comal*, Tula; (k) gadrooned plain ware, Tula; (l) handled censer, Tula; (m) black-on-orange ring stand, Aztec I; (n) X Fine Orange, incised and painted in black, Chichén Itzá; (o) hobnail-decorated coarse ware, Tula; (p) red-on-brown jug, Tula; (q) black-on-orange jar, Aztec II; (r) Tlaloc incense burner, Tula. (From the following sources: a, k, q, Acosta, 1945; b, c, d, e, f, i, j, l, o, p, r, Acosta, 1956–1957; g, h, n, Brainerd, 1941; m, Piña Chán, 1960.)

person except for his head, which protrudes from its jaws. Dismembered arms and legs are enmeshed with the serpent's body.

One ball court is still unexcavated, but another, larger one, cleared and restored, is a variation of others already mentioned. It lies across the northern plaza from Building B and possesses a drainage system so remarkable that, freed of debris, it continues to function today. Panels and friezes once faced the ball court, but these were carried off by the later Mexica. Originally, stone rings through which the ball had to pass protruded from the walls, but today only the empty holes for their insertion are visible. No one knows the purpose of the niches placed diagonally at the ends of the court, but similar ones are found in the courts at Monte Albán and Atzompa in Oaxaca.

There is still much to excavate at Tula, and many questions remain unanswered. The central cluster of buildings occupies only a bit more than one square kilometer, but many unexcavated mounds and plazas are scattered about the surrounding hills. We have no estimates of the population of Tula at its apogee, but it certainly never reached the proportions of Teotihuacán. In 1880 a French visitor, Désiré Charnay, reported some habitation remains a few miles distant that had rooms connected by passageways, stuccoed floors, and walls. Our knowledge of settlement patterns and house sites has not progressed since that time.

Plate 11.   Toltec period pottery

a. Mold-made polychrome Mazapan figurine. Height: 4 inches. Courtesy of the Museo Nacional de Antropología, Mexico.

b. Clay spindle whorls (*malacates*), incised decoration, Central Mexico. Diameter largest: 2½ inches. Courtesy of the Museum of the American Indian, Heye Foundation (22/8559).

c. Vessel with ring-stand and handle representing Tlaloc, painted blue. Height: 5⅛ inches. Courtesy of the Museo Nacional de Antropología, Mexico.

d. Negative-painted *olla*, Tlacotepec, State of Mexico: Early Postclassic period. Height: 5½ inches. Courtesy of the Museum of the American Indian, Heye Foundation (8/8773).

e. Mazapan red-on-buff bowl. Height: 5 inches. Courtesy of the Museo Nacional de Antropología, Mexico.

f. Large orange ware tripod with stamped decoration. Height: 11 inches. Courtesy of the Museo Nacional de Antropología, Mexico.

g. Plumbate effigy vessel, Department of Suchitepéquez, Guatemala. Height: 5 inches. Courtesy of the Museum of the American Indian, Heye Foundation (16/3463).

Also left to speculation is the meaning or purpose of the curious sculpted stone figures known as *chacmools* (Plate 12c) that are found in some of the colonnaded halls. These life-sized figures, always resting in a reclining posture with legs flexed, hold either a receptacle or flat slab on their abdomens as they gaze vacantly off to one side. Whatever role they played in ceremonial life seems to have been fundamental to the Toltecs. We find *chacmools* among their contemporaries and descendants until Conquest times. These figures are prominent among the Postclassic Tarascans, Aztecs, and Maya.

chacmools — Toltecs

a

Few doubt that Tula was the capital of the legendary Quetzalcóatl. His name and attributes are amply recorded for us in a variety of forms including feathered-serpent columns and Tlahuizcalpantecuhtli carved in relief panels. In addition, the central motif of the *coatepantli* represents the planet Venus or Quetzalcóatl as the Morning Star. All the processional figures in the benches advance toward a central figure — Quetzalcóatl himself. The symbol of the planet Venus is carved in one remaining slab belonging to Building C. The immortality of Quetzalcóatl was guaranteed by a carving on a rock above Tula, which bears the date 1 Reed 8 Flint, or A.D. 980. This was indeed his city. What then of his victorious rival, the scurrilous Tezcatlipoca? Of him, not a trace remains!

Artisans at Tula may have been plentiful, but the quality of the workmanship is not extraordinary, despite Toltec claims of superiority (Plate 11). Coyotlatelco ware, popular among valley peoples after the destruction of Teotihuacán, continued to be used under the Toltecs. Ceramicists initiated new styles of their own, among them Mazapan (Plate 11e), derived from the earlier Coyotlatelco red-on-buff pottery. Other diagnostic wares are Fine Orange and Plumbate (Shepard, 1948), both widely traded in Mesoamerica (Figure 28g, h, n; Plate 11g). Metallurgy finally made its entrance into Mesoamerica around A.D. 900, very possibly in a two-pronged intrusion from Guatemala and through western Mexico or coastal Guerrero, where excellent craftsmen worked with tin, gold, copper, and silver ores, exhibiting great sophistication in their control of alloying and cold-working of metals (Pendergast, 1962a,b; Brush, 1969). These regions were all well situated to receive stimulation from

Plate 12.   Toltec stone carving

a. A Toltec warrior. Courtesy of the Museo Nacional de Antropología, Mexico.

b. Jaguar carved in stone relief. Height: approximately 4 feet. Courtesy of the Museo Nacional de Antropología, Mexico.

c. *Chacmool* figure, life-size, usually thought to be associated with the rain god, Tula, Hidalgo. Courtesy of the Museo Nacional de Antropología, Mexico.

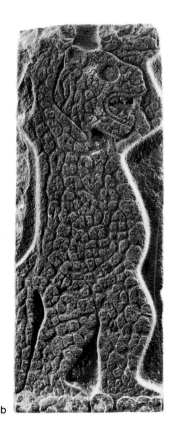

b

c

Central or South America via the Pacific Ocean. Few articles of metal have been found at Tula itself, but gold and copper ornaments began to appear at other early Postclassic sites.

Clay smoking pipes were an innovation at this time (Figure 26c) (Thompson, 1970). The typical Tula pipe is of orange ware with a small conical bowl, short flaring platform, and long stem decorated by an undulating serpent. Tobacco was used for medicinal purposes, taken as snuff, and smoked by both North and South American Indians at the time of the Conquest, but clay smoking pipes dating prior to the Postclassic period are rarely found in Mesoamerica. Several pipes in private collections are attributed to Tlatilco, and others to the Olmec culture. Peter Furst (personal communication) reports that stone pipes decorated with animal and human effigies from northern Jalisco are dated at about A.D. 100–200. In addition to this possible early evidence, representations of smoking cigars or tubular pipes are known from the Classic Maya, but it is not until the Postclassic period that pipe smoking attained an appreciable popularity. Even then the habit was not universal in Mesoamerica, as the distribution of clay smoking pipes follows an arc from the Pacific, through the basin of Mexico, to the Gulf coasts (Porter, 1948). Since pipe smoking was a well-established practice among the Indians of the southeastern United States prior to A.D. 900, it may be that this practice diffused southward from this region to Mesoamerica (Porter, 1948; Thompson, 1970). Switzer (1969) has recently dated California stone pipes at around 4000 B.C., which, if correct, makes the west another possible source.

Other innovations are the *malacate* or spindle whorl, a perforated round disk of clay used as a weight in spinning thread, and the *molcajete* (Figure 28e, f), a tripod pottery bowl with a heavily scored interior floor for grinding fruit and chile. Preclassic "grater bowls" presumably made for this same purpose are sometimes called *molcajetes* also but are easily distinguishable (compare Fig. 5e with Fig. 28e and f).

The most significant change, and one that deeply affected all subsequent Mesoamerican peoples, was the rising concern with militarism, which was reflected in art, settlement patterns, architecture, and consumer goods. Tula, although close to Teotihuacán, is located outside the basin of Mexico in an arid region necessitating irrigation and, by implication, a firm administrative authority, as was implied at Teotihuacán. There is a strong secular flavor to Toltec culture. Toltec expansion was a military operation coupled with intensive agriculture and the beginning of confiscation of food surpluses, which was later formalized as tribute payments. We believe that the capital of Tula swept many different peoples of diverse languages into the Toltec fold and that Mesoamerica's frontier was pushed northward as people learned the benefits of agriculture along with those of warfare, garrisoned troops, and "civilization." The three hundred years between A.D. 1000 and 1300 saw the maximum northward extension of Mesoamerica's boundaries, probably owing to optimum conditions for farming (Armillas, 1969). This was the time of Huastec colonization or at least strong influence in San Luis Potosí, as seen at the site of Buenavista Huaxcama. To the west, the farming belt extended along the eastern flanks of the Sierra Madre Occidental to the southern boundary of Chihuahua.

The eventual violent destruction of Tula was probably due largely to a dramatic climatic change that resulted in the dessication of northern central Mexico. Unable to continue farming and faced by drought and starvation, Chichimeca groups were forced to leave their lands. Their mass exodus in turn exerted pressure on more established settlements, of which the most vulnerable was, of course, Tula. The accounts we read of ideological struggles, civil disorders, and political disaster are probably due in large part to the very real ecological problems that faced the farmers. As a result, splinter groups of Toltecs tried to create smaller centers of power, resulting in inevitable conflicts, competitions, and reshufflings of population. In the Valley of Mexico, groups claiming Toltec ancestry settled at Azcapotzalco, Xicco, Culhuacán, Texcoco, and Xaltocan, but of these the most legitimate Toltecs were those of Culhuacán (Wolf, 1959). In the Valley of Puebla, Toltecs and Chichimeca together drove out the Olmeca-Xicalanca and liberated Cholula in 1292 (Jiménez Moreno, 1955).

The Huasteca

The northeastern periphery of Mesoamerica, the region of northern Veracruz and eastern San Luis Potosí known as the Huasteca, reached its real peak of cultural attainment not in the Classic period as might be expected but in Postclassic times. The close bond between the Huasteca and southern Veracruz, Tabasco, and the lowland Maya region that existed during the earlier Preclassic horizon had been abruptly severed, perhaps by the intrusion of Náhuat-speaking peoples into central Veracruz during the Classic period. It will be remembered that the Tajín and Remojadas cultures were strongly influenced by Teotihuacán. Although the Huasteca, lying immediately to the north of this area, also reflects these events (as seen in "portrait"-type figurines and negative or resist painting), the most significant Huastec development took place after A.D. 900. This could be the result, possibly indirect, of Toltec movements and shifting of peoples, new religious beliefs, and the ideas of weaponry and militarism that swept across all of northern Mesoamerica. This is Las Flores phase in the Huasteca sequence (Ekholm, 1944) (see Chart 3).

We do not know the nature of Huastec exposure to Toltec culture, but it does not seem to have been through outright conquest. Ceramic resemblances with central Veracruz could be the result of contact along a route passing from this area through Cholula to the Valley of Mexico. Pánuco pottery is similar to Fine Orange wares from the Isla de Sacrificios, Veracruz, and other details are shared with El Tajín and Cerro Montoso in Veracruz, Cholula, and early Mexica pottery. True Plumbate, however, has not been reported from the Huasteca. For the first time, objects of copper, clay smoking pipes, stamps, *malacates*, engraved shells, and wheeled figures are found. With the exception of the wheeled objects, most of the other artifacts have parallels at Tula as well as in the far western cultures of coastal Sinaloa. Lines of communication seem to have been well established across northern Mesoamerica at this time, very possibly a reflection of Toltec influence.

In addition to the relationships that link the Huasteca with major developments in highland Mexico in this early Postclassic period, local innovations gave unique distinction to this northeast periphery. The use of asphalt as paint or glue is found here as well as in the Classic Veracruz cultures such as Remojadas. Thin layers of asphalt were also used to cover floors and even to surface mounds from the Late Classic period onward. The application of asphalt, regardless of how desirable it might

Photo 45. Huastec stone stela with attributes of Quetzalcóatl, Castillo de Teayo, Veracruz. Height: approximately 12 feet. Courtesy of the Museo Nacional de Antropología, Mexico.

have been, depended entirely on natural seepages, so of necessity the technique was geographically limited. Stone carving is one medium that reflects a totally new artistic expression (Photo 45), the style of which is flat and slab-like. Figures often wear a conical-shaped headdress backed by a fan-like shield, and a cavity in the chest may have held an inlay of some kind.

Perhaps the Huasteca is most famous for its round structures, which are found here in greater numbers than in any other region of Meso-america and are the prevalent form of architecture. At the sites of Las Flores, Pavón, and Tancol, round structures predominate. Numerous others have been reported from the mountains as well as the coast and from as far west as Buenavista Huaxcama and San Luis Potosí. Round structures, wherever found in Mesoamerica, are generally associated with Quetzalcóatl in his aspect as the wind god, Ehécatl. Quetzalcóatl is also closely linked to the east as a cardinal point. The great concentration of round structures suggests that this east coast region was a likely center of origin (Ekholm, 1944). One asphalt-surfaced conical structure at the Pavón site is estimated to date from the Late Classic period; others may prove to be of even earlier origin.

Round structures are known from various sites in central and southern Mesoamerica but are never common and generally date from the Toltec or Mexica periods. Notable exceptions are the structure shaped like a fluted cone at La Venta and the conical structure at Cuicuilco. It may be that not all round structures were associated with Quetzalcóatl, and thus there need not necessarily be a connection between these Preclassic pyramids and later Huasteca developments.

Huasteca pottery and figurines followed local styles of development. Basically the clay was fired very well, and has a characteristic cream or pinkish color. In late Postclassic times a very distinctive black-on-white decoration became extremely popular (see Figure 31m, Chapter 8). Styles incorporating teapot forms, flat ribbon-like handles, and spouts were common. This new pottery has no counterpart elsewhere and does not have a long tradition in the Huasteca region itself. It appears fully developed. Sudden changes in the archaeology of this area are frequent, and the region is still very inadequately known. It remains a challenging peripheral area that retained a local flavor throughout its long history of occupation. By Conquest times, a few towns in the south had succumbed to the Mexica yoke, but on the whole the Huasteca was its own master.

The geographical position of the Huasteca makes it the best potential link between Mesoamerica and the southeastern cultures of the United States. But in sharp contrast to the northwestern frontier of Mesoamerica, which shows a blending into the southwestern United States, the northeastern seaboard seems to have had but sporadic contact with its northern neighbors. This point will be taken up again in Chapter 9, which examines Mesoamerica's relationships with cultures beyond her borders.

The West and the North

The role of western Mexico in Mesoamerica has yet to be clearly defined (Lister, 1955). Although it falls within the geographic boundaries of the sixteenth century (Kirchhoff, 1943), a question may be raised as to its inclusion prior to the Postclassic period. We know that people in this region shared the common substratum of agriculture and exploited estuaries and marine life even earlier. In other respects, however, the region remained aloof and followed an independent development more pronounced than, for example, the Huasteca. The well-known ceramic sculptures of human beings, plants, and animal forms from this area are not just amusing or documentary examples of humanistic art but have religious and supernatural connotations (Furst, 1970). The deep shaft-and-chamber tombs have no parallel in the rest of Mesoamerica prior to Mixteca examples (Bernal, 1965), and may not be connected. This is a region untouched by Olmec excursions and unresponsive to the development of hieroglyphic writing, the growth of urban centers, organized trade, and formalized religious beliefs shared by the other areas. Western Mexicans went their own way on the periphery of the more complex cultures. In the Postclassic years, however, there is evidence that this region was drawn into the main current of events. Such involvement could have been triggered by the introduction of metallurgy from the west, as well as by Toltec expansion out of Tula. What is the evidence for this supposition?

Within the Sinaloa sites, distinctions are apparent. Chametla is believed to be the oldest manifestation or phase of the Aztatlán complex; Culiacán overlaps in part and follows chronologically with a greater range of traits; and Guasave represents the most recent and richest phase of all with its iron pyrite beads, onyx and alabaster vases, paint cloisonné, and turquoise mosaics, pendants, beads (Kelley & Winters, 1960).

Paint cloisonné is a technique of decoration applied to gourds and is associated with thirty-four graves at Guasave. This process of decoration consists of applying a layer of paint to the surface and cutting away the paint of the design area, then filling in the hollow with another color. The result is a perfectly smooth surface. The same technique is used by modern Tarascans of Uruapan and the Lake Pátzcuaro region of Michoacán to decorate wood and gourds. It is possible that this modern lacquer work represents the survival of an ancient pre-Columbian craft. The technique has a wide distribution in the New World, and examples are known from Snaketown, Arizona and all through western Mexico, in-

Photo 46. Pyramid of Chalchihuites culture at La Quemada, Zacatecas. Courtesy of the Instituto Nacional de Antropología e Historia, Mexico.

cluding the northwestern cultures of Chalchihuites and even the Valley of Mexico. It is interesting that far to the south, among the Inca cultures of Peru, a similar paint cloisonné decoration was applied to wooden cups (Ekholm, 1942).

Probably related to this technique is a variation in which two layers of paint are applied and part of the top one is cut away to expose the color beneath. In this case the design feels raised to the touch. Pre-Columbian stone *metates* and *manos* and conch shells decorated in this way have been found near Queréndaro, Michoacán. The technique, still applied today to wood and gourds, is a popular craft of Olinalá, Guerrero.

Paint cloisonné is an ingredient of the Aztatlán complex, which has features of the Mixteca-Puebla culture (see page 199). This influence in the western and northern regions can best be explained by some cultural movement from central Mexico to the west coast around A.D. 900, probably an actual migration of peoples passing through the Valley of Toluca, Cojumatlán, Michoacán, and Ixtlán del Río, Nayarit, as a few of the traits are found along this path. Why certain cultural traits were selected for transplant to the exclusion of others has never been explained. Whatever the reason, the effects were short-lived in Sinaloa, where the elaborate Aztatlán symbolism was soon replaced by geometric motifs.

As sometimes happens, the coastal Sinaloa sequence has been clarified and elaborated by work in a neighboring area. Just over the mountains, along the eastern foothills of the Sierra Madre Occidental, lay a corridor-like area inhabited by sedentary farmers that extended north through the states of Zacatecas and Durango to the southern boundary of Chihuahua. This narrow region of cultivation, limited on the west by the juniper, pine, and oak forests of the foothills and by the great interior desert plateau on the east, has been found to have a great number of archaeological remains consisting of fortresses combined with ceremonial centers. The fortified settlements are usually situated on hilltops, village farming communities occupying the valleys below. These remains are known as the Chalchihuites culture (Kelley, 1956).

The oldest phase of this culture, Alta Vista, dates back to the Classic period, and both La Quemada in Zacatecas and the Shroeder site farther north in Durango may have some Early Classic beginnings (Kelley & Winters, 1960). The pyramid and many constructions at the Shroeder site are believed to belong to the Ayala phase, estimated as Late Classic. Although many settlements may have their roots in the Classic period, the greatest development was after A.D. 900 during the Postclassic period. At this time the Toltecs had their greatest impact on these northern peripheral cultures of Mesoamerica.

La Quemada, Zacatecas, is the best-known and largest site. It is situated at an altitude of 6500 feet, and the ruins cover most of a large hill. A great stone wall encircles the hilltop, while lower on the hillside are stone masonry pyramids, colonnaded courts, and rooms reminiscent of those at Tula. A large I-shaped ball court adjoins a nontruncated pyramid that terminated in an apex and never supported a temple (Photo 46). The large colonnades and much of the construction are built from small flat slabs of stone. Ninety miles northwest of La Quemada are the ruins of Alta Vista de Chalchihuites, located on a low hilltop. This was not a fortress nor are there any pyramids, but there are walls, rooms, platforms, and a kind of hall with crude columns. The ruins at the Shroeder site in

Durango are distributed over two hills and boast at least one tiered pyramid. There is a large central court surrounded by rooms and raised platforms. Well-dressed stones, some monolithic in size, were used in construction. The small ball court at this site, together with the large one at La Quemada, are the only courts known from this northern region.

Such sites are numerous throughout this agricultural belt and extend to Zape, Durango, some 135 miles northwest of the Durango Valley. The area shows a cultural unity in the pottery, which correlates both with Tula and with the Aztatlán complexes of Sinaloa. Red-on-buff tripods and plain bowls are common throughout. More distinctive is the paint-cloisonné decoration applied to tripod vessels. Engraved and plain *malacates* are found, but incised ones from this area are dated much earlier as belonging to the Ayala phase, A.D. 450–700. Copper bells, obsidian flaked blades, and a number of stone artifacts are also diagnostic of the Chalchihuites' Toltec period.

The Postclassic horizon of the Chalchihuites culture has been broken down into three phases following Ayala: the Las Joyas phase (A.D. 700–950), the Río Tunel phase (A.D. 950–1150), and the Calera phase (A.D. 1150–1350) (see Chart 3). The dates are approximate. This seemingly endless division into phases may seem tedious, but it was through just such minute examinations of chronological differences that correlations were found with coastal Sinaloa sites, thus clearing up discrepancies previously existing on the coast. In like manner these phases have permitted correlation with the Hohokam culture of Arizona, where some of the red-on-brown wares, mosaic plaques, copper bells, and varied stone complexes may be traced to either trade or inspiration from Chalchihuites. Eventually Sinaloa also influenced these northern groups.

The Chalchihuites culture is about the last truly Mesoamerican culture encountered going north. Beyond, in Chihuahua, the remains become simpler, and as one proceeds north, archaeological evidence indicates the increasing influence of the Hohokam and Mogollon cultures of Arizona. For example, the Loma San Gabriel culture, which follows the pattern of a hilltop ceremonial center with small valley farms, is poorly known but certainly lacks the stone masonry, paint cloisonné, copper objects, and *malacates* of its southern neighbors. As a much simpler manifestation, it is probably transitional to the Río Conchas–Bravo Valley cultures, which culturally belong to the southwestern United States. There is no gap, no great hiatus, between the two culture areas throughout the continuous sedentary occupation. Features of both regions mingle until eventually, upon reaching Chihuahua, the emphasis swings away from Mesoamerica (J. C. Kelley, 1956, 1960). The important remains at Casas Grandes, Chihuahua properly belong to a discussion of the southwestern United States (pages 279–280, Chapter 9).

The Chalchihuites culture received its greatest stimulation from the Toltecs, who pushed northward extending military and commerical operations possibly by means of a merchant group carrying a new religious cult. The northern regions reciprocated by providing salt, alum, incense, and raw copper. After the destruction of Tula, these northwestern provinces did not prosper under the rising Mexica (Aztec) power. As we shall see, Mexica interests lay largely in the richer areas of the east and south, and by A.D. 1400 the Chalchihuites culture and the cultures of its neighbors had largely withered away.

Photo 47. Interior of palace structure showing stone mosaic wall panels, Mitla, Oaxaca. Photographed by the author.

Oaxaca

The southern extension of Toltec influence is less well known, but it may have included the Mixtecs. Certainly one group of Toltecs mingled with the Mixtecs and may even have conquered them. In the Codex Nuttall, the pictorial history of a Mixtec leader, Eight Deer, shows him in typical Toltec dress, while those surrounding him are clearly Mixtecs. Eight Deer is believed to have ruled over Tilantongo, a separate Mixtec domain from A.D. 1030 to 1063 (Spores, 1967), that is, prior to the collapse of Tula. To judge from one *codex*, Eight Deer actually made a trip to Tula for his investiture of office, which suggests that Tula exercised some influence over the region, but in general, certainly as far as material goods are concerned, Tula made little impact on the Oaxaca area.

Interesting because of their absence from the Valley of Oaxaca are a whole range of objects we have come to associate with the Early Postclassic horizon. Oaxaca produced no *chacmools* or Atlantean figures and no stone sculptures of Toltec influence. Also lacking or extremely few in number are smoking pipes, *malacates*, circular pyramids, *molcajetes*, pottery flutes, whistles, and *omechicahuastlis* (bone rasps). Two Plumbate vessels have been found, and some Fine Orange ware was copied locally, but the impact of the Toltecs and later Mexica on Oaxaca was not as strong as that of the earlier Teotihuacán civilization.

In the Oaxaca area, this early Postclassic period is called Monte Albán IV, but it is very inadequately known. Lambityeco, on the highway between Oaxaca City and Mitla, may have been one site that was occupied about the time Monte Albán was abandoned. Archaeologically, the material seems to be of Early Postclassic date and representative of a period of cultural decadence. Many large mounds and multichambered homes have been identified but not yet excavated. Sculpting of burnt limestone plaster while it was still soft is a clue that these people were somehow influenced by the Maya rather than the local Zapotecs, who did not use this technique. The carbon-14 dates from this site would place these remains in the seventh or eighth centuries. For some reason, all the carbon-14 dates from Oaxaca seem earlier than warranted, and I have followed the relative chronology based on archaeological inferences and cross ties. This is not easy because the Mixtecs influenced the Valley of Oaxaca in varying degrees at different times, and stratigraphic studies are not neatly arranged, with Mixtec pottery directly sealing Monte Albán III or IV. It does seem, however, that the Mixtec culture spread to the Valley of Oaxaca in the tenth century and was at least partly contemporaneous with Zapotec culture (Paddock, 1966).

Thus, the well-known site of Mitla in the eastern part of the Oaxaca Valley is probably Zapotec with Mixtec influence, a mingling of traits also repeated at Yagul (Bernal, 1965). Mitla consists of five groups of buildings, still not completely excavated. A typical group is made up of rectangular patios bordered by apartments of long, narrow rooms. The core of the construction was mud and stone, which was covered with plaster or well-cut trachyte. The facades and door frames are decorated with mosaics of small stones combined to form a wide variety of geometric patterns such as the stepped fret (Photo 47). Beams from wall to wall supported the roofs, which were covered with small slabs, then gravel, and finally plastered over. Roofs were made with a gentle slope to direct the rain water toward the patio. At nearby Yagul, in a more attractive setting on the slopes of the hill northeast of Tlacolula, the buildings are constructed in exactly the same way, but the workmanship is not as fine. Tombs, often elaborate cruciform structures with antechambers, are similarly built. Enormous rectangular slabs on the roofs were heaved into final position by ropes passed through small holes. These tombs are probably the result of mingled Mixtec and Zapotec influences in the valley.

The Yagul ball court, partially decorated with stone mosaics, is larger than the ball court at Monte Albán and, unlike the latter, has no niches, central stone markers, or rings. Even in Mixtec *códices*, ball courts are illustrated without rings. The *códices* also show a variety of other structures such as temples, palaces, shrines, and even sweat baths. The structures at Yagul and Mitla are overwhelmingly civic rather than religious in nature, conforming to the general trend toward secularization seen elsewhere in Postclassic times.

The Maya Area

If there is little evidence of the Toltecs in the region of Oaxaca, more is found further south. We know that the Toltecs who settled at Tula were only the best known of many groups that claimed the name. Probably a group from central Mexico that eventually settled in El Salvador and Nicaragua was also Toltec. Their descendants in historic time are known as the Pipils. These migrations may have resulted from the Olmeca-Xicalanca takeover of Cholula around A.D. 800 and would thus account for the presence of many Mexican features and place names that persisted until Spanish times in these Central American regions.

The highland Maya states of the Quiché and Cakchiquel were among those that claimed Toltec ancestry (Recinos & Goetz, 1953). We do not know for certain whether these claims were real or fictitious, but it is entirely possible that as some Toltecs made their way to Yucatán by land, others may have branched off to remain in the Guatemalan highlands. Certainly some Toltec penetration of the Maya highlands about this time made a strong impact and these communities retained a Toltec flavor until the Conquest. The general shift in emphasis from a religious to a secular orientation on the rise elsewhere in Mesoamerica at this time affected the settlement patterns and architecture of these highland people (Shook & Proskouriakoff, 1956; Smith, 1955). In the Early Postclassic period villages occupied hilltop sites and tongues of land surrounded by deep ravines. By the Late Postclassic phase they not only remained in these strategic defensible positions, but were heavily fortified. Ball courts were built with side benches as the older ritual function was replaced by a spectator sport. The presence of twin temples atop pyramids with double balustrades are generally ascribed to foreign Mexican influences. The interest in commerce and craft specialization reached a new peak, and the demand for Tohil Plumbate kept potters under pressure to increase production. The western highland sites of Zaculeu and Zacualpa must have been lively commercial centers. The Conquest interferred with the goals of two highland peoples, the Quichés and Cakchiquels, who had developed well-organized aggressive kingdoms and were bent on military and economic expansion. The smaller Pokomam, Zutughil, and Mam nations were of lesser importance but equally proud to attribute the good things in life to their Toltec heritage.

Turning again to the dispersal of the Toltecs from Mexico, groups undoubtedly traveled by both land and sea to penetrate the Maya region at various times. Remember that trade routes were already established in Classic times, that the influence of Teotihuacán can be seen at Uxmal, and that representations of a feathered serpent and the Mexican Tlaloc are sprinkled throughout Classic Maya sites as far south as Copán. Toward the end of the Classic period there is evidence of Putún traders and the development of an empire centering in Tabasco and Campeche. These Putún Maya intermarried with their Mexican neighbors and were naturally receptive to foreign ideas. These ideas in turn were spread by the Putún as they traveled by sea and pushed their way up the inland waterways (Thompson, 1970).

What is commonly and rather ambiguously referred to as the Mexican period in Yucatán are the years from A.D. 987 to 1224, when Chichén Itzá came under heavy Toltec domination (Photo 48). It is not easy to trace movements of peoples and correlate conflicting historical sources with archaeology and the Mayan calendar, which by now recorded only Short Count dates, an abbreviated date-recording system which replaced the earlier Long Count (see page 107, Chapter 5). Bishop Landa (Tozzer, 1941), our most important Spanish source, for example, is unclear as to whether the Itzás arrived with Kukulcán and conquered Chichén Itzá, or came prior to, or even following, this event. Itzá history is reconstructed from a few historical narratives mentioned by sixteenth-century Spaniards and from historical references in the katun prophecies. These are largely contained in the Books of Chilam Balam, written during Colonial times in the Maya language using Spanish script. The complicated blending of Toltec and Yucatec traditions has been newly interpreted by Thompson (1970). Aided greatly by the scholarly writings of Ralph Roys (Scholes & Roys, 1948; Roys, 1966), I have leaned heavily on the chronicles and colonial period source material, in piecing together the following order of events.

It has already been pointed out that the Itzás were a branch of the Putún or Chontal Maya who made their way by sea around Yucatán to Cozumel and eventually established themselves in Chichén Itzá by the year A.D. 918, which is prior to the arrival of Kukulcán, or Quetzalcóatl and the Toltecs. These early Itzás brought with them some Mexican influences, as seen in Tlaloc representations at Uxmal and warriors with *atlatls* on the door jambs of Kabah that are almost certainly of Late Classic date. At Chichén Itzá both the inner structure of the Castillo and the

Photo 48. Aerial view of Chichén Itzá
showing the Temple of the Warriors (in foreground) and Kukulcán. Courtesy of Compañia Mexicana de Aerofoto, S. A.

Photo 49. View of Toltec Chichén Itzá
with the ball court and Temple of the Tigers
in the foreground, the Temple of Kukulcán
at right, and the Temple of the Warriors at
rear. Courtesy of the Instituto Nacional de
Antropología e Historia, Mexico.

High Priest's Grave are Mexican rather than Toltec. We now think that these were the work of the Itzá—Putún Maya from Tabasco and Campeche, who maintained contact with their homeland. Perhaps Chichén Itzá was only another local capital of an outlying Putún province.

The history of the Toltecs in Yucatán tends to support the arrival of Kukulcán in the year A.D. 987; that is, of the two chronologies of Tula, the one based on the *Anales de Cuauhtitlán* fits best. The exact route of the Toltecs is not clear. Little evidence of their culture has been found in the Putún heartland, and it is likely that their passage through this area was relatively swift as they fled from their enemies. As Thompson points out, their passage could have been greatly facilitated by the fact that the Putún, already well disposed toward Mexicans, could have conducted this group to Chichén Itzá, another area of their domain, along already well-established routes. Thus, a second group of Putún Itzá is believed to have accompanied Kukulcán and his band of Toltecs to Chichén Itzá in A.D. 987, katun 8 Ahau. That the trip was made rapidly is suggested by the fact that Toltec traits are transplanted to Yucatán almost unaltered.

A whole new section of the site was added, created in the image of Tula (Photo 49). Chichén Itzá had been an active ceremonial center during Classic times, when it was characterized by typical Maya sculpture, hieroglyphs, and Puuc-flavored buildings with vertical facades covered by elaborate stone mosaic masks. The arrival of Kukulcán and his second group of Itzás resulted in a new building surge. The structures known as the Temple of the Warriors, Group of a Thousand Columns, Temple of Kukulcán or the Castillo, the Tzompantli or Skull Rack, Temple of the Chacmool, and the great ball court are predominantly Toltec in design and inspiration but were executed in Maya technique.

Ruz (1951) tells us that the Toltec structures were enclosed by a wall forming an irregular polygon with entrances at the four cardinal directions, the sides of which were faced with dressed stone. The wall is now

Photo 50. View looking down the central playing alley of the great ball court of Chichén Itzá. Note the position of stone rings high on the lateral walls. Courtesy of the Instituto Nacional de Antropología e Historia, Mexico.

entirely destroyed so it is not known if it had a parapet nor can its dimensions be estimated. But the inhabitants of Postclassic sites were often concerned with fortifications, and the residents of Chichén Itzá may have felt that some precaution was necessary to protect their sacred zone. Having selected the site for the glorification of Kukulcán and solar deities, they may well have chosen a wall as an ideal means of protection on the flat Yucatecan plain.

Within the Toltec compound, however, there was no feeling of limitation or crowding of buildings (Morley, 1956). On the contrary, they were widely dispersed along a consistent orientation seventeen degrees east of north, the common arrangement in central Mexico. Earlier Maya ceremonial structures were built with thick walls, narrow door ways, and dark, mysterious interiors symbolizing the heart of the earth from which the priests would emerge to transmit messages to the waiting congregations. The Toltecs introduced a new concept in religion that replaced the earth gods with celestial worship of the sun, moon, and stars; consequently, they constructed buildings and courts open to the heavens for more effective mass communication between the gods and men. Emphasis was placed on human sacrifice, carried out for the glory of the group and for the benefit of all, and therefore expedited under conditions of maximum spectator participation, pomp, and ceremony.

The great ball court on the northern edge of the site, one of seven known to exist, has a playing alley 480 feet long and 120 feet wide — the giant of all Mesoamerican courts (Photo 50). Two long vertical walls rise twenty-seven feet in height and have stone rings still set in place. Six carved reliefs show a ball player being decapitated. A small temple is located at either end, but the most imposing structure is the Temple of the Jaguars above the east wall. Feathered-serpent columns support the lintels, above which, on the exterior facade, a procession of jaguars carved in relief calls to mind the prowling jaguars of Pyramid B at Tula. Frescoes decorating the inner walls portray the gory details of a battle scene that is often considered to represent the Toltec invasion of Yucatán. Thompson (1970) has presented another interpretation. He points out that the attackers' dress shows some elements of Toltec attire but that their round shields and feathers denote another group, which he identifies as Putún Itzá. The people they are attacking are not Yucatec Maya, and therefore this scene did not take place in Chichén Itzá. Rather, several different ethnic groups are shown, making it likely that this commemorative mural records an attack by the Putún Itzá on groups in Tabasco. Near the ball court is a macabre *tzompantli*, or skull rack, completely decorated with carved human skulls, a constant reminder of man's obligation to supply the deities with human hearts and blood.

The Temple of Kukulcán, usually called the Castillo, is only a short walk south from the ball court, and forms the center of Toltec Chichén. Nearly square, with steep staircases leading up all four sides, the temple commands one of the best views of the entire site. A blend of Toltec and Maya features is seen in this temple — corbelled vaulting combined with reliefs of Toltec warriors. Within the pyramid a temple attributed to the earlier Putún Itzá preserves a famous stone throne in the form of a red jaguar encrusted with spots, with eyes of jade and shell fangs. The Temple of Kukulcán is impressive for its severe but simple style. Greatly contributing to its grandeur is the fact that it rises in lonely splendor from an immense clearing. Thousands could have gathered on every side to share in the spectacle of the music, fires, and processionals and to hear the voices of the gods. From the height of the Temple of Kukulcán one can look across at the Temple of the Warriors and observe that the plan is basically the same as the Temple of Quetzalcóatl at Tula. Here, however, it is enlarged and more skillfully executed, for the Maya pupils far surpassed their Toltec instructors. As at Tula, maximum spaciousness, light, and air were admitted through great colonnaded courts, which perhaps served as meeting places or council halls as suggested by the dais or thrones. The Group of the Thousand Columns, a huge open plaza of several acres, is completely surrounded by colonnades. The great plaza may well have served as a marketplace, for certainly there must have been a central area designed for exchange of goods and ideas. One enters the Temple of the Warriors by passing through one of these great colonnaded courts of square columns, which are carved on all sides with typical Toltec warriors (Figure 26e). Climbing the wide staircase, one is greeted by the ever-present *chacmool* at the entrance to the temple, again supported by feathered-serpent columns at the doorway. At the back of the temple is a shrine or altar supported by small Atlantean figures such as we know existed once at Tula (Figure 26a). The walls were frescoed with battle scenes between the Putún and groups of Maya. Other murals depict canoes peacefully passing by a village whose distinctive house type helps place the village in Tabasco, the home of the Putún. The Temple of the Warriors contains an earlier structure known as the Temple of the Chacmool. Paintings on the benches of this structure clearly depict two protagonists: Toltecs seated on jaguar thrones and Maya nobles holding scepters, seated on jaguar skins thrown over stools. The latter may not be Yucatec Maya, judging by the dress, ornamentation, and paraphernalia.

Minor structures such as two dance platforms are completely Mexican in flavor. Their sloping *talud* and vertical *tablero* are not unlike the profile of Xochicalco and are covered with Toltec themes of eagles and jaguars eating human hearts. Although these low platforms are not to be compared with the great ceremonial structures, they were undoubtedly an important integrative factor in religious life. Here, Bishop Landa tells us, dances and public spectacles were held, thus affording vicarious participation by the populace.

Although located outside the Toltec compound at Chichén Itzá near the older section of Puuc buildings, the Caracol or Observatory has some Toltec touches. This curious structure, considered by some to be a monstrosity, consists of a round tower perched on two rectangular terraces. The interior spiral stairway (*caracol* in Spanish) leads to a small observation chamber in the tower. Square openings in the walls seem to correspond to lines of sight at the vernal and autumnal equinoxes, but the structure may have been destined for other purposes as well. This building was remodeled by the Mexicans, who added some exterior decoration.

The Toltec influence at Chichén Itzá can be summed up in the presence of the following features, which appear in a variety of forms and combinations with Maya traits, and are considered to be Toltec because of their occurrence at Tula, Hidalgo (Figure 26) (Tozzer, 1957):

1. Temple structures with interior columns.
2. Long colonnaded courts.

3. Processions of warriors with nearly identical weapons and clothing.
4. Feathered-serpent columns.
5. *Chacmool* reclining figures.
6. Jaguars, eagles, skulls and cross bones, and human hearts.
7. Atlantean figures with upraised arms supporting altars or sanctuary repositories.
8. Architectural features such as the sloping *talud* and *tablero*.
9. Large-scale human sacrifice.
10. Militarism, not unknown before, but now shown on a large scale in scenes from murals.
11. Art portraying scenes and events involving groups rather than individual representations.

Although the Toltec impact is startling and unmistakable, Maya features persist. The innovations were Toltec, but the execution was Maya, and basic techniques remained unchanged. Religions blended, and we find the cult of Kukulcán mingling with the Mayan long-nosed deity Chac; corbelled vaulting is combined with interior columns and wooden beams; eagle and jaguar warriors are shown side by side with Maya in their typical attire. Ceramics too show the fashionable imported X-type Fine Orange ware from Tabasco and southern Veracruz and Tohil Plumbate ware from the Guatemalan highlands as well as the characteristic slate wares of Yucatán. Toltec Mazapan pottery is unknown. Copper and gold objects, although few in number, are attributed to this period and have been recovered from the waters of the Sacred Cenote. These must have been brought in through trade, since Yucatán was well removed from any center of metallurgy.

There is little doubt that these Toltecs, after firmly establishing their seat of power at Chichén Itzá, soon managed to dominate Yucatán, a simple task in view of the backing and sponsorship of the Putún Itzá. Thus, a kind of Toltec empire developed in Yucatán that spread the cult of Kukulcán and continued to promote commercial interests from Tabasco to Honduras. Yucatán was well located for trade. It produced materials that were much in demand, including cotton cloth, salt, honey, and also slaves. Salt was a major commodity, and shallow lagoons along the north coast of Yucatán were an excellent source. Yucatán could also provide slaves, since agricultural labor was not needed during a good part of each year. On the other hand, slaves were always needed to work in the *cacao* groves of Tabasco and Honduras.

As Chichén Itzá rose to power, Uxmal and other Puuc sites were abandoned. Details of the Toltec hegemony are still unclear. Although the Maya aristocracy seems to have maintained its identity during the Toltec period, it was subsequently lost, for by the sixteenth century all the upper classes claimed Mexican descent. The Toltec period was remembered nostalgically as a golden age of peace, justice, and religious worship. Prisoners, sacrifices, and battles had been forgotten. By the year A.D. 1224 (Katun 6 Ahau), Chichén Itzá was abandoned by the Toltecs for reasons unknown to us, and they vanish from our record, probably completely absorbed into the Maya way of life. From that time on, the inhabitants of Chichén Itzá are referred to merely as the Itzás.

8

Strife, Empires, and Europeans: The Late Postclassic Period

T HE SITE OF CHICHÉN ITZÁ HAD PROBABLY ORIGINALLY been chosen because of its proximity to one of the great natural wells or *cenotes* on the northern plains of Yucatán. Eventually a cult evolved around this sacred *cenote* that reached its peak in Postclassic times. Even after the Spanish Conquest it was a center of pilgrimages. The *cenote* measures some two hundred feet in diameter and is seventy feet deep. The symmetrical walls rise sharply from the water to the ground level, some sixty-five feet above. Into this depth both human victims and valuable objects were thrown as offerings to the rain god and as a form of divination to predict abundance of future crops. A small temple at the edge of the *cenote* marks one end of a causeway connecting the pool with the Temple of Kukulcán. Presumably, sacrifices were made from this point (Tozzer, 1957). The romantic idea that young Maya virgins were the sacrificial victims was hastily discarded once a sample of skeletons was studied by Dr. Ernest Hooton of Harvard University. The great majority proved to be children, a fair number were adult males, and the few women were beyond the normal age of marriage. Along with the skeletons, dredging brought up great amounts of jade, gold, and copper objects, jewelry of all types, weapons, copal, and rubber objects, wearing apparel, and fragments of textiles and baskets. Apparently, anything of value was offered to the gods in the hope of increasing precipitation.

Chichén Itzá was not the only center that attracted pilgrims. The Island of Cozumel was famous for the shrine of Ix Chel, goddess of medicine and patron deity of women. A paved road connected the nearest point on the mainland to Tabasco, Xicalanco, Champotón, and Campeche. A third shrine, honoring the sky god Itzamná, was located at Izamal, to which people swarmed to be cured of disease. Izamal was always a rich center owing to the excellent salt beds on the nearby coast. As a religious shrine, it prospered from Classic times until the eventual fall of Mayapán (see Inset, Map 3, Chapter 6).

Mayapán and the Last of Maya Civilization

In katun 13 Ahau (A.D. 1263–1283) a joint government was established at Chichén Itzá (Roys, 1966). This was an important step that involved organizing local states according to varying degrees of influence and power. At the same time some Itzás moved west and founded the city of Mayapán (see Map 4), which became the capital of Yucatán in 1283. Following a brief revival of the Kukulcán cult, a period of great debauchery set in. Legends are filled with tales of sorcery, adultery, homosexual practices, and much erotic conduct apparently associated with the *plumería* flower (frangipani). An Itzá lineage by the name of Cocom enlisted the aid of Mexican mercenaries from Tabasco and, with their help, seized the reins of government in Mayapán. The mercenaries are usually credited with introducing the bow and arrow into Yucatán, where it met with great success. Prior to its introduction, *atlatls* and darts brought in by the Toltecs, spears, blowguns, and traps were used. Under the leadership of the Cocoms, Mayapán gained control of all northern Yucatán. A prosperous period followed, led by rulers who were reputedly just and benevolent. The centralized government in Mayapán brought all the heads of other city states to live in the capital. By this means, coupled with their control of Chichén Itzá and Izamal, they eliminated their rivals.

The ruins of Mayapán cover an area of about two square miles (Pollock, Roys, Proskouriakoff, & Smith, 1962). Nine kilometers of defensive walls completely surrounded the city, which had only two entrances and interior steps leading up to the parapet. The Cocoms could thus have maintained a tight control over the inhabitants of the 3600 structures that have been mapped within the walls. Most of these were house sites arranged around small courtyards without any discernable master pattern. Religious structures, degenerate in scale and construction, were concentrated in a small ceremonial center at the heart of the city. A tiny temple dedicated to Kukulcán is a miserable replica of the one at Chichén Itzá, and some sort of round structure once existed where rubble stands today. Religion must have occupied a minor position in the lives of men and was largely reduced to individual household shrines. No one bothered to raise corbelled vaults, and columns were crudely assembled, with mistakes camouflaged by stucco. No ball courts have been found. Ceramics are largely monochrome; typically crude and ostentatious incense burners bear representations of both Mexican and Maya deities. Poor taste characterizes Mayapán, and cultural manifestations sank to an all-time low.

The population has been estimated at around 11,000–12,000. With local rulers forced to reside at Mayapán, luxury goods flowed in as tribute and a brisk trade seems to have been carried on. It is believed that, aside from the nobility, the residents were craftsmen, merchants, and soldiers. Farmers would have had to live in the country and carry their products into the city.

Probably about this time the east coast cultures engaged in a flurry of activity. Although they were fairly well isolated from their contemporaries at Mayapán, their architecture, art, and ceramics (including V-type Fine Orange) are shared with northern Yucatán. Clay figurines at Santa Rita in British Honduras are almost indistinguishable from those at Mayapán. Such sites as Ichpaatum near Chetumal, Quintana Roo, and Tancah near Tulum have histories reaching back into the Classic period, when their cultural isolation was impressive, but Tulum itself is exclusively Postclassic (Sanders, 1960).

Tulum (Lothrop, 1924) has a dramatic setting. Perched on a cliff overlooking the blue waters of the Caribbean, its other three sides are effectively protected by a massive, eight-hundred-meter-long wall that is two meters high and has five gates and interior stairs at various points. In contrast to Mayapán, Tulum looks like a planned city. It is organized around a main-street axis bordered by both civic and residential buildings and includes a marketplace. Stone palaces suggest a greater interest in secular than religious structures, which were located within a walled enclosure. Both Tulum and Mayapán are examples of a concentrated town pattern of Late Postclassic date in which residences are packed around the ceremonial center.

Bishop Landa (Tozzer, 1941) described such a pattern in sixteenth-century Yucatán: "the natives lived together in towns . . . in the middle of the town were their temples with beautiful plazas, and all around the temples stood the houses of the lords and the priests and then [those of] the most important people . . . and at the outskirts of the town were the houses of the lowest class . . . [p. 62]."

Xelhá, just north of Tulum on the coast, was a smaller fortified town, and Ichpaatum near Chetumal was a walled settlement with columned palaces like Tulum. Xcaret was also walled. It has been suggested that town walls could have been symbolic in nature rather than truly a tactical defensive measure.

Tulum and Santa Rita in British Honduras have frescoed murals that are more Mexican, specifically Mixtec, than Mayan in technique, although the themes are clearly Mayan. Here again is an example of the Putún culture that encircled the peninsula of Yucatán. A great loss is the glyphic text that once accompanied the murals at Santa Rita, the only one ever reported. Although these sites are the best known, the entire Caribbean coastline is strewn with ruins, an indication that this area supported a considerable population.

Meanwhile, at Mayapán the Itzá empire under Cocom leadership was being undermined. A Mexican group known as the Xiu had, according to Landa, wandered about Yucatán for some forty years and eventually settled near the old ruins of Uxmal. They made friends with their neighbors and, by exercising a little diplomacy, managed to participate in the administration of Mayapán, becoming second in power to the Cocoms. The end of the Itzá occupation of Yucatán is related in the often-told tale of Hunac Ceel, a Tabascan mercenary imported by the Cocoms who rose to leadership at Mayapán. This colorful figure had become something of a hero by surviving the sacrificial ordeal of the Sacred Cenote at Chichén Itzá. After being thrown in the pool, he somehow survived all night and brought back to the world on the following morning the prophecy of the rain god concerning prospects for a good crop in the forthcoming year. Once he became chief of Mayapán he schemed to rid himself of his rivals at Chichén Itzá. Through the aid of sorcery, he persuaded the ruler of Chichén Itzá to abduct the bride of the chief of Izamal during the wedding feast. Then full of feigned indignation, Hunac Ceel and some Mexicans drove the Itzá from Chichén.

Fleeing from the conflicts of Yucatán, the Itzás eventually made their way south through the Petén jungle to settle in peace on five small islands in Lakes Petén and Ekixil. Their main settlement was at Tayasal, a peninsula opposite Noh Petén, today known as Flores. Here their descendants were visited many years later, in 1524, by Hernán Cortés, who was on his way to put down a revolt in Honduras. They were not actually conquered by the Spanish until 1697. These Itzá were ruled jointly by a head chief and a high priest. Under them were four minor officials, *batabs*, each of whom presided over a *barrio*, which was in turn subdivided. At the time of their conquest, they were well aware of their ancestral background in Yucatán, worshiped several of the same ancient deities, retained the katun count, and still practiced human sacrifice (Thompson, 1951).

Turning our attention once more to Mayapán, we find that the Cocom's victory over the Itzá was short-lived. The nobles of Mayapán soon rose up in revolt, with the full cooperation of the Xiu. All the Cocoms were overwhelmed and summarily put to death, except for one son who was off on a trading expedition to Honduras. This reportedly occurred in another katum 8 Ahau, probably not historically accurate.

The Xiu then improved their position by moving south of Mayapán to a well-populated area offering better resources than Uxmal. They established a small but powerful kingdom at Maní. When the Spanish arrived, they remained bystanders until they saw which way the tide was turning, whereupon they allied themselves with the foreigners.

The collapse and destruction of Mayapán in A.D. 1441 marks the end of the last centralized government in Yucatán. Thereafter political control was of three different types (Roys, 1966). In one case a single lord reigned as a kind of monarch over his town and was recognized by a few others. In case of need, he could call all warriors to battle. Examples of this type of authority are found at Maní, Sotuta, Ah Kinchel, and Cochuah. The second type of political organization was a kind of lineage rule such as that of the Canul and Cupul, two lineages or name groups. This was a rather loose arrangement whereby the heads of groups of towns belonged to the same lineage and would unite to defend each other when necessary. Finally, in the third form, towns might simply ally themselves to form a kind of province. They sometimes aided one another, but this was not obligatory. The area of Chakan, which included Mérida, was such a region.

This political situation endured for almost one hundred years, from the fall of Mayapán to the conquest of the northern end of the peninsula. These years are filled with accounts of petty quarrels, local competitions, and struggles. Chichén Itzá continued to be the object of pilgrimages but supported no concentrated population. Mayapán, in shambles, shuddered with relief to be rid of the Cocoms and no one else chose to live there. The Puuc cities had been abandoned for many years. Dzibilchaltún managed to maintain itself, though with no particular distinction. Surely these surviving Maya must have felt abandoned and cast out by their gods as disaster after disaster befell them. In 1464 they weathered a devastating hurricane, followed in 1480 by a plague. Worse still was the smallpox epidemic that swept through Yucatán in 1514, three years after some shipwrecked Spaniards had been cast ashore. Is it any wonder that, with the exception of a few bloody uprisings, the Spanish Conquest of Yucatán met with little resistance?

By the time the Spanish had arrived and Landa wrote his account of the Yucatecan Indians, the greatest period of Maya development had passed. He found the Maya leading a simple village life, competing with neighboring towns for prestige and constantly warring over any trivial dispute. Central Mexican influences had made considerable impact two or three centuries earlier and by now were thoroughly blended with native Maya culture. The ancient calendar had been condensed and reduced to recording only a katun ending date, the Short Count. Many drastic changes had taken place in Maya life since the peak of her civilization, but we have written documentation for only the last centuries of life in Yucatán (Roys, 1965). Even the existing *códices* are thought to date from the Postclassic period and were probably painted in Yucatán. European influences are usually easily spotted, but those from central Mexico are less easily seen, for, after all, Mesoamerican cultures shared many basic features and attitudes. However, Maya culture had a special flavor, and from sixteenth-century accounts we can make inferences about the earlier Classic civilization. The risks are not as great as one might think at first, for there is a marked continuity of the Mesoamerican pattern from the time it was formulated in the Preclassic period until the sixteenth century.

Agriculture, for example, was basically the same everywhere in its reliance on the cultivation of maize, chili peppers, beans, squash, cotton, and fruit trees, although techniques varied according to local conditions. Some plants such as *cacao*, which needed well-drained land, heavy rainfall, and limited sunlight, could only be grown in particular locations and had to be traded to other regions. Landa speaks of individual houses as having gardens and fruit trees where papaya, custard apple, avocado, and the *ramon* tree were grown. Agricultural lands were located away from the centers of population. Dogs and turkeys were the only domesticated animals known, and were raised for food. Native stingless bees were important to the Maya because honey was a prominent export commodity and the wax was used in rituals. In addition to gathering wild honey in the woods, most families kept hives of bees. Hollowed tree trunks served as hives, the ends of which were closed with mud or a piece of wood or stone so that the honey could be easily extracted; the bees entered through a small hole in the side. Honey was also combined with water and soaked with the pounded bark of the *balché* tree to make a fermented ceremonial drink. Although bee keeping was probably limited to Yucatán, the practice of slash-and-burn agriculture, house garden plots, and the general range of cultivated plants are all features found in the Classic Petén.

Commerce was always vitally important to every region. Chief commodities in Yucatán were slaves, honey, salt, and cotton cloaks. Trade was carried out on land by foot travel using tumplines (head or chest straps), but probably even more merchandise was moved by sea, for we know that the Maya had large dugout canoes with sails capable of carrying forty people, and that they traveled from the Bay of Honduras around Yucatán to the big port at Xicalanco. The Putún distinguished themselves as merchant seamen as early as A.D. 850. This long-distance trade will be more fully described when we deal with the *pochteca*, the Aztec merchants. It is assumed that the Maya had equivalent traders, although an association such as that of the *pochteca* is not described. Maya merchants operated under the auspices of Ek Chuah, God of the North, who was their patron. He can easily be identified in the *códices* by his black face (Figure 29).

There is no reason to believe that the Maya house in Classic times was any different from that seen today in villages of Yucatán. Rectangular, often with rounded corners, houses were set on stone-faced platforms with walls made of stone rubble and plaster, sometimes combined with poles. The roofs were of thatched palm and floors were covered with gravel or plaster. This is the same house as that depicted in the mosaic stone facade of the Nunnery at Uxmal, and it has been constructed by the Maya for centuries.

Landa's description of towns has been mentioned earlier. It is not certain how long the Maya had been living in tightly nucleated centers. Classic settlements present a great variety of patterns due in some cases, but not all, to the local topography. Because houses of mud, reed, and plaster are not preserved, we have little information on the arrangements and distribution of private homes prior to Postclassic Yucatecan settlements. There is some indication that Tikal may have resembled the late urban city of Mayapán in having an ungridded residence pattern and structures scattered about at random. The contrasting terrain of these cities could account for some differences, and the defensive wall of Mayapán reflects the troubled times of Postclassic years. Haviland sees in Mayapán a logical outgrowth of earlier Petén settlements in contrast to central Mexican city planning, which was very different (Haviland, 1969).

Technology likewise remained stable for hundreds of years. It was based on the digging stick, *metate* and *mano*, bark beaters, and the use of obsidian, flint, granite, limestone, and quartzite for knives, pounders, polishers, and scrapers. The *atlatl* may have been in use during the latter part of the Classic period, but its manufacture was given new impetus as a result of the Toltec invasion. The bow and arrow was introduced even more recently, probably from the area of Tabasco. Metals were also a Postclassic addition, as the Classic Maya had relied exclusively on stone tools.

All this information is documented archaeologically. The patterns of ritual, religion, and social and political organization, however, are much more inferential, and for this information we rely heavily on written accounts of sixteenth-century Yucatán to look for either supporting evidence or lack of it from the archaeological record. There is no question that Maya society was strongly stratified. Landa reports ruling families and tells of the great respect with which chiefs and lords were treated. Society was highly structured with the nobles at the top, an aristocracy that contained the civic, religious, and military leaders. Merchants and artisans were next in rank, followed by the peasants or commoners and slaves. Only the priests and lords knew the art of writing, and they were in charge of educating sons of the first families in writing, astronomy, calendrics, and astrology. With the exception of military leaders, for whom there is little evidence at present, the structuring of society applies equally well to what we know of life in late Classic times, as evidenced in the richness of tombs and paintings of elaborately attired individuals who must have belonged to the hierarchical elite (Adams, 1970).

The Maya conception of the world is not well known and has been interpreted from the written documents, legends, sculptures, and painted representations of deities and ceremonies. It is possible that the Maya, like the Aztecs, believed that the world rested on the back of a huge alligator in the center of a pond (Barrera Vásquez & Morley, 1949; Thompson, 1970).

The Maya pantheon was crowded with deities, and these seem to have become more prolific in later years. As is natural for an agricultural people, the most prominent gods were those controlling the forces of nature. The Maya conceived of groups of deities, who were both individual and multiple at the same time. Maya gods are not as well known as Aztec ones, and the data at hand refer largely to Yucatán (Morley, 1956; Thompson, 1954, 1970). Representations of deities are found in stone stucco, pottery, and in the three surviving *códices* (Figure 29).

Itzamná, a sky god, was the supreme deity who, with his wife Chebel Yax, creation goddess, begat all the other gods and goddesses. Itzamná, who is the father of science and the arts, is shown with the face of an old man; he has a prominent Roman nose and a single tooth.

Kukulcán, the feathered-serpent deity of Yucatán, was known as Gucumatz among the highland Quichés. He did not assume prominence until early Postclassic times and is closely associated with the Toltec invasion. Feathered serpents are present earlier, however, in sculptures of many Classic sites, including Tikal.

Figure 29. Maya deities.

From left to right, top to bottom:

Itzamná, the head of the Maya pantheon, patron of day Ahau, the last and most important of the 20 days.

Chac, the rain god.

Ah Mun, the god of corn and agriculture, usually shown as a young man, often with an ear of corn or corn plant as a headdress.

Yum Cimil, the god of death, patron of the day Cimi, shown with a skull for a head and fleshless body with bare ribs and exposed vertebrae.

Ek Chuah, the black war captain with a large drooping underlip; also the god of merchants.

Xaman Ek, the god of the North Star, shown with a snubnosed face, who somewhat resembles a monkey.

(From the following sources: Itzamná, Ah Mun, Yum Cimil, Xaman Ek, Codex Dresden, Villacorta & Villacorta, 1930; Chac, Ek Chuah, Codex Tro-Cortesiano, Villacorta & Villacorta, 1930.)

Itzamná   Chac   Ah Mun

Yum Cimil   Ek Chuah   Xaman Ek

Yum Cimil or Hun Cimil was the god of death, and can be identified in the *códices* by his fleshless backbone, skull head, and body with black spots denoting decay. An owl or the Moan bird often accompanies him. Other deities dealt with epidemics, mass deaths, suicides, death by hanging, and being caught in a trap. The war god seems to have also presided over human sacrifice and violence.

The Nature deities were very important, for they were vitally concerned with man's subsistence activities such as agriculture and fertility. Cosmic and celestial bodies, wind, water, and vegetation all had patron deities. Chac, the rain god, was unrivaled in importance. Associated with the five cardinal points — east, west, north, south, and the center of the universe — he was at the same time benefactor, creator, and father of agriculture. It is his long hooked nose that adorns the Puuc buildings. His helpers, the Bacabs, stood at the four sides of the world and held up the sky.

The sun god, Kinich Ahau, is usually shown with filed teeth and large square eyes. He was the patron deity of Izamal, where at noon time he took the form of a macaw and swooped down to devour any offerings made to him.

Of almost equal importance and prominence in the Maya pantheon is Ah Mun, the corn god, represented as a handsome young man who often has a maize plant sprouting from his head.

Although there were a great number of deities, power was concentrated in a few; the others were remembered on special occasions when their help was needed. The gods were not particularly charitable, as their favors were dispensed in exchange for offerings of incense, food, and blood. No important move was made without consulting their wishes, and they indicated the most propitious time for planting and harvesting. They regulated marriages, baptisms, and the selection of names and advised when to embark on a trip or trading expedition, when to fish, and when and where to hunt. Supplications were made in public and in private, but the activities of continence, fasting, prayer, and making offerings went on incessantly. The Maya were very supersititious and exhibited a real concern with lucky and unlucky days, charms, amulets, and magic. Eclipses of the sun or moon caused great fear, which was partly alleviated by banging on doors or seats and making as much noise as possible.

Some beliefs recorded by the Spanish are not typical of aboriginal American thinking and may well represent the teachings of the Spanish friars. We suspect that one example of this is the concept of reward and punishment meted out in a heaven or hell depending on how one behaved on earth. However, the practices of baptism, incense burning, and a kind of confession were already part of native Indian religion, which facilitated the substitution of Catholicism in the sixteenth century.

The Maya were as vain as we are today, and went to great lengths to improve their natural appearance. Elongated heads with receding foreheads forming a straight line with the nose were so admired that infants' skulls were artificially deformed to produce the coveted profile. This was accomplished by lashing two boards together, one flat against the back of the head, the other on the forehead. Four or five days of this treatment was sufficient to permanently alter the shape of the skull. Head deformation has a very long history in the Maya region, including the Classic period years. Greatly admired too were squinting and slightly crossed eyes, which could be induced by suspending a little stone or ball of resin between the eyes. Other beauty aids included filing the teeth to create interesting patterns and incrusting them with jade or iron pyrites. Finally, the body might be decorated by tattooing, scarification, or painting. Much of this may have had symbolic or ritual significance as well, for we know that colors had special meanings. These traits, along with hair styles and modes of dress, are documented by clay figurines and murals. Figurines from Jaina and the murals of Bonampak show styles of skirts, turbans, mantles, flowing robes, animal skins, and masks as well as the expressions, stances, and gestures of the various social ranks (see Plate 8h, i, j; Photos 24, 25 in Chapter 6).

The Maya loved their children and believed in discipline. Children were punished by pinching their arms and ears or rubbing chili pepper on them. Marriages were arranged by a professional matchmaker and the spouse was chosen from a prescribed group, usually when a young man was about twenty. After a wedding feast the husband lived with his father-in-law for five or six years, an indication of matrilineal ties. However, property was passed on patrilineally and family ties were important for joint enterprises such as exchange of labor. The ability to trace both parents' descent groups was a necessary key to prestige in the community. Usually a man had only one wife, but desertion and divorce were common. On the whole women were chaste and hard working but extremely jealous and prone to erupt into violent rages. Men and women ate and danced separately. We are told that the Maya loved dancing and banquets. A dinner invitation incurred an obligation to return the favor, and presents were exchanged. Music was produced by wooden drums, flutes, whistles, conch shell trumpets and rattles.

Upon the death of a person, relatives showed signs of great distress. During the day they wept in silence, but at night they howled and cried aloud. People were usually buried in the house or just behind it, and the dwelling was then deserted unless the family was so large that desertion was impractical. This long-standing practice of deserting a house upon death of a member of the family has caused some anxiety among archaeologists when using house mound counts to estimate ancient populations (see the discussion on pages 155, 156, Chapter 6; Thompson, 1971). The more privileged members of society were cremated and their ashes placed in an urn. The Cocoms of Mayapán preserved the head by cooking it, removing the flesh, and sawing it in half from top to bottom. The front half was covered with wax and modeled to resemble the deceased. This then was kept in the family shrine and revered, where it was provided with offerings from time to time.

Warfare was common during the last years before the Conquest, although it does not seem to have played a major role until late Classic times, when weapons consisted of clubs and a kind of battle axe. Later the bow and arrow and *atlatl* were introduced from Mexico with great success. The cotton quilted armor described for Yucatán may have been inspired by the central Mexicans. Wars were fought in the day time, and war paint, along with much shouting and hissing, was designed to frighten the enemy.

Thompson (1954) characterizes the spirit of the Maya as devout, exercising moderation, and possessing great discipline. These qualities, combined with a profound respect for authority, would have been important factors in the emergence of a theocratic government. This opinion is based on his long acquaintance with the archaeology of the Maya, as well as many years of contact and residence among the Maya of British Honduras. Other scholars, such as M. D. Coe (1966), feel that this picture is not realistic. Coe sees them instead as quarrelsome, doting on warfare, and fiercely competitive in their struggle for political gain. The archaeological facts appear to bear out a strong theocratic organization in the early years of Maya history, for the constant building and rebuilding of religious structures seem to reflect the genuine devotion and widespread participation which would logically accompany a *cargo*-type system of socio-political organization (see pages 166, 167, Chapter 6). In Late Classic and Postclassic years, however, human sacrifice became more prevalent, defensive walls were raised around Yucatán cities, weapons were more plentiful and diversified, and actual scenes of battles were portrayed in murals. Then the secular trend acquired more and more power at the expense of the religious hierarchy. This same trend is paralleled in central Mexico, where it culminated in the civilization of the Aztecs.

The Aztecs or Mexica

One of the most exciting chapters of history is the story of how Hernán Cortés with a few hundred Spaniards conquered the Aztecs and their king, Moctezuma. The story of how the white man penetrated the New World and overcame thousands of savage Indians thrills every adventurer, but in this case, the tale is enhanced further by a beautiful Indian girl who served Cortés as mistress and interpreter. The ingredients are provided by history itself and need little embellishment by the imagination.

By recalling what we now know of earlier peoples in Mesoamerica, we can view, hopefully with some perspective, the culture of the Aztecs as it was in the year A.D. 1519, an Aztec year of Ce Acatl 1 Reed. The Aztecs are often considered to be "the" Indians of Mexico, but they were actually only one of many groups inhabiting Mesoamerica at that time. It is true that by subduing the Aztecs the Spaniards cut down the most powerful resistance that could have been offered at that time, but the subjugation of Mesoamerica was not due to their defeat alone, for theirs was not the only independent political center.

At the head of the great Aztec nation was Moctezuma, whose name needs some explanation. The Moctezuma of 1519 was Moctezuma Xocoyotzin, or Moctezuma II, son of Axayácatl and great-grandson of Moctezuma Ilhuicamina or Moctezuma I. It is a mere accident of history that these names received world-wide publicity. Had the Spanish arrived fifty years earlier, we would be learning instead about the wonderful world of Texcoco and the benevolent rule of King Nezahuacóyotl, studying the earliest code of law in the New World, and marveling at native philosophy and poetry. The Aztecs, despised for their unsavory customs and relentless thirst for sacrificial victims, would very possibly have appeared in the record only as Texcoco's war-mongering neighbors. It would have been as difficult to foresee the rapid emergence of the Aztec empire under Moctezuma Ilhuicamina's three grandsons as it would be for us to predict events if the Spanish had delayed their arrival until fifty years after 1519. Perhaps, as some suggest, the Aztecs would have eventually conquered the Maya and developed a closely consolidated empire with an efficient power structure capable of controlling the economic, social, and religious complexities of a strong political state. But the alternative is also possible: The Aztecs could have suffered a fate like that of Tula or Teotihuacán — a devastating collapse.

But it was in 1519 that the Spanish came, precisely at the hour of Aztec strength. Tenochtitlán, the Aztec capital, and not Texcoco or Azcapotzalco, was the goal of the invaders, the center of interest of the Spanish chroniclers.

Early History

The early history of the Aztecs is sketchy, and until the reign of Nezahuacóyotl in Texcoco in the fifteenth century, we trace events in the Valley of Mexico through oral traditions. Later history is pieced together from the Spanish chronicles and the pre-Hispanic and Colonial *códices.* Excellent ethnographic data and genealogic and chronologic information abound in the writings of Conquest witnesses such as Cortés (1908), Sahagún (1946), and Diaz del Castillo (1944), and later authors such as Torquemada (1943) and Durán (1867–1880). Best of the native sources are the *Tira de la Peregrinación, Historia de los Mexicanos por sus Pinturas,* Codex Xólotl, the Tlotzin and Quinatzin maps, and the interpretations of Ixtlilxóchitl (1891), for despite exaggerations and confusions resulting at times from the bias of the latter author, an essentially coherent picture emerges. In the Aztec period, we are dealing with historical archaeology; history and archaeology merge, confirming and amplifying one another. For more recent works dealing with this period see Acosta Saignes (1945, 1946), Barlow (1949), Caso (1958, 1967), M. D. Coe (1962), Cook (1947), Jiménez Moreno (1962), Kelly and Palerm (1952), Kirchhoff (1954–1955), Krickeberg (1961), León-Portilla (1963), Monzón (1949), Peterson (1959), Soustelle (1964), Wolf (1959), and Wolf and Palerm (1955).

Accordingly, we know that after the destruction of Tula, a great Chichimec leader, Xólotl, settled first at Tenayuca and later moved his capital to Texcoco, which was to play a vital role in the history of the Valley of Mexico. Of several Toltec groups, the lineage at Culhuacán was the most prestigous and the most sought out for marriage. Before long, the best land for cultivation in the basin of Mexico was in use, the lake shore settled by Náhuat- and Otomí-speaking peoples and descendents of refugees from the old abandoned centers of Teotihuacán and Tula. With the choice areas already taken, no one welcomed an additional band of immigrant Chichimecas with the unpleasant habits of stealing women and practicing human sacrifice. These latecomers were not to pass unnoticed, however. We know them as the Aztecs or Mexica.

This group we call Aztec probably never heard the word. We think it stems from Aztlán, "place of the seven legendary caves," which spawned these "Warriors of the Sun." They were known at various times as Tenochca, Mexica, or, more specifically, the Culhua-Mexica. As Tenochca they followed their early tribal leader Ténoch, under whom they straggled into the Valley of Mexico as unwanted squatters and for whom they later named their city Tenochtitlán. They eventually became known as the Culhua-Mexica, Culhua showing their association with the Toltec lineage at Culhuacán. But they are frequently called simply the Mexica, a name that came to be known and dreaded from coast to coast.

The story of the Aztecs or Mexica rise to power is a dramatic rags-to-riches tale. This miserable band, despised by all, was driven from one location to another around the western lake shore, living as it could on fly eggs, snakes, and other vermin. The king of Culhuacán engaged their aid in a war against neighboring Xochimilco, but he was repelled by their barbarous customs, such as the severing of ears from each prisoner as proof of their prowess in war. On another occasion they flayed the king's daughter in honor of Xipe Totec, and when he arrived for the marriage festivities, he was confronted instead by a priest dancing about in his daughter's skin. To escape the fury of the Culhuacanos, the Aztecs took refuge in the tall reeds of the lake shore, and finally in desperation moved to some swampy islands in the lake.

According to legends, their tribal war god, Huitzilopochtli, led them to this place. Here an eagle, sitting on a cactus with a serpent in its beak, told them to build their temples and nourish the sun with the sacrifice of human victims. This became the destiny of every Aztec, his purpose and mission in this world, and here it was to be fulfilled. The legend is depicted on the Mexican flag today.

Accounts vary as to the date of the founding of Tenochtitlán, but it probably occurred close to A.D. 1345. An eagle may or may not have been waiting, but the fact remains that the Aztecs had exhausted the tolerance of their littoral neighbors and were badly in need of refuge. Another settlement, Tlatelolco, was already in existence on the northwestern part of the island, so Tenochtitlán was founded south and east of it. These two cities were to thrive side by side for many years, the former becoming a great mercantile center, the latter growing steadily in military strength. Rivalry between the twin cities was unavoidable, and Tlatelolco was finally taken over by the Mexica under Axayácatl in A.D. 1473 after 128 years of jealous, competitive coexistence.

The rise of Mexica power and events in the Valley of Mexico can be followed by tracing the succession of kings and outstanding personalities of the times. Although preceded by tribal leaders, Acamapichtli was the first king and the founder of a lineage because of his kinship ties with Culhuacán. In the genealogical chart that follows, the numbers represent the order of succession:

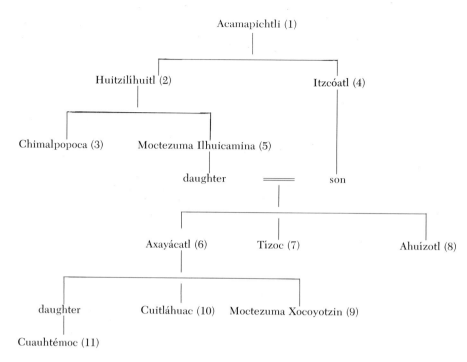

Figure 30. Genealogy of Mexica rulers.
This genealogy is not complete, showing only the probable relationship between rulers. There often are conflicting accounts in the chronicles. For example, some sources list Chimalpopoca rather than Huitzilíhuitl as the father of Moctezuma Ilhuicamina, and Itzcóatl as the son of Huitzilíhuitl rather than his brother. (For a detailed description of source material, see notes in Gillmor, 1964; adapted from Gillmor, 1964.)

Social Structure

When one king died, the next was elected from the royal lineage by a council composed of nobles, titled warriors, and important priests. Although the council gathered to "elect" a new king, the foregoing genealogical chart illustrates how tightly the reins of succession were held, usually passing from brother to brother before descending to the following generation. The hereditary nobility, from which the king was chosen, reckoned its descent from the Toltecs and enjoyed certain privileges not shared by others. The king claimed that he was selected by the god Tezcatlipoca and was his representative on earth. Furthermore, he claimed descent from deified ancestors, not real ones. As might be expected, the king had special insignia and the finest clothing. He, as well as his own court, was permitted to have many wives and send his male children to the *calmécac,* a strict, elite school where formal education was given in the arts and sciences, but emphasis being placed on basic religious instruction. There were six such institutions in Tenochtitlán, at which much time was devoted to sacrifice, prayers, ritual purification, bloodletting, and autosacrifice, wherein the students pierced their ears and tongues with the sharp spines of the maguey. These young boys became the *pillis* and *tecuhtlis,* a privileged group including the king, from which people were chosen to occupy posts as governors, ministers of justice, and coordinators. This group owned land but did not work it themselves. Although they formed a hereditary nobility, another group of nobility was eventually created. A warrior who distinguished himself in battle might be singled out for honors and thus be elevated to a special group of nobility, no longer being bound to his *calpulli* or required to work its lands. There is some indication that this nobility was somewhat in conflict with the hereditary one (Monzón, 1949).

Commoners and laborers, known as *macehuales*, were, of course, very poor. They had only one wife, and their meager belongings consisted of stones for grinding corn, a *petate* to sleep on, and the clothes they wore. Their male children might attend the *telpochcalli* schools, of which there was one in each district of Tenochtitlán. This was a popular school, less severe than the *calmécac*. Boys were instructed in the arts of warfare and were given some religious training. There were other schools that taught dance, song, and the playing of musical instruments, but all were basically religious in orientation. Girls were educated in separate schools.

Another social group was the *mayeques* or bondsmen, often called slaves. Of these there were different categories and for some the status was only temporary. A person might voluntarily go into slavery or temporarily place his children in bondage to pay off a debt. Women and children captured in war were treated as slaves, as were criminals, who were sometimes forced to work for the family they had offended. The children of *mayeques* were free, and we even hear of *mayeques* owning land and slaves of their own. This, then, was a special, fluctuating social category. As a servile group, they worked the lands of the *pillis*.

Much has been written about the *calpulli*, which originally was a kind of tribal organization. The twenty *calpullis* in Tenochtitlán seem to have been based on kin groups or clans with endogamous tendencies; thus, they were permanent, land-holding groups with hereditary headmen. Not all *calpullis* had equal status; some owned more land than others and embraced all kinds of people (Monzón, 1949). Early in Mexica history all lands were owned by the *calpullis*, but as public or state offices emerged and the *pillis* grew to include not only descendants of kings but even some people from powerful foreign groups, private land holdings emerged. The crucial step that provided the *pillis* with economic as well as political power was made possible by the resounding defeat of the Tepanecs, described below. Only then did the Mexica gain access to property on the mainland and begin their rise to political power.

In the earliest period of their power the Aztecs were led by Acamapichtli, his son Huitzilíhuitl, and his grandson Chimalpopoca. During this time the Aztecs served as mercenaries to the Tepanecs, the people of Azcapotzalco, who were led by a ruthless but extraordinarily gifted ruler, Tezozómoc. Undoubtedly the Aztecs benefited greatly under this master warrior and administrator, while at the same time seething under the yoke of tribute and subjugation. Tensions were eased somewhat by intermarriage with the Tepanecs, only to worsen under Chimalpopoca, when the Aztecs were accused of becoming arrogant and demanding. Accounts vary as to whether Chimalpopoca was poisoned, strangled, starved in a cage, or committed suicide, but in all likelihood the Tepanecs were responsible (Ixlilxóchitl, 1891, Vol. 2).

Emergence as a Political Power

The subsequent election of Itzcóatl in Tenochtitlán took place after the tyrant Tezozómoc had died in Azcapotzalco, and with his rule a new phase was initiated. Aided by Texcoco and Huexotzingo, Azcapotzalco was finally conquered, ruthlessly sacked, and its people brutally massacred. All the pent-up vengeance of years gone by was unleashed on the defeated Tepanecs. The surviving Tepanec town of Tlacopan, today's Tacuba, had been sufficiently neutral to be selected as the weakest member of the Triple Alliance formed with Tenochtitlán and Texcoco. Henceforth, all three cities were to receive part of the tribute exacted from subservient towns; Tenochtitlán and Texcoco were entitled to two-fifths each, and Tlacopan received the remaining fifth.

Itzcóatl, Obsidian Snake, was a strong ruler himself and his rein is intimately associated with two of the most important figures in the history of the Valley of Mexico: Tlacaélel and Nezahuacóyotl. Tlacaélel, a half-brother of Moctezuma Ilhuicamina, occupied a position of power, an office known as the *cihuacóatl*, or Snake Woman. In early times this office included some priestly duties along with acting as advisor to the king, but eventually the religious aspect seems to have been discarded. Tlacaélel was a famous *cihuacóatl* who served under three successive kings. He emerges in history as a very able administrator who exercised great influence. To him we may owe the book burning that took place during Itzcóatl's reign. At that time the Mexica gained their freedom from the Tepanecs, and it was decided to wipe out their inglorious and degrading past and to rewrite history to their liking. Thus, every available record of conquered peoples was destroyed and a new indoctrination begun extolling the glories of the Warriors of the Sun.

Nezahuacóyotl of Texcoco is linked with both Itzcóatl and his successor in Tenochtitlán, Moctezuma Ilhuicamina. When only a child, Nezahuacóyotl, from his hiding place in a tree, witnessed the murder of the king, his father, at the hands of the Tepanecs. He grew up in exile knowing that he was responsible for carrying on the ancient Chichimecan lineage. Helpless against the powerful Tepanecs, he sought refuge with eastern friends and relatives in Tlaxcala and Huexotzingo, secretly visiting Texcoco and Tenochtitlán to plot his rightful restoration of power. Allying himself with Itzcóatl, he took part in the destruction of Azcapotzalco, which effectively ended Tepanec power in the Valley. One by one other cities fell around the lake shore: Culhuacán, Xochimilco, Huexotla, Coatlichan, and Coatepec. After subduing all the Tepanec strongholds in the Texcocan region, Nezahuacóyotl returned to his home covered with glory and was restored to power as king of Texcoco in a great ceremony at Tenochtitlán. His reign was unparalleled in cultural achievements and learning. He codified Texcocan law, which was more severe than that of the Mexica, and constructed a great dike across Lake Texcoco to hold back the brakish water of this lake from the fertile *chinampas* (a system of agriculture, see page 245) of the sweet water of Lake Chalco. He initiated an intricate system of canals and dams to increase agricultural production; he helped Moctezuma Ilhuicamina build the aqueduct that carried sweet water to Tenochtitlán from Chapultepec; and he stimulated arts and crafts, offering prizes for the finest achievements in gold and feather working, music, and poetry. His summer residence at Texcotzingo, in ruins today, still retains elements of the former beauty of its stairways, temples, fountains, aqueducts, and baths, which were either cut out of bedrock or constructed of mortar.

It is said that commoners and nobles were equally represented on Nezahuacóyotl's governing councils, and merchants were consulted on economic affairs. The early chroniclers stress his monotheistic tendencies and opposition to human sacrifice. Nezahuacóyotl preferred an invisible god who had both masculine and feminine qualities and who could not be represented materially. This god, Tloque Nahuaque, lived in the highest point in the heavens and all things depended on him. He did not intervene directly in man's affairs; therefore, Tloque Nahuaque was never very popular. We know, however, that although Nezahuacóyotl did erect a large temple to this one almighty god, in which there was no sacrificial stone, he also honored other deities. Nezahuacóyotl emerges as a very fair administrator and an exceptional thinker and poet, yet he too participated in many battles and, as a product of his times, ordered sacrifices and executions. Under Texcocan law, his favorite son was put to death as a traitor, because even the king's son could not be an exception. While Texcoco, under his administration, became famous as a center of learning, Tenochtitlán grew in military strength and eventually prevailed as a political power.

Tenochtitlán undoubtedly owes more to Texcoco than is usually admitted. Texcoco had its own history of conquests and tribute rolls prior to Mexica supremacy (Palerm & Wolf, 1954–1955). After the fall of Azcapotzalco, it was through Texcoco's leadership that the eastern regions were brought under control of the Triple Alliance. Texcoco and Huexotzingo were long-standing friends, and it was the towns in the Puebla Valley that gave refuge and support to Nezahuacóyotl and enabled him to regain the throne. Thus, some conquests claimed by Tenochtitlán had already been achieved by Texcoco. Unwittingly or not, Texcoco was gradually dispossessed of its role as leader and upstaged by its aggressive island neighbor.

The Triple Alliance provided Tenochtitlán with a base for its scramble to power. Under Itzcóatl's nephew, Moctezuma Ilhuicamina, Archer of the Sky, the Mexica began their great expansion. Their domain was extended to the Gulf Coast, an area of special commercial interest. Influenced and aided by his friend and ally Nezahuacóyotl, Moctezuma built botanical and zoological gardens. Every known plant, bird, and animal was collected at Huastepec, Morelos. It was also during his reign, about A.D. 1450, that Tenochtitlán suffered privation under a great four-year drought. Hunger was so great that the Mexica became frantic; wild animals emerged from the forests and attacked people for lack of food. So desperate was the situation that many Mexica sold themselves as slaves to the lowland Totonacs of Veracruz, where corn was plentiful. Later they were to serve as spies reporting vital information about the alien country. In a final spasm of desperation, the Mexica appealed to their powerful gods through mass human sacrifice. To provide the necessary victims, a pact, known as the "Flowery War," was established with the Tlaxcalans and Huexotzincas. Battles were even set up by appointment, but actual conquests were never made. From this time on, human sacrifice on a large scale formed part of the Mexican pattern of life. The two great leaders, Moctezuma Ilhuicamina and Nezahuacóyotl, died within a few years of each other, and the stage was set for the final thrust of Mexica militarism.

Axayácatl, the first of Moctezuma Ilhuicamina's grandsons to succeed him, spent much time reconquering territory and suppressing rebellions. He attempted western expansion, only to be met with firm

Photo 51. *Chinampa* at Míxquic, Valley of Mexico. Courtesy of Victoria Bach.

resistance from the Tarascans (see Map 4, Chapter 7). But he finally took Tlatelolco, which from A.D. 1473 on was governed from Tenochtitlán. Upon his death, his brother Tízoc reigned, but only for a short time. Tízoc has been branded in history as a coward because his love of battle did not match that of his brothers. However, the third brother, Ahuízotl, throve on war. Under him Mexica influence was extended from coast to coast to include the Balsas basin and coastal Guerrero, and he pressed his claims to the Guatemalan border. He was especially gifted as a military leader. At home he managed to complete the Main Temple of Tenochtitlán, dedicated jointly to Huitzilopochtli and Tlaloc, each of whom was honored by a temple atop a pyramid with a double stairway, the hallmark of Mexica architecture. So important were the dedication ceremonies, which lasted four days, that 20,000 victims were stretched over the sacrificial blocks to have their hearts removed while multitudes watched and rejoiced.

The Mexica in 1519

Moctezuma Xocoyotzin, son of Axayácatl, is remembered largely for his tragic fate and forced surrender of Tenochtitlán to the Spanish. Usually unnoticed is the fact that he was a very powerful, well educated, and able ruler who continued military expeditions in the area of Oaxaca and adjacent regions and dealt with his share of uprisings. In his day, Tenochtitlán was transformed into a beautiful city with a great concentration of population, estimated at between 200,000 and 300,000, that embraced hereditary nobles, priests, specialized artisans in a variety of crafts, merchants, and an enormous peasantry.

The Spaniards' first glimpse of this great metropolis came after they had ascended to the *altiplano* from coastal Veracruz and passed between the snow-covered volcanoes of Popocatépetl and Ixtaccíhuatl. There, spread beneath them, stretched the vast sweep of the basin of Mexico, some 3000 square miles, enclosed by forested mountains and embracing in the center a chain of five lakes. Coming closer they saw an island city with towering temple-pyramids connected to the mainland by three great causeways, a city of canals rather than streets.

Banding the island were *chinampas*, a kind of floating mattress of reeds and water lilies covered with silt. These were among the most fertile gardens of the New World (Photo 51) (West & Armillas, 1950). Here the Mexica grew corn, squash, beans, chile, *chia*, amaranth, innumerable vegetables, and flowers. Produce was loaded daily into canoes for transport to the markets. The *chinampas* were cultivated from Tenochtitlán and Tlatelolco south to the shore of Lake Xochimilco and then east into Lake Chalco, and it is possible that *chinampas* were utilized even during Classic times (M. D. Coe, 1964). Today they are still in use at Xochimilco and Míxquic, and are popularly called the Floating Gardens. Actually they do not float, as the layers of silt and reeds are held in place by trees that put down roots and serve as anchors. Xochimilco, for example, could not have grown up at random, for aerial photography reveals a grid network of canals. Thus, the canals were carefully planned and formed by draining the swampy shore, which was fed by freshwater springs. The orientation of these canals is seventeen degrees east of true north, the same as the streets of Teotihuacán, mentioned in Chapter 4.

We know that the Mexica worked hard to protect these valuable lands. The greatest threat to their existence was the possibility of infiltration of nitrous salts from the eastern part of Lake Texcoco. With the summer rains the danger of flooding was acute. Thus, great aqueducts built of stones, earth, poles, and branches were constructed to serve as dikes. To make a good *chinampa* one must have sweet water of little depth so that the garden can be covered periodically with rich mud from the bottom. This ingenious method of agriculture was made to order for island dwellers because it provided tillable land and easy transportation. Owing to the constant renewing of the soil, *chinampas* never "wore out."

At the center of Tenochtitlán was a great court enclosed by a *coatepantli* or serpent wall, within which were the main religious structures, seventy-two according to Sahagún's count (Photo 52). The main temples of Huitzilopochtli and Tlaloc and those dedicated to Tezcatlipoca, Xipe Totec, and Quetzalcóatl, together with the ball courts, grisly *tzompantlis,* altars, houses of retreat, and minor structures, were all located within the walls. Outside this main center were the sumptuous palaces of the nobility, lay buildings, humble dwellings, plazas, and marketplaces, all interlaced by canals. The latter separated the different private holdings in the city. Sweet water was carried to the Main Temple by an aqueduct from Chapultepec. What a magnificent spectacle it must have been, this island-city with its painted temples and whitewashed houses gleaming in the bright Valley sun! What a pity that it was so completely ruined!

In the ninety-day siege against the Spaniards, many buildings were destroyed to fill in the canals. The Mexica hurled stones and debris from temples, houses, and bridges in a desperate attempt to save their city. The battle was heroic but futile. Cortés had much more on his side than the obvious superiority of weapons. Moctezuma Xocoyotzin, who had been a student at the *calmécac,* had trained for the priesthood, and was thoroughly indoctrinated in his Toltec ancestral history, knew well the prophecy of Quetzalcóatl to return in a year Ce Acatl. Thus, when the fair and bearded Cortés arrived in Veracruz precisely in that year, who could be certain that Quetzalcóatl had not returned? In addition to the monarch's own superstitions, uncertainty, and apprehension, which were heightened by numerous bad omens, the centralized government of Tenochititlan did not extend throughout the Aztec "empire." The decisive impetus was given by the Tlaxcalans, who joined the Spaniards and contributed both their manpower and knowledge of native warfare.

It is not clear exactly how Moctezuma Xocoyotzin met his death in the year 1520, but surely he must have felt that his gods had failed him. Having welcomed the Spanish into the city, he soon found himself their prisoner. In the heat of a bloody battle in which the Spaniards were forced to flee the city and retreat to Veracruz, Moctezuma Xocoyotzin perished. He was succeeded by his brother Cuitláhuac, who ruled only four months and died of illness the same year. Their nephew Cuauhtémoc, the last of the Mexica kings fought savagely in the defense of Tenochtitlán and is regarded today as a national hero. In the final death throes of Tenochtitlán, every Mexica fought valiently, persistently, but vainly. The city was shattered in the struggle and, after the battle ended, the Spaniards completed the destruction of its temples and idols to facilitate the substitution of a new order. Still not feeling completely secure, however, Cortés took Cuauhtémoc on an expedition to Honduras rather than risk leaving him behind. In the jungle country of Chiapas the last Mexica king was cruelly hanged in A.D. 1524.

Archaeology

What can archaeology add to the wealth of data provided by the chroniclers? We know, for example, that the religious center of Tenochtitlán underlies the civic center of modern Mexico City. The exact location of some of the structures has been identified. One example is the Main Temple of Tenochtitlán, which lies near the cathedral under the streets of Guatemala and Licenciado la Verdad. Similar work across the city has uncovered part of the great temple at Tlatelolco. Tons of stone sculpture, pottery, and artifacts of all kinds have poured out of

Photo 52. Reconstruction of the ceremonial center of Tenochtitlán. Courtesy of the Instituto Nacional de Antropología e Historia, Mexico.

Photo 53. Pyramid of Tenayuca, Tlalnepantla. Courtesy of the Instituto Nacional de Antropología e Historia, Mexico.

each freshly dug foundation and street construction as well as from the excavations for the new subway, which passes through the heart of the ancient capital. Tenochtitlán lies hopelessly beyond the possibility of restoration, although confirmation of the city planning, its layout, and location of prominent structures has been made.

There are, however, numerous remains of the Mexica's ancient contemporaries from surrounding sites such as Tenayuca, Tezcotzingo, Calixtlahuaca, Malinalco, Teopanzolco, Tepozteco, and Cholula. These give an excellent idea of the final Mesoamerican construction and are easily accessible today from Mexico City.

Tenayuca, that old settlement of Xólotl near the modern town of Tlalnepantla, was enlarged many times (Photo 53). The temple's final construction with a double staircase was probably very similar to that of the main temple of Tenochtitlán. Three sides of this pyramid are encircled by a curious *coatepantli* consisting of once brightly colored coiled serpents made of mortar with great carved heads. Two large fire serpents with crested heads are coiled on either side of the stairways. Only three kilometers away is the small pyramid of Santa Cecilia, completely restored even to the stone temple on top. It is one of the finest visible examples of late Postclassic architecture (Photo 54).

Calixtlahuaca in the Valley of Toluca, home of the Matlatzinca, was a center closely allied first to the Tepaneca and then to the Mexica. Particularly outstanding is a round structure believed to have been dedicated to Quetzalcóatl as the wind god Ehécatl. Southeast of Toluca, near the modern town of Tenancingo, is Malinalco, which was incorporated into the Mexica domain by Axayácatl. Its unique main temple was actually hewn out of the bedrock of the mountainside. Jaguar sculptures flank the main staircase, which leads to a circular chamber through a doorway shaped like the jaws of a serpent. The interior shrine resembles the *kiva* (the ceremonial chamber) of the southwestern United States in several features. Sculptures of eagles, jaguars, and serpents abound. Malinalco was a very holy place, and to judge from its unique features it must have been a very special Mexica shrine.

In the state of Morelos, another twin pyramid can be seen at Teopanzolco, across the tracks from the railroad station at Cuernavaca. But far more spectacular, owing to its setting, is the simple pyramid of Tepozteco, which clings to the cliffs overlooking the village of Tepoztlán.

In addition to the Mexica ruins themselves, all the small objects used in routine daily living, as well as a vast array of ceremonial paraphernalia, have been unearthed (Plate 13). Díaz del Castillo (1944) mentions that multicolored pottery vessels were especially favored by the rulers. We know that this reference is to the famous Cholula polychrome or Mixteca-Puebla ware (Figure 31a–d, f; Plate 13a). The plates, goblets, bowls, cups, and pitchers are truly worthy of royalty. Although these prized wares were manufactured either by Mixteca-Puebla residents of Tenochtitlán or imported from their eastern homeland, the Mexica also made great quantities of a well-fired pottery decorated in black on orange. The tripod forms, plates, and pitchers made by earlier groups were continued, but supports now were either thin solid slabs or sharp spikes. *Molcajetes* with deeply scored interiors are common (Figure 31i). A fine, highly polished red ware sometimes decorated in black is very characteristic. Stamps (Plate 14j), smoking pipes (Plate 14g), *malacates* (see Plate 11b, Chapter 7), and mold-made figurines representing deities

(Plate 14h) were all very standardized, produced in great quantities, and rather monotonous. The finest wares are the imports, of which many, such as elaborate long-handled censers (Figure 28l, Chapter 7), were designed strictly for ceremonial use.

The greatest artistic expression of the Mexica was achieved in stone carving. It is here that symbolism is seen as an important dimension in Mesoamerican art. The free-standing figures of Aztec deities are true idols, and are characterized by a high degree of realism rarely found in the earlier cultures. Most stand rigidly on a small pedestal base, but some are kneeling or seated cross-legged. A chin may rest pensively on a hand or be cocked at an angle. Attire, hair styles, sandals complete with knotted thongs, loin cloths, and *quexquemitls* are typically portrayed in figures of the gods. Truly monumental sculptures of gods, such as the Coatlícue, Our Lady of the Serpent Skirt, are excellent examples of Mexica art. Gruesome and hideous, Coatlícue is a figure with two facing serpent heads, wearing a skirt of snakes and a necklace of human hearts and hands. Macabre and awesome even on her pedestal in the National Museum of Anthropology of Mexico, she must have terrified even the staunchest heart when lit by firelight or torch and worshipped

Photo 54. Restored pyramid and temple of Santa Cecilia at Tenayuca. Courtesy of the Instituto Nacional de Antropología e Historia, Mexico.

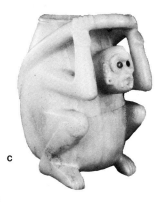

a

b

c

d

e

f

g

Plate 13.   Mexica period vessels

a. Cholula polychrome vessel with ring stand. Height: 9⅞ inches. Courtesy of the Museum of the American Indian, Heye Foundation (16/3394).

b. Polychrome goblet with humming bird, Tomb 2, Zaachila, Oaxaca. Height: 3½ inches. Courtesy of the Museo Nacional de Antropología, Mexico.

c. Onyx monkey-effigy vessel with inlaid obsidian eyes, Isla de Sacrificios, Veracruz. Height: 5 inches. Courtesy of the Museo Nacional de Antropología, Mexico.

d. Onyx tripod vessel, Isla de Sacrificios, Veracruz. Height: 8½ inches. Courtesy of the Museo Nacional de Antropología, Mexico.

e. Tlaloc brazier, central Veracruz: Late Postclassic. Height: 5 feet. Courtesy of the Museo Nacional de Antropología, Mexico.

f. Red-ware "teapot" vessel with stirrup-spout handle, Michoacán: Tarascan culture. Height: 8 inches. Courtesy of the Museum of the American Indian, Heye Foundation (24/3025).

g. Black-on-white spouted vessel, Veracruz: Huasteca culture. Height: 7⅞ inches. Courtesy of the Museum of the American Indian, Heye Foundation (66/46).

to the accompaniment of rattling bones and drumbeats. Another example, also in the National Museum of Anthropology, is a head of Coyolxauhqui, moon goddess and sister of Huitzilopochtli, beautifully executed in polished green diorite, who is shown after her death by decapitation, executed by the sword of her brother. The Mexica liked to see their deities and have them about in their temples and sacred places, so scores of gods and goddesses were realistically sculptured in their various aspects (Photos 55 and 56).

The famous so-called Calendar Stone, a relief carving nearly twelve feet wide, is actually a representation of the sun god Tonatiuh, who gazes out of the central symbol for earthquake, which, according to legend (Codex Chimalpopoca, 1945), is the next catastrophe this world may expect. Jaguar, wind, rain, and water, each responsible for a disaster wiping out former worlds, are also represented, and all of this is enclosed by a band of the twenty day signs, solar symbols, and two serpents. It is believed that this huge relief was prepared for a prominent place in a temple, but the carving was never completed. Another monumental stone is that of Tízoc, which is actually a gigantic round *cuauhxicalli*, a receptacle for burning human hearts. The sides are elaborately carved with scenes depicting Tízoc's conquests.

Atlantean figures and *chacmools*, a survival of Toltec art forms, continued to be carved. The latter often represent Tlaloc and are characteristically more elaborate than the known Toltec examples. Although most sculptures are life size or even larger, there are a series of smaller outstanding carvings of coyotes, serpents, grasshoppers, and plant forms. All have a religious connotation and were probably cult objects placed in sacred areas, for Mexica art was highly symbolic and the gods often assumed animal forms.

Figure 31. Ceramics of Late Postclassic period.
(a), (b), (c), (d), (f) Cholula polychrome; (e) red-on-white bowl, skull-and-crossbones motif; (g) polished black-on-red pitcher; (h) black-on-red goblet; (i) black-on-orange *molcajete*; (j) black-on-orange tripod; (k) monochrome unslipped censer, with a circular central vent in the base, Burial 5, Tikal; (l) Ixpop polychrome tripod vessel, rattle supports, surface debris, Temple II, Tikal; (m) black-on-white vessel, Huasteca culture.

(From the following sources: a, Piña Chán, 1960; b, d, Noguera, 1965; c, Noguera, 1950; e, Covarrubias, 1957°; f, g, Toscano, 1952; h, j, m, Marquina, 1951; i, Museum of the American Indian, Heye Foundation, specimen 8/8694; k, l, Adams & Trik, 1961.)

There are also stone blocks, perhaps used as pedestals, and stone boxes. Even wooden drums (*huéhuetl*) and the *xiuhmolpilli* or year bundle (representing the completion of a fifty-two year cycle) were copied in stone. We know that these were also carved in wood and buried. As Nicolson (1970) has pointed out, friezes and panels, popular among earlier peoples, became rare. Much of Mexica art is macabre, typified by the horrendous Coatlícue, but this aspect has probably been exaggerated. Nicolson stresses symbolism and free-standing sculpture as characteristics of Mexica art.

For craftsmanship in textiles, wood, and feathers, one must rely on descriptions rather than actual specimens. We know that feathers were worked into cloaks and shields and were highly valued. A few weathered examples have survived in European museums, but the selection cannot possibly be representative of what once existed. Some beautiful wooden drums, undoubtedly made for ceremonial use, have been preserved. Wooden drums were of two kinds. One was the *huéhuetl*, a vertical drum over the top of which a skin was stretched (see Photo 24, Chapter 6). It was played with the palms and fingers like an Afro-Cuban bongo drum.

° Redrawn from *Indian Art of Mexico and Central America*, by Miguel Covarrubias. Copyright © 1957 by Alfred A. Knopf, Inc. Reprinted by permission of the publisher.

a

b

c

d

e

f

g

h

i

j

Plate 14

Plate 14. **Miscellaneous small artifacts of the Post-classic period**

a. Obsidian lip plugs or labrets, showing front, lateral, and inferior surfaces, Aztec culture. Length: 1⅛ inches. Courtesy of the Museum of Primitive Art, New York.

b. Ground obsidian ear spool associated with grave, Tzintzuntzan, Michoacán. Courtesy of the Museo Nacional de Antropología, Mexico.

c. Pair of obsidian ear plugs: Aztec culture. Height each: 1⅜ inches. Courtesy of the Museum of Primitive Art, New York.

d. Necklace of pink shell beads, Oaxaca. Courtesy of the Museo Nacional de Antropología, Mexico.

e. Necklace of rock crystal beads: Mixtec culture. Courtesy of the Museo Nacional de Antropología, Mexico.

f. Carved jaguar bone: Mixtec culture. Length: 5 inches. Courtesy of the Museo Nacional de Antropología, Mexico.

g. Mexica polished red clay pipe, Federal District of Mexico. Height: 2⅝ inches. Courtesy of the Museum of Primitive Art, New York.

h. Mold-made clay figurine, Valley of Mexico: Aztec culture. Height: 6 inches. Courtesy of the Museum of the American Indian, Heye Foundation (22/1025).

i. Conch shell pendant, carved in design of warrior, Veracruz: Huastec culture. Length: 6¼ inches. Courtesy of the Museum of the American Indian, Heye Foundation (23/9573).

j. Clay stamps or seals. Dimensions of specimen on right: 2 by 2½ inches. Courtesy of the Museum of the American Indian, Heye Foundation (upper: 23/5490, lower: 23/5489).

Photo 55. Stone statue of Xipe Totec, Tlalpan, Valley of Mexico. Height: 30 inches. Courtesy of the Museum of the American Indian, Heye Foundation (16/3621).

Photo 56. Aztec water goddess. Height: 13 inches. Courtesy of the Museum of Primitive Art, New York.

The other, the *teponaztli*, was a horizontal cylinder in the top of which one or two tongues of wood were carved (Plate 15f). These tongues were struck with sticks, the points of which were covered with rubber. The different length of the tongues produced different sonorous and penetrating sounds. Some of these were beautifully carved with religious motifs and were probably sacred instruments. Small drums made of pottery are also known. Music also was made by striking a turtle shell with splinters of deer bone. Rattles, copper bells, bone rasps, conch shell trumpets, pan pipes, whistles, and *ocarinas*, along with various kinds of simple and composite flutes, were all utilized in honoring the gods. Music was probably not used for aesthetic enjoyment; rather, it constituted one of the emotional props in religious fanaticism. No funeral procession, ritual, or warfare took place without its appropriate musical setting (Plate 15) (Martí, 1968).

The very finest gold work is usually attributed to the gifted Mixtecs of northwestern Oaxaca, who perfected the "lost wax," or *cire perdue*, method of gold working to produce the greatest masterpieces of this type in the New World. The labrets and ear spools, beads, nose and breast ornaments, pendants, and rings made by these skilled metallurgists are nothing short of exquisite. Pearls, jade, turquoise, amber, rock crystal, and amethyst were combined with gold or obsidian. Even ceremonial vessels might be fashioned of jade or rock crystal. The famed Tomb 7 of Monte Albán yielded some of the finest grave goods of this type ever recovered in the New World (see Plate 16) (Caso, 1965a). The use of copper and silver was less spectacular but these metals were also worked into jewelry.

With the possible exception of those made by the Tarascans, who excelled in copper and bronze work, tools had changed but slightly since Preclassic days. The digging stick, *manos* and *metates*, bark beaters, pounders, and obsidian blades, knives, and scrapers remained standard equipment.

Religion

To understand the Mexica attitude toward many of their activities and the functioning of their society, it is necessary to know something of their religious beliefs. Indeed, commerce, warfare, and religion were the most time-consuming occupations of the Mexica. Because all aspects of a functioning society are interrelated and integrated, it is impossible to discuss one feature as an isolated entity. It is necessary, for example, to realize that warfare was both a privilege and duty of every able-bodied man and was carefully reinforced by religious beliefs. After important battles honors and titles were handed out for bravery or for capturing four or five prisoners; in this way nobility could be achieved. Every young man was considered to be a potential warrior dedicated to providing prisoners of war for sacrifice. The sacrifice of human hearts was the "food" necessary to sustain the sun in its daily flight across the sky, and was not the sun necessary to life itself?

Mexica religion seems to us an exaggerated polytheism (Caso, 1958). Full of fear, dread, and apprehension, the Mexica mirrored in their gods their own preoccupation with magic and divination and forces of good and evil. With the exception of Nezahuacóyotl's Tloque Nahuaque, the multitude of gods were represented in human form and were felt to have human problems and weaknesses. The war god, Huitzilopochtli,

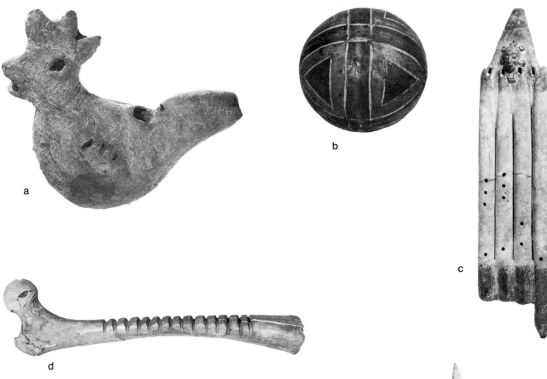

Plate 15.   Mesoamerican music

a. Clay whistle in the form of a bird, Tlatilco. Length: 4 inches. Photographed by Spence Gustav. Author's collection.

b. Rattle in the shape of a game ball, Tlacotepec, Toluca Valley. Diameter: 3½ inches. Courtesy of the Museum of the American Indian, Heye Foundation (8/8752).

c. Pottery pan pipes, Tabasco, Mexico. Length: 22½ inches. Courtesy of the Museum of the American Indian, Heye Foundation (23/902).

d. *Omichicahuaztli* (bone rasp) made of human femur, Valley of Mexico. Length: 14 inches. Courtesy of the Museum of the American Indian, Heye Foundation (2/6719).

e. Incised conch shell trumpet, Oaxaca: Mixtec culture. Length: 9½ inches. Courtesy of the Museum of the American Indian, Heye Foundation (22/6377).

f. Carved wooden *teponaztli* drum, Axzotla, Puebla. The base is hollowed out and the top is slitted to form two tongues. Length: 17¼ inches. Courtesy of the Museum of the American Indian, Heye Foundation (16/3373).

was the Mexica's alone, but in general their religion had great flexibility and a unique capacity to embrace deities of both ancestral peoples and contemporaries. Thus, the ancient gods of fire (Huehuéteotl), rain and water (Tlaloc), springtime (Xipe Totec), and the feathered serpent (Quetzalcóatl) still occupied important roles, although their meaning and symbolism may well have undergone reinterpretations (Figure 32).

Tezcatlipoca (Smoking Mirror), a sky god, is familiar from Toltec days as the adversary of Quetzalcóatl. Under the Mexica, Tezcatlipoca had perhaps the greatest variety of attributes and prerogatives. He was intimately associated with the night and therefore the stars and moon, but he also had affinities with death, evil, and destruction. Eternally young, he was the patron deity of magicians and robbers. The overlapping of roles of this and other deities sometimes seems a hopeless jumble. For example, Tezcatlipoca of the east was red and associated with Xipe, while Huitzilopochtli, both war and sun god, was at the same time the blue Tezcatlipoca of the south. The white Tezcatlipoca of the west was one form of Quetzalcóatl. The night deity, of course, was none other than a northern black Tezcatlipoca.

Much confusion arises because one god could appear in different forms. Quetzalcóatl, for example, might be the wind god, god of life, god of the morning, the planet Venus, or god of twins and monsters, and he could only be recognized by particular attributes that distinguish his various names: Ehécatl, Tlahuizcalpantecuhtli, Xólotl, or Ce Acatl. It is difficult for us to understand the complexities of Mexica religion if we try to visualize the deities as distinct entities, which they were not. The concept of duality, the forces of good and evil being represented by different aspects of the same deity, was a common feature of this religion. Common people busied themselves with satisfying their immediate household deities and looked to the priests for guidance, interpretation, words of caution, and advice in such religious matters.

All Mexica were aware that they were living under the constant threat of doomsday, which they tried to ward off as long as possible by human sacrifices. Although many cultures have some kind of blood sacrifice, there is probably no historical parallel that can be made to the attitude of the Mexica, expressed in such acts as the slaughter of 20,000 victims at the dedication of the Great Temple of Tenochtitlán under Axayácatl. How was it possible to create this state of mind?

The beliefs surrounding Quetzalcóatl and Huitzilopochtli are good examples of the fanatic Mexica preoccupation with war, blood, and death, into which every child was indoctrinated from birth. Quetzalcóatl, god of air and life, went down to the underworld and, gathering up all the bones of past generations, sprinkled them with his own blood, and thus recreated humanity. Since man's very existence depended on the gods, he had to insure their well-being by providing them with human sacrifices, which supplied that magic substance of life found only in blood and human hearts.

In his aspect as the sun, Huitzilopochtli, is a young warrior, who is born every morning in the womb of the earth and who dies every night to illuminate the underworld of the dead. Each morning the young warrior, armed with his fire serpent, has to fight off his sister, the moon, and his brothers, the stars. By winning this daily struggle, he ensures a new day of life for man. Victorious, he is borne to the center of the heavens by the souls of those glorious warriors who have had the good fortune

Figure 32. Mexica deities.

Tlaloc, the god of rain and lightning, probably one of the oldest gods; known as Chac among the Maya, Tzahui among the Mixtecs, and Cocijo among the Zapotecs.

Xipe Totec, the Flayed One, god of planting, springtime, and jewelers; in his honor, victims were flayed and their skins worn by a priest. He is also the red Tezcatlipoca.

Quetzalcóatl, the feathered-serpent deity, god of learning and the priesthood. He is also god of life, the morning, the planet Venus, and twins and monsters. In various aspects, he may be called Ehécatl, Tlahuizcal-pantecuhtli, Ce Acatl, or Xólotl.

Tezcatlipoca, the Smoking Mirror, appears in many forms. He is associated with the nocturnal sky, the moon, and the forces of evil, death, and destruction.

(From the following sources: Tlaloc, Codex Telleriano-Remensis 1889; Xipe Totec, Codex Borbónico 1899; Quetzalcóatl, Codex Fejéváry-Mayer, 1830–1848; Tezcatlipoca, Stone of Tizoc, drawn after Tozzer, 1957, Courtesy of the Peabody Museum, Harvard University.)

Tlaloc

Xipe Totec

Quetzalcóatl

Tezcatlipoca

to perish either in battle or on the sacrificial block. In the afternoon, the souls of women who died in childbirth, that is, in giving their lives for a warrior, carry the sun to the west, where he is now visualized as an eagle who falls and dies, only to be gathered up by the earth. This daily struggle of Huitzilopochtli was the Mexica's struggle, for they were the people of the sun, chosen to be warriors. From birth, children learned that their reason for existence was to prepare for the sacred war necessary to nourish Huitzilopochtli. Thus, man's collaboration with the gods was indispensible.

Several types of sacrifices were performed. Most common was that of stretching a victim over a convex sacrificial stone at the entrance to the temple, where four priests held the limbs while the fifth made a sharp slice through the chest and, reaching in, wrenched out the still palpitating heart. Placed in a special stone eagle vase, or *cuauhxicalli*, it was burned for the gods' consumption. Flaying the victim was a sacrifice performed in honor of Xipe Totec. Another form was a "gladiatorial combat" in which the prisoner, tied to a gigantic stone, was forced to defend himself with a wooden club against Mexica warriors armed with obsidian-edged swords. Occasionally his defense was so excellent that the victim was spared. A special sacrifice involved tying the prisoner to a wooden frame and shooting him with arrows. Whatever form was chosen, however, the sacrifice was always carried out to nourish the gods and for the eternal glorification of the Mexica.

Religion touched almost every aspect of Mexica society. Art, of course, was almost exclusively of a religious and symbolic nature, and religious instruction was an integral part of education for both sexes. Even games were played under divine guidance. Sahagún tells us that the two ball courts in Tenochtitlán were dedicated to the sun and the moon. The game *tlachtli* had been known in some form for probably 2000 years, and a match always met with enthusiastic anticipation. Which side would the gods favor? All knew that the decision was made in the heavens.

The game of *patolli* also had religious overtones and was played under the auspices of the god of games. *Patolli* is surprisingly like the game of pachisi (or the modern Parcheesi), which spread to the Western world from India. Both are played on a similar cross-shaped board with safety zones and progression of counters. The Mexica used marked beans instead of dice. Many years ago the striking similarities caught the attention of one of the early anthropologists, Edward B. Tylor, setting off a lively discussion of the principles of diffusion as a cultural process. Students are still fascinated by the pachisi–*patolli* game, without ever having settled its history or histories of development (Erasmus, 1950).

The area devoted to the *volador* occupied a prominent place near the center of Tenochtitlán. Not a dance, and certainly not a game, it was more of a spectacular ritual ceremony involving a giant pole capped by a kind of revolving platform. The *códices* illustrate men dressed as birds or gods who threw themselves off the revolving frame and descended to earth with the aid of a rope fastened to the waist, which unwound as they "flew." Today the *volador* is still performed by the Totonac Indians of the Papantla region of Veracruz and in parts of the state of Puebla. One man remains on top of the pole and stomps out a dance while playing a flute and beating a drum. The music gives the signal for the "flyers" to begin their perilous flight to earth.

The Mexica lived in such constant fear of the gods that they were perhaps reluctant to enjoy worldly pleasures. Thus, mothers withheld outward manifestations of pride in their sons and the long-distance traders known as *pochteca* dressed humbly so as not to incite wrath or jealousy on the part of the gods (or perhaps the nobility). Strict religious discipline may help to explain the high moral code of the Mexica. As man respected the gods, so he also respected his superiors and his parents. Discretion and sobriety were expected and demanded, as were women expected to be chaste and faithful to their husbands. A good *macehual* obeyed the harsh laws, met his tribute deadlines promptly, had only one wife, and carefully observed the rules of sexual continence and drinking restrictions. Drunkenness was a crime against the state, and only after the age of seventy was drinking to excess permitted.

Law and Justice

At the time of the Conquest, the highest authority was, of course, the king himself, who was considered to be semidivine and so supreme that only those of the very highest rank were permitted to look at him directly. When approaching the king, one must first touch the ground and then his mouth with his hand, a sign of humility and reverence. The king ate alone and received visitors and foreign dignitaries only after they had removed their sandals and covered their fine clothes with a humble maguey fiber cape. The king was carried about in a litter and did not touch his foot to the earth. How many changes had taken place since the first unwanted Aztecs had straggled into the Valley of Mexico under the command of their tribal leader!

A complex juridical system grew out of early customs and was probably influenced by Nezahuacóyotl, king of nearby Texcoco, whose far-reaching code of law has been preserved (Ixtlilxóchitl, 1891). Aztec law dealt with all aspects of human relations — civil, criminal, and legal matters as well as foreign affairs of the state. The entire structure of the legal system was taught at the *calmécac*.

The advisory position of *cihuacóatl* (Snake Woman), was originally one of considerable power with administrative and juridical authority. Probably the most famous *cihuacóatl* was Tlacaélel who served as advisor to Moctezuma Ilhuicamina, and participated in all major decisions. However, thereafter the monarch's power increased and the position of *cihuacóatl* gradually declined in importance. One of the chief duties of the *cihuacóatl* was to preside over a supreme court, which was composed of four judges. A very difficult case could be referred to the king who was the ultimate authority. He was aided by thirteen wise men who formed a special high court that met about every twelve days. Their verdict was passed on to the king who then pronounced judgment. There were also lower courts of justice, provincial courts, and a kind of local judge in each town. Sahagún (1946) stresses that these offices were filled from the ranks of well-qualified nobles, who had been educated in the *calmécac*.

Because of the nature of Mexica law, there was little need for jails or prisons. Most crimes were punished by some kind of death: flogging, sacrifice, decapitation, or by being placed in slavery either temporarily or for life, depending on the nature of the offense. Small wooden cages housed those who committed minor crimes. If Mexica law seems brutal today, it was clearly understood by the society that the law-abiding citizen was protected and could feel secure under the justice of the land. The law was harsh, yet it contained certain rather charming exceptions. For example, stealing corn was punishable by death, but a person in need was permitted to help himself to four ears from those rows planted along the road for his immediate use without castigation. An interesting concept of Mexica law was that the severity of punishment was measured in accordance with the offender's station in life. A high priest would be put to death for a crime that might be tolerated by a bondsman. That is, a man of high office assumed greater moral responsibilities and his conduct was expected to be beyond reproach. Laws were designed to preserve the family, the society, and the state. Nobles had the right to defend themselves and be heard in private, but they were duly punished if found guilty. Under no circumstance was the individual permitted to take action or settle a dispute on his own. The state only was authorized to make decisions and mete out punishment.

A good law-abiding Mexica was careful about his conduct and was anxious to do what was right and appropriate as well as gain approval of others. He wanted to be highly regarded, but his conduct on earth was in no way connected with a belief in reward or punishment after death (León-Portilla, 1963).

Commerce

The greatest unifying factor among the diverse areas of Meso-america continued to be commercial activity. The strong desire for products of other regions goes back at least to Preclassic times. Trade stimulated contact among different groups and forced lines of communication to remain open, regardless of competition or warfare. The establishment of commercial relations provided a natural vehicle for the exchange of, or at least exposure to, all forms of cultural activity. The structure of Mexica trade relations is well documented in the literature. We suspect that this complex system had been gradually elaborated through the years by predecessors of the Mexica.

Basically, two kinds of trading systems operated simultaneously but independently (Chapman, 1959). The local market system, which functioned like a neighborhood general store, was carefully preserved by the Spanish and has survived to our day in native Latin America. Daily local markets were held in such cities as Tenochtitlán, Texcoco, and Cholula, with larger gatherings every fifth day. The urban centers had huge markets with as many as 60,000 in attendance, but smaller settlements too had local markets for their daily needs. The market at Tlatelolco particularly dazzled the Spanish, for it was held in the wide paved area that stretched before the great temple of Huitzilopochtli, where boats could draw up in the canal at one side to unload their merchandise. Every imaginable product was available and occupied its designated place; vendors of vegetables, fish, and fruit products squatted in orderly rows with their merchandise in neat piles before them on *petates* (Sahagún, 1946, Vol. 2). Merchandise included not only finished products such as mantles, baskets, pottery, tools, jewelry, and feather work, but also slaves and raw materials such as unrefined gold ore, stone, untanned hides and skins, lime, and wood. From the list of commodities offered, it would seem that not everyone built his own house, produced his own food and tools, and wove his own cloth, but that specialists and middlemen existed. The goods were taxed as they were brought in and sales were carefully regulated by special courts and judges, and for this reason transactions were forbidden outside the markets. Misdemeanors were severely punished; anyone caught pilfering was immediately stoned to death. Accordingly, business was orderly and the marketplace respected. It also functioned as a social and religious gathering place for gossip and worship (Sahagún, 1946, Vol. 2; Torquemada, 1943; Chapman, 1959; Acosta Saignes, 1945).

A favorite drink of the nobility, *cacao*, or chocolate, was also used as a medium of exchange. Other types of money were cotton cloaks, quills filled with gold dust, and small copper axes. Because of the widespread use of *cacao* both as money and as a beverage, the areas of production were of considerable importance. The most productive regions were Tabasco and northern Oaxaca, central and southern Veracruz, southern Chiapas, southwestern Guatemala, and Honduras. We believe that *cacao* had been produced for at least 1000 years prior to the Conquest, and it was a product often listed on the tribute rolls (Millon, 1955).

Another type of trade was carried on over long distances by professionally trained merchants known as *pochteca* (Acosta Saignes, 1945; Chapman, 1959). As we shall see, they also acted as spies and confidence men. They dealt exclusively with foreigners and imports outside the

Mexica domain. Once an area was conquered, however, trade became tribute, which was no concern of the *pochteca*. Occupying a special status in Mexica society roughly equal to that of skilled craftsmen, they were granted private ownership of a piece of land, like the *pilli*, but they were not nobles. The *pochteca* of eighteen towns in the Valley of Mexico banded together in a kind of association and resided in Tlatelolco. Theirs was a hereditary occupation. They had their special god, Yiacatecuhtli, and their own rites, feasts, courts, hierarchy, and insignia. *Pochteca* were not allowed to bathe, wash, or cut their hair.

If the day was auspicious for a trade caravan to leave Tenochtitlán, the band of merchants would travel together to Tochtepec in Oaxaca, laden with such goods as gold ornaments and precious stones, rich garments, slaves, obsidian knives, and copper bells, needles, and combs. Tochtepec was the end of the first lap of the journey. Here the caravan split, part heading east, the others south to meet their counterparts at a specified location where fleets of canoes and other caravans converged from foreign regions.

The return to Tenochtitlán was carefully planned so that the *pochteca* arrived at night on a day of good luck. A merchant would deposit his acquired goods, typically raw materials such as feathers, precious stones, *cacao*, animal skins, and gold, in the home of a relative and would then report to the officials. One wonders at this furtive nocturnal entry. In addition to being a protective measure, it may have served to conceal success, for the *pochteca* were careful not to appear too prosperous. We know that those who were conspicuous about accumulating wealth were put to death. A model *pochteca* was humble, self-effacing, and stayed well within the limits of propriety.

Long-distance trade was a separate institution from that of the daily market. The former was organized for dealing with luxury items and took place at special geographical locations called ports of trade. Near lagoons or rivers for convenient access by canoe, these meetings places were located in areas traditionally removed from political conflict. The most important were Xicalanco in Tabasco, Soconusco on the Pacific coast of Guatemala, the region of Acalán on the lower Usumacinta River, and more distance areas on the Bay of Chetumal and Gulf of Honduras (see Map 4, Chapter 7). In all these areas, with the exception of Xoconusco, Putún traders had been active around A.D. 900 (Thompson, 1970), so that the regions had a very long history of commercial transactions. The *pochteca* probably dealt with professional counterparts in Xicalanco, who handled the trade to the south, traveling around Yucatán by sea to the Bay of Chetumal. These sea-going traders along the coasts of Yucatán and Honduras reportedly used large canoes eight feet wide by fifty feet long in which the heaviest cargo could be carried. It must be remembered that on land all goods were transported on human backs. The maximum load permitted was fifty pounds per person. One would like to feel that such a limitation shows some concern by the state for the welfare of its people, but the limitation may simply have proved to be most efficient in the long run. It is interesting that the Spanish allowed this long-distance trade to dry up, since they had no use for it, whereas they themselves depended on the market system, which has consequently survived to the present day.

The Mexica were materialistic. Seemingly insatiable, they demanded cotton, *cacao*, feathers, and raw materials such as jade, gold, and precious stones to manufacture all the luxury items ably produced in Tenochtitlán for the delight of the nobility and the enrichment of the temples and religious hierarchy. The *pochteca* doubled as government spies, and often the Aztec war council would act on their information. When the order went out for war, every able-bodied man received his weapons and paraphernalia from the local storehouse as no standing army was maintained. The weapons were obsidian-edged wooden swords, *atlatls,* spears, bows and arrows, slings, and blow guns. Shields were made of reeds and feathers and sometimes jewels. The Mexica warrior decked himself out in fantastic headdresses, nose and ear ornaments, and cotton quilted armor, and the outfits of the nobility were even more dazzling. Thus geared for war *pillis* and *macehuales* alike plunged into battle to the music of trumpets and drums. Warfare, justified partly on religious grounds, is more readily understood in the light of economics, for lively commerce was essential to the support of the rapidly growing administrative and religious urban center at Tenochtitlán. Expansion and conquest were designed primarily to increase the flow of goods into Tenochtitlán. Tribute was mandatory, and accounts of its volume are almost beyond belief. An extreme example is Soconusco, five hundred miles from Tenochtitlán, which paid two hundred loads (five tons) of *cacao* alone every six months in addition to other items (Millon, 1955).

Slaves were often used as beasts of burden, but not exclusively. Women and children taken in war became slaves, but male prisoners were sacrificed to the gods. Women were valuable assets because they could increase yields of both agricultural and manufactured products.

Both kinds of trade were carried out under the auspices of particular gods, but trade was primarily a business operation of a secular nature. The empire was, as we shall see, largely a design for exercising the threat of force over defeated towns for economic exploitation.

The Mexica Empire

The Mexica "empire" was a curious thing indeed. "Sphere of influence" is in one sense a more descriptive term, but it does not convey the oppression, cruelty, and harsh demands inflicted by the Mexica on their conquered peoples. Military expeditions were two-fold in purpose. The first and foremost goal was to exact heavy tribute to meet the increasing demands in Tenochtitlán for all the food, cloth, feathers, metals, and slaves necessary to maintain the highly structured social organization of the island city. The second goal was to maintain an every-ready supply of sacrificial victims to satisfy the gods. A coordinated, centralized political empire never emerged, but the strong state power of Tenochtitlán maintained itself through force and threat of force.

The lack of any true, cohesive political empire is seen in the fact that many towns were constantly reconquered. Once a town was taken, the Mexica sent tribute collectors, but otherwise the region usually continued under the same local rule. When the *pochteca* reported signs of unrest, or were themselves captured or put to death, immediate retribution would follow in the form of a sweeping attack by the dreaded Triple Alliance or the Mexica, to which resistance was useless. The defensive sites and fortifications of these towns were built in strategic areas such as hilltops, and walls and moats were undoubtedly constructed with an eye to defense. But there is nothing in the record to indicate permanent occupation by troops or a professional army. Tenochtitlán itself was not a fortified city. The best means of defense was its natural position in the lake, and it possessed no special military structures. In the battle for its life, fighting raged from housetops, temples, aqueducts, and bridges (Díaz del Castillo, 1944; Sahagún, 1946).

Mexica warfare may seem like a senseless exercise in which military campaigns were fought only to be fought again. By establishing a permanent army and a politically centralized cohesive government, the Mexica could almost certainly have achieved a real conquest state, but they may not have felt this necessary or particularly desirable. It may have been deemed convenient to have a ready enemy such as Tlaxcala to serve the purpose of a Flowery War, initiated in time of crisis but continued thereafter, which may partially explain the independence of the Tlaxcalans. However, the Mexica may also have had little incentive to force its conquest. It is well known that the Tlaxcalans were well prepared for war and that they possessed fortifications and a good mercenary army of Otomís and refugees from the basin of Mexico eager for revenge (Byam Davies, 1968). Possibly more important than the uncertainty of success in an all-out military effort was the fact that Tlaxcala represented no great economic prize. From the time that Moctezuma Ilhuicamina extended the Mexica empire to the Gulf Coast, cutting off the Tlaxcalans' communications and supplies with this eastern region, they became notoriously poorly clothed and suffered from lack of salt. Indeed, the area offered so little in the way of economic resources that their conquest may not have been worth the effort involved. Ixtlilxóchitl (*Historia Tolteca-Chichimeca*, 1947) relates that Moctezuma Xocoyotzin observed one battle while sitting on a hill, whereas his predecessors had actively led the assaults. This suggests that Tlaxcala was perhaps worth fighting from time to time but that it did not merit the effort necessary for conquest. Indications are, however, that enmity was real and feelings strong on both sides; it is not true, as some have thought, that the two cities maintained a friendly arrangement for battle engagements (Byam Davies, 1968).

The Mexica sphere of influence lay east and south of its capital Tenochtitlán. As we have seen, these were the areas of greatest economic interest. The vast north and northwest, so ably exploited by the Toltec, were largely ignored by the Mexica, to whom they seemed of little economic value. The land of the Tarascans, immediately to the west, was a different matter. Here conquest was desired and attempted but never accomplished. The Mexica were ever aware of a large independent kingdom located directly at their backs.

The Mexica in Retrospect

The Mexica civilization reaped the benefits of all the advances that had been made by its Teotihuacán and Toltec predecessors and even earlier groups. Thus, the Aztecs had urbanization; hydraulic control, and *chinampa* agriculture; metallurgy; institutionalized trade and commerce; state control of land and other property; codified law; a strict moral code; formal educational institutions; and a carefully structured society with clubs or brotherhoods, craft guilds, and a formally organized religion.

Considerable space has been devoted here to Mexica culture, in which commerce and religion have been emphasized. Warfare was vitally important too, and was closely related to these other features. So much research has been devoted to the complex Mexica religion that it is often thought of as the very backbone of their culture. I believe, however, that commerce was equally fundamental to the growth and maintenance of this unique civilization. Its roots reach back at least 2000 years to a time when the Olmec elite exhibited a discriminating taste for jade and fine ceremonial objects.

In most respects the Mexica were the natural end product of a long heritage. Their material culture and technology continued traditions established by their predecessors. The new pottery styles and designs are well within expected variations, and display a monotony, repetition, and standardization inherent in any mass production, although technologically they leave little to be desired. As for social organization, we cannot be certain which features were Mexica innovations because earlier social structures—although we must rely more on inferences in interpreting them—nonetheless exhibited a clearly defined class stratification. That differences in rank existed from ancient times is indicated by many examples of rich tombs, palatial dwellings, and special caches. Slaves and prisoners are shown in the Bonampak murals; distinction in dwellings is noticeable at Teotihuacán. The difference between Mexica society and that of Classic Tikal or Teotihuacán and Postclassic Tula or Mexican Chichén Itzá may be only a matter of degree. Centralized authority of some kind and a strong priesthood have long histories. Warfare, as opposed to smaller raids, was common toward the end of the Classic period and has been amply demonstrated for the Early Postclassic period. The calendrical system, fifty-two-year cycle, and counting were Preclassic and Classic achievements from which the Mexica benefited.

In view of their rich inheritance, what did the Mexica themselves contribute? What if anything was unique in their civilization? To these city-island dwellers we attribute the following:

1. A special, fanatic elaboration of an older religious pattern that allowed for incorporation of other deities into an already crowded pantheon.
2. Large-scale or mass human sacrifice.
3. An elaboration of a distinctive religiously oriented monumental stone-carving style.
4. A variation in temple-pyramid architecture consisting of double staircases and twin temples.
5. The imposition of tribute on a large scale.

In addition, it should be remembered that in this period some of the finest examples of gold work and lapidary art ever achieved in the New World were produced, though here the credit properly belongs to the Mixtecs, who were the masters in this field. The history of Mexica features, such as *chinampa* agriculture, the *pochteca* as an organized institution, and the establishment of ports of trade, is not yet fully known, but I am inclined to feel that this knowledge dates well back into Classic days if not earlier, though perhaps in another form and under another name. Recalling the steps in the emergence of the Mesoamerican cultural pattern and the rise of the great centers of civilization that preceded this final phase, one may view the Mexica as the final expression of a very long tradition to which they added their own particular style.

Had the Spaniards not interrupted the reign of Moctezuma Xocoyotzin when they did, what would have become of the Mexica? Other strong groups, such as the Mixtecs and Tarascans, might conceivably have challenged the island city at some time in the future. Or perhaps the Mexica might have eventually consolidated their empire and become the masters of Yucatán.

The Mixtecs

To the Mixtecs the Mesoamericans owed many of the finer things of life. For the most beautiful examples of pottery, exquisite work in metallurgy, and fine lapidary art of all kinds, we turn to the Mixtecs who were the teachers of the Texcocans and Mexica. Their crafts were in great demand by the Mexica nobility, and the finest jewels sent to Charles V of Spain were undoubtedly turned out by their expert hands.

The Mixtec region, often called simply the Mixteca, consists of three subareas. The Mixteca Baja is centered in western and northwestern Oaxaca. To the east and south lies the Mixteca Alta, an area of high, cold, fertile valleys surrounded by mountains. This region borders on and is most intimately related to the Zapotec remains. Finally there is the Mixteca de la Costa or the coastal lowlands of Oaxaca (Spores, 1967).

Confusion often arises because the term Mixteca-Puebla culture is used to refer to the development around Cholula and Tlaxcala in Toltec and Aztec times (Nicolson, 1961). The elaborate polychrome pottery of Cholula is indistinguishable from the sumptuous wares manufactured in the Mixteca Alta (Plate 13a, b). The red-on-cream pottery may be Coyotlatelco-derived, and Mixtec figurines certainly resemble those of Mazapan and later Mexica ones. Many features of native writing are also shared with groups in the Puebla region.

Cholula may be the home of the lacquered polychrome ware that appeared there immediately after the Teotihuacán horizon, but an equally strong case can be made for a Mixtec origin and northward spread (Bernal, 1965). We do know that after this ware ceased to be made in Cholula, it continued in use in the Mixteca. Despite close interaction with the Puebla–Tlaxcala region, the Mixtecs had a distinctive culture of their own, and although it is hard to pinpoint exactly when and where this culture first emerged, it is a Postclassic development.

This Mixtec culture centered in the Mixteca Alta. It never produced a major ceremonial center of the magnitude of Monte Albán, but eventually mingled with Zapotec culture, spread throughout parts of the Valley of Oaxaca, and occupied sites such as we have seen at Mitla and Yagul on the eastern edge of the valley. These towns, built by Zapotecs in Monte Albán IV, incorporated some Mixtec ideas.

There is more information, archaeologically speaking, about Coixtlahuaca and Tilantongo than about any other sites in the Mixteca Alta. Little is known of the architecture, but some Zapotec influence is represented in walls covered with mosaics, such as those of Mitla and Yagul. A very common pottery vessel is an open bowl decorated with red or brown geometric designs on the natural base color. Curiously enough, though many aspects of Mixteca culture spread to the Valley of Oaxaca, this vessel did not. The elegant polychrome wares shared with the Valley of Puebla are particularly outstanding but are not associated with tomb material of the Mixtecs.

One exceptional tomb at Coixtlahuaca consisted of three chambers with a common entrance, but this design is unique. The usual Mixtec tomb was not constructed but simply dug into the *tepetate*, much like the shaft-and-chamber tombs of western Mexico, only very much smaller (Bernal, 1965).

No ball courts are known from either Coixtlahuaca or Tilantongo, but the Mixtecs must have known the game because courts are amply represented in their *códices*. This apparent absence may be due to inadequate excavation or a lack of recognizable traces on the surface.

In the Valley of Oaxaca we know that Monte Albán was almost deserted by Postclassic times. Period V remains found there are limited to tombs, burials, and offerings from the Mixtec occupation.

Mixtec craftsmanship was highly prized and greatly sought out by others (Plate 14d, e, f; Plate 16b, d, e), and this area was a great center for the production of small, fine luxury items such as gold objects, jade and turquoise mosaics, small carvings in hard stone, and beautiful polychrome ceramics. Turquoise was as favored by Mixtec jewelers as jade, which had always been the preferred precious stone of earlier cultures.

The most fabulous treasure ever recovered in the New World is that of Tomb 7 at Monte Albán (Caso, 1965a). The tomb itself was Zapotec, constructed in Period IIIb and reused by the Mixtecs to inter a high official. Thereafter it remained undisturbed until Alfonso Caso discovered it in 1932. Twenty-four silver objects, 121 gold objects, and 8 vessels of *tecali* were found as well as necklaces formed of beads of jet, jade, pearl, amber, coral, and shell. Other finds, including rock crystal jewels and vases, disks, rings, ear and nose ornaments, obsidian ear plugs less than one millimeter thick, and beautifully carved jaguar

Plate 16.   Mesoamerican metallurgy

a. Copper bells from Ulua River Valley, Honduras. Length of largest: 3½ inches. Courtesy of the Museum of the American Indian, Heye Foundation (left to right: 4/312, 18/4724, 20/3469, 4/3920, 4/3921).

b. Gold filigree ring representing an eagle, Monte Albán V, Oaxaca: Mixtec culture. Height: ⅞ inch. Courtesy of the Museum of the American Indian, Heye Foundation (16/3447).

c. Copper figurines, Michoacán: Tarascan culture. Courtesy of the Museo Nacional de Antropología, Mexico.

d. Gold necklace, Oaxaca: Mixtec culture. Length: 20 inches. Courtesy of the Museum of the American Indian, Heye Foundation (16/3451).

e. Gold labret representing jaguar head with flexible tongue, Ejutla, Oaxaca: Mixtec culture. Length: 2¼ inches. Courtesy of the Museum of the American Indian, Heye Foundation (18/756).

f. Pendant, needles, and pins of copper from graves at Tzintzuntzan, Michoacán. Courtesy of the Museo Nacional de Antropología, Mexico.

g. Copper axe hafted to wooden handle from grave at Tzintzuntzan, Michoacán. Courtesy of the Museo Nacional de Antropología, Mexico.

h. Copper tweezers, Michoacán: Tarascan culture. Courtesy of the Museo Nacional de Antropología, Mexico.

a

b

c

d

e

f

g

h

bones, demonstrate the beauty, precision, and superb craftsmanship of the Mixtec artists. The cylindrical drill had long been known, but perfection in stone working was achieved by cutting with flint, using special sands as abrasives, and polishing with wood, bone, and bamboo. No finer gold work was ever achieved in the Americas. Techniques of hammering, fusing, soldering, filigree, repoussé, overlaying of metals, and gilding were all known. The most exquisite gold work was made by the "lost wax" or *cire perdue* method.

Contrary to popular belief, metal working was not exclusively limited to jewelry. Tin and lead were known in addition to gold, silver, and copper. The extensive list of practical tools includes such items as hoes, axes, spades, chisels, helmets, awls, punches, shields, tweezers, needles, pins, and lances. We do not know to what extent bronze was used. It may have been restricted to the coastal regions of Guerrero, Nayarit, and the Tarascan region (Brush, 1969). Studies in this field are still in progress. There is no doubt, however, that the Mixtecs were very sophisticated craftsmen in the arts of metallurgy and lapidary (Plate 16b, d, e).

At the same time they made thousands of crude little human figures of stone, known as *penates*. Carved from a greenish or white stone, their features summarily indicated by straight incised lines or drilled circles, they are the antithesis of the beauty and perfection of the jewels just described. They may have been mass-produced to satisfy a large popular demand. Caso (1965a) has suggested that they might represent dead ancestors. They are very characteristic of the Mixtec period (Monte Albán V).

Talent of another kind is reflected in writing and calendrical inscriptions. The Códices Vindobonensis, Nuttall, Bodley, Colombino, Seldens and Beckers are all beautiful examples of picture writing from this area and provide nearly ten centuries of continuous history. In contrast to the Maya *códices*, for example, these deal primarily with genealogies and historical data. The writing is fundamentally symbolic and iconographic, but Caso believes there is some phonetic value associated with toponyms (place names). Many personal and place names, dates, representations of astral bodies, geographical localities, and animals can all be interpreted. Of particular interest are the prized ethnographic data provided by illustrations of houses, temples, palaces, weapons, dress, ornaments, and evidence of rank. Although these *códices* are closely related to those from Puebla–Tlaxcala, they retain a distinctive flavor. The Mixtec calendar was of the typical Mesoamerican system already described (see Chapter 5). The earlier use of a bar to represent five was replaced by both the Zapotecs and Mixtecs with dots up to thirteen (Caso, 1967).

The Mixtecs were a proud people with royal lineages and a class structure based on an intricate ranking system. At the top were a privileged kin group, the ruler who was an absolute monarch, and his immediate family. This small class of nobility was succeeded in rank by the great mass of commoners, with servants and slaves occupying the lowest positions in the social scale. Through historical sources we know that marriages were contracted to strengthen alliances and to preserve and limit prerogatives. The careful structuring of society was duplicated in each valley that formed a distinct political entity (Spores, 1967). At the time of the Conquest, one of the most important centers was Tilan-tongo. The lords of Tilantongo exercised such power that they could appoint members of their royal family to fill vacancies in certain towns where the ruling *cacique* or lord, had no legitimate offspring. This royalty was supported by farmers who produced maize, squash, beans, and chile in the bottom lands and on artificial terraces. This diet was supplemented by the gathering of wild plants, fruits, roots, and herbs and to a minor extent by hunting deer and birds.

Although the Mixtec and Zapotec cultures mingled and overlapped in certain areas of Oaxaca, each had a very individual development (Dahlgren, 1954). The Mixtecs seem to have been as secular as the Zapotecs were religious. No great center of urban life comparable to Tenochtitlán ever emerged, nor do we find any truly extensive ceremonial centers. The settlement pattern was one of rather limited valley enclaves. As there was no incentive to conquer territory, warfare was probably never more than a matter of raids and local intervillage wars. Ability in warfare was well developed nonetheless, and the Mixtecs were not easily conquered. Numerous sites, such as Diquiyú, were mountaintop settlements that served well as defensive positions. The Mixtec communities were so well known for their wealth of jewels, precious stones, plumes, and fine mantles that they made prime targets for the economically ambitious Mexica (Barlow, 1949). At one point the Mixtecs banded together with the Zapotecs to deal the Mexica a resounding defeat from a fortified hilltop near Tehuantepec, but eventually, in the fifteenth century, the greater part of the Mixteca Alta fell to the forces of Tenochtitlán. Taking Coixtlahuaca was one of Moctezuma Ilhuicamina's greatest victories; this town and Tlaxiaco were the richest of the tribute provinces in the region. Thereafter, the native rulers of the Mixteca were allowed to retain their power (Spores, 1967), but in humiliation they watched their subjects, heads bent against the weight of the tumpline, make their long journey through the mountains bearing tribute eagerly awaited in Tenochtitlán.

The Tarascans and Late Developments in the West

The western Mexican development we know most about in Late Postclassic years is the culture and empire of the Tarascans, centered at Lake Pátzcuaro and thriving at the time of the Spanish Conquest. Source material for this region is not as extensive as that for the Mexica because the conquerors of Michoacán left no personal history. Fortunately, the Spanish monarchs requested geographical and historical information about New Spain, and these records, called the "Relaciones," provide invaluable data for us. Other early sources are the traditions recorded by members of the religious orders, sixteenth-century *códices* and land titles, and references to the Tarascans in the Mexican *códices*. We know of no pre-Columbian Tarascan *códices*. The sixteenth century *codex* called the Lienzo de Jucutácato, found near Uruapan, shows definite Hispanic influence. Both a Nahua and Tarascan document, it traces a migration of peoples from Veracruz to the Valley of Mexico and hence to Zacapu and Uruapan. Eventually they split up into four groups: three went off to look for mines and one headed for the Pátzcuaro region. The basic work on the Tarascans is the *Relación de Michoacán*, believed to have been written by a Franciscan friar around 1538 (Brand, 1943; León, 1904). Reference has already been made to the Tarascans as the group that repeatedly repelled the Mexica warriors who probed their eastern frontier, undoubtedly with an eye on their fine copper and bronze tools as well as other excellent Tarascan products.

The Tarascans were people who mingled with Chichimeca and occupied the northern shores of Lake Pátzcuaro in the twelfth century, after the fall of Tula. The affinities of the Tarascan language are unknown, but some similarities have been noted with the far-flung Quechua of South America. Today the language is still spoken by the descendants of the Tarascans, who occupy the land of their forefathers, the richly endowed modern state of Michoacán. Proud of their Chichimec dynasty, the Tarascans made their capital at Tzintzuntzan on the shores of Lake Pátzcuaro. Here they constructed a huge platform on the slopes of the mountainside to support a tight row of five temple-pyramids called *yácatas*. Each *yácata* was roughly T-shaped, combining a rectangular with a circular structure, the first tier being common to all five structures (Photo 57). From this religious and administrative center, the Tarascan kings waged wars of exploitation against their neighbors from A.D. 1370 to 1522, and reputedly conquered the northwestern part of Michoacán and adjacent Jalisco, part of the *tierra caliente*, the hot lowlands of Michoacán and northwestern Guerrero. Both the Tarascans and the Mexica maintained a line of forts separating their domains. These were usually situated on hills or promontories commanding views of the rivers, and also served as signal stations. The Tarascan military expeditions were probably similar to those of the Mexica. A favorite eastern raid had as its goal the fine salt deposits of Ixtapan. Tarascans

Photo 57. Panoramic view of the giant ceremonial platform supporting five *yácatas* at Tzintzuntzan, Michoacán. Courtesy of Román Piña Chán.

were also interested in deposits of copper, gold, and silver; cinnabar; and products of the Balsas and Tepalcatepec rivers such as honey, cotton, *cacao*, feathers, hides, skins, and oleoresins like copal. It is uncertain how far south of the Balsas River the Tarascans reached, but they never crossed the Sierra Madre to the Costa Grande of Guerrero. To the north, their frontier fluctuated from time to time as they endeavored to push back the Chichimeca and Otomís. Raids reached as far west as Guadalajara, Jalisco, but the "empire" itself probably included only the lands in modern Michoacán (Brand, 1943).

Among the Tarascans, the most ancient and revered deity was the fire god Curicaueri and his feminine counterpart. These gods throve on human sacrifice, and in their honor the Tarascans drew blood from their ears and threw it into the fire. Because the sun is a great ball of fire, Curicaueri was logically the sun god too. As among the Mexica, a vast pantheon of deities is found, each with many attributes and prerogatives associated with colors, animals, directions, and certain calendrical days. We do not know the names of the Tarascan days, but we do know that at least in the area of Lake Pátzcuaro the Tonalpohualli employed symbols similar to those of the Mexica (Caso, 1967).

Today the five *yácatas* of Tzintzuntzan command a view of the lake over the mestizo pottery-making village below. Because no mortar was used in building, the interiors, formed of small slabs, easily collapse once the outer cut-stone facings are gone, making restoration work hazardous. Nonetheless, several *yácatas* have recently been reconstructed. Excavations at the site have yielded much resist-painted pottery and many stirrup handles and teapot spouts (Plate 13f), miniature tripods, and clay smoking pipes. Notched bones are also common, as are axes, copper bells, and ornaments. Although none has been found at Tzintzuntzan itself, *chacmools* form part of the Tarascan complex. The nearby site of Ihuatzio across the lake has rectangular *yácatas* and has produced some rather charming simple sculptures of coyotes rearing up on their hind legs.

Excavations by the Instituto Nacional de Antropologia e Historia in the patios of Yácata V (that is, in the angles where the round structure joins the rectangular one) revealed rich multiple burials (Rubín de la Borbolla, 1944). The five burials in the southwest patio contained female skeletons and were probably secondary graves. Offerings consisted of many miniature objects of ritual use. Some vessels had been "killed" by chipping a small hole through the bottom. Many copper objects were found, including brooches decorated with animal heads and two dangling bells, simple bells, needles, and a lip plug of rock crystal (Plate 16f). The east patio was more complex. A primary multiple grave with nine skeletons had been interred beneath a layer of stones. The arm of each skeleton was interlocked with that of his neighbor. They had been placed upon *petates*, with pottery vessels at their heads. Copper bells were found near their ankles, and copper bracelets on their wrists. Also found were long-stemmed clay smoking pipes, obsidian lip and ear plugs of incredible perfection, and a pair of silver tweezers (Plate 16h). We know from early descriptions that tweezers were customarily worn around the neck of a priest. Another body was buried with a copper axe hafted to a wooden handle, which was partially preserved by the oxidation of the copper (Plate 16g). Two gold earrings, simply made and bearing one flat square pendant, were found with this skeleton. In more recent excavations multiple graves with objects of obsidian, gold, rock crystal, and turquoise were recovered in the patio of Yácata IV.

How can we account for these simultaneous burials, in which several bodies were interred with distinctive goods? The descriptions of the colorful funeral services of a Tarascan king in the *Relación de Michoacán* (León, 1904) and the writings of Torquemada (1943) provide a reasonable answer. When the king died, we read, he was washed and clothed elegantly. His ankles were adorned with gold bells, his wrists with bracelets of turquoise, and his head with an elaborate jeweled and plumed headdress. He also wore elegant necklaces and ear plugs of gold. Two gold bracelets were tied on his arms and a green lip plug put in place. The body then was placed on a platform and attention turned to selecting those who were to accompany him in the next world. According to law, when the king died, those servants that were to attend him in the hereafter must also die. They were selected by the new king from both sexes. Seven women were chosen to occupy the following positions: chamber maid or jewel keeper, caretaker of the lip plugs, server of drinks, caretaker of water for washing hands, the cook, and her servants. The men to be killed were more numerous: caretaker of clothes, hairdresser, garland weaver, chair carrier, woodcutter, adventurer, shoemaker, incense carrier, boat oarman, boatman, doorman for the king and doorman for the women, feather worker, silversmith, custodian of the bows and arrows, two or three mountain climbers, several doctors, storyteller, musicians, and dancers. It is said that all these people offered to die willingly and volunteered spontaneously. It may well be that they felt treatment at the hands of their chief in the next world would be preferable to that offered by his successor in this one.

Precisely at midnight the bier was brought out of the palace, preceded by all those who were to perish. They wore garlands of flowers on their heads and played crocodile bones on turtle shells. Amid many lights, the trumpets and shells sounded, the tones mingling with voices raised in song. Those who did not take part in the ceremonies were busy sweeping and cleaning off the paths leading to the patios of the temple, where the bier was placed on a huge pyre of dry wood. While the king burned, all his future servants were killed. First they were intoxicated to remove the fear of death, and then were killed with clubs and knives of wood edged with obsidian. They were buried behind the temple with all their adornments, jewels, and instruments. By sunrise the great bier had been reduced to ashes, and all the jewels and precious stones that had escaped the fire were bound up together with the bones and, adorned with a mask and gold shield, were placed inside a large funeral urn. This was set on a wooden couch in a tomb decorated with very fine *petates* and surrounded by many *ollas* and jars filled with food and drink. Fine cloaks and robes were thrown on top, and the rest of the tomb was filled in with bundles of feathers and ornaments worn by the king during festivities. Finally the tomb was carefully covered over with beams and planks.

The account does not say where the tombs were located, but they still await discovery somewhere at Tzintzuntzan. The retainers who were "buried in the patios behind the temples" are in all likelihood the multiple burials. Instead of graves, excavations of other patios have yielded remains of walls and earlier structures. A cemetery with primary graves with much more modest offerings was located on a lower hillside.

Secondary burial (that is, bones interred after decomposition of the flesh) and cremation were also practiced at Tzintzuntzan.

When the Spaniards were making their way up to Tenochtitlán, the Mexica sent some emissaries to the Tarascans to ask for aid. The latter, not knowing what to do, solved this dilemma by sacrificing the visitors. Later, when Tenochtitlán lay in ruins, they belatedly questioned their hasty actions. When their own turn came to face the Spaniards in A.D. 1522, the last Tarascan king, Tangaxoan II, offered little resistance.

The Tarascans are probably representative of many groups of Meso-americans at the time of the Conquest. They left no evidence of truly urban centers, yet they undoubtedly had a structured society with nobil-ity, commoners, and slaves; craft specialization; and commercial in-terests. We do not know of any ports of trade in this area, but exploitation of the hot country was important to them. Of their material goods, we would like to know where they found the inspiration for their stirrup-spouted handles on pottery vessels and their advanced techniques of metallurgy. Some of the answers may be provided by the coastal regions, where many influences converged.

The vast amount of gold reported by the chroniclers from western Mexico has never been substantiated archaeologically. From numerous field seasons at Tzintzuntzan some gold jewelry and tweezers were found, but gold is even more rare at other western Mexican sites. Rather, copper ornaments and tools are found in quantity. Gilding of copper has been reported from Tzintzuntzan (Rubín de la Borbolla, 1944) and from Amapa, Nayarit (Pendergast, 1962a), and now some artifacts from Michoacán have proved to be bronze. The addition of tin to copper makes it yellowish in appearance, which, together with gilding, may account for the widespread reports of gold in the sixteenth century.

Quantities of metal have been found near Zihuatanejo on the coast of Guerrero. The finds consist of hundreds of open rings, often hooked together in jumbles, along with bells, thin sheets of gold, a grey metal resembling silver, and two pieces of slag. Ellen and Charles Brush ex-cavated nearby at the Barnard site and recovered metal associated with polychrome pottery and large quantities of *malacates*. They believe the site to have been occupied briefly just after A.D. 900 (Brush, 1969).

Analysis of the metal shows that much of it is bronze, probably deliberately compounded of copper and tin alloy. Tumbaga, an alloy of copper and gold, was also found, the only sample known outside Oaxaca. The bronze was recovered from household refuse, an indication that it was not a luxury product. We do not yet know how extensively bronze was used in Mexico, but upon analysis some "copper" objects from Michoacán have proved to be bronze. Should this account for the renowned superiority of the Tarascans in warfare, it might imply that the knowledge of bronze was restricted. Chunks of slag found at the Barnard site indicate that smelting was performed on the spot. There are traces of silver, copper, tin, and gold, and alloyed ores do exist in the region.

Amapa, Nayarit, was another metal-working center active by A.D. 900. A great variety of artifacts have been recovered including fishhooks, ear spools, axes, awls, knives, pins, needles, numerous kinds of bells, and plaques. Located about thirty miles from the Pacific Coast on the north bank of the Santiago River, Amapa would have been as accessible to commerce by sea as coastal Guerrero.

Metal artifacts in Mesoamerica have been studied in depth by Pendergast (1962a, b), who has suggested some patterning in their distribution. Two areas seem to have functioned as primary metal-working centers. One was the southern Maya region, which influenced other Maya groups as well as southern, eastern, and central Mexico. A second center, in western Mexico, included coastal Nayarit and Guerrero, from where the art is believed to have spread rapidly to central Mexico, in particular to areas in the far north reaching into the southwestern United States. The inhabitants of the Oaxaca region, able craftsmen though they were, apparently had less influence on surrounding areas than might be expected.

The concept of metal working was understood in these areas by A.D. 900 and became widespread in Mesoamerica shortly thereafter. This is considerably later than in South America, where the knowledge was well advanced by A.D. 300. Although specific resemblances have been pointed out between Amapa artifacts and some from Ecuador, others can be found with Central America. The almost simultaneous appearance of metal-working centers in the southern Maya area and on the Pacific coast of Mexico lends support to maritime travel as the means of introduction.

Another area of western Mexico, known largely from the excavation of one site, is the Tepalcatepec basin, lying northwest of Guerrero in the *tierra caliente* of Michoacán. This area, somewhat isolated from others discussed, lies in a depression bordered by the escarpment of the highland plateau on the north and the mountains of the Sierra Madre del Sur on the south. Here, at Apatzingán, Kelly (1947) identified a sequence of cultural remains chronologically extending from Classic to Conquest times. Ring stands, *molcajetes*, resist painting, pyrite mirrors, and copper smelting are widespread Postclassic Mesoamerican features, but in addition Apatzingán has a distinctive local flavor that isolates it in many ways from Tarascan sites and the Jalisco–Colima complex. Now, more than twenty-five years after the publication of the Apatzingán report, there is little archaeological knowledge that can be added, a fact that emphasizes the need for intensive field work in western Mexico.

Other Kingdoms

Although the Aztec, Mixtec, and Tarascan states were largest and most powerful at the time of the Conquest, smaller, less well-defined kingdoms, located east and south of the Valley of Mexico (see Map 4, Chapter 7), existed. It is by no means clear how much autonomy or political unity these areas enjoyed, but they do not appear to have paid tribute to Tenochtitlán.

The history of the Puebla region is intimately tied to events in the basin of Mexico as well as to the Spanish Conquest itself. Tlaxcala was as traditionally the good friend of Texcoco as it was the enemy of Tenochtitlán. Therefore, the rise of Tenochtitlán in the Triple Alliance naturally increased the hostility of the latter toward Tlaxcala.

Although Tlaxcala was the dominant center in the Valley of Puebla at the time of the Conquest, the towns of Huexotzingo and Cholula were earlier leaders. The independent kingdom of Tlaxcala therefore should be remembered as possessing three centers, with a very old history that reached back to the time of Teotihuacán supremacy. Cholula, once dominated by the Olmeca-Xicalanca, who were thrown out by the Tolteca-Chichimeca, was at one time the leading political and mercantile power in the area. Huexotzingo eventually conquered Cholula in A.D. 1359 and retained its position of strength until the reign of Moctezuma Ilhuicamina. After the long and bitter war over Chalco in the Valley of Mexico, many people from Chalco took refuge in Huexotzinco, contributing to its importance. In the wars of Mexica expansion that resulted in the isolation of the Tlaxcala–Huexotzinco area, these refugees did not take a firm stand or active role, but encouraged other towns to resist the Mexica.

Gradually Tlaxcala emerged as the most important center in Puebla and actively engaged Tenochtitlán in battle. How was it possible for such a small group to maintain its independence? Partial explanation has already been given (see page 263), from the viewpoint of the Mexica. As for Tlaxcala itself, the economic problems created by its isolation did not greatly affect its effectiveness in warfare because few imports were needed. It is also possible that the Mexica encirclement was not as effective on the eastern side as on the west. There is some evidence that around the time of the Conquest Mexica patience was finally wearing thin and that they were actually attempting to strangle Tlaxcalan independence and complete their domination of the Puebla–Tlaxcala *altiplano*.

Two other kingdoms lay north and south of Tlaxcala (Byam Davies, 1968). To the north lay Meztitlán, a region embracing parts of the modern states of Puebla, Tlaxcala, Hidalgo, and Veracruz. The invasion of the Mexica divided the area into two parts, Meztitlán and Tototepec. It was a region rich in agricultural land but poor in salt.

To the south lay Yopitzinco, which, unlike Meztitlán with its two centers or Tlaxcala with three, was more like a confederation of tribes with no true urban settlements. Located in the harsh, mountainous environment of Oaxaca and Guerrero, it is believed to be the homeland of that famous deity Xipe Totec (Caso & Bernal, 1952) (Figure 32; Photo 55). Perhaps the region had some special religious and traditional significance for the Mexica, which could have been a factor in maintaining its autonomy.

In contrast, Tototepec del Sur, with well-defined borders and single capital, had greater cohesion as an independent kingdom. Both Toltec and Mixtec influences met and mingled in this coastal region of Oaxaca, the childhood home of the famous Mixtec king, Eight Deer. The Codex Nuttall depicts scenes from his youth in a temple and ball court of Tototepec, which can be identified by the accompanying name glyph. Apparently the region reached its greatest extension in the years between the Toltec and Mexica supremacies. After the Mixtecs formed a confederation following the rule of Eight Deer, Tototepec established itself as a separate kingdom. Its boundaries were reduced as a result of Mexica expansion, but it retained its independence.

The political status of Teotitlán del Camino, an area lying between Oaxaca and Tlaxcala, is not clear. It may have been subject to the Mexica yoke at the time of the Conquest. Support for this belief comes from the Mexica themselves, who traditionally invited their enemies to Tenochtitlán on special occasions to witness great sacrifices. As Teotitlán del Camino was not included in the invitations, it already may have been subservient to the Mexica (Byam Davies, 1968).

I N VIEWING MESOAMERICA AS A MAJOR CULTURE AREA IN
the New World and the northern center of Nuclear America, one
should note that its boundaries did not function as cultural barriers and
that contacts were maintained with neighboring areas. The reverse is
often the unfortunate impression given by culture area maps in which
boundaries of necessity are clearly and decisively drawn. Such maps
have the advantage of facilitating the grouping of tribes and concen-
trating or clustering traits for study, but they do not reflect the blending
of cultures that takes place in peripheral regions.

In this chapter, the relationship of Mesoamerica to neighboring
cultures is briefly summarized, followed by comparative comments on
more distant regions. In so few pages, the complex question of diffusion,
and the processes and implications involved, cannot be adequately
treated. Scarcely more than a few similarities and possible inferences
can be presented. The aim is to give some perspective to Mesoamerica
within the total context of New World cultures rather than to abandon
its cultural history at the sixteenth-century frontiers. Mesoamerican
studies should not be bounded by these limitations, and it is becoming
increasingly clear that the civilization of Mesoamerica needs to be
viewed in the broader context of New and Old World cultures in order
to understand its evolutionary development.

Mesoamerica and the Southwestern United States

It has already been pointed out that no great gap existed between the
cultures of northwestern Mesoamerica and southwestern United States.
Between 7000 and 5000 B.C. these two areas shared features of the
Desert preceramic cultural tradition and were probably indistinguishable. It was after 5000 B.C. that peoples of Mesoamerica began to culti-
vate plants such as the bottle gourd, squash, corn, cotton, and beans,
their appearance antedating that in the Southwest. *Chapalote* maize
reached the Southwest as early as 3000 B.C. and was introduced to the
ancestral people of the Mogollon culture. The impact was hardly
noticeable, however, for sedentary villages did not grow up among the
desert people of the Hohokam in the arid basin-and-range lowlands of
Arizona until *teocinte* was added and a hybrid form of maize produced
that could grow at lower elevations and in more arid regions. This event
took place around 100 B.C. or slightly earlier. At the same time the
sedentary Mogollon people of the semiarid mountains of southeastern
Arizona and southwestern New Mexico were making pottery and
figurines, also inspired by their high-culture southern neighbors. The
Hohokam culture could have derived its knowledge of pottery making
and village farming either from the Mogollon or from a separate Mexican
stimulus. However the introduction of diffused ideas took place, it was
the Hohokam rather than Mogollon peoples who ultimately manifested

the strongest and most enduring ties with Mesoamerica. Excellent discussions of the relationships between these cultures and areas are to be found in the publications by Jennings (1968), J. C. Kelley (1956, 1960, 1966), Sears (1964), Sociedad Mexicana de Antropología (1944), and Willey (1966).

There were two main routes by which we believe that people, ideas, and artifacts might have made contact. One path lies along the Pacific coastal plain of Nayarit and Sinaloa to Sonora, where the river drainage pattern could be followed northward to southwestern United States. The other lies along the eastern slopes of the Sierra Madre Occidental range, which was occupied by farming communities of the Chalchihuites and Canutillo cultures. Although these western regions are not considered to form part of Mesoamerica proper until the Postclassic period, they were important as transmitters of culture traits.

Opinions vary regarding the process by which diffusion took place. Large direct group migration, small sporadic group contacts, trade excursions, and individual journeys have all been suggested as mechanisms. Probably various patterns, involving both direct and indirect diffusion, were employed, because these two routes seem to have been used for a very long period of time.

The coastal route may have been the first used. There are some vague similarities between the San Blas complex of Nayarit and the Pioneer period of the Hohokam in pottery decoration (or lack of it), clay human figurines, and stone ornaments (Mountjoy, 1970). There may well be other such estuary settlements to the north that will reveal a greater extension of Preclassic population in this region.

Inland along the eastern edge of the Sierra Madre Occidental, farming villages of the Chalchihuites and Canutillo cultures stretched in an unbroken line northward from Zacatecas, Durango, and Chihuahua, providing a kind of cultural corridor for the movement of trade items and ideas. Because the whole region shared the same basic environment, the diffusion of cultigens would have been very easy. The southwestern cultures of the United States were located at the northern end of this route.

Following A.D. 600 Mesoamerican flavor is seen in Hohokam design motifs such as positive- and negative-painted small animals, simple and interlocking plain and fringed scroll designs, quadrant bowl interior patterns, vessel supports, and basket handles, but perhaps above all in the red-on-buff pottery itself. Other such items include stone bowls, mortars, three-quarter grooved and polished stone axes, troughed *metates*, shell work, conch-shell trumpets, and turquoise mosaics. The ball game and ball courts, mosaic pyrite mirrors, *chacmool*-like figures carved in stone, and cotton weaving are further evidence of Mesoamerican influence, along with platform mounds of earth and adobe. The copper bells are Mesoamerican in shape and were manufactured by the "lost wax" method of casting. In view of the early tradition of metal working at Amapa, Nayarit (Mountjoy, 1969; Pendergast, 1962a), the coastal route would have been the most logical for the diffusion of these copper bells, which arrived in the Southwest by A.D. 1000. Hohokam canal irrigation may be a local development and is not necessarily derived from Mesoamerica.

It will be remembered that around A.D. 900 coastal Sinaloa was the center of the extraordinary Aztatlán development, which reflects a close relationship with the central Mexican Mixteca-Puebla cult (Ekholm, 1942). During the Aztatlán horizon the Anasazi southwestern expansion took place, bringing the two groups closer together and thus facilitating interaction (Kelley & Winters, 1960).

Many Mesoamerican motifs—life forms and mythological beings such as ceremonial mural art with birds, masked dancers, eagle men, stylized plumed serpents, sun symbols, crosses, and feathers—are very significant features in the Southwest. It has been suggested that the *katchina* ceremonialism (*katchinas* were supernatural beings of the pueblos of southwestern United States) may have been introduced from Mesoamerica as a variant of the Tlaloc cult (Kelley, 1966). It is difficult to trace specific sources in this case, since the Aztatlán complex shared many features of the Chalchihuites cultures to the east, and both of these in turn were related to cultures further south. Somewhere in western Mexico the stirrup-spout bottle is believed to have lingered on after its early occurrences in Colima, at Tlatilco and, later, Chupícuaro. Its appearance in the Anasazi cultures of the Southwest is believed to be the result of diffusion out of Mesoamerica. Eventually the form traveled eastward, via the Arkansas River trade route, where it became popular among late cultures in the Mississippi Valley after A.D. 1200 (Ford, 1969).

The Puebloan Southwest developed a rich style of its own, which grew out of an infiltration of Mesoamerican ceremonialism with concepts of fire, sun, and a twin war god associated with an early Quetzalcóatl and a basic rain fertility cult.

Around A.D. 1350 the Guasave phase on coastal Sinaloa collapsed and disappeared, and the inland Chalchihuites cultures rapidly followed suit. In the Southwest, the Pueblo cultures retreated, and in the intermediate area of southern New Mexico, Arizona, and Sonora, a cultural and geographic hiatus developed that had not existed previously. This resulted in the virtual isolation of the Pueblo cultures. As we have seen, it was at this time also that Mesoamerica turned its attention to the east and south under Mexica leadership.

It is therefore particularly interesting that the Casas Grandes culture in the northwestern part of Chihuahua close to the border of New Mexico reached such extraordinary complexity after A.D. 1300. As the fertile Casas Grandes valley parallels the main range of the Sierra Madre Occidental, the mountains provided useful natural resources for valley farmers who settled along the rivers. Here one could find stands of pine to be used for building and fuel, quartz and sandstone to be quarried, natural outcroppings of raw copper, and white kaolin deposits to make fine pottery. Deer and turkeys were hunted, the latter sometimes kept in pens in the valleys (Di Peso, 1966).

Of the three main periods of development at Casas Grandes, Mesoamerica exerted a strong influence only in the last one. Prior to A.D. 1000 the Viejo period inhabitants were in contact with southwestern peoples as seen in their pit-house dwellings, pottery, and the *kiva* or underground ceremonial chamber. In the succeeding Medio period, grave goods were more plentiful, the people commonly being buried beneath the house floors, and polychrome pottery was added to earlier styles. The population probably increased during this time, for the water systems were more elaborate, now including irrigation canals and subterranean drains. Towards the end, a building boom resulted in the erection of walls and stairs, with the ceremonial *kiva* retaining its importance.

However, Casas Grandes reached its maximum complexity after A.D. 1300 in the Tardio period. A number of Mesoamerican features suddenly appeared—I-shaped ball courts, platform mounds, truncated pyramids, town courts, and round stone houses, and human sacrifices—presenting a startling new orientation with a Mesoamerican flavor. The plumed-serpent motif, copper bells, and needles also may have been Mexican-derived. But Casas Grandes also exhibits some non-Mesoamerican characteristics during this period. An extraordinary polychrome pottery produced in abundance was probably locally inspired, while the multiroomed and multistoried dwellings have their closest parallel among the southwestern Anasazi people. Di Peso (1966) suggests that the Mesoamerican influence could have resulted from a take-over by a powerful religious group from central Mexico. It is also possible, however, that inhabitants of the Mimbres region to the north migrated south to Casas Grandes, and subsequently were heavily influenced by Mesoamerica (Willey, 1966). At the height of prosperity, Casas Grandes, with its master building plan, religious architecture, specialized labor, and intricate water system and communication network, ranks as the most powerful center of the northern mountain area. Its natural resources and strategic location in northwestern Chihuahua could have established Casas Grandes as a major trading center. Surely its influence was far reaching and has yet to be fully understood.

In the final phase of its pre-Columbian history, a rapid architectural decline took place at Casas Grandes, manifested by makeshift and flimsy construction, which was followed by razing and burning. Although located in a region intermediate between Mesoamerica and southwestern United States, this site apparently had little contact with Mesoamerica until the Tardio period, which would make it too late to have been a factor in the earlier diffusion of Mesoamerican traits to the Hohokam peoples. Casas Grandes rightfully belongs to the cultural sphere of the southwestern United States.

Thus far, we have dealt largely with the diffusion of Mesoamerican influence to the north and west. What if anything, did the southwestern United States area contribute to Mesoamerica? One possibility is the domesticated turkey, which appears earlier in this region than in Mesoamerica, where our first record of it is found in the Palo Blanco phase of the Tehuacán Valley (MacNeish, 1967). Another interesting possibility is the smoking pipe. Conical stone pipes were smoked on the California coast as long ago as 4000 B.C., the earliest documented evidence of pipe smoking in the Americas (Switzer, 1969). From here the use of pipes diffused into the Great Basin and into the Southwest where they attained great popularity. Tubular basalt pipes have been found in pit houses in western New Mexico in the Pine Lawn Valley as early as 500–400 B.C. Although clay smoking pipes are largely a Postclassic feature in Mesoamerica, the antiquity of Mexican smoking pipes is difficult to trace owing to the possible existence of perishable early instruments. At the present time, the southwestern United States is at least as likely a source of clay smoking pipes as any other.

Whatever the origin of the smoking pipe, it is entirely possible that many of the religious beliefs and concepts surrounding the ceremonialism of pipe smoking entered the southwest from Mexico. The Tlalocs and their assistants, the Tlaloques, closely parallel the Pueblo rain chiefs, who also were concerned with rainmaking and identified with mountain tops. Switzer (1969) believes that some of the Mexican religious concepts could have spread to areas of southwestern United States at a very early time, along with corn and squash. This supposition in no way conflicts with the history of the smoking pipe since there is no necessary correlation of the spread of agriculture and the use of tobacco for chewing and smoking.

Mesoamerica and the Eastern Cultures of the United States

Peoples of eastern United States also felt the impact of the strong neighboring civilizations during both the Woodland and Mississippi traditions, and possibly even as early as the Late Archaic period (Griffin, 1966; Jennings, 1968; Ford, 1969; Willey, 1966).

Prior to 8000 B.C. these eastern peoples shared the hunting tradition of other North American groups, but thereafter a shift can be seen in which local groups exploited their immediate environments in a pattern much like that of Mesoamerica's Tehuacán and Tamaulipas cave dwellers. The earliest pottery from southeastern United States is a crude, fiber-tempered ware, dated at about 2400 B.C. It was found at a site on the Georgia coast called the Stallings Island complex. The shapes and decorations of these vessels have some parallels in the very early Valdivia pottery of coastal Ecuador. Ford (1969) has speculated that the resemblances are the result of contact with maritime voyagers who made their way along the eastern coast of Panama and, aided by the Gulf Stream, were able to navigate through the straits of Yucatán and Florida to the Georgia coast. According to Ford, another settlement, the Orange complex, located some 150 miles south of Stallings Island on the Florida coast, likewise is related to Ecuador. The first possible Mesoamerican influence is reflected in pottery made after 1300 B.C., when wide, flat rims on flat-based vessels are found in the early Atlantic coastal sites. These early features are also shared with northern South America.

About this time the Olmecs rose to prominence in Mesoamerica, and some of their influence could have reached the lower Mississippi Valley soon after 1200 B.C. The curious site of Poverty Point appears to have been occupied from 1300 to 200 B.C. Mesoamerican-type *manos* and *metates* have been found, and these, together with material from the inland living sites, provide indirect evidence of maize cultivation. Earth mounds forming concentric ridges are located eight degees left of the true cardinal directions, an orientation paralleled by construction at the Olmec sites of La Venta and Laguna de los Cerros. The long prismatic flakes struck from prepared cores found at these sites are objects unparalleled in Mesoamerica, but the work in jaspar is much like the Olmec lapidary art in jade. Both cultures share unzoned rocker stamping and the *tecomate* vessel form. Despite careful excavations, Poverty Point is still hard to fit into the more general scheme of southeastern archaeology (Ford, 1969; Jennings, 1968).

As this early period, sometimes called Archaic, blends into the early Woodland culture, exemplified by the Baumer and Red Ocher sites in Illinois and Tchefuncte in Louisiana, pottery making and construction of burial mounds became very widespread. Wicke (1965) interprets the latter as being Mesoamerican inspired. The cord-marked, rocker-stamped, zone-decorated Woodland pottery is often seen as the result of stimulation from northeastern Siberia, although it also resembles pottery found in some Middle Preclassic Mesoamerican sites. Scandanavia has been proposed as an alternate source of this Woodland pottery, as the pottery was found at an appropriate chronological depth (Kehoe, 1962). The perplexing possibility of outside stimulation on these eastern cultures therefore remains very much open at the present time.

By 1000 B.C. attention shifts to the Woodland cultures of the Ohio River Valley and Great Lakes area. Both mound building and maize agriculture seem to have preceded pottery making in this area. A carbonized ear of maize from an Adena burial in Ohio has been dated with radiocarbon at 280 B.C. Also found in the Adena remains was skeletal material showing the intrusion of a brachycephalic population that practiced occipital and frontooccipital head deformation. Here a direct migration of peoples from the south, possibly even from Central America, is implied, for earlier eastern populations were dolichocephalic. Other traits that may have diffused northward from Mesoamerica are the celt axe form, perhaps conical mounds over cremations on floors (which has some parallel at La Venta), sandstone saws, bird motifs, and ear spools. Flat tablets (stamps?) and finger rings probably should also be included.

The Hopewell culture replaced that of Adena and flourished until A.D. 300. It spread over a large area but most significantly southward, to Louisiana and Mississippi. Though somewhat retarded, Olmec influence can be found even here, in such traits as the bent-knee stance of figures, burial of green stone celts, and tombs made of logs that are similar to the basalt column tombs of La Venta and the log tombs of Kaminaljuyú. Pan pipes and blades struck from prepared cores represent further southern influence. As noted above, the rocker-stamped pottery of this culture need not be derived from Mesoamerica. Indeed, it more closely resembles the ceramics with zoned stamping of the Chavín horizon in Peru, or may even stem from entirely different Siberian or Scandanavian traditions (Jennings, 1968).

From a southern Hopewellian manifestation called Marksville emerged the Mississipian culture, in which the peoples of the eastern United States after A.D. 600 attained their greatest complexity of development. Although its geographic center lay along the Mississippi Valley from Natchez, Mississippi, to St. Louis, Missouri, related cultures extended from Oklahoma to Florida and Georgia and north to Michigan. Temple-pyramids, enlarged many times, were found grouped around plazas in a layout familiar to every student of Mesoamerica. This period is well described and summarized by Jennings (1968).

Of particular interest to us is the wave of Mesoamerican influence that can be recognized in this culture around A.D. 900 or 1000. Contact is believed to have been made via the overland route rather than through coastal settlements, although Wicke (1965) thinks that maritime contacts are a good possibility. That contact was made is generally conceded, but the circumstances under which it took place are largely speculative. The areas lying between northeastern Mexico and Texas were poorly suited for early agriculture, and there was no uniform environmental corridor of farming peoples uniting the areas, as we have just noted in the case of northwestern Mexico and southwestern United States. Nevertheless, the most likely overland route passed from northern Mexico across Texas and eastward to the Mississippi Valley. The Gulf Coast would not have offered a useful route as the shore line consists of mud flats and sand dunes, and could not have supported a year-round occupation of peoples.

A number of Mexican artifacts have been recovered in the area between Mesoamerica and southeastern United States, but these are usually isolated discoveries without any associations and are difficult to place chronologically. One of the most significant features shared by both regions was an engraved pottery design into which red paint was rubbed. This technique was centered in the so-called Caddoan area that extended from eastern Oklahoma to the Mississippi Valley and is believed to be the result of contact with Mesoamerican peoples around A.D. 700–900, in the early part of the Mississippi period, which lasted until the seventeenth century.

The Mississippi period after A.D. 900 is probably the best-known eastern culture. An intensive agricultural village life with temples and mounds arranged around a central plaza reflects the typical Mesoamerican pattern. This configuration is almost certainly related to new agricultural developments. A number of traits attributed to Mesoamerica are found in this Mississippi tradition. The most outstanding features relevant to this discussion have been outlined by Griffin (1966) and are briefly reviewed here.

Negative painting as a decorative technique was known earlier but only became common in the period from A.D. 1000 to 1500. In Mexico its long history currently dates back to 1200 B.C. (Tolstoy & Paradis, 1970). The eastern examples most closely resemble those of Mesoamerica's Late Classic and Early Postclassic periods, which would be chronologically compatible with the influx of other Mesoamerican features. For example, tooth mutilation was common in Classic and Postclassic Mesoamerica, and occurs after A.D. 1000 in Illinois. Some very close parallels in art styles are seen in the combination of skull–hand–heart and long-bone motifs relating to the religious and ceremonial ideology of Postclassic Mesoamerica. The Southeast Ceremonial complex, dated at A.D. 1000–1400, contains many features of this nature. Perhaps ties were strongest of all during the Early Postclassic period, when the Toltec peoples were more concerned with the northern frontier and peripheral regions than the succeeding Mexica. The Toltecs also smoked tobacco in pottery pipes, and during their day pipe smoking was taken up by certain groups in Mesoamerica. The smoking of pipes has a long history among eastern peoples of the United States, and the chronological distribution of pipes suggests this region as a source for their diffusion to Mesoamerica (Griffin, 1966). Another possibility, as we have seen, could have been southwestern United States. Cord-marked pottery may represent a very late diffusion from the area of the United States to Mexico. Although some examples have been reported from Soconusco and Veracruz at a very early time (M. D. Coe, 1961), it was never important in Mesoamerica until the Aztec period.

In Late Mississippi cultures, the shoe-shaped vessel and stirrup-spout bottle occur, the latter having been ultimately derived from Mesoamerica via the Southwest (Ford, 1969). There are undoubtedly many more specific resemblances that could be mentioned, but the most significant contribution of Mesoamerica to this area was the knowledge of agriculture and the religious and cultural ideas associated with it, which were reflected in the material culture. The result, however, was not the spread of Mesoamerican civilization, but the emergence of a distinctive pattern of southeastern cultures that chose a very different life style.

The Caribbean

Despite the fact that Yucatán is located only 120 miles from Cuba, there is scant evidence to suggest that much contact occurred between these two regions prior to the arrival of the Spanish. It is believed that the Lesser and Greater Antilles were largely populated from various parts of northern South America, and archaeological evidence indicates that the closest ties were with mainland Venezuela. In the reconstruction of Caribbean history it is a significant fact that the remnants of the earliest and simplest inhabitants, the Ciboney, are found on the westernmost tip of Cuba, which geographically lies closest to Mesoamerica. More complex cultures, those of the Arawak and later Carib, are found in the central region, and on the islands of Hispaniola and Puerto Rico.

Should Ford (1969) prove to be correct, sea-going travel has a very long history among aboriginal Americans. We know that the Caribs had fine canoes, and that Arawak canoes were outfitted with sails and oars and carried forty to fifty people. Mesoamericans also had the technical knowledge to make long voyages, for we know that merchant ships skirted the eastern coastline and transported merchandise to and from Xicalanco from ports in Yucatán and Honduras. Despite this knowledge of navigation, neither archaeological studies nor early written sources lead us to believe that contacts were either regular or frequent between the Caribbean islands and the Mesoamerican mainland.

The Chilam Balam of Chumayel (Roys, 1933) mentions that some unclothed strangers arrived in Yucatán about 1359 "looking for people to eat." Occasionally a ship strayed off its course, and sporadic shipwrecks were inevitable. Such accidents would account for the presence of a Jamaican Indian girl found on the island of Cozumel by the Spaniards in A.D. 1518. She told of strong currents that had swept a fishing group off course two years earlier, carrying their canoe west to Cozumel, where all the men ended up on the sacrificial block.

Pertinent archaeological evidence pointing to possible contact revolves around a discussion of maize agriculture, *metates* and *manos*, and the ball game, hammock, and certain religious beliefs (Rouse, 1966). Although maize was grown by the Arawak, it was not the staple crop of the islands and was always second in importance to manioc. The Arawak preferred roasting ears of corn in the fire to the Mesoamerican method of preparation, which was based on soaking it in lime water overnight to be subsequently ground on the *metate* and made into tortillas. The *metates* and *manos* found in Cuba, Jamaica, and Puerto Rico resemble those of southern Central America more than Mesoamerican ones. If Mexico was the source of Caribbean maize, it probably reached them via Central America and northern South America.

The best evidence of direct contact is provided by the ball game. Arawak courts were not bordered by elaborate stone construction as in Mesoamerica, but they did outline courts with earth or slab walls, which was not done in South America. Ekholm (1961) has argued convincingly that Arawak stone "collars" and "elbow stones" were in all probability used as protective ball-game belts, in much the same way as the Mexican "yokes." The presence of these belts and the delineation of courts supports direct diffusion as the means of introduction. On the other hand, the game itself was played more like that of the modern Arawak of the Orinoco Valley, thus providing some basis for the postulated introduction of the game into the Antilles via South America.

The hammock may well be a Caribbean import to Mesoamerica, either directly or indirectly through Central American peoples. It is hard to ascertain when the hammock was introduced into Yucatán, but its pre-Columbian presence is documented by a painting on a Late Classic Maya vase that shows a chief in a jaguar-skin hammock.

Rouse (1966) believes that the best ties between the two areas in the fields of religion and social organization are yet to be found. However, it does not seem likely that the Caribbean and Mesoamerican peoples ever maintained contact to any significant degree. This may not be true in the case of South America.

The Intermediate and Andean Culture Areas

South of Mesoamerica, a blending of its culture with that of its neighbors took place, primarily in the last centuries before the Spanish Conquest. We have historical evidence of the late migration of Náhuatl-speaking peoples into Central America, and therefore it comes as no surprise to find there stylistic resemblances in pottery, the spread of Mexican religious beliefs, and the use of *cacao* as a media of exchange. More significant relationships, which may have been basic to the development of Mesoamerica, are found much further south and are much earlier in time.

Many years ago, Spinden (1917) postulated the existence of an early "archaic" culture that spread from Mexico to the Andean area and involved such shared traits as maize agriculture, pottery, and clay figurines. At that time, it was felt that the area of initial maize domestication would also prove to be the heartland of the other features, which together formed a complex that spread throughout this vast geographical area. Now we know that maize was not the first cultivated plant, but probably had multiple origins, and that in the case of Mesoamerica, cultivated plants preceded pottery making by several thousand years. Still, in one way Spinden's vision of a common "archaic" (now called Preclassic or Formative) period may have been prophetic, for indeed it is during this horizon, prior to A.D. 300, that the greatest evidence of contact and most pronounced similarities among centers of Nuclear America are to be found. The following discussion is based on recent writings of Meggers (Meggers *et al.*, 1965), Reichel-Dolmatoff (1965), Lanning (1967), Lathrap (1966, 1970), Willey (1962b, 1971a), Grove (1971), and Ford (1969), all of whom have studied this problem.

The most important Preclassic or Formative sites in these areas for which we have reliable chronological information are the following, listed from north to south:

Panama: Monagrillo, a shell midden on the Pacific coast of Panama on the Parita peninsula (2140 B.C.) (Willey & McGimsey, 1954).
Colombia: Puerto Hormiga, east coast between the Magdalena and Sinú rivers (3000 B.C.); nearby Momíl (600 B.C. to A.D. 1) (Reichel-Dolmatoff, 1965).
Ecuador: Valdivia, coastal site on the Guayas peninsula (3000 B.C.); Machalilla phases at nearby coastal sites (2000–1500 B.C.); Chorrera phase sites located along rivers, inland on the Guayas Peninsula (1500–500 B.C.) (Meggers *et al.*, 1965).
Peru: coastal sites: Guañape, Las Haldas, and Asia (1500 B.C.); Cupisnique, Ancon (900 B.C.) (Lanning, 1967).

highland sites: Waira-jirca Kotosh (1800–600 B.C.) (Izumi & Sono, 1963); Chavín de Huantar (900 B.C.) (Bennett, 1944).

eastern lowland sites: Tutishcainyo (1800 B.C.) (Lathrap, 1958, 1970).

It is interesting to note that all except Kotosh and Tutishcainyo are coastal or near-coastal sites, a fact that may not be entirely the result of archaeological sampling but may reflect early settlement patterns. It has long been felt that in Early Preclassic times the general direction of influence flowed predominately from north to south, that is, from Mesoamerica to South America. However, according to the present records, pottery making and certain pottery forms and decorations appear earliest in northwestern South America. With the finding of early maize in the highlands of Peru in dry caves near Ayacucho (MacNeish, 1969), early animal domestication, and a semisedentary existence, we recognize a familiar pattern roughly paralleling that of the Tehuacán Valley. Just as each ecosystem in Mesoamerica was developing its own program of exploitation of resources and cultivation of local plants, so throughout Nuclear America there must have been any number of local cultures responding in a variety of ways to their environmental potentials. Because of the great distances between the small village communities of this period, it is all the more remarkable to find that Preclassic peoples of Nuclear America were in contact with one another, probably by sea as well as land (Edwards, 1969; West, 1961).

The earliest known pottery in the New World is that from Valdivia and Puerto Hormiga on the Ecuadorian and Colombian coasts, respectively. Meggers believes that the art of pottery making, along with certain decorative techniques, was ultimately derived from the Old World, specifically Japan, where she sees early parallels between the Jomon pottery of Japan and that of Valdivia. At Puerto Hormiga on the east coast of Colombia, shell-mound dwellers made pottery, some of which resembles that of Valdivia, around 3000 B.C. Rocker stamping is found on the oldest wares in each case; it is unzoned in Ecuador, while both zoned and dentate in Colombia. By 2140 B.C. this same technique is found on pottery from Monagrillo, Panama, along with excising and the *tecomate* vessel form (Willey & McGimsey, 1954).

The Machalilla phase of coastal Ecuador is represented at sites north of Valdivia extending into the Manabí province. Although chronologically overlapping with Valdivia sites and dating from 2000–1500 B.C., this phase shows distinctive traits that stem from an unknown source. This is of interest to us here because of the early appearance of the stirrup spout and bottle forms (Evans & Meggers, 1966). These also occur together at Kotosh, Peru, about 1100 B.C. and are a well-known ingredient of the Chavín horizon pottery.

More early evidence is known from Ecuador and Colombia. A striking similarity was noticed by M. D. Coe (1961) and Meggers (Meggers *et al.*, 1965) between Ocós pottery from coastal Guatemala and that from the Chorrera phase of Ecuador, sites approximately equivalent in date. This phase succeeds the Valdivia and Machalilla phases already mentioned. Both Ocós and Chorrera yield pottery decorated by a kind of iridescent painting in bands or circles. In the same Ecuadorian phase, Meggers interprets the napkin-ring ear spools, annular bases, and obsidian flakes and blades as being influenced by Mesoamerica. Again, rocker stamping occurs. Sea trade along the Pacific Coast is postulated as the means of contact.

The period during which the greatest resemblances are found between Mesoamerica and Peru is perhaps from 1500 to 800 B.C. A number of shared traits can be listed: ear spools; finger rings; mirrors; effigy vessels; stirrup spouts; flat-based, straight-sided bowls; *tecomates;* and the decorative techniques of zoning, paneling, burnishing, and roughening of fields using rocker stamping, excising, and punctating. It may be significant that in both areas the first great art styles, those of Chavín and the Olmecs, were spreading. The presence of the jaguar or feline motif is often pointed out as a recurrent theme in both these styles. Although this motif predominates in both cultures, there are highly significant differences. The Olmec jaguar is usually a were-jaguar, more human than animal, whereas in Chavín the animal overshadows the human attributes. The style and execution are very different in both areas, and Willey (1962b) has argued against a close relationship other than a possible sharing of ancient mythological concepts, which, if they existed at all, have left no trace in the intermediate areas. For example, neither Puerto Hormiga or the later site of Momíl on the northern Colombian lowlands has produced any artifacts reflecting the jaguar art theme although Mesoamerican influence is much in evidence.

The early Momíl inhabitants of around 700 B.C. were sedentary villagers who planted manioc and baked it on large, circular, rimmed griddles. They already were decorating some vessels with negative or resist painting, which has a long tradition in Nuclear America. However, in Momíl II a few hundred years later (around 200 B.C.) maize agriculture was practiced, as evidenced by stone *metates* and *manos*. Other Mesoamerican-like traits appearing at this time are bowls with basal flanges, mammiform-shaped supports, tall solid tripods, tubular spouts, red-zoned incisions, red pigment rubbed in incised lines, flat and cylindrical stamps, and zoomorphic whistles.

Later influence and contact appear to be more sporadic and less generalized. It seems possible that Mesoamerican settlers colonized the Pacific coast of Colombia from time to time. After 500 B.C. the Tumaco culture near the border of Ecuador had a well-defined complex of ceramic traits resembling some on the Gulf coast of Mesoamerica. Other similarities have been found in such diverse areas as Oaxaca, the highlands of Mexico, and Guatemala, and in some Central American cultures. We find thin, red-slipped, and incised pottery, double-bridged spouts, basal flanges, white-on-red painting, thin pointed vessel supports, anthropomorphic figurines, and large *metates* and *manos* without any antecedents in the older local tradition. Reichel-Dolmatoff (1965) believes that this complex moved eastward away from the coast and gradually spread up the river valleys to the intermountain valleys near the headwaters of the Magdalena River, introducing such traits as deep-level pit graves, elaborate figurines, head deformation, vessel supports, and perhaps double-spouted jars, stamps, *malacates*, and whistles. Here the inhabitants of San Agustín and Tierradentro carved great shaft-and-chamber or sepulchral tombs into the earth, a local specialization closely paralleled in western Mexico. Colombian shaft tombs were probably built around 500 B.C. but their chronological range is still undetermined. It is in this region that a sub-Andean culture pattern eventually developed. By Conquest times, some political cohesion had been achieved, and many late customs are similar to those seen in Mesoamerica: warfare for the purpose of capturing sacrificial victims; sacrifice by removal of the heart, flaying, and arrows; exhibition of trophy skulls; frontooccipital head deformation; tooth mutilation; and bee keeping. Chibcha traditions speak of a bearded man who brought the knowledge of arts and crafts to his people before eventually ascending to the sky, calling to mind once again the legend of Quetzalcóatl.

At the northern end of Nuclear America, the situation in Mesoamerica is still unclear, but resemblances to South American culture are found to occur sporadically in a disarticulated fashion. At the present time we can only compile a rather jumbled list of suspected South American features that in no way form a related complex. It seems significant to me that most of these are found in Guerrero and western Mexico, which are Pacific coastal regions favorably endowed for maritime contacts.

I will briefly summarize here the case for South American influence on Mesoamerica. Archaeological evidence seems to be strongest in two areas that would logically reflect two routes of introduction or contact. The first of these could be either overland via lower Central America utilizing the Ulua and Motagua river drainages as a route to highland Guatemala and to the Pacific coastal sites of La Victoria and Altamira, or directly to Soconusco by sea from northwestern South America, or both. The earliest hint of contact with South American cultures may be Green and Lowe's postulated manioc economy at Altamira on the Pacific coast of Chiapas (Green & Lowe, 1967; see Chapter 4).

Preclassic ceramic resemblances between Soconusco and northwestern South America are as follows: the Barra phase pottery of Altamira (red slip, incising, grooving, fluting, zoned decoration, cord marking) ties in with Machalilla, Ecuador, and with Puerto Hormiga and Barlovento, Colombia; the Ocós phase of La Victoria (flaring-wall bowls, dentate and plain rocker stamping, cord marking, zone burnishing, iridescent painting) is related to the Chorrera phase of Ecuador; zoomorphic effigy representations of Ocós parallel those of Puerto Hormiga and Momíl; the long, solid vessel supports (spider-leg tripods), also shared by Tlatilco, are found in Momíl II and Early Tutishcainyo. Sometimes the *tecomate* form and flat-bottomed vessels, with either vertical or outward-sloping walls, are seen as Mesoamerican influence in Peru at such early sites as Las Haldas and Early Guañape on the coast. These are also the predominant forms at Kotosh in the highlands. These features are not found, however, in pottery of the early cultures in Ecuador and Colombia, so the relationship is tenuous. Grove (1971) believes the term *tecomate* should be applied only to vessels with a thickened, comma-shaped rim, as distinct from any bowl with an incurved rim. It is not yet clear if this distinction is archaeologically significant. In any case, *tecomates* are not found in northwestern South America. A somewhat parallel situation exists with clay figurines. Those from Las Haldas show similarities to some from the Mexican Gulf Coast region, but have nothing in common with the Valdivia or Momíl I figurines. Of course, it is possible that the latter areas were bypassed either by land or sea, but the general relationship remains in question. Clay figurines in South America never attained the importance they must have had in Mesoamerica, where they are very abundant and have a long tradition of manufacture, particularly north and west of the Isthmus of Tehuantepec.

The question of Olmec–Chavín relationships has been widely discussed for many years and already has been touched on here. I am now much less convinced of a direct relationship between the Olmecs and Chavín people than I was many years ago (Porter, 1953), because subsequent material discovered from the upper Amazon basin (Lathrap, 1970; Willey, 1971a) and highland Peru (Izumi & Sono, 1963) shows the existence of a widespread early tradition in South America that possesses many of the ceramic decorations and techniques shared by Nuclear America. In other words, there is no need to look beyond Colombia, Ecuador, or eastern Peru for examples of the stirrup-spout vessel form, resist painting, excising, zoning, pattern burnishing, or application of specular hematite paint. On the other hand, the Olmec–Chavín relationship was postulated in part on the assumption that the unusual features at Tlatilco were Olmec. As has been noted (Chapter 4) we believe that some of the Olmecs briefly inhabited the basin of Mexico and buried some of their dead at Tlatilco, but the stirrup-spouted vessels, long-necked and composite bottles, and effigy pots have proved to be not Olmec traits but of a different cultural strain derived from western Mexico. While the finds in western Mexico are admittedly limited, intensive excavations in the Olmec heartland during the last twenty years have turned up little evidence of central Mexican influence. The result is a strengthening and clarification of Mesoamerican–Andean relationships via western Mexico, while at the same time a weakening of the case for direct connections between the Olmecs and Chavín peoples. Western Mexico is the second major region through which we think influences from South America were transmitted to Mesoamerica.

The Preclassic material suggesting outside influence in this area is still scarce, but only a few years ago we would have said that there was none. Since then Isabel Kelly has recovered a Capacha stirrup-spouted vessel, and the Morret red-and-white zoned ware is suspiciously similar to that of the Chorrera and Tejar phases of Ecuador (Meighan, 1969). Some of the shaft-and-chamber tombs of western Mexico resemble those from the Cauca Valley and central Andes of Colombia. In Mesoamerica, the shaft tombs are almost entirely limited to the states of Jalisco, Colima, and Nayarit. Contact must have taken place by 100 B.C. or possibly earlier (see pages 77, 78, Chapter 4). Such tombs represent a considerable expenditure of time and effort, and would indicate great dedication to some special belief or ritual. Meighan (1969) feels the shaft tombs represent a diffusion northward from South America, again by sea.

Knowledge of metal working, which became widespread after A.D. 900, is probably the most significant feature believed to be an import from Central or South America, or both. The Tarascans were famed metal workers, as were the Mixtecs. Two possible centers of introduction have already been mentioned: the southern Maya area and western Mexico (Pendergast, 1962b), which would mean that the old Preclassic lines of communication were kept open. Mountjoy (1969) has drawn attention to specific similarities between metal artifacts from Amapa, Nayarit, and those from Ecuador. Not only are metal objects, mostly copper, abundant, but the fact that they were used for common domestic implements such as tweezers, fish hooks, and needles shows that metal was not a luxury but had become accessible to everyone. This idea is further supported by the discovery of discarded metal objects in ordinary refuse, as well as the fact that the crescent-shaped "money" knives used in other parts of Mesoamerica are not found in western Mexico. Metal had become an everyday article. An important point advanced by Meighan is that Andean metal workers may have spent some time on the west coast in order to demonstrate technological knowledge rather than merely engaging in trading objects. There is some archaeological evidence of metallurgy workshops at the Barnard site on the Pacific coast of Guerrero, west of Acapulco (Brush, 1969).

Two striking specific similarities with Peru have been pointed out in the *chimera* decoration—an imaginary monster in Mochica art, which was used as a pottery design on a bowl from Amapa, Nayarit (Meighan, 1969), and the Nazca-style gold disks of western Mexico (Furst, 1965a). Guerrero has produced several isolated features that hint of southern origins. For example, at Arcelia, a small mound explored by looters exposed an interior, three-storied adobe structure, the trapezoidal doorway of which is very Incan in form. Polychrome pottery from the Yestla–Naranjo area of central Guerrero is strongly reminiscent of Nicaraguan and Costa Rican wares. This same ware, at times with loop supports, is known from the coastal Barnard site. Characteristic of both Postclassic Guerrero and Central America is a design consisting of a row of dots bordered by vertical lines. Also on a Late Postclassic horizon are the little male figurines seated on four-legged stools or benches. In this case, the concept, not specific representations, is shared. Both South and Central American influence is evident in the Mixteca-Puebla culture, some features of which spread westward through Jalisco to Guasave, Sinaloa, and can be seen in the Aztatlán complex. One Mixteca-Puebla polychrome vessel in the National Museum of Anthropology of Mexico is decorated with an interlocking serpent motif much in the style as textile designs from coastal Peru. Finally, the linguists, with understandable caution, tell us that the Tarascan language, with no known relative in Mesoamerica, may be affiliated with Penutian languages, which also embrace the Quechua-Aymara in Bolivia (Swadesh, 1956; see the discussion in Wolf, 1959). More recently Mary L. Foster (1971) has found linguistic evidence for the relationship of Tarascan to Japanese based on linguistic reconstruction. If we are to believe that early Japanese fishermen brought pottery styles to Ecuador, it logically follows that conversation ensued.

In summary, the evidence for contact between centers of Nuclear America is found from early to late horizons. Maize agriculture, head deformation, and resist painting of pottery all are among the most ancient traits common to both centers. Pottery making, rocker stamping, and the stirrup spout were current earlier in northwestern South America than in the north. Mesoamerican features that look intrusive in South America are *metates* and *manos*, the *tecomate* and flat-based vessel form, ear spools, and clay stamps. Common to both areas are a number of Chavín–Olmec ceramic traits including certain forms, decorations, techniques, and styles: miscellaneous small objects, and the jaguar art theme. Contacts were continued, perhaps intermittently, until the Conquest, and highland Colombia seems to have been particularly affected by Mesoamerican ideas in late years.

In reviewing the whole subject of pre-Columbian contacts between Mesoamerica and South America I am impressed not so much with Nuclear American relationships (that is, Mesoamerica and the Andean region) as with the whole area of northwestern South America (the Intermediate Area). Colombia and Ecuador appear to have been the hearth of many cultural innovations that spread to both centers of Nuclear

America. If overland travel by foot or voyages by sea at this early time seem incredible, the task of defending any alternative explanation is a burden of equal proportion. In a study of possible maritime contacts, Edwards (1969) points out that sea travel would not have been as difficult as is often depicted. The trip could have been made directly by sea, in large oceangoing rafts or canoes, and if the course was in doubt, one could easily have tacked toward land now and then to check progress. The trip was also possible in a smaller craft such as a dugout by following a course close to shore and running up on a beach to search for food or to wait out an impending squall.

If we accept the establishment of early trade, it would seem that Mesoamerica was largely on the receiving end, particularly in regard to western Mexico. Mesoamerica must have had some worthwhile attraction to warrant the danger, expense, and time incurred by these early traders. One cannot look at a Mexican-style figurine from Las Haldas or a clay stamp, whistle, or ear spool and be convinced that these were the prime objectives of ocean voyages. If however, these apparently minor traits represented the spread of a major religious cult or system, one might be on firmer ground. As yet there is little evidence to substantiate such a belief. Mountjoy may have touched on an interesting possibility when, in looking for some highly desirable commodity, he suggests peyote or some other narcotic plant (Mountjoy, 1969). Peyote could have survived the trip either in its natural button form or powdered, as it is light in weight, small, and easily transported. Also as the Andean peoples are notorious for their use of *coca*, a local narcotic plant, from which cocaine is derived, this drug would have found a receptive market. This is no more than a reasonable suggestion, but by accepting early contact as a fact, we are now able to direct our thoughts and research toward promising new fields.

Reflecting on the emergence of civilization in Mesoamerica, one wonders what influence this outside contact might have had. Of the features under discussion, many are trivial and nonessential in nature, and would hardly have affected the on-going equilibrium. Metallurgy, perhaps the most significant import, arrived long after the patterns of civilization had crystallized, and served only to enrich an elaborate society already set in its ways. Of greater importance than identification of what diffused is the knowledge that interaction and exchange of ideas formed part of the early economic processes.

Trans-Pacific Contacts

Similar problems concerning the effect of possible diffusion arise in relation to the current trans-Pacific studies, which attempt to trace Old World influences on New World cultures. Here interest centers around an old question in archaeology: Did New World civilizations arise independently, or were their origins and development significantly influenced by the Old World?

When similarities are found in different cultures, they may be explained on the basis of convergence. That is, if environments pose similar problems to different peoples, they might be expected to solve them in similar ways, leading to independent inventions of the same custom or technique. On the other hand, a cultural trait may have been shared or widely copied, resulting in its geographical spread by the process called diffusion. For example, most people have no difficulty in accepting the diffusion of agriculture from Mesoamerica to southwestern United States where chronological, ecological, and geographical factors reinforce the archaeological data. The assumption of diffusion between such widely spaced areas as the New and Old Worlds, however, has set up a lively controversy. To admit the intrusion of an Old World trait into the western hemisphere is felt by many to somehow deprive our cultures of their native genius or to undermine the status of New World civilizations. Part of the controversy involves such intangibles as the very nature and "psychic unity" of man. For example, some feel that pottery making is so unique a concept that it could only have been invented once in the history of the world. Others see it as a simple technique easily explained by a number of possible origins, including inspiration by natural forms such as gourds, imitation of stone receptacles, or accidental invention resulting from the observation of clay drying in the sun or hardening through proximity to fire.

Those who have difficulty in accepting the idea of trans-Pacific contacts want to know how man managed to transport himself across the Pacific Ocean and ask for explanations of time, place, and means of contact. They feel that such traits as metallurgy and pottery making are not so complex that they could not have had multiple origins, and they cite numerous historical cases of reinvention. Stylistic convergences can, and have been known to, occur. The fact that we do not have at present any local antecedents of the Olmec culture, for example, need not mean that they will not be found eventually, and thus it is not necessary to invoke voyages across the Pacific to provide their roots. The discovery of an ancient wild maize in the Mexican highlands has proved that domestication of maize could have taken place locally, and New World domestication of plants is no longer challenged. Finally, even if sporadic contacts did somehow take place, the foreign influence may not have been sufficiently early or significant enough to be decisive in influencing the emergence of New World civilizations (Phillips, 1966).

Those favoring trans-Pacific contacts are not dismayed by these challenges. They believe that early voyages did take place, perhaps accidentally in some instances, as a result of voyagers being swept off course and carried away by currents. They admit that evidence will be difficult if not impossible to produce, but they do not see transportation as an overriding problem in view of the convincing nature of the evidence itself. Meggers believes that an excellent case for diffusion can be supported by such factors as the uniqueness of a trait, the lack of local antecedents, the absence of functional causality, and the clustering of traits. In this view, Old World influence in Mesoamerica is reflected primarily in styles and motifs and in some technical processes. The brief summary presented here is based largely on the writings of Ekholm (1964), Heine-Geldern (1959, 1966), D. H. Kelley (1960, 1969), and Tolstoy (1963).

The oldest trans-Pacific influence in Mesoamerica is postulated for the Early Preclassic period, corresponding to the Early Bronze age in China during the Shang dynasty (1700–1027 B.C.). At this time the art of jade working and the jaguar or feline motif could have been introduced to Mexican lowland cultures. Tolstoy (1963) has made a strong case for the introduction of stone beaters for making bark cloth from Asia into upper Central America and the Isthmus of Tehuantepec around 1000 B.C. This study is backed by statistical analyses of detailed attributes and takes into account the alternatives, nonessential aspects, and degrees of similarity. More recently, Kelley (1969) has attempted to derive the Mesoamerican calendar from the Chinese lunar zodiac.

The cylindrical tripod vessel of Early Classic Teotihuacán has parallels in the bronze and pottery vessels of the Han period in China. Details of form, the conical lid, and the frequent use of a bird at the apex, as well as the use of a mold for producing appliqued ornaments, are shared by both regions. During the Classic period clay figurines were produced in molds, replacing the earlier hand-modeled technique. Might not this change represent a new application of the mold originally used to make the bronze vessels? About the same time the distinctive Tajín art style spread its interlaced design through most major centers of Mesoamerica. This scroll pattern is paralleled in late Chou art in China. The fresco technique for decorating walls and pottery and wheeled clay figures as miniature reproductions of bronze carts are both traced to Han China by Ekholm (1964).

Ekholm sees a second wave of influence during the Late Classic and Postclassic periods in Mesoamerica that seems to stem not from China but from the Hindu–Buddhist civilizations of India and Southeast Asia. This influence is seen in phallic sculptures and themes in bas-relief panel carvings such as the lotus motif, tiger thrones, and the "tree of life." The relief carvings of Palenque contain much of this flavor, and some is present in later periods at Chichén Itzá and in central Mexico. As interest in this old field of research has been renewed, many scholars have recently engaged in comparative analyses of conch shells, panpipes, metal casting, calendrical concepts, mythology, architecture, sacrifice, languages, and botanical studies. There is interest in the transfer of knowledge as an event and also in diffusion as an explanation of culture change.

If we now restate the problem of diffusion in the light of the latest studies, we are left with a very basic question: Assuming that contact did occur, how far does it go toward explaining such basic factors as the function and configuration of the socioeconomic pattern of Mesoamerica, the "core" features of its culture, and its rise to civilization? To substantially affect basic cultural development, the influence would presumably have been absorbed early in the Preclassic horizon, before the pattern of civilization crystallized. Second, the influence would have had to be of a nature that would affect the existing equilibrium in the religious, political, social, or economic systems. To present evidence in support of this thesis is a difficult task, but the present atmosphere of challenge, discussion, and weighing of evidence is producing stimulating results. Trans-Pacific contacts have yet to be proven convincingly, but analytical studies in progress mark the first step in a truly scientific approach that is replacing the older, emotional one.

B Y NOW THE READER HAS BECOME FAMILIAR WITH TIKAL, Tlatilco, Dzibilchaltún, and Kaminaljuyú, and an endless assortment of names difficult to retain and harder to spell. Does it matter which people painted their pots and which added legs? Are pipes and Plumbate worth remembering? The answer must indeed be yes, for just as every piece is necessary to complete a puzzle, so in archaeology each bit of evidence is precious and has its rightful place in the record. Interrelated and arranged chronologically, these fragments of knowledge, pieces of culture, form the factual record from which inferences and interpretations of the history of Mesoamerican civilization are drawn. Thus, this record will serve as a testing ground for the ultimate disproof or verification of the ever-increasing number of hypotheses and models, regardless of source. Furthermore, and even more important, this systematic knowledge is a necessary prerequisite toward an understanding of the processes at work in the evolution of a civilization, wherever it may be found.

Civilization Defined: The Mesoamerican Example

It is time to see what is meant by the term "civilization" and in what way it applies to Mesoamerica. It is commonly felt that a "civilized" person is one who is a member of a permanent, large, complex society with an orderly government, as contrasted with a member of a small independent group, perhaps leading a nomadic or primitive life. The inference here is that the concept of civilization is closely related to that of the state, which is true. This political aspect is only part of its character, however. In attempting to define what is meant by civilization, the views of anthropologists often reflect their particular regional interests. For example, Childe (1952a, 1952b), whose primary concern has been with Old World cultures, in particular those of the Near East, feels that writing and urbanism are achievements correlated with civilization. Often mention is made of specific techniques such as metallurgy, use of the wheel, and domestication of beasts of burden. However, if we try to apply these kinds of criteria to cultures throughout the world we run into difficulty for some New World civilizations clearly do not conform to this pattern. Furthermore, the simple possession of one or more such features does not indicate the existence of a highly complex society as some of these traits may be found among very primitive people. To embrace all civilizations of both the Old and New Worlds such a definition must be cased in more general terms to express a quality or style of life. The forms that these may take are the specific characteristics of each individual civilization unique to it. Among those general qualities implicit in the word "civilization" we find many relating to a well-developed social structure, such as stratification of rank; complex division of labor resulting in occupational specialization; intensive agriculture; efficient methods for the distribution of food, raw materials, and luxury items;

10

Mesoamerican Civilization and Archaeology

some large concentration of population; monumental architecture; and political and religious hierarchies in whose hands rests the administration of the state. Some form of writing or recording device seems functionally very important for administrative purposes, and a high art in which sophistication, symbolism, and language of form are present, characterizes civilized societies. If a culture embraces not only one or two but all of these features, we say it has attained that degree of complexity called civilization.

There is further agreement among scholars that a civilization must have as its base sufficient efficiency in food production to produce a surplus so that some members of the community can dedicate their full time to crafts, trade, religious, administrative or other pursuits, by which means advances are made in technological, political, and social control. The fact that agriculture is practiced by many simple cultures does not necessarily imply that a surplus of food is produced. Some motivation must be present to produce more food than is needed for mere subsistence. When the reasons for such a motivation are exposed, more will be known about the processes that lead to the rise of civilization, an issue which we will take up shortly.

Let us look at Mesoamerica as a civilization. It possesses all the general complexities mentioned above, excelling particularly in monumental public works and scientific and intellectual achievements. I shall try to outline what I consider to be the fundamental aspects of Mesoamerican civilization—those ingredients that give it its particular style. First, it possessed an elaborate religious hierarchy closely integrated with a formalized political system, wherein lay the administrative powers. The belief in a fatalistic cosmology was accompanied by man's perpetual struggles to influence the deities on his behalf. Special features became of primary importance in carrying out man's mission in life such as human sacrifice, the ritualistic ball game, a special complex calendrical system and method of counting, periodic markets, and institutionalized trade. In this civilization the principle of the wheel was never put to any practical use nor was any beast of burden domesticated. The first case is not easily explained because the wheel could have been used to great advantage both by ceramicists and for transporting goods. Its absence is all the more remarkable since an excellent working model existed in miniature wheeled objects. In the second case, the lack of a suitable native animal to domesticate is one obvious explanation. This situation indicates that domesticated animals as a source of energy are not a determining factor in the growth of civilization. Metallurgy, usually considered to be a vital technology, was introduced to Mesoamerica from cultures further south. However, this occurred long after the attainment of its cultural climax, and therefore is not seen as either a prerequisite or an inducement to the rise of civilization in this part of the world. Another special characteristic of Mesoamerican civilization as a whole is the multiplicity of centers of development. Never in its long cultural history was there one capital, one political center, or seat of power. In earliest times, small cultural centers were the general rule, and these were eventually succeeded by larger settlements, some of which reached urban proportions. At no time, however, was there a centralization of administration that can approach that of the Inca state in Peru, for example. As a result specific civilizations within Mesoamerica can be identified. One can properly speak of an Olmec civilization in

Preclassic times; the Classic Teotihuacán, Zapotec, and Maya civilizations; and numerous Postclassic examples. All share fundamental concepts that give a cultural unity to Mesoamerica. Notwithstanding the great diversity and local specializations just emphasized, I think it can also be said that Mesoamerican culture shows remarkable stability from beginning to end, not only in technology and subsistence patterns, but in many of the other features that characterize this area. Evolution followed a particular direction or pattern that emerged in Preclassic times and never basically changed thereafter. Viewing the cumulative effects of two thousand years of development at the time of the Conquest, we see an elaboration of the early cultures, but few major changes.

Causal Factors in the Rise of Mesoamerican Civilization

The causes of the phenomenon called "civilization" have intrigued scholars for generations. Early ideas about a specially endowed people who produced a great leader, or environmental determinism implying a cause-and-effect relationship between environment and culture, are no longer taken seriously. A much more likely suggestion is that a self-contained region where farm land is limited is a breeding ground for competition and conflict, which results in more complex social institutions, a strong authority, and eventually civilization. Or one can search for evidence of diffusion from outside sources. The latter, however, provides no adequate explanation in itself, for the processes in the rise of civilization are the same, whether inspired from within or without a culture, and still must be discovered. The phenomenon of civilization stems not from any single cause but from the interaction of multiple factors that vary with the individual ecosystem analyzed. The fact that each civilization arose from a different setting and the specific ingredients are dissimilar does not mean that the search for an understanding of their evolution is meaningless. On the contrary, each emerged through orderly processes that can be analyzed scientifically. In this field of investigation Mesoamerican civilization is particularly illuminating. An examination of where and under what circumstances civilization was achieved should shed some light on the cultural processes involved.

It is generally conceded that the first Mesoamerican civilization was that of the Olmecs in the Preclassic period. The truth of this statement depends to some extent on how civilization is defined. All the features usually associated with civilization—managerial skills and control of production; social stratification; specialization of crafts; organized trade and commerce; a central authority perhaps synonymous with religious leadership; institutionalized religion; intellectual achievements in the realm of numbers, writing, and the calendar; the attainment of highly sophisticated and conceptualized art styles—can be found taking shape prior to A.D. 300. We do not know if the political organization can be justly described as a "state," but this is certainly possible in the case of the Olmecs. Those looking for the full development of writing, elite residences, and urbanization are more inclined to view this period as one of preparation for the great civilizations of the Classic period that followed. It is interesting that two factors often associated with civilization, hydraulic agriculture and urbanism, are not identified with the Olmecs. By hydraulic agriculture we refer to large-scale public works for the control of water as opposed to the simpler techniques of rainfall utilization or rudimentary irrigation canals for agricultural purposes. That the Olmecs did control water in some way is evident from their great construction of drains, but more complicated irrigation works are unknown and would have served little purpose in this region. Nor is there any evidence of great concentrations of population.

In the following Classic period, however, Sanders and Price (1968) attribute the population increase and the resultant urbanism of Teotihuacán to the interaction of two factors. Of primary importance is the existence of hydraulic agriculture concentrated in the Teotihuacán Valley in an extremely competitive social environment. Public works in this dry valley would have required larger aggregations of people for cooperative labor, and this in turn would logically lead to increased social stratification, which is essentially Wittfogel's theory (Wittfogel, 1957) applied to highland Mexico. Another major factor in the growth of Teotihuacán is called economic symbiosis (Sanders & Price, 1968), that is, the interdependence of groups in the effective distribution and redistribution of surpluses, whether raw materials or finished products. Of course, this symbiosis is intimately related to the variety of sharply defined ecological niches and resulting craft specialization and organized trade. Such economic symbiosis is a vital catalyst in the development of all Mesoamerican cultures, and in highland Mexico it seems to be correlated with complex irrigation works, urbanism, and civilization. Sanders and Price, however, extend their thesis further to suggest that pressures from the highland urban hydraulic civilization on lowland cultures led to the latter's rise to comparable heights. There is little agreement on this particular point. The control and distribution of water certainly cannot be denied, as the reservoirs at Tikal, for example, must have been an important factor in maintaining the large resident population. This activity would not be described as a large-scale water work however, and there is no evidence that irrigation was important to the lowland Maya. Moreover, in this case administrative controls probably would have resulted from rather than caused an increase in population. Attempts to account for the Maya civilization in terms of highland hydraulic urbanism are not very convincing on the basis of present archaeological evidence. Rather within the Mesoamerican pattern, the lowland Maya constitutes another model of civilization, reached through adaptation to an entirely different ecological niche. The rise of Maya civilization grew out of the same generalized Preclassic base as Teotihuacán but evolved in a different direction.

Maya civilization emerges during the Early Classic period to culminate in the Late Classic. An examination of the environmental potential of this lowland area reveals a general uniformity, a situation contrasting sharply with the closely spaced ecological zones of highland Mexico. As we have seen (pages 167, 168, Chapter 6), Rathje (1971) has proposed a feasible explanation for the origin of Maya civilization in northeastern Petén, the area most isolated and in greatest need of essential goods. The complex sociopolitical organization of the Maya could have resulted as a response to this demand, and would help to explain the spread of the Classic Maya culture throughout the lowlands. Irrigation and water works have no part in this explanation, and it is interesting that the key area is not the one bordering the sources of materials, but the region farthest removed from them. Instead of one major center such as Teotihuacán, many centers grew up, each with some distinction.

A special kind of urbanism grew up at Tikal, which was located in this remote nuclear zone; but with this exception, the ceremonial center-type settlement seems to have been more typical. It is not yet clear from the excavations whether Tikal was the most powerful center of the Classic Maya, exercising political control over a large area. Before any judgment can be made concerning the political status of the Petén centers, more information comparable to that from Tikal is needed. The present data on Tikal are so extensive that our perspective is unbalanced. It is clear, however, that surplus food was essential to maintain Maya "cities," and that foods other than maize, squash, and beans were consumed, some requiring much less time and energy than slash-and-burn agriculture. Although the environmental homogeneity of the Petén has been noted, in the particular example of Tikal the fine local flint supply may have contributed to its importance. Perhaps because of an unwillingness to move away from this abundant flint, which was a great economic asset as a trade commodity, the early pattern of shifting villages was replaced by one of permanence. Such permanent settlement forced the population to augment their food supply, at which point the residents of Tikal took advantage of the nutritious breadnut tree (Haviland, 1970). With subsistence assured and essential goods flowing in from distant centers, the population increased sharply, and craft specialists, as well as an aristocratic hierarchical elite, prospered.

Highland central Mexico and the lowland Petén region provide only two dramatic examples of very different ecological adaptations within Mesoamerica. There are many more situations to be examined that will undoubtedly point to other growth factors of which we are still unaware. These examples, however, will hopefully lead to greater flexibility in future studies of civilization. The causal factors here as in the case of every civilization were a combination of interrelated ingredients, some cultural and some noncultural, but always the product of unique ecological adaptations. Thus, it should come as no surprise to find very diverse configurations of cultural growth in an area of such pronounced ecological contrasts.

In the highlands the diversity of microenvironments led to a local market economy, whereas the more environmentally homogeneous lowlands reached out for long-distance commercial relationships. This desire for goods not locally available, which Rathje hypothesizes led to pronounced social stratification, centralization of authority, and the attainment of the status of civilization, is applicable not only to the lowland Maya but also to the earlier Olmecs (Rathje, 1971). Viewed in this light, the shift of power that took place in late Preclassic times from the Gulf Coast region to highland Mexico can be more readily understood, for in finding themselves part of a commerical network the highlanders then had distinct advantages of resources and the setting for true urbanism (see Willey, 1971b). However materialistic these people may seem to have been, the cast of Mesoamerican civilization is still thoroughly religious. I join Willey (1971b) in my feeling that in addition to whatever sociopolitical effects trade may have had, it also provided the mechanism for the spread of religious ideology, and these religious beliefs were vital to the growth of civilization and the kind of civilization that emerged in Mesoamerica. Archaeologically it may be easier to document the movement of material goods than to understand the significance of a deep-rooted religious ideology, but the latter is consistently omnipresent from early Olmec art to the last victim sacrificed by the Mexica. Without an appreciation of its religious base, Mesoamerican civilization would make no sense at all.

In the final analysis, Mesoamerican civilization was a very special phenomenon as regards its content, specific stylistic elaboration, and pattern—all of which argues for its development independent of outside influence, in the sense of this influence being a determining factor. On the other hand, I believe the forces leading to the rise of civilization in this part of the world to be basically the same processes operative in the growth of other great civilizations.

Problems and Trends in Mesoamerican Archaeology

If by any chance this history of cultural events in Mesoamerica seems logical, smooth, and simple, I have, in striving for clarity, greatly overstated the case. It is nothing of the kind. In an attempt to link the archaeological facts into a convenient framework for study, gaps in knowledge have been glossed over and many problems and subjects of controversy touched but lightly. The general outline and sequence of events is, I believe, sound, but as field work continues, it becomes increasingly clear how urgent the need is for more data. With each new discovery Mesoamerican history becomes increasingly more complex, more challenging, and more interesting. For the young, well-trained archaeologist, this field promises rich intellectual rewards.

Despite years of research and study, there are many long-standing problems still unresolved. Where, and who, for example, are the ancestors of the Olmecs? The sites of San Lorenzo Tenochtitlán and La Venta have contributed a wealth of information for which there is no known precedent in the archaeological record. Clues to Olmec origins may still await discovery in the southern Mexican jungles, having inadvertently been skipped by the shovel and not yet exposed to the magnetometer. Perhaps we do not know what to look for or where. Can it be possible that antecedents do not exist in Mesoamerica at all, and that this culture was suddenly introduced from outside sources? No one can say at present, but this is one of the most tantalizing and challenging questions to be answered. Of great interest too is the final fate of the Olmecs. The archaeological record at San Lorenzo shows they were replaced by other groups, but who were they to interfere with the jaguar's people, under what circumstances, and why? The Olmecs have left us a heritage of puzzles.

The Classic period has been eulogized for years and the great sites have consumed more time, effort, cement, and money than any others. To the archaeologists' delight there were vast public buildings in a multitude of ceremonial centers to be excavated and restored, simple and lavish living quarters to explore, common graves, and rich tombs and caches filled with abundant treasures. Furthermore, the accommodating lowland Maya even dated their monuments. Why then with such an abundance of material should there be so much speculation, so many uncertainties and mysteries concerning life at this time? In the case of the lowland Maya, the tropical climate has destroyed many remains to which the archaeologist feels entitled, but this is only a partial excuse. No one is completely satisfied with the explanations surrounding the dramatic collapse and abandonment of the Petén region at the close of the Classic period. Unfortunately, considerably less attention has been devoted to the catastrophe that befell Teotihuacán, which, since it occurred first, could provide a clue to understanding the upheavel in both areas. Relationships between all the leading centers at this time remain to be clarified, and in the process we are certain to hear more about competition and conflict. The development of warfare and growth of trade have yet to be researched in depth, and the results of such studies could have a significant bearing on settlement patterns and social structure. The whole question of correlation between the Maya and Christian calendar has never been definitively settled, and consequently it is sometimes difficult to bring the chronologies of Yucatán and Oaxaca in step with other key areas. And the possibility of translating an original Maya hieroglyphic text, if a phonetic writing system can be worked out, may produce a whole new generation of epigraphers.

A region of great expectations in the near future is that of Puebla–Tlaxcala. It has always been a center of diverse cultural activity, but until very recently was bypassed by archaeologists in their enthusiasm to explore the Aztec capital and the more spectacular Teotihuacán. Cholula, under excavation at the present time by the Mexican Instituto Nacional de Antropología e Historia, is proving to be far more complex than anticipated. Excavations at this site and elsewhere in the Valley of Puebla should help to clarify the interrelationships between lowland and highland peoples from the earliest Pleistocene hunters to the coming of the Spanish, giving a true chronological crosssection of Mesoamerica.

The area of western Mexico could satisfy every problem-oriented archaeologist. The intriguing questions of cultural relationships with the southwest of the United States and maritime contacts with outside areas remain to be settled, and vast expanses of land still await sampling. The two great rivers of the Balsas and Lerma–Santiago are known to be avenues of travel and communication, but their roles in the cultural development could be focused much more sharply. Western Mexico is unique in that this area remained relatively independent until its eventual incorporation into Mesoamerica around A.D. 900. Probably the whole redefinition or segmentation of its cultural development should be outlined anew because this is one of the most obscure, disjointed, and least understood areas in our record. The region has received much more attention from adventurous pot hunters than archaeologists, a situation that fortunately is being rapidly remedied by systematic excavations carried out by a team of archaeologists from the University of California at Los Angeles and by the independent work of Isabel Kelly.

From the valley of Oaxaca new information on early cave sites, settlement patterns, and irrigation is complementing or rounding out earlier work at the great site of Monte Albán. Hundreds of sites have been mapped; comparatively few have been dug. This situation too is rapidly changing. To the southeast, the New World Archaeological Foundation has already devoted some twenty years to mapping, surveying, and digging in the hitherto little-known regions of Chiapas and the Isthmus of Tehuantepec. Through generous financial support for concentrated methodical excavation and prompt publication of information, the archaeological progress has been enormous in this region. To judge from preliminary reports and the number of newly discovered sites, digging here has just begun.

Many questions have undoubtedly arisen in the mind of the reader. I have mentioned only a few of the most obvious and urgent problems in order to point out that the gathering of data is far from finished. No one has ever heard his field director say, "Pack up your trowels and whisk brooms, there is nothing more we can learn here." The packing is done because the rains come, jaundice sets in, or the money runs out, but always with the hope and expectation to return the following season with more workers, more funds, and more time. Field work still essentially involves competent control of the digging and careful observation because accurate recording of all information is, after all, the point of departure for the next phase of the work: interpretation.

In a sense archaeology in Mesoamerica is entering a whole new phase of development. Recently some new trends have developed, not so much in the actual digging of sites as in theoretical approaches, refinement of techniques, and orientation of research, all of which result in more sharply focused, precise interpretations. In Mesoamerica we are just beginning to see the results of this new line of thought, which are stimulating even the most dedicated classifier of points and potsherds to stand back and rethink his procedures and purpose.

One technique which has proved to be astoundingly successful is the effective collaboration among scientists from a number of fields, such as those specialists that carried out the excavations in the Tehuacán Valley. This milestone in archaeology has already been described (page 27, Chapter 3). In this approach they attempted to reconstruct the various available microenvironments and to see how they were utilized by ancient residents of the valley. The results, still in the process of publication, consist of precise and detailed information in a number of specialized fields of research—a far cry from the older inventory-type descriptive monograph that used to signal completion of work on a particular site. The many years of pioneer work were, nonetheless, a necessary preliminary phase in this relatively new science of archaeology. Current scholars should remember that they can achieve brilliant results only because of the hard labor put in by their predecessors, and if we come upon errors and misinterpretations in the past record, we can be sure that future generations will be carping about our own.

Great technological advances have been made in processing field data by computers and perfecting methods for establishing more precise chronologies. Carbon dating, though not flawless, has been used extensively in Mesoamerica along with relative dating techniques. Other methods, such as obsidian dating and thermoluminescence, are still under study. Pollen analysis, fluorine dating, and geomagnetic surveying have all provided new and valuable information. Furthermore, use is being made of mathematical techniques such as seriation analysis and factor analysis. Flannery's application of the general system theory to the early food gatherers and food producers in Mesoamerica is rapidly becoming a classic (Flannery, 1968b).

Other approaches involve application of other new theoretical viewpoints. Not content to just rethink and rework older interpretations, new theories, hypotheses, and models are being formulated that remain to be tested by using the archaeological record. Many of these models are derived from ethnographic data, and by analogy can be applied to situations in ancient times. Such studies are enjoying great popularity at the moment, but the technique must be used with caution, for example, in attempting extensive inferences about social behavior. The widespread enthusiasm with which this approach has been greeted is understandable because the method provides the means to put meat on an archaeological skeleton, fill in those aspects of culture long considered beyond recovery. One of those to make use of ethnographic analogy in the archaeology of Mesoamerica is Peter Furst, with, I believe, considerable success. Hopefully one of the benefits to be reaped from this current trend will be a greater use of the rich and very extensive literature of the Colonial period. In the case of Mesoamerica we are extraordinarily lucky to have fallen heir to a wealth of ethnohistory. The native documents, Colonial chronicles, and ancient and modern ethnographies have yet to be profitably exploited by the archaeologists. Is it not reasonable that cultural parallels represent survivals from the ancient to the historic peoples? Coe believes that modern Mexico owes much to its pre-Spanish heritage, dating back to the Olmecs (M. D. Coe, 1968b), and Thompson (1970) implores the reader to look beyond Landa's account of the Maya to writings of early Spanish officials, reports, and anonymous papers that found their way to Spain to discover for himself the continuity that has persisted from the early days of the Classic Maya to the present.

Mesoamerican archaeologists are fortunate to have the opportunity to work amid the natural beauty and native charm of Mesoamerica and its peoples. Countries such as Mexico and Guatemala, which have such an abundant wealth of archaeological treasures, shoulder an enormous responsibility to their own people and to the world at large. It is to their everlasting credit that this burden is fully appreciated and that they have created schools, institutes, and museums to train personnel, conduct research, and display their treasures. Conscious of the scope of the task, the governments of Guatemala and Mexico have collaborated with foreign scholars for many years and issued permits to innumerable foreign institutions to enable field work and research to progress. Mexico has almost become a field laboratory for budding archaeologists in the United States as well as for linguists and cultural anthropologists. However, with all the archaeological treasures they offer, these countries are not spared the problems of the twentieth century. Ancient ball courts, plazas, and pyramids are obliterated by the rapidly expanding cities, and frequently there is little or nothing left to salvage. Superhighways and airports mushroom where convenient. Tenochtitlán of course, was completely devastated by the Spanish, who immediately moved right in and settled on top of the ruins. Now the Aztec capital has sunk into the former lake bed and is buried beneath two and a half centuries of modern living. The excavation for a new building, a trench or pit of any kind, even a fresh road cut, may produce an incense burner, a battered *chacmool*, or a few pipes and pots, but with greater luck it could also be a life-size basalt Xipe Totec or Quetzalcóatl. In recent excavations for the Mexico City subway, no less than twenty tons of archaeological remains were unearthed! Another vanishing city is that of Kaminaljuyú, but its modern destruction began only in the last thirty years, a victim of the rapid westward expansion of Guatemala City. The few mounds that remain give the visitor no idea of the size and importance of this great site which can be best appreciated by reading the publications of the Carnegie Institution of Washington and perusing the collections of the National Museum of Guatemala. In regions free from urban "progress" invaluable sites have been destroyed by oil drills and dredges, dams, and land reclamation projects, the operating and contruction deadlines of which permit little time for even salvage archaeology. For those unfortunate sites, time has already run out. Furthermore, the exotic lowland jungle makes ruins and monuments difficult to locate. Branches and roots topple temples and all manner of structures, and travel through the mass of vegetation is slow and difficult. A few misguided steps and one can be lost for hours or days probing one's way through the dense growth. In this area ruins not visited for some length of time have been lost and rediscovered years later.

Other frustrations originate with our fellow man, who is no easier to control than the jungle. Pot hunting and looting have proved to be such lucrative pastimes that sites are plundered by acquisitive looters as soon as rumors of a newly discovered tomb or cemetery spread. Again and again the archaeologist arrives on the scene to find a once rich grave hopelessly destroyed, bones scattered, and vessels smashed and trampled in the rush to find a marketable item. Each year hundreds of articles make their way to the United States and to other foreign lands to be handled by art dealers and department stores as primitive art. Some are purchased by museums, where they are beautifully displayed with the disappointing label, "Provenence Unknown." One sees illustrations of fashionable living rooms and country homes frequently adorned with a few pieces of pottery sculpture, which more often than not, were partial contents of a looted Jalisco shaft tomb. This illicit trade is not limited to small *objets d'art*. Entire stone stelae may be offered for sale, as well as enormous lintels, sizable fragments of frescoed walls—everything short of a complete pyramid. The material thus lost to archaeological science is beyond calculation. The swiftest effective remedy would be to dry up the market, but there is always some shop, museum, or private party who succumbs to temptation, thus encouraging further destruction. The faker's crime is somewhat less serious, as his work can be done in the basement. Attempts to produce "original" ancient works are often so bizarre they are easily spotted. Fakers usually copy the originals, and in the process may make telltale mistakes. Expert forgeries can create at least temporary confusion and be of considerable irritation. Much to the archaeologist's glee, new technological advances in dating processes are plunging the faking profession into its worst known economic recession.

Archaeology has been called the science of dead cultures. This is not true of archaeology in Mesoamerica, where the proud traditions of the Maya, Mexica, and their contemporaries are a vital part of daily living. Ancient motifs may have lost or changed their meaning, but are faithfully reproduced in modern textiles, jewelry, ceramics, and sculpture. Every Mexican looks up with wonder and respect at the proud figure of Cuauhtémoc on his pedestal, presiding over a busy intersection in Mexico City. Crowds flock to Teotihuacán at night for a glimpse of ancient ritual and dances reenacted among the illuminated pyramids. The new National Museum of Anthropology, occupying 450,000 square feet of Chapultepec Park, has returned some objects to their original resting places, for in these same ancient woods of *ahuehuete* trees Huémac took his own life, the Mexica celebrated a New Fire Ceremony, and carved images of their rulers in the rocks at the base of the hill. Of the thousands of visitors that come to see this modern tribute to Mexico's past and enter the courtyard with its giant umbrella fountain of water to begin their three-mile trip through exhibit halls, none are more interested, more respectful than the Mexicans themselves. This unique museum traces the indigenous Mexican tradition from its ancient beginnings to the present. Here, one can observe a young girl in *quexquemitl* standing in silent contemplation before a model of her own image. To one side she sees the pole-and-thatch hut she has just left behind, and the *metate* and *mano* that await her return. She knows the pottery griddle and fiber mats well, but so does the archaeologist who could show her examples two thousand years older. Yet some say that little has survived from the pre-Hispanic cultures. They could not have been present in 1964 the day it rained. When the National Museum of Anthropology opened in Mexico City that year, the 168-ton stone Tlaloc from Coatlinchan near Texcoco was moved to its present location on the Paseo de la Reforma at the driveway entrance. On that day the rain fell in torrents unprecedented in man's memory. Who could doubt that Tlaloc had spoken?

Ah Mun   Maya god of maize, symbolized by day glyph Kan and associated with the number eight. Represented in the *códices* as a handsome young man often with maize plant sprouting from his head. Classic and Postclassic representations (Figure 29).

Bacabs   four Maya deities, brothers, who held up the sky. Atlantean figures may represent Bacabs and date back to Classic period. Bacabs associated with the fate of the incoming year, bees, and the apiary.

Bolon-ti-Ku   nine Maya Lords of the Underworld, who ruled in unending sequence over a cycle of nine nights. Glyphs included in Long Count inscriptions (Figure 16).

Centéotl, see also Chicomecóatl   Mexica god of the maize plant, as distinguished from Xilonen (goddess of the young tender ear of corn) and Ilamatecuhtli (goddess of the old dried ear of corn). The three were intimately associated with Chicomecóatl, general goddess of sustenance. All may be distinguished by some attribute of the maize plant. Possibly derived from Olmec God II.

Chac, see also Tlaloc   Yucatec name of rain god or group of rain deities. Rain god cult is very old lowland tradition recorded in inscriptions and códices. Many concepts parallel the Mexican Tlaloc such as the ancient association of rain deities with the snake. Chac represented with long pendulous nose, a scroll beneath the eye, often toothless. Four Chacs were associated with the cardinal points: east, west, north, and south with colors red, black, white, and yellow, respectively. Many lesser Chacs (Figure 29).

Chebel Yax   wife of the great Maya creator, Itzamná. Depicted in *códices* as the old red goddess with hank of cotton or cloth, presiding over weaving activities.

Chicomecóatl   most important of Mexica vegetation deities, whose name signifies "seven serpent," also called "seven ears of corn." Sculptured in stone, she often holds two ears of corn in each hand.

Coatlícue   Mexica earth goddess and mother of Huitzilopochtli, typically shown wearing a skirt made of entwined serpents. She presided over the rainy season which was directly related to her concern with the soil and agriculture.

Cocijo, see Tlaloc   (Plate 7g).

Coyolxauhqui   Mexica moon goddess and ill-fated sister of Huitzilopochtli. Decapitated by her brother.

Curicaueri   Tarascan fire and sun god. Postclassic, western Mexico.

Ehécatl, see also Quetzalcóatl   Quetzalcóatl in his aspect as the wind god, shown with a projecting mouth mask. Mexica (Figure 11b).

Ek Chuah, see also Xamen Ek   Yucatec god of merchants and cacao, normally painted black and often shown traveling with a staff and back pack. Possibly of Putún origin. Classic and Postclassic periods (Figure 29).

Gucumatz, see Quetzalcóatl

Huehuéteotl   the old fire god, also known as Xiuhtecuhtli. One of the most ancient of Mesoamerican deities, often shown as an old man with wrinkled face and toothless, who bears a brazier on his head. Traced back to Preclassic cultures in the basin of Mexico and God I of the Olmecs.

Huitzilopochtli   special war and sun god of the Mexica, chief deity of Tenochtitlán. Identified by his special weapon, the fire serpent. He is also the blue Tezcatlipoca, associated with the south.

Itzamná   most important and supreme deity of Maya, abundantly represented in Classic and Postclassic art. Creator deity with multiple aspects affecting every phase of man's life. Both celestial and terrestial associations (Figure 29).

Itztlacoliuhqui   god of curved obsidian knife, variant of Tezcatlipoca as deity of the ice and cold, of sin and misery. Represented in Teotihuacán and Mexica art.

Ix Chel   leading Putún deity with great shrine at Cozumel. Goddess of the moon, childbirth, procreation, and medicine, associated with lakes, wells, and underground water. Wife of Yucatec sun god, Kinich Ahau.

Kinich Ahau   Yucatec name of sun god. Sun deity is abundantly represented in Classic and Postclassic Maya art with a square eye and prominent Roman nose, closely associated with Itzamná as the old sun god in the sky. His head glyph personifies the number four. The sun may also appear as a young man with an almond-shaped eye, personifying the day Ahau.

°*Based primarily on Caso, 1958, Joralemon, 1971, Sahagún, 1946, and Thompson, 1970.*

Selected List of Mesoamerican Deities°

Kukulcán, see also Quetzalcóatl   the feathered-serpent deity in Yucatán. The Codex Dresden relates the feathered serpent to the planet Venus, or Quetzalcóatl as the morning star. Many associations link the cult to the Putún Maya who brought it to Yucatán in the tenth century.

Mictlantecuhtli   Mexica God of death who resided in the underworld in darkness. He is usually represented wearing a mask in the form of a skull. Possibly derived from Olmec God VIII.

Quetzalcóatl, see also Kukulcán   the feathered-serpent deity, bearded god of learning and the priesthood, father and creator, brother of Xipe Totec, Tezcatlipoca, and Huitzilopochtli. He brought to man all knowledge of the arts, agriculture, and science. His many different aspects include: the wind god (Ehécatl), the morning star (Tlahuizcalpantecuhtli), and the evening star (Xólotl, his twin). Counterparts: Kukulcán and Gucumatz among the Maya. A feathered-serpent deity is prominent throughout Mesoamerican art, Classic and Postclassic periods. Preclassic representations include Olmec God VII (Figure 32; Photo 45).

Tezcatlipoca   a god of creation possessing many diverse forms, often identified by a smoking mirror which replaces his foot which was wrenched off by the earth monster. God of night closely associated with deities of death, evil, and destruction. Patron deity of sorcerers and robbers. Very important because of his direct intervention in the affairs of man. Attains prominence among Toltecs as the adversary of his brother, Quetzalcóatl. Revered later not only in Tenochtitlán but as the tutelary god of Texcoco and known in many parts of Mexico. Depicted on columns at Chichén Itzá (Figure 32).

Tlahuizcalpantecuhtli, see also Quetzalcóatl   Quetzalcóatl, the planet Venus as the morning star. He appears with two faces: that of a living man and the other a skull. Postclassic Central Mexico.

Tlaloc, see also Chac   rain god, "he who makes things grow." Mexica. Associated with serpent, mountains, flooding, drought, hail, ice, and lightning. Probably one of most ancient Mesoamerican deities, traced to Olmec God IV. Rings around the eyes, fangs and a volute over the mouth are frequent distinguishing characteristics. Counterpart among other Mesoamerican cultures: Chac (Lowland Maya), Tajín (Totonacs), Tzahui (Mixtecs), Cocijo (Zapotecs). Tlaloc representations are known from Classic Copán, Petén, and Puuc sites, and in Postclassic Chichén Itzá (Figures 28r, 32; Plates 2e, 9j, 13e).

Tloque Nahuaque   abstract invisible god revered in Texcoco under Nezahuacóyotl. Supreme deity who could not be represented materially. Worshipped in temples without idols.

Tonatiuh   the sun god of the Mexica, closely associated with the young warrior, Huitzilopochtli, the sun himself. Best known representation is that of the so-called "calendar stone" in which the central figure is Tonatiuh who clutches in his taloned eagle claws, hearts of human beings, his sustenance.

Xamen Ek, see also Ek Chuah   Maya god of the north star and the guide of merchants, logically associated with Ek Chuah. His name glyph is the hieroglyph for cardinal point north. Frequently represented in *códices* (Figure 29).

Xipe Totec   Mexica god of springtime, seeding and planting; the red Tezcatlipoca associated with the west. In his honor a priest dressed in the skin of a flayed victim, a ritual signifying the renewal of vegetation in the spring. Also called Yopi. Believed to have been brought to central Mexico from Oaxaca-Guerrero borders. Ultimate origins may be found in Olmec God VI. Revered in central Mexico, especially Tlaxcala. Represented also in Maya area in Campeche, Oxkintok, Chichén Itzá and Mayapán (Figure 32; Plate 7e; Photo 55).

Xólotl, see also Quetzalcóatl   Mexica god of the planet Venus as the evening star, twin brother of Quetzalcóatl. Represented as having the head of a dog. Postclassic central Mexico.

Yiacatecuhtli   Mexica god of the long-distance merchants. Shares some attributes with Quetzalcóatl. Symbol is a bamboo staff. Postclassic central Mexico, especially Cholula, Tenochtitlán–Tlatelolco.

Yum Cimil   Maya god of death and evil who presides over luckless days. In the *códices* his head often replaced by a skull; the ribs and backbone are exposed to view. Associated with the south, the color yellow, the number ten and day sign Cimi. Other names: Cizin and Hun Ahau (Figure 29).

Terms Frequently Used in Mesoamerican Archaeology

aguadas   seasonal water holes in lowland Maya region.

Atlantean figures   figures of men used as supporting or decorative columns (Toltec) (Figure 26a; Photo 44).

atlatl   spear thrower; a short, grooved stick with handles at one end used to propel a dart or lance (Figure 4h; Plate 10d).

bajos   broad, swampy depressions in Petén area that fill with water during summer months.

baktun   See Long Count.

calendar round   52-year cycle, produced by the permutation of the 260-day cycle and the 365-day true year.

calmécac   strict Mexica school for the male children of the king and nobility.

calpulli   kin units, "conical clans," division of Mexica tribe of which there were 20 in Tenochtitlán, occupying designated sectors of the city.

candelero   small clay incense burner (Figure 22d).

celt   ungrooved axe, popular wood-working tool.

cenote   natural underground well in Yucatán, a major source of water for drinking and bathing (Photo 3).

chacmool   life-size stone figure in reclining position, legs flexed, hands holding receptacle on abdomen, head turned to one side (Postclassic) (Plate 12c).

champ-levé   decorative ceramic technique in which part of the design area is heavily carved, characteristic of Classic Teotihuacán.

chapalote   ancient indigenous race of Mexican maize.

chinampa   very productive system of agriculture; artificial island of layers of mud and aquatic plants built out into a lake and rooted in place by trees. Popularly called "floating gardens" in the basin of Mexico (Photo 51).

chultun   bottle-shaped underground cistern in northern Yucatán, used for water storage; in the southern lowland Maya area, smaller lateral chambered *chultuns* were used for food storage, particularly of the breadnut.

cloisonné   method of decorating pottery, wood, or gourds in which a layer of paint is applied to the surface. A design is marked off and the paint cut out within the design area. The hollow spaces are then filled in with another color and the surface remains smooth. Several layers of paint can be worked in this way (cultures of northern and western Mexico).

coa   digging stick, principal farming instrument.

coatepantli   serpent wall, forming part of sacred precincts in Postclassic highland Mexico.

codex (plural: *códices*)   painted book made from bark paper or deer skin that folds like a screen (Photos 11, 12).

comal   clay griddle for frying tortillas (Figure 28j).

cord marking   decorative technique in which a fine cord was wrapped around a paddle and pressed against an unfired clay vessel, leaving a characteristic imprint.

Coyotlatelco ware   distinctive red-on-buff pottery tradition of Postclassic horizon.

cuauhxicalli   so-called "eagle cup," stone receptacle for burning and storing of human hearts (Mexica).

Danzantes   life-size carvings in bas-relief on stone slabs at Monte Albán (Plate 2d).

double-line break   incised decoration on pottery in which one or two lines run parallel to the lip or rim and then turn sharply and disappear over the edge (Figure 5e).

excising   decorative technique applied to pottery in which deep grooves, channels, or fields were carved from the surface; recessed areas often left rough and coated with red cinnabar (Preclassic) (Figure 5k; Plate 4c).

Fine Orange ware   Early Postclassic fine-grained paste pottery with several distinct varieties, V, X, Y and Z (Figure 28g, h, n).

florero   pottery jar with tall restricted neck and flaring rim (Classic Teotihuacán) (Figure 22f).

Haab   Maya calendar year of 365 days, corresponding to Mexica Xihuitl.

hacha (thin stone head)   beautifully carved stone, associated with the ball game cult, often with a notch or projecting tenon at back for attachment (Classic Veracruz cultures) (Plate 9g).

huéhuetl   vertical drum with skin head, played with palms and fingers (Photo 24).

Initial Series   see Long Count.

Glossary

katun   see Long Count.

kin   see Long Count.

Long Count   Total number of days elapsed from a mythical starting point in the past, 3113 B.C. (GMT correlation); recorded by the Maya in number of baktun (144,000 days or 20 katuns), katun (7200 days or 20 tuns), tun (360 days or 20 uinals), uinal (20 days or 20 kins), and kin (1 day) (Classic Lowland Maya) (Figure 16; Plate 6b).

"lost wax" (*cire perdue*)   method of casting metals; the desired form was carved in wax, coated with charcoal and clay; the wax was melted and ran out a duct as molten metal was poured into the casing of clay (Plate 16e).

macehual   commoner or laborer (Mexica).

malacate   spindle whorl, usually of clay; a perforated round disk used as a weight in spinning thread (Plate 11b).

mano   see *metate*.

mayeque   bondsman or "slave" in Mexica society.

metate   stone trough-like basin (quern) for grinding maize, accompanied by a hand stone (*mano*) (Figure 4s).

molcajete   bowl, usually tripod, with interior scoring or roughening for grinding fruits and vegetables (Figure 31i).

Nahua   language of Uto-Aztecan group; also applied to people.

Náhuat   an old linguistic form of Nahua, in contrast to the more recent close relative, Náhuatl, the language of the Mexica.

Náhuatl   language derived from Nahua which became the *lingua franca* of Mexica.

negative painting   see resist painting.

Nemontemi   five unlucky days at year end, Mexica calendar, corresponds to the Maya Uayeb (glyph, Figure 13s).

olla   pottery jar with flaring neck (Figure 4p).

omichicahuaztli   musical instrument made of a notched bone, often human or deer, played by rasping a stick along the serrations (Plate 15d).

palma (palmate stone)   carved fan-shaped stone with smooth dorsal surface, associated with ball game cult (Classic Veracruz cultures) (Plate 9h).

patolli   game played by Mexica on cross-shaped board much like modern Parcheesi.

penate   small stone figure produced in large quantity by the Mixtecs, serving as an amulet (?).

petate   woven straw mat.

pilli   privileged class in Tenochtitlán.

Pipil   term applied rather loosely to the speech and culture of migratory Náhuat-speaking groups in Central America.

pisote   coati (*Nasua*), a small, raccoon-like arboreal animal.

Plumbate   fine textured ware with a high percentage of iron compounds; upon firing, the surface acquires a hard, lustrous vitrified finish, often with a metallic iridescence. Two varieties: San Juan (Classic Maya), Tohil (Postclassic Maya) (Plate 11g).

"pot" irrigation   irrigation of cultivated plots of land where the water table is high by sinking wells at intervals in fields; water is drawn out by buckets or scoops and distributed around plants.

Putún   Chontal Maya inhabiting southern Campeche and delta regions of the Usumacinta and Grijalva rivers of Tabasco; outstanding seamen and merchants who extended their commercial interests throughout the Yucatán peninsula.

quexquemitl   cape-like blouse without sleeves.

resist painting (negative painting)   technique of decoration of pottery in which the design is covered before firing with some substance, probably wax, and paint applied; the wax is subsequently removed, revealing the design in base color. An alternative method is by firing vessel and then applying clay slip over design area; vegetable substance is then rubbed on and a low heat applied. The clay slip can subsequently be rubbed off, creating the same effect (Plates 4g, 11d).

rocker stamping   decorative technique in which a curved sharp edge, probably shell, is "walked" back and forth on pottery vessel, creating a curved zigzag incised line (Preclassic) (Figure 5o; Plate 4k).

roof comb (or crest)   a tall stone superstructure built on roof of lowland Maya temples, adding height and grandeur to the temple-pyramid complex. Openings were sometimes made to relieve the massive weight. Roof combs were often elaborately stuccoed, carved, and painted (Figure 24, Tikal, Palenque; Photos 22, 29).

sacbé   Maya causeway constructed of huge blocks of stone, leveled with gravel and paved with plaster.

Short Count abbreviated date recording system utilized by the Maya in Late Post-classic Yucatán, consisting of 13 katuns (13 × 7200 days or 256¼ years), each katun bearing the name of the day on which it ended, always Ahau. Thus, a Short Count date (as referred to in the Books of Chilam Balam) might read katun 9 Ahau, or katun 7 Ahau.

slash-and-burn agriculture swidden agriculture, in which fields are cleared, burned, and planted until yield decreases, then allowed to lie fallow for several years to regain fertility.

Soconusco (Xoconusco) geographical province of Pacific coastal plains of Chiapas and Guatemala, an important port of trade in the Late Postclassic period (Map 4).

stela (plural: *stelae*) stone column monument (Plate 6).

stirrup spout distinctive ceramic form with two hollow tubes that rise from the body of the vessel to form a single spout (Preclassic) (Figure 5ff; Plate 13f).

talpetate see *tepetate*

talud–tablero architectural feature consisting of a sloping apron (*talud*) surmounted by a horizontal, rectangular panel (*tablero*) (Teotihuacán) (Figures 21, 25).

tecali Mexican onyx, either a banded calcite, travertine, or alabaster (Plate 10k).

tecomate spherical pottery vessel with restricted opening and no collar (Figure 5m, o, s; Plate 4c).

tecuhtli privileged class in Tenochtitlán.

telpochcalli Mexica schools for *macehuals*, standard training, instruction in warfare.

temescal sweat bath, often used for ritual purification.

tepetate (*talpetate*) a fine-grained compact yellowish substance of volcanic origin.

teponaztli horizontal cylindrical wooden drum with slotted tongues, struck with tongs (Figure 17b; Plate 15f).

Thin Orange ware fine-paste, thin-walled pottery, widely traded in the Classic period (Plate 7c).

tlachtli ancient ritual ball game.

tlacolol agriculture a variant of the slash-and-burn system in which cultivable land is divided into sectors, some of which are planted for two to three years, then left to fallow for three to four years; usually practiced on slopes.

Tonalpohualli 260-day cycle, Mexica, composed of 20 days combined with 13 numbers, corresponding to the Maya Tzolkin.

Tripsacum wild grass that will hybridize with maize.

tumpline carrying strap passed over either the chest or forehead, facilitating transportation of a burden packed on the back (see figure heading, Chapter 2).

tun see Long Count (glyphs, Figure 15).

Tzolkin 260-day cycle, Maya, composed of 20 days combined with 13 numbers, corresponding to Mexica Tonalpohualli.

tzompantli skull rack, usually located near temple, to which heads of sacrificial victims were skewered (Postclassic).

Uayeb remaining five unlucky days at year end, Maya; known as Nemontemi among the Mexica (glyph, Figure 12).

uinal see Long Count (glyphs, Figure 15).

Usulután ware pottery decorated with a resist technique producing groups of wavelike yellowish lines on a dark orange or brown background; the center of manufacture is thought to have been Usulután, El Salvador (Plate 4g).

volador ceremony in which men dressed as gods or birds descend to earth from a rotating platform erected at the top of a high pole; the men were tied at the waist by ropes that unwound as they circled to earth.

white-rimmed black ware pottery with a contrast in surface color produced by differential firing (Preclassic).

Xicalanco Gulf coast region of Tabasco, important port of trade in the Late Postclassic period (Map 4).

Xoconusco see Soconusco.

Xihuitl Mexica calendar year of 365 days, corresponding to Maya Haab.

yácata Tarascan mound or pyramid (Photo 57).

yoke U-shaped stone, often elaborately carved, believed to be imitation of the protective belt worn by ball players (Plate 9k).

Bibliography

Abbreviations used for frequently cited publications

AA	American Anthropologist
AAA-M	American Anthropological Association, Memoir
AATQ	American Antiquity
AMNH-AP	American Museum of Natural History, Anthropological Papers
APS-P	American Philosophical Society, Proceedings
APS-T	American Philosophical Society, Transactions
BAE-B	Bureau of American Ethnology, Bulletin, Smithsonian Institution.
CA	Cuadernos Americanos
CIW-P	Carnegie Institution of Washington, Publication
CIW-C	Carnegie Institution of Washington, Contribution
DO-CO	Dumbarton Oaks Conference on the Olmec, Trustees for Harvard University, Washington, D.C., 1968
DO-SPAA	Dumbarton Oaks, Studies in Pre-Columbian Art and Archaeology, Trustees for Harvard University, Washington, D.C.
EX	Expedition, Bulletin of the University of Pennsylvania, Philadelphia, Pennsylvania
HMAI	*Handbook of Middle American Indians,* R. Wauchope, (General Ed.), Austin, Texas: University of Texas Press.
IA	Ibero-Americana
ICA	International Congress of Americanists
INAH	Instituto Nacional de Antropología e Historia, Mexico, D.F.
INAH-A	Instituto Nacional de Antropología e Historia, Anales
INAH-B	Instituto Nacional de Antropología e Historia, Boletín
INAH-M	Instituto Nacional de Antropología e Historia, Memorias
KAS-P	Kroeber Anthropological Society, Papers
NWAF-P	New World Archaeological Foundation, Papers. Brigham Young University, Provo, Utah.
PM-P	Peabody Museum, Harvard University, Archaeological and Ethnological Papers
PMNW	*Prehistoric Man in the New World.* J. D. Jennings and E. Norbeck (Eds.), Chicago, Illinois: University of Chicago Press, 1964
PSP	*Prehistoric Settlement Patterns in the New World.* G. R. Willey (Ed.). Viking Fund Publications in Anthropology, No. 23, 1956
PTV	*Prehistory of the Tehuacán Valley.* D. S. Byers (Ed.), Austin, Texas: University of Texas Press
RMEA	*Revista Mexicana de Estudios Antropológicos,* Mexico, D.F.
SCA	*Smithsonian Contributions to Anthropology,* Washington, D.C.
SWJA	*Southwestern Journal of Anthropology*
VFPA	Viking Fund Publications in Anthropology, Chicago, Illinois: Aldine
WA	World Archaeology, Oxon, England

ACOSTA, J. R.
1941 Los últimos descubrimientos arqueológicos en Tula, Hgo. 1941, *RMEA,* **5,** 239–248.
1945 La cuarta y quinta temporada de excavaciones en Tula, Hidalgo, 1943–1944, *RMEA,* **7,** 23–64.
1956 Resumen de las exploraciones arqueológicas en Tula, Hidalgo, durante los VI, VII y VIII Temporadas 1946–1950. *INAH-A,* **8,** 37–116.
1956– Interpretación de algunos de los datos obtenidos en Tula relativos a la época Tol-
1957 teca, *RMEA,* **14,** 75–110.
1964 El Palacio del Quetzalpapálotl, *INAH-M,* **10.**
1965 Preclassic and Classic architecture of Oaxaca, *HMAI,* **3,** 814–836.
ACOSTA SAIGNES, M.
1945 Los Pochteca, *Acta Antropológica,* **1,** No. 1.
1946 Los Teopixque, *RMEA,* **8,** 147–205.
ADAMS, R. E. W.
1970 Suggested Classic period occupational specialization in the southern Maya lowlands, *PM-P,* **61,** 487–498.
ADAMS, R. E. W., & TRIK, A. S.
1961 Temple 1 (Str. 5D-1): Post-constructional activities, *Tikal Reports,* No. 7, *Museum Monographs,* The University Museum, Philadelphia, Pennsylvania.
ADAMS, R. M.
1961 Changing patterns of territorial organization in the central highlands of Chiapas, Mexico, *AATQ,* **26,** No. 3, 341–360.
1967 *The Evolution of Urban Society.* Chicago, Illinois: Aldine.

ANDERSON, W. F.

1971   Arithmetic in Maya numerals, *AATQ*, **36**, 54–63.

ANDREWS, E. W.

1960   Excavations at Dzibilchaltún, northwestern Yucatán, Mexico. *APS-P*, **104**, No. 3, 254–265.

1965   Archaeology and prehistory in the northern Maya lowlands, *HMAI*, **2**, 288–330.

ARMILLAS, P.

1950   Teotihuacán, Tula, y los Toltecas, *Runa*, **3**, 37–70.

1964   Northern Mesoamerica, *PMNW*, pp. 291–330.

1969   The arid frontier of Mexican civilization, *Transactions of the New York Academy of Sciences, Series II*, **31**, 697–704.

AVELEYRA ARROYO DE ANDA, L.

1950   *Prehistoria de Mexico*, Mexico, D.F.: Ediciones Mexicanas.

1956   The second mammoth and associated artifacts at Santa Isabel Iztapan, Mexico, *AATQ*, **22**, 12–28.

1963   *La estela teotihuacana de la Ventilla, Mexico*. Mexico, D.F.: Museo Nacional de Antropología.

1964   The Primitive Hunters, *HMAI*, **1**, 384–412.

AVELEYRA ARROYO DE ANDA, L., & MALDONADO-KOERDELL, M.

1953   Association of artifacts with mammoths in the Valley of Mexico, *AATQ*, **18**, 332–340.

BARLOW, R. H.

1949   The extent of the empire of the Colhua-Mexica, *IA*, No. 28.

BARRERA VÁSQUEZ, A., & MORLEY, S. G.

1949   The Maya chronicles, *CIW-C*, No. 48.

BENNETT, W. C.

1944   The north highlands of Peru: Excavations in the Callejón de Huaylas and at Chavín de Huantar, *AMNH-AP*, **39**, Part 1.

BENNYHOFF, J. A.

1967   Chronology and periodization: Continuity and chance in the Teotihuacán ceramic tradition. *Teotihuacán, Onceava Mesa Redonda*. Mexico, D.F.: Sociedad Mexicana de Antropologia. Pp. 19–30.

BERLIN, H.

1958   El glifo "emblema" en las inscripciones mayas. *Journal de la Société des Americanistes*, **47**, 111–119.

BERNAL, I.

1965   Archaeological synthesis of Oaxaca, *HMAI*, **3**, 788–813.

BLOM, F.

1932   The Maya ball-game *pok-ta-pok* (called *tlachtli* by the Aztec). Middle American Research Institute, Tulane University, Publication No. 4, 485–530.

BLOM, F., & LA FARGE, O.

1926–   Tribes and temples, Middle American Research Institute, Tulane University,
1927   Publication No. 1. 2 vols.

BORHEGYI, S. F.

1965   Archaeological synthesis of the Guatemalan highlands, *HMAI*, **2**, 3–58.

BRAINERD, G. W.

1941   Fine Orange pottery in Yucatán, *RMEA*, **5**, 163–183.

BRAND, D. D.

1943   An historical sketch of geography and anthropology in the Tarascan region, Part 1. *New Mexico Anthropologist*, **6, 7**, 37–108.

BRANIFF, B.

1970   Oscilación de la frontera septentrional mesoamericana. Paper presented at the 35th Annual Meeting, Society for American Archaeology, Mexico, D.F.

BRONSON, B.

1966   Roots and the subsistence of the ancient Maya, *SWJA*, **22**, No. 3, 251–279.

BRUSH, C. F.

1969   A contribution to the archaeology of coastal Guerrero, Mexico. Unpublished doctoral dissertation, Columbia University, New York.

BRUSH, E. S.

1968   The archaeological significance of ceramic figurines from Guerrero, Mexico. Unpublished doctoral dissertation, Columbia University, New York.

BULLARD, W. R., Jr.

1960   The Maya settlement pattern in northeastern Petén, Guatemala, *AATQ*, **25**, 355–372.

1970   Topoxte, a Post-Classic Maya site in Petén, Guatemala, *PM-P*, **61**, 245–307.

BYAM DAVIES, C. N.
1968   Los señoríos independientes del imperio azteca, *INAH*, Serie Historia 19.

CANBY, J. S.
1951   Possible chronological implications of the long ceramic sequence recovered at Yarumela, Spanish Honduras. In S. Tax (Ed.), *The Civilizations of Ancient America, Selected Papers of the 29th International Congress of Americanists.* Pp. 79–85.

CARNEIRO, R. L.
1960   Slash and burn agriculture: A closer look at its implications for settlement patterns. In F. C. Wallace (Ed.), *Men and Cultures*, Philadelphia: University of Pennsylvania. Pp. 229–234.

CARR, R. F., & HAZARD, J. E.
1961   Map of the ruins of Tikal, El Petén, Guatemala. *Tikal Reports*, No. 11, *Museum Monographs*, The University Museum, Philadelphia, Pennsylvania.

CASO, A.
1942   El paraiso terrenal en Teotihuacán, *CA*, **1**, No. 6.
1958   *The Aztecs, People of the Sun.* Norman, Oklahoma: University of Oklahoma Press.
1965a Lapidary work, goldwork and copperwork from Oaxaca, *HMAI*, **3**, 896–930.
1965b Zapotec writing and calendar, *HMAI*, **3**, 931–947.
1965c Mixtec writing and calendar, *HMAI*, **3**, 948–961.
1967   *Los Calendarios Prehispánicos.* Mexico, D.F.: Universidad Nacional Autónoma de México, Instituto de Investigaciones Históricas.

CASO, A., & BERNAL, I.
1952   Urnas de Oaxaca, *INAH-M*, **2.**
1965   Ceramics of Oaxaca, *HMAI*, **3**, 871–895.

CASO, A., BERNAL, I., & ACOSTA, J. R.
1967   La cerámica de Monte Albán, *INAH-M*, **13.**

CHAPMAN, A. M.
1959   Port of Trade Enclaves in Aztec and Maya Civilizations. In K. Polanyi & C. M. Pearson (Eds.), *Trade and Market in Early Empires.* Glencoe, Illinois: Free Press of Glencoe. Pp. 114–153.

CHILDE, V. G.
1952a The birth of civilization, *Past and Present*, No. 2, 1–10.
1952b *New Light on the Most Ancient East.* London: Routledge & Kegan Paul.

CODEX BORBÓNICO
1899   In M. E. T. Hamy (Ed.), *Manuscrit Mexicain de la Bibliotéque de Palais Bourbon.* Paris.

CODEX BOTURINI
1830– In Lord E. K. Kingsborough, *Antiquities of Mexico.* Vol. I. London: Robert Havel
1848   & Calnaglie, Son & Co.

CODEX CHIMALPOPOCA
1945   *Anales de Cuauhtitlán y Leyenda de los Soles,* translated from Náhuatl by Primo F. Velazquez. Mexico, D.F.: Universidad Nacional Autónoma de Mexico, Instituto de Historia.

CODEX DRESDEN
1930   In J. A. Villacorta and C. A. Villacorta, *Códices Maya.* Guatemala City: Tipografia Nacional.

CODEX FEJÉVÁRY
1830– In Lord E. K. Kingsborough, *Antiquities of Mexico.* Vol. III. London: Robert
1848   Havel & Calnaglie, Son & Co.

CODEX FLORENTINO
1905   In Fray B. de Sahagún, Francisco del Paso y Troncoso (Ed.), *Historia General de las Cosas de Nueva España, Facsimile Edition of Vol. 5.* Madrid: Hauser y Menet.

CODEX MAGLIABECCHIANO
1904   *Manuscrit Mexicain Post-Colombien de la Bibliothèque National de Florence.* Rome: Duke of Loubat.

CODEX MATRITENSE de la REAL ACADEMIA de la HISTORIA
1907   In Fray B. de Sahagún, Francisco del Paso y Troncoso (Ed.), *Historia General de las Cosas de Nueva España, Facsimile Edition of Vol 8.* Madrid: Hauser y Menet.

CODEX MENDOZA
1830– In Lord E. K. Kingsborough, *Antiquities of Mexico.* Vol. I. London: Robert Havel
1848   & Calnaglie, Son & Co.

CODEX NUTTALL
1902   In *Facsimile Edition,* Introduction by Zelia Nuttall. Cambridge, Massachusetts: Peabody Museum of American Archaeology and Ethnology.

CODEX TELLERIANO-REMENSIS
  1889 In *Facsimile Edition,* Commentary by E. T. Hamy. Paris: Duke of Loubat.
CODEX TRO-CORTESIANO
  1930 In J. A. Villacorta and C. A. Villacorta, *Códices Maya.* Guatemala City: Tipografía Nacional.
COE, M. D.
  1957 Cycle 7 monuments in Middle America: A reconsideration, *AA,* **59,** 597–611.
  1961 La Victoria, an early site on the Pacific Coast of Guatemala, *PM-P,* **53.**
  1962 *Mexico.* New York: Praeger.
  1964 The chinampas of Mexico. *Scientific American,* July, 90–98.
  1965a Archaeological synthesis of southern Veracruz, and Tabasco, *HMAI,* **3,** 679–715.
  1965b The Olmec style and its distribution, *HMAI,* **3,** 739–775.
  1965c *The Jaguar's Children: Preclassic Central Mexico.* New York: Museum of Primitive Art.
  1966 *The Maya.* New York: Praeger.
  1968a San Lorenzo and the Olmec civilization, *DO-CO.* Pp. 41–71.
  1968b *America's First Civilization: Discovering the Olmec.* New York: American Heritage.
  1970 The archaeological sequence at San Lorenzo, Tenochtitlán, Veracruz, Mexico. *Contributions of the University of California, Archaeological Research Facility,* No. 8, 21–34.
COE, M. D., & COBEAN, R.
  1970 Obsidian trade at San Lorenzo, Tenochtitlán, Mexico. Paper presented at the 35th Annual Meeting, Society for American Archaeology, Mexico, D.F.
COE, M. D., & FLANNERY, K. V.
  1964 Microenvironments and Mesoamerican prehistory, *Science,* **143,** 650–654.
  1967 Early cultures and human ecology in south coastal Guatemala, *SCA,* **3.**
COE, W. R.
  1957 Environmental limitation on Maya culture: A re-examination, *AA,* **59,** No. 2, 328–335.
  1959 Piedras Negras archaeology: Artifacts, caches, and burials, *Museum Monographs,* The University Museum, Philadelphia, Pennsylvania.
  1962 A summary of excavation and research at Tikal, Guatemala, 1956–1961, *AATQ,* **27,** 479–507.
  1965 Tikal: Ten years of study of a Maya ruin in the lowlands of Guatemala, *EX,* **8,** No. 1, 5–56.
  1967 *Tikal: A Handbook of the Ancient Maya Ruins.* Philadelphia: University of Pennsylvania.
COE, W. R., & McGINN, J. J.
  1963 The North Acropolis of Tikal and an Early Tomb, *EX,* **5,** No. 2, 24–32.
COOK, S. F.
  1947 The interrelation of population, food supply and building in pre-Conquest central Mexico, *AATQ,* **13,** 45–52.
CORTÉS, H.
  1908 *The letters of Cortés to Charles V* (F. A. MacNutt, translator). New York and London: Oxford University Press. 2 vols.
COVARRUBIAS, M.
  1946 El arte "Olmeca" o de la Venta, *CA,* **28,** No. 4, 153–179.
  1957 *Indian Art of Mexico and Central America.* New York: Knopf.
COWGILL, G. L.
  1964 The end of Classic Maya culture: A review of recent evidence, *SWJA,* **20,** 145–159.
COWGILL, U. M.
  1962 An agricultural study of the southern Maya lowlands, *AA,* **64,** No. 2, 273–286.
CULBERT, T. P.
  1965 The ceramic history of the central highlands of Chiapas, Mexico, *NWF-P,* No. 19.
  1970 Sociocultural integration and the Classic Maya. Paper presented at the 35th Annual Meeting, Society for American Archaeology, Mexico, D.F.
DAHLGREN DE JORDAN, B.
  1954 *La Mixteca, su Cultura e Historia Prehispánica.* Mexico, D.F.: Imprenta Universitaria.
DE TERRA, H., ROMERO, J., & STEWART, T. D.
  1949 Tepexpan Man, *VFPA,* No. 11.
DIAZ DEL CASTILLO, B.
  1944 *Historia Verdadera de la Conquista de la Nueva España.* Mexico, D.F.: Editorial Pedro Robredo. 3 vols.

DIBBLE, C. E.
1940   El antiguo sistema de escritura en Mexico, *RMEA*, **4**, 105–128.
DI PESO, C. C.
1966   Archaeology and ethnohistory of the northern sierra, *HMAI*, **4**, 3–25.
DIXON, K. A.
1959   Ceramics from two Preclassic periods at Chiapa de Corzo, Chiapas, Mexico, *NWF-P*, No. 5.
DRUCKER, P.
1943a Ceramic sequences at Tres Zapotes, Veracruz, Mexico, *BAE-B* 140.
1943b Ceramic stratigraphy at Cerro de las Mesas, Veracruz, Mexico, *BAE-B* 141.
1952   La Venta, Tabasco: A study of Olmec ceramics and art, *BAE-B* 153.
DRUCKER, P., & HEIZER, R. F.
1960   A study of the *milpa* system of La Venta Islands and its archaeological implications, *SWJA*, **16**, 36–45.
DRUCKER, P., HEIZER, R. F., & SQUIER, R. J.
1959   Excavations at La Venta, Tabasco, 1955, *BAE-B* 170.
DUMOND, D. E.
1961   Swidden agriculture and the rise of Maya civilization, *SWJA*, No. 4, 301–316.
DURÁN, D.
1867– J. F. Ramirez (Ed.), *Historia de las indias de Nueva España y islas de tierra firme.*
1880   Mexico, D.F.: J. M. Andrade & F. Escalante. 2 vols. and atlas.
DUTTON, B. P.
1955   Tula of the Toltecs, *El Palacio*, **62**, 195–251.
EDWARDS, C. R.
1969   Possibilities of pre-Columbian maritime contacts among New World civilizations. *Mesoamerican Studies*, No. 4, 3–10. Carbondale, Illinois: Research Records of the University Museum, Southern Illinois University.
EKHOLM, G. F.
1942   Excavations at Guasave, Sinaloa, Mexico, *AMNH-AP*, **38**, 23–139.
1944   Excavations at Tampico and Pánuco in the Huasteca, Mexico, *AMNH-AP*, **38**, 321–509.
1948   Ceramic stratigraphy at Acapulco, Guerrero, In *El Occidente de México, Mesa Redonda*. Mexico, D.F.: Sociedad Mexicana de Antropologia. Pp. 95–104.
1961   Puerto Rican stone "collars" as ballgame belts. In S. F. Lothrop *et al.* (Eds.), *Essays in Pre-Columbian Art and Archaeology*. Cambridge, Massachusetts: Harvard University Press. Pp. 356–371.
1964   Transpacific Contacts, *PMNW*. Pp. 489–510.
EKHOLM, S. M.
1969   Mound 30A and the Early Preclassic ceramic sequence of Izapa, Chiapas, Mexico, *NWAF-P*, No. 25.
ERASMUS, C. J.
1950   Patolli, pachisi and the limitation of possibilities, *SWJA*, **6**, 369–387.
EVANS, C., & MEGGERS, B. J.
1966   Mesoamerica and Ecuador, *HMAI*, **4**, 243–264.
FLANNERY, K. V.
1967   *The Vertebrate Fauna and Hunting Patterns*. Vol. 1. *PTV*, Pp. 132–177.
1968a The Olmecs and the valley of Oaxaca: A model for inter-regional interaction in formative times, *DO-CO*. Pp. 79–110.
1968b Archaeological systems theory and early Mesoamerica. In B. J. Meggers (Ed.), *Anthropological Archaeology in the Americas*. Washington, D.C.: The Anthropological Society of Washington, Pp. 67–87.
FLANNERY, K. V., KIRKBY, A. V., KIRKBY, M. J., & WILLIAMS, A. W.
1967   Farming systems and political growth in ancient Oaxaca, Mexico, *Science*, **158**, 445–454.
FORD, J. A.
1969   A comparison of formative cultures in the Americas, *SCA*, **11**.
FOSTER, M. L.
1971   American Indian and Old World languages: A model for reconstruction. Paper presented at the 70th Annual Meeting of the American Anthropological Association, New York.
FURST, P. T.
1965a West Mexico, the Caribbean and northern South America: Some problems in New World interrelationships, *Antropológica*, No. 14.
1965b West Mexican tomb sculpture as evidence for shamanism in prehispanic Mesoamerica, *Antropológica*, No. 15.

1968 The Olmec were-jaguar motif in the light of ethnographic reality, *DO-CO*. Pp. 143–174.

1970 Paper presented at Before Cortés Symposium, Metropolitan Museum of Art, New York, October 5–9.

GARCÍA PAYÓN, J.

1955 *Exploraciones en el Tajin, temporadas 1953 y 1954*. Mexico, D.F.: Instituto Nacional de Antropología e Historia.

1957 *El Tajin, Guia Oficial*. Mexico, D.F.: Instituto Nacional de Antropología e Historia.

GAY, C. T. E.

1967 Oldest paintings in the New World, *Natural History*, **76**, No. 4, 28–35.

GILLMOR, F.

1964 *The King Danced in the Marketplace*. Tucson, Arizona: University of Arizona Press.

GLASS, J. B.

1966 Archaeological Survey of Western Honduras, *HMAI*, **4**, 157–179.

GRAHAM, I.

1967 Archaeological Explorations in El Petén, Guatemala, *Middle American Research Institute, Publication 33*, Tulane University, New Orleans, Louisiana.

1971 *The Art of Maya Hieroglyphic Writing*. Cambridge Massachusetts: Harvard University Press.

GREEN, D. F., & LOWE, G. W.

1967 Altamira and Padre Piedra, Early Preclassic Sites in Chiapas, Mexico, *NWAF-P*, No. 20.

GRIFFIN, J. B.

1964 The northeast woodlands area, *PMNW*. Pp. 223–258.

1966 Mesoamerica and the eastern United States in prehistoric times, *HMAI*, **4**, 111–131.

GROVE, D. C.

1968a Chalcatzingo, Morelos, Mexico: A reappraisal of the Olmec rock carvings, *AATQ*, **33**, 486–491.

1968b The Preclassic Olmec in central Mexico: Site distribution and inferences, *DO-CO*. Pp. 179–185.

1970a The Morelos Formative: Cultural stratigraphy and implications. Paper presented at the 35th Annual Meeting, Society for American Archaeology, Mexico, D.F.

1970b The Olmec paintings of Oxtotitlán Cave, Guerrero, Mexico. *DO-SPAA*, No. 6.

1970c The San Pablo pantheon mound: A Middle Preclassic site in Morelos, Mexico. *AATQ*, **35**, 62–73.

1971 The Mesoamerican Formative and South American influences. Primer Simposio de Correlaciones Antropológicas Andino–Mesoamericano, Salinas, Ecuador. Mimeographed copy

GROVE, D. C., & PARADIS, L. I.

1971 An Olmec stela from San Miguel Amuco, Guerrero, *AATQ*, **36**, 95–102.

HAVILAND, W. A.

1966 Social integration and the Classic Maya, *AATQ*, **31**, 625–631.

1969 A new population estimate for Tikal, Guatemala, *AATQ*, **34**, 429–433.

1970 Tikal Guatemala and Mesoamerican urbanism, *WA*, **2**, No. 2, 186–198.

HEINE-GELDERN, R.

1959 Chinese influence in Mexico and Central America: The Tajín style of Mexico and the marble vases from Honduras, *Actas del 33 Congreso Internacional de Americanistas, San José, Costa Rica*, **1**, 195–206.

1966 The problem of transpacific influences in Mesoamerica, *HMAI*, **4**, 277–295.

HEIZER, R. F.

1960 Agriculture and the theocratic State in Lowland Southeastern Mexico, *AATQ*, **26**, 215–222.

1968 New observations on La Venta, *DO-CO*. Pp. 9–36.

HEIZER, R. F., & BENNYHOFF, J. A.

1958a Archaeological Investigation of Cuicuilco, Valley of Mexico, *Science*, **127**, 232–233.

1958b Excavations at Cuicuilco in 1957. Unpublished manuscript.

HEIZER, R. F., & COOK, S. F.

1959 New Evidence of Antiquity of Tepexpan and other Human Remains from the Valley of Mexico, *SWJA*, **15**, 32–42.

HISTORIA TOLTECA-CHICHIMECA
   1947   *Anales de Quauhtinchan* (prologue by P. Kirchhoff). Mexico, D.F.: Antiqua
          Librería Robredo, de José Porrua e Hijos.
IXTLILXÓCHITL, F. DE A.
   1891   Alfredo Chavero (Ed.), *Obras Históricas*. Vol. 1. *Relaciones*. Vol. 2. *Historia Chi-
          chimeca*. Mexico, D.F.: Oficina Tipográfica de la Secretaria de Fomento.
IZUMI, S., & SONO, T.
   1963   *Andes 2: Excavations at Kotosh, Peru, 1960,* University of Tokyo, Scientific Ex-
          pedition to the Andes. Tokyo: Kadokawa Publ.
JENNINGS, J. D.
   1968   *Prehistory of North America*. New York: McGraw-Hill.
JIMÉNEZ MORENO, W.
   1941   Tula y los Toltecas según las fuentes históricas, *RMEA*, **5,** 79–83.
   1942   El enigma de los Olmecas, *CA*, **1,** No. 5, 113–145.
   1955   Síntesis de la historia precolonial del Valle de México, *RMEA*, **14,** Part 1, 219–
          236.
   1962   La historiografía Tetzcocana y sus problemas, *RMEA*, **18,** 81–85.
JORALEMON, P. D.
   1971   A study of Olmec ïconography, *DO-SPAA*, No. 7.
KEHOE, A. B.
   1962   A hypothesis on the origin of northeastern American pottery, *SWJA*, **18,** No. 1,
          20–29.
KELLEY, D. H.
   1960   Calendar, animals and deities, *SWJA*, **16,** 317–337.
   1962a Glyphic evidence for a dynastic sequence at Quiriguá, Guatemala, *AATQ*, **27,**
          323–335.
   1962b Fonetismo en la escritura Maya, *Estudios de Cultura Maya*, **2,** 277–318.
   1962c A history of the decipherment of Maya script, *Anthropological Linguistics*, **4,**
          No. 8.
   1969   Culture diffusion in Asia and America. In H. A. Moran and D. H. Kelley, (Eds.),
          The Alphabet and The Ancient Calendar Signs. Palo Alto, California: Daily Press.
          Pp. 125–139.
KELLEY, J. C.
   1956   Settlement Patterns in North-Central Mexico, *PSP*. Pp. 128–139.
   1960   North Mexico and the Correlation of Mesoamerican and Southwestern Cultural
          Sequences. In A. P. C. Wallace (Ed.), *Selected Papers, 5th International Congress
          of Anthropological Sciences, Philadelphia, Pennsylvania*. Pp. 566–573.
   1966   Mesoamerica and the Southwestern United States, *HMAI*, **4,** 94–110.
KELLEY, J. C., & WINTERS, H. D.
   1960   A revision of the archaeological sequence in Sinaloa, Mexico. *AATQ*, **25,** 547–561.
KELLY, I. T.
   1938   Excavations at Chametla, Sinaloa, *IA*, No. 14.
   1947   Excavations at Apatzingán, Michoacán, *VFPA*, No. 7.
   1945– The archaeology of the Autlán-Tuxcacuesco area of Jalisco: I: The Autlán zone,
   1949   II: The Tuxcacuesco Zapotitlán zone, *IA*, No. 26, 27.
   1970   Preclassic material from Colima. Paper presented at the 35th Annual Meeting,
          Society for American Archaeology, Mexico, D.F.
KELLY, I. T., & PALERM, A.
   1952   The Mexican conquests in *The Tajín Totonac*, Part 1, Publication 13. Washington,
          D.C.: Smithsonian Institution, Institute of Social Anthropology. Pp. 264–317.
KIDDER, A. V.
   1947   The artifacts of Uaxactún, Guatemala, *CIW-P* 576.
KIDDER, A. V., JENNINGS, J. D., & SHOOK, E. M.
   1946   Excavations at Kaminaljuyú, Guatemala, *CIW-P* 561.
KINGSBOROUGH, LORD E. K.
   1830– *Antiquities of Mexico*. London: Robert Havel & Calnaglie, Son & Co. 9 vols.
   1848
KIRCHHOFF, P.
   1943   Mesoamerica, *Acta Americana*, **1,** 92–107.
   1954– Land tenure in ancient Mexico, *RMEA*, **14,** Part 1, 351–362.
   1955
   1955   Quetzalcóatl, Huémac y el fin de Tula, *CA*, **84,** No. 6, 163–196.

KNOROZOV, Y. V.
  1958   The problem of the study of the Maya hieroglyphic writing, *AATQ*, **23**, 284–291.
  1967   *The Writing of the Maya Indians (Russian Translation Series)*. Vol. 4. Cambridge, Massachusetts: Harvard University Press.
KRICKEBERG, W.
  1961   *Las Antiguas Culturas Mexicanas*. Mexico, D.F.: Fondo de Cultura Económica.
KROEBER, A. L.
  1948   *Anthropology*. New York: Harcourt.
KUBLER, G.
  1967   The iconography of the art of Teotihuacán, *DO-SPAA*, No. 4.
  1970   Paper presented at Before Cortés Symposium, Metropolitan Museum of Art, New York, October 5–9.
LANNING, E. P.
  1967   *Peru before the Incas*. Englewood Cliffs, New Jersey: Prentice-Hall.
LATHRAP, D. W.
  1958   The cultural sequence at Yarinacocha, eastern Peru, *AATQ*, **23**, 379–388.
  1966   Relationships between Mesoamerica and the Andean areas, *HMAI*, **4**, 265–276.
  1970   *The Upper Amazon*. New York: Praeger.
LEÓN, N.
  1904   *Los Tarascos*. Mexico, D.F.: Museo Nacional.
LEÓN-PORTILLA, M.
  1963   *Aztec Thought and Culture, a Study of the Ancient Náhuatl Mind*. Norman, Oklahoma: University of Oklahoma Press.
LINDSAY, A. J. JR.
  1968   Current research, *AATQ*, **35**, 418.
LINNE, S.
  1934   Archaeological researches at Teotihuacán, Mexico, Publication No. 1. Stockholm: Ethnographical Museum of Sweden.
  1942   Mexican highland cultures: Archaeological researches at Teotihuacán, Calpulalpan, and Chalchicomula in 1934–1935, Publication No. 7. Stockholm: Ethnographical Museum of Sweden.
LISTER, R. H.
  1955   The present status of the archaeology of western Mexico: A distributional study, *University of Colorado Studies, Series in Anthropology*, No. 5. Boulder, Colorado.
LONGYEAR, J. M., III.
  1952   Copán ceramics: A study of southeastern Maya pottery, *CIW-P* 597.
  1966   Archaeological Survey of El Salvador, *HMAI*, **4**, 132–156.
LORENZO, J. L.
  1970   Cronología y la posición de Tlapacoya en la prehistoria americana. Paper presented at the 35th Annual Meeting, Society for American Archaeology, Mexico, D.F.
LOTHROP, S. K.
  1924   Tulum, An archaeological study of the east coast of Yucatán, *CIW-P* 335.
LOWE, G. W.
  1959   Archaeological exploration of the upper Grijalva River, Chiapas, Mexico, *NWAF-P*, No. 2.
LOWE, G. W., & MASON, J. A.
  1965   Archaeological survey of the Chiapas coast, highlands and upper Grijalva Basin, *HMAI*, **2**, 195–236.
MacNEISH, R. S.
  1954   An early archaeological site near Pánuco, Veracruz, *APS-T*, **44**, Part 5, 543–646.
  1958   Preliminary archaeological investigations in the Sierra de Tamaulipas, Mexico, *APS-T*, **48**, Part 6.
  1961   First annual report of the Tehuacán archaeological botanical project, Project Reports No. 1. Andover, Massachusetts: R. S. Peabody Foundation.
  1962   Second annual report of the Tehuacán archaeological botanical project, Project Reports No. 2. Andover, Massachusetts: R. S. Peabody Foundation for Archaeology.
  1967   A summary of the subsistence, *PTV*, **1**, 290–309.
  1969   First annual report of the Ayacucho archaeological botanical project. Andover, Massachusetts: R. S. Peabody Foundation for Archaeology.
  1970   Megafauna and man from Ayacucho, Highland Peru, *Science*, **168**, 975–977.
MacNEISH, R. S., & NELKEN-TEMER, A.
  1967   Introduction, *PTV*, **2**, 3–13.

MacNEISH, R. S., & PETERSON, F. A.

1962 The Santa Marta rock shelter, Ocozocoautla, Chiapas, Mexico, *NWAF-P*, No. 14, Publication 10.

MacNEISH, R. S., PETERSON, F. A., & FLANNERY, K. V.

1970 Ceramics, *PTV*, **3**.

MALDONADO-KOERDELL, M.

1964 Geohistory and paleogeography of Middle America, *HMAI*, **1**, 3–32.

MANGELSDORF, P. C., MacNEISH, R. S., & GALINAT, W. C.

1964 Domestication of corn, *Science*, **143**, 538–545.

1967 Prehistoric wild and cultivated maize, *PTV*, **1**, 178–200.

MARQUINA, I.

1951 Arquitectura prehispánica, *INAH-M*, **1**.

MARTÍ, S.

1968 Instrumentos musicales precortesianos, *INAH*.

MAUDSLAY, A. P.

1889– Archaeology, *Biologia Centrali-Americana*. London: E. Du Cane Godman &
1902 Osbert Salvin. Text in 4 vols.

MEDELLIN ZEÑIL, A.

1960 *Cerámicas del Totonacapán: Exploraciones en el centro de Veracruz*. Jalapa, Veracruz: Universidad Veracruzana, Instituto de Antropología.

MEGGERS, B. J., EVANS, C., & ESTRADA, E.

1965 Early Formative period of coastal Ecuador: The Valdivia and Machalilla phases, *SCA*, **1**.

MEIGHAN, C. W.

1969 Cultural similarities between western Mexico and Andean regions, *Mesoamerican Studies*, No. 4, 11–25. Research Records of the University Museum, Southern Illinois University, Carbondale, Illinois.

MILES, S. W.

1965 Sculpture of the Guatemala-Chiapas Highlands and Pacific slopes and associated hieroglyphs, *HMAI*, **2**, 237–275.

MILLON, C.

1966 The history of mural art at Teotihuacán. Paper presented at 11th Mesa Redonda, Mexico, D.F., August 10.

MILLON, R.

1955 When money grew on trees. Unpublished doctoral dissertation, Columbia University, New York.

1957 Irrigation systems in the valley of Teotihuacán, *AATQ*, **23**, 160–166.

1967 Extensión y población de la ciudad de Teotihuacán en sus diferentes períodos: Un cálculo provisional, *Teotihuacán, Onceava Mesa Redonda*. Mexico, D.F.: Sociedad Mexicana de Antropología. Pp. 57–78.

MONZÓN, A.

1949 *El Calpulli en la Organización Social de los Tenochca*. Mexico, D.F.: Universidad Nacional Autónoma de Mexico, Instituto de Historia.

MORLEY, S. G.

1915 An introduction to the study of the Maya hieroglyphs, *BAE-B* 57.

1920 The inscriptions of Copán, *CIW-P* 219.

1935 Guide book to the ruins of Quiriguá, *CIW Supplementary Publication* No. 16.

1937– The inscriptions of Petén, *CIW-P* 437. 5 vols.
1938

1956 *The Ancient Maya* (3rd ed. revised by G. W. Brainerd). Stanford, California: Stanford University Press.

MORRIS, E. H., CHARLOT, J., & MORRIS, A. A.

1931 The Temple of the Warriors at Chichén Itzá, Yucatán, *CIW-P* 406. 2 vols.

MOUNTJOY, J. B.

1969 On the origin of west Mexican metallury, *Mesoamerican Studies*, No. 4, 26–42, Research Records of the University Museum, Southern Illinois University, Carbondale, Illinois.

1970 The San Blas complex ecology. Paper presented at the 35th Annual Meeting, Society for American Archaeology, Mexico, D.F.

NEELY, J. A.

1967 Organización hidráulica y sistemas de irrigación prehistóricos en el valle de Oaxaca, *INAH-B*, No. 27, 15–17.

NICOLSON, H. B.

1961 The use of the term "Mixtec" in Mesoamerican archaeology, *AATQ*, **26**, 431–433.

1970   Paper presented at Symposium, Before Cortés, Metropolitan Museum of Art, New York, October 5–9.

NOGUERA, E.

1942   Exploraciones en El Opeño, Michoacán, *Proceedings 27 ICA*, Pp. 574–586.

1950   El horizonte Tolteca-Chichimeca, *Enciclopedia Mexicana de Arte*, No. 4. Mexico, D.F.: Ediciones Mexicanas.

1954   *La Cerámica Arqueológica de Cholula*. Mexico, D.F.: Editorial Guaranía.

1965   La cerámica arqueológica de Mesoamerica. No. 86. Mexico, D.F.: Universidad Nacional Autónoma de México, Instituto de Investigaciones Historicas.

OVIEDO Y VALDÉS, G. F.

1851–   *Historia general y natural de las Indias, Islas y Tierra Firme del Mar Océano.*
1855   Madrid: Imprenta de la Real Academia de la Historia. 4 vols.

PADDOCK, J.

1966   Editor, *Ancient Oaxaca: Discoveries in Mexican Archaeology and History*. Stanford, California: Stanford University Press.

1968   Current research, *AATQ*, **33**, 122–128.

PALERM, A.

1955   The agricultural basis of urban civilization in Mesoamerica. In J. H. Steward (Ed.), *Irrigation Civilizations: A Comparative Study, Pan American Union.* Pan-American Union, Social Science Monographs, No. 1. Washington, D.C. Pp. 28–42.

PALERM, A., & WOLF, E. R.

1954–   El desarrollo del area clave del imperio Texcocano, *RMEA*, **14**, 337–349.
1955

PARSONS, L. A.

1967   Bilbao Guatemala: An archaeological study of the Pacific coast Cotzumalhuapa region, *Publications in Anthropology*, No. 11. Milwaukee, Wisconsin: Milwaukee Public Museum.

PENDERGAST, D. M.

1962a Metal artifacts from Amapa, Nayarit, Mexico. *AATQ*, **27**, 370–379.

1962b Metal artifacts in Prehispanic Mesoamerica, *AATQ*, **27**, 520–545.

PETERSON, F. A.

1959   *Ancient Mexico: An Introduction to the Pre-Hispanic Cultures*. New York: Capricorn Books.

PHILLIPS, P.

1966   The role of transpacific contacts in the development of New World pre-Columbian civilizations, *HMAI*, **4**, 296–315.

PIÑA CHÁN, R.

1955   *Las culturas Preclásicas de la Cuenca de México*. México, D.F.: Fondo de Cultura Económica.

1958   *Tlatilco*, Serie Investigaciones, No. 1, 2. Mexico, D. F.: Instituto Nacional de Antropología e Historia.

1960   Mesoamerica, *INAH-M*, No. 6.

1965   Chalcatzingo, Morelos, *INAH*, Informes 4.

1968   *Jaina*. Mexico, D. F.: Instituto Nacional de Antropología e Historia.

POLLOCK, H. E. D.

1965   Architecture of the Maya Lowlands, *HMAI*, **2**, 378–440.

POLLOCK, H. E. D., ROYS, R. L., PROSKOURIAKOFF, T., & SMITH, A. L.

1962   Mayapan, Yucatán, Mexico, *CIW-P*, 619.

PORTER, M. N.

1948   Pipas precortesianas, *Acta Antropológica*, **3**, No. 2.

1953   Tlatilco and the preclassic cultures of the New World, *VFPA*, No. 19.

1956   Excavations at Chupícuaro, Guanajuato, Mexico. *APS-T*, **46**, Part 5.

PROSKOURIAKOFF, T.

1946   An album of Maya architecture, *CIW-P* 558.

1950   A study of Classic Maya sculpture, *CIW-P* 593.

1954   Varieties of Classic Central Veracruz sculpture, *CIW-C*, No. 58, 63–100.

1960   Historical implications of a pattern of dates at Piedras Negras, Guatemala, *AATQ*, **25**, 454–475.

1961   The lords of the Maya realm, *EX*, **4**, No. 1, 14–21.

PULESTON, D. E.

1965   The Chultunes of Tikal, *EX*, **7**, No. 3, 24–29.

PULESTON, D. E., & CALLENDER, D. W., JR.

1967   Defensive earthworks at Tikal, *EX*, **9**, No. 3, 40–48.

PULESTON, D. E., & PULESTON, O. S.

1971   Ecological approach to the origins of Maya civilization, *Archaeology*, **24**, 330–337.

RANDS, R. L., & SMITH, R. E.

1965   Pottery of the Guatemalan highlands, *HMAI*, **2**, 95–145.

RATHJE, W. L.

1970   Socio-political implications of lowland Maya burials: Methodology and tentative hypotheses, *WA*, **I**, No. 3, 359–374.

1971   The origin and development of lowland Classic Maya civilization, *AATQ*, **36**, 275–285.

RECINOS, A.

1950   *Popol Vuh: The Sacred Book of the Ancient Quiché Maya.* Norman, Oklahoma: University of Oklahoma Press.

RECINOS, A., & GOETZ, D.

1953   *The Annals of the Cakchiquels.* Norman, Oklahoma: University of Oklahoma Press.

REICHEL-DOLMATOFF, G.

1965   *Colombia.* New York: Praeger.

ROUSE, I.

1966   Mesoamerica and the eastern Caribbean area, *HMAI*, **4**, 234–242.

ROYS, R. L.

1933   The Book of Chilam Balam of Chuyamel, *CIW-P*, 438.

1965   Lowland Maya native society at Spanish contact, *HMAI*, **3**, 659–678.

1966   Native empires in Yucatán, *RMEA*, **20**, 153–175.

RUBÍN DE LA BORBOLLA, D. F.

1944   Orfebrería Tarasca, *CA*, **3**, 127–138.

RUPPERT, K., THOMPSON, J. E. S., & PROSKOURIAKOFF, T.

1955   Bonampak, Chiapas, Mexico, *CIW-P* 602.

RUZ LHUILLIER, A.

1951   Chichén Itzá y Palenque, ciudades fortificadas, *Homenaje al doctor Alfonso Caso.* Mexico, D.F.: Imprenta Nuevo Mundo, S.A. Pp. 331–342.

1952   Estudio de la cripta del Templo de las Inscripciones en Palenque, *Tlatoani*, **1**, Nos. 5–6, 3–37.

1960   *Palenque, Official Guide.* Mexico, D.F.: Instituto Nacional de Antropología e Historia.

1963   *Uxmal, Official Guide.* Mexico, D.F.: Instituto Nacional de Antropología e Historia.

SÁENZ, C. A.

1961   Tres estelas en Xochicalco, *RMEA*, **17**, 39–65.

1962   Xochicalco, Temporada 1960. *INAH Colección Informes*, No. 11.

SAHAGÚN, FRAY B. DE

1946   *Historia General de las Cosas de Nueva España.* Mexico, D.F.: Editorial Nueva España. 3 vols.

SALAZAR, P.

1966   Maqueta prehispánica teotihuacana, *INAH-B*, **23**, 4–11.

SANDERS, W. T.

1956   The central Mexican symbiotic region, *PSP*. Pp. 115–127.

1960   Prehistoric ceramics and settlement patterns in Quintana Roo, *CIW-C*, No. 60.

1962   Cultural ecology of Nuclear Mesoamerica, *AA*, **64**, 34–44.

1967   Life in a classic village, *Teotihuacán, Onceava Reunion de Mesa Redonda.* Mexico, D.F.: Sociedad Mexicana de Antropología. Pp. 123–143.

SANDERS, W. T., & MICHELS, J. W.

1969   The Pennsylvania State University Kaminaljuyú Project – 1968 Season. Part 1 The Excavations. *Pennsylvania State University, Occasional Papers in Anthropology*, No. 2.

SANDERS, W. T., & PRICE, B. J.

1968   *Mesoamerica: The Evolution of a Civilization.* New York: Random House.

SATTERTHWAITE, L.

1965   Calendrics of the Maya Lowlands, *HMAI*, **3**, 603–631.

SCHOLES, F. V., & ROYS, R. L.

1948   The Maya Chontal Indians of Acalán-Tixchel, *CIW-P* 560.

SEARS, W. H.
  1964   The southeastern United States, *PMNW*. Pp. 259–287.
SÉJOURNÉ, L.
  1966   *Arqueología de Teotihuacán, la Cerámica.* Mexico, D.F.: Fondo de Cultura
         Económica.
SELER, E.
  1901– *Codex Fejéváry-Mayer.* Berlin and London: Duke of Loubat.
  1902
SHEPARD, A. O.
  1948   Plumbate, a Mesoamerican trade ware, *CIW-P* 573.
SHOOK, E. M.
  1951   The present status of research on the Preclassic horizons in Guatemala. In. S. Tax
         (Ed.) *The Civilization of Ancient America, Selected Papers of the 29th Inter-
         national Congress of Americanists.* Pp. 93–100.
  1958   The Temple of the Red Stela, *EX,* **1,** No. 1, 26–33.
  1960   Tikal, Stela 29, *EX,* **2,** No. 2, 28–35.
  1965   Archaeological Survey of the Pacific Coast of Guatemala, *HMAI,* **2,** 180–194.
SHOOK, E. M., & KIDDER, A. V.
  1952   Mound E-III-3, Kaminaljuyú, Guatemala, *CIW-C,* No. 53.
SHOOK, E. M., & PROSKOURIAKOFF, T.
  1956   Settlement patterns in Mesoamerica and the sequence in the Guatemalan high-
         lands, *PSP.* Pp. 93–100.
SOCIEDAD MEXICANA DE ANTROPOLOGÍA
  1944   El norte de México y el sur de Estados Unidos, *Tercera Reunión de Mesa Redonda,
         Mexico, D.F.*
SOUSTELLE, J.
  1964   *The Daily Life of the Aztecs.* London: Pelican Books.
SMITH, A. L.
  1950   Uaxactún, Guatemala: Excavations of 1931-7, *CIW-P* 588.
  1955   Archaeological reconnaissance in central Guatemala, *CIW-P* 608.
SMITH, A. L., & KIDDER, A. V.
  1951   Excavations at Nebaj, Guatemala, *CIW-P* 594.
SMITH, R. E., & GIFFORD, J. C.
  1965   Pottery of the Maya Lowlands, *HMAI,* **2,** 498–534.
SPENCE, M. W.
  1967   Los talleres de obsidiana de Teotihuacán, *Teotihuacán, Onceava Reunión de
         Mesa Redonda.* Mexico, D.F.: Sociedad Mexicana de Antropología. Pp. 213–218.
SPINDEN, H. J.
  1917   The origin and distribution of agriculture in America, *Proceedings 19 ICA,*
         Washington, D.C. Pp. 269–276.
SPORES, R.
  1967   *The Mixtec Kings and Their People.* Norman, Oklahoma: University of Oklahoma
         Press.
STIRLING, M. W.
  1943   Stone monuments of southern Mexico, *BAE-B* 138.
STONE, D. Z.
  1957   The archaeology of central and southern Honduras, *PM-P* 49, No. 3.
STROMSVIK, G.
  1947   Guide book to the ruins of Copán, *CIW-P* 577.
STRONG, W. D., KIDDER, A. V., & PAUL, A. J. D.
  1938   Preliminary report on the Smithsonian Institution-Harvard University Archaeo-
         logical Expedition to Northwest Honduras, 1936. *Smithsonian Miscellaneous
         Collections,* **97,** No. 1.
SWADESH, M.
  1956   Problems of long-range comparisons in Penutian. *Language,* **32,** 17–41.
SWITZER, R. R.
  1969   Tobacco, pipes, and cigarettes of the prehistoric Southwest. Special Report No.
         8, El Paso Archaeological Society.
TAYLOR, R. E., BERGER, R., MEIGHAN, C. W., & NICOLSON, H. B.
  1969   West Mexican Radiocarbon Dates of Archaeologic Significance. In J. D. Frierman
         (Ed.), *The Natalie Wood Collection of Pre-Columbian Ceramics from Chupi-
         cuaro, Guanajuato, Mexico.* Los Angeles, California: University of California.
         Pp. 17–30.

THOMPSON, J. E. S.

1939   Excavations at San José, British Honduras, *CIW-P* 506.

1942   *The Civilization of the Mayas*, Leaflet 25. Chicago, Illinois: Field Museum of Natural History, Anthropology.

1943   A trial survey of the southern Maya area, *AATQ*, **9**, 106–134.

1945   A trial survey of the northern Maya area, *AATQ*, **11**, 2–4.

1948   An archaeological reconnaissance in the Cotzumalhuapa region, Escuintla, Guatemala, *CIW-C*, No. 44.

1950   Maya hieroglyphic writing, introduction. *CIW-P* 589.

1951   The Itzá of Tayasal, Petén, *Homenaje al doctor Alfonso Caso*. Mexico, D.F.: Imprenta Nuevo Mundo, S.A. Pp. 389–400.

1954   *The Rise and Fall of Maya Civilization*. Norman, Oklahoma: University of Oklahoma Press.

1959   Systems of hieroglyphic writing in Middle America and methods of deciphering them, *AATQ*, **24**, 349–364.

1962   *A Catalogue of Maya Hieroglyphs*. Norman, Oklahoma: University of Oklahoma Press.

1965a Archaeological synthesis of the southern Maya lowlands, *HMAI*, **2**, 331–359.

1965b Maya hieroglyphic writing, *HMAI*, **3**, 632–658.

1970   *Maya History and Religion*. Norman, Oklahoma: University of Oklahoma Press.

1971   Estimates of Maya population: Deranging factors, *AATQ*, **36**, 214–216.

TOLSTOY, P.

1963   Cultural parallels between Southeast Asia and Mesoamerica in the manufacture of bark cloth, *Transactions of the New York Academy of Sciences, Series II*, **25**, No. 6, 646–662.

TOLSTOY, P., & PARADIS, L. I.

1970   Early and Middle Preclassic Culture in the Basin of Mexico, *Science*, **167**, 344–351.

1971   Early and Middle Preclassic culture in the basin of Mexico. In R. F. Heizer and J. A. Graham (Eds.), *Observations on the emergence of civilization in Mesoamerica*, *Contributions of the University of California Archaeological Research Facility*, No. 11. Pp. 7–28.

TORQUEMADA, J. DE

1943   *Monarquía Indiana* (facsimile edition). Mexico, D.F.: Editorial Chávez Hayhoe. 3 vols.

TOSCANO, S.

1952   *Arte Precolombino de Mexico*. Mexico, D.F.: Universidad Nacional Autónoma de Mexico.

TOURTELLOT, G.

1970   The peripheries of Seibal, an interim report, *PM-P*, **61**, 407–420.

TOZZER, A. M.

1941   Landa's Relación de las Cosas de Yucatán, a translation, *PM-P*, **18**.

1957   Chichén Itzá and its *cenote* of sacrifice, *Peabody Museum Memoirs*, **12**.

VAILLANT, G. C.

1930   Excavations at Zacatenco, *AMNH-AP*, **32**, 1–197.

1931   Excavations at Ticomán, *AMNH-AP*, **32**, 199–439.

1935   Excavations at El Arbolillo, *AMNH-AP*, **35**, 137–279.

VAILLANT, G. C., & VAILLANT, S. B.

1934   Excavations at Gualupita, *AMNH-AP*, **35**, 1–135.

VILLACORTA, J. A., & VILLACORTA, C. A.

1930   *Códices Maya*. Guatemala City: Tipografía Nacional.

VILLAGRA CALETI, A.

1949   Bonampak, la Ciudad de los Muros Pintados, *INAH-A Suppl.*, **3**.

VOGT, E. Z.

1968   Some Aspects of Zinacantan Settlement Patterns and Ceremonial Organization. In K. C. Chang, (Ed.), *Settlement Archaeology*. Palo Alto, California: Natural Press Books. Pp. 154–173.

WALLRATH, M.

1967   The Calle de los Muertos Complex: A Possible Macrocomplex of Structures near the Center of Teotihuacán, *Teotihuacán, Onceava Mesa Redonda*. Mexico, D.F.: Sociedad Mexicana de Antropología. Pp. 113–122.

WEAVER, M. P.

1967   Tlapacoya Pottery in the Museum Collection, *Indian Notes and Monographs*,

Miscellaneous Series, No. 56. New York: Museum of the American Indian, Heye Foundation.

1969   A Reappraisal of Chupícuaro. In J. D. Frierman (Ed), *The Natalie Wood Collection of Pre-Columbian Ceramics from Chupícuaro, Guanajuato, Mexico*. Los Angeles, California: University of California. Pp. 3–15, appendix Pp. 81–92.

WEIANT, C. W.

1943   An introduction to the ceramics of Tres Zapotes, *BAE-B* 139.

WEST, R. C.

1961   Aboriginal sea navigation between Middle and South America, *AA*, **63**, 133–135.

1964   The natural regions of Middle America, *HMAI*, **1**, 363–383.

WEST, R. C., & ARMILLAS, P.

1950   Las chinampas de Mexico, *CA*, **5**, 165–182.

WICKE, C.

1965   Pyramids and temple mounds: Mesoamerican ceremonial architecture in eastern North America, *AATQ*, **30**, 409–420.

WILLEY, G. R.

1962a   Mesoamerica, In *Courses toward Urban Life*. VFPA, No. 32. Pp. 84–105.

1962b   The early great styles and the rise of the pre-Columbian civilizations, *AA*, **64**, 1–14.

1966   *An Introduction to American Archaeology*. Vol. 1, *North and Middle America*. Englewood Cliffs, New Jersey: Prentice-Hall.

1970   Type descriptions of the ceramics of the Real Xe complex, Seibal, Petén, Guatemala, *PM-P*, **61**, 315–355.

1971a   *An Introduction to American Archaeology*. Vol. 2, *South America*. Englewood Cliffs, New Jersey: Prentice-Hall.

1971b   Commentary on: The Emergence of Civilization in the Maya Lowlands. In R. F. Heizer and J. A. Graham (Eds.), *Observations on the Emergence of Civilization in Mesoamerica, Contributions of the University of California Archaeological Research Facility*, No. 11. Pp. 97–111.

WILLEY, G. R., & BULLARD, W. R., JR.

1965   Prehistoric settlement patterns in the Maya lowlands, *HMAI*, **2**, 360–377.

WILLEY, G. R., BULLARD, W. R., JR., GLASS, J. B., & GIFFORD, J. C.

1965   Prehistoric Maya settlements in the Belize Valley, *PM-P*, **54.**

WILLEY, G. R., CULBERT, T. P., & ADAMS, R. E. W.

1967   Maya lowland ceramics: A report from the 1965 Guatemala City Conference, *AATQ*, **32**, 289–315.

WILLEY, G. R., & McGIMSEY, C. R.

1954   The Monagrillo culture of Panama, *PM-P*, **49**, No. 2.

WILLEY, G. R., & SMITH, A. L.

1969   The ruins of Altar de Sacrificios, Department of Petén, Guatemala, an introduction, *PM-P*, **62**, No. 1.

WITTFOGEL, K. A.

1957   *Oriental Despotism: A Comparative Study of Total Power*. New Haven, Connecticut: Yale University Press.

WOLF, E. R.

1959   *Sons of the Shaking Earth*. Chicago, Illinois: University of Chicago Press.

WOLF, E. R., & PALERM, A.

1955   Irrigation in the old Acolhua domain, *SWJA*, **11**, 265–281.

1957   Ecological potential and cultural development in Mesoamerica. In *Studies in Human Ecology*. Washington, D.C.: Pan-American Union. Pp. 1–37.

Numbers in *italics* refer to the pages on which the complete references are listed.

Author Index

Smith, A. L., 130, 172, 221, 230, *322*, *324*, *326*

Smith, R. E., 42, 82, 130, *323*, *324*

Sono, T., 289, *319*

Soustelle, J., 238, *324*

Spence, M. W., 75, 128, *324*

Spinden, H. J., 25, 285, *324*

Spores, R., 220, 265, 268, *324*

Squier, R. J., 52, *317*

Stewart, T. D., 69, *316*

Stirling, M. W., 54, 57, 83, 152, *324*

Stone, D. Z., 88, *324*

Stromsvik, G., 170, *324*

Strong, W. D., 40, 88, *324*

Swadesh, M., 290, *324*

Switzer, R. R., 213, 280, 281, *324*

T

Taylor, R. E., 79, *324*

Thompson, J. E. S., 86, 87, 88, 93, 104, 108, 109, 110, 152, 156, 167, 168, 170, 172, 173, 175, 176, 182, 185, 195, 213, 222, 225, 231, 234, 237, 303, 307, *323*, *325*

Tolstoy, P., 62, 64, 72, 283, 292, *325*

Torquemada, J. de, 238, 260, 272, *325*

Toscano, S., 251, *325*

Tourtellot, G., 174, *325*

Tozzer, A. M., 208, 226, 229, 230, 255, *325*

Trik, A. S., 251, *313*

V

Vaillant, G. C., 42, 61, 65, 67, 72, *325*

Vaillant, S. B., 61, *325*

Villacorta, C. A., 96, 235, *325*

Villacorta, J. A., 96, 235, *325*

Villagra Caleti, A., 176, *325*

Vogt, E. Z., 166, *325*

W

Wallrath, M., 75, 124, *325*

Weaver, M. P., 42, 77, *325*, *326*

Weiant, C. W., 57, *326*

West, R. C., 8, 12, 14, 91, 245, 286, *326*

Wicke, C., 281, 282, *326*

Willey, G. R., 85, 91, 153, 154, 166, 167, 168, 172, 182, 195, 278, 280, 281, 285, 286, 287, 289, 299, *326*

Williams, A. W., 58, *317*

Winters, H. D., 217, 218, 279, *319*

Wittfogel, K. A., 298, *326*

Wolf, E. R., 6, 7, 128, 144, 145, 214, 238, 243, 290, 322, *326*

Numbers in *italics* refer to the pages on which the entries appear in either the Selected List of Mesoamerican Deities or the Glossary.

Subject Index

Carib, 284, *see also* Caribbean area
Caribbean area, 284–285
Carnegie Institution of Washington, 115, 169, 171, 303
Casas Grandes, 219, 279–280, *see also* Chihuahua; United States, southwestern
Cascade point, 18, *see also* Early man
Ceiba, 12
Celt, 309, *see also* Axe
Cempoala, 57
Cenote, 13, 227, 229, 231, *309*
Central America, 212, 274, 282, 284, 285, 288, 290, 292
Ceremonial centers, 74, 75, 150, 151, 152, 166, 218, 224, 230, 269, 283, 299, 300, *see also* individual site name
  appearance, 36–37
  defined, 154
  function of, 36–37
Cerro Chavín, 150, 190
Cerro del Tepalcate, 73, 76
Cerro de las Mesas, 145
Chac, 83, 185, 227, 235, *307*, *see also* Deity, rain god; Tlaloc
Chacmool, 211, 220, 226, 227, 250, 271, 278, *309*
Chalcatzingo, 56, 61, 62, 63, 64, *see also* Morelos, Olmecs, Preclassic period
Chalchihuites, 77, 202, 217–219, 278, 279
Chamelecón River, 12
Chametla, 217, *see also* Western Mexico
Champ-levé, *see* Pottery, decorative techniques
Chanchopa, 78, 79, *see also* Colima, Western Mexico
Chapalote, see Maize, races of
Chapultepec, 204, 242, 246, 304
Chavín, 282, 286, 287, 288, 289, 290, *see also* Nuclear America, South America
Chebel Yax, 234, *307*, *see also* Deity
Chenes, *see* Architecture, style
Chetumal, 195, 230
Chia, 5, 245
Chiapa de Corzo, 45, 148
  phases at, 45, 85
  pottery, 45, 85, 150
  stone architecture, 45
Chiapas, 10, 15, 31, 246, 260, 288
  Classic period at, 148, 150–151
  Preceramic remains, 26, *see also* Santa Marta rock shelter
  Preclassic period at, 40, 45
Chicanel (phase), 86–88, 152, 153, *see also* Petén, Preclassic period
  architecture, 86–87
  pottery, 86
  in Yucatán, 87
Chichén Itzá, 115, 169, 293, *see also* Putún Maya
  architecture, 188, 222, 224–225

ball court, 224–225
Classic period at, 188–190
fortification of, 224–225
founding of, 182, 192, 195, 222, 224, 229
government, 229
Long Count, 190
Postclassic period at, 193, 222–227, 229–233
society, 264
Toltec influence at, 222–227
Chichimeca, 145, 202, 204, 214, 239, 242, 270, 271
Chihuahua, 6, 22, 213, 218, 219, 278, 279, 280, *see also* Casas Grandes
Chilam Balam (books of), 3, 96, 110, 112, 195, 222, 284
Chili pepper (*Capsicum annuum* or *Capsicum frutescens*), 27, 29, 30, 32, 233, 236, 245, 269
Chimalpopoca, 240, 241
China, 144, 145, 292–293, *see also* Trans-Pacific contact
Chinampa, 5, 242, 245, 263, 264, *309*, *see also* Agriculture, Mexica
Chixoy River, 172
Chocolate, *see* Cacao
Cholula, 214, 221, 260, 265, 274, 275, 301, *see also* Puebla, Tlaxcala
  architecture, 142, 196
  Classic period at, 136, 142, 191
  historic Olmecs at, 50, 197, 214, 221, 274–275
  mural paintings, 142
  outside influence at, 197, 199
  Postclassic period remains at, 196–199
  pottery, 198–199, 248
  Preclassic period at, 196
  stone carving, 145
Chorrera (phase), 285, 286, 288, *see also* Ecuador
Chultun, 85–86, 180, *309*
Chupícuaro, 76–77
  burial customs, 76–77
  chronology, 77
  external relationship of, 73, 77, 120, 279
  figurines, 73, 76–77, 120
  pottery, 73, 77, 120, 279
Cihuacóatl, 242, 259
Civilization, 295–300, *see also* Maya civilization, Nuclear America, Olmecs, Teotihuacán
  definition of, 295–296
  factors leading to, 25, 297–300
  Mesoamerica and, 296–300
  urbanism and, 117, 297–299
Classic period, *see also* Civilization, Maya civilization, Olmec civilization, individual site name
  chronology, 93, 107, 117, 148, 153
  civilization, 297
  decline of, 142, 180, 190–193
  key areas, 120, 167
  summary of, 117–120, 191–193

Soconusco, 45
South America, 287, 288
western Mexico, 78–79
Fine Orange ware, 151, 152, 173, 199, 212, 214, 220, 227, 230, 309, see also Pottery
Fire drill, 106
Fish, 14, 31, 42, 50, 65, 68, 81, 112, 134, 160, 170, 260
Flint, 161
  eccentric, 83, 150
  source of, 155, 157, 168, 299
  tools of, 21, 28, 29, 31, 57, 128, 158, 234, 268
Floral Park (phase), see Protoclassic Period, lowland Maya
Florero, 131, 146, 149, 309, see also Teotihuacán, pottery
Florida, 281
Flowery War, 243, 263, see also Tlaxcala
Flute, 77, 79, 220, 236, 254, 258, see also Music
Folsom point, 18, 22, see also Early man
Formative period, see Preclassic period
Frog, 68, 82, 83, 113, 114, see also Toad

G

Gold, 62, 212, 227, 229, 242, 254, 260, 261, 264, 266, 268, 271, 272, 273, see also Metallurgy
Goodman–Martínez–Thompson correlation, see Calendar, correlation system
Grasshopper, 110, 250
Grijalva River, 12, 46, 169, 173
Gualupita, 61, see also Morelos, Preclassic period
Guanajuato, 76, 204
Guasave, 217, 279, 290, see also Sinaloa, Western Mexico
Guatemala City, see Kaminaljuyú
Gucumatz, 234, 308, see also Deity, Kukulcán, Quetzalcóatl
Guerrero, 10, 12, 27, 31, 38, 129, 131, 270, 273, 288, see also Balsas River, individual site name
  cave paintings, 63
  figurines, 40, 63, 137
  metallurgy, 212, 268, 273, 290
  Mexica in, 244
  Olmecs in, 63
  pottery, 40, 63, 137
  resources, 62, 137
  Teotihuacán influence in, 137
Guilá Naquitz Cave, 31
Gulf Coast, 36, 45, 46, 58, 61, 85, 282, 299, see also Huasteca, Olmecs, Veracruz cultures
  cultures of, 50–58, 142–145, 214–216
  conquered by Mexica, 243, 263

H

Haab, 103, 309, see also Calendar

Hacha (thin stone head), 144, 152, 309, see also Ball game, paraphernalia
Hammock, 284–285
Hematite, 50, 51, 54, 58, 64, 150, 158, 160, 289
Hieroglyph(s), 6, 57, 60, 83, 87, 117, 144, 151, 153, 160, 161, 168, 171, 172, 176–178, 195, 199, 231, see also Calendar, Códices, Writing systems, individual site name
  decipherment of, 57, 109–115
  distribution, 96, 182
  emblem, 115
  historical, 113–115
  ideographic, 109, 110, 113
  logographic, 113
  phonetic, 110–113, 115
  sources of, 96, 99
  syllabic, 109, 112
Hochob, 169, 183
Hohokam, 77, 78, 219, 277, 278, see also United States, southwestern
Holmul, 87, 152, 169
Honduras, 5, 12, 15, 22, 26, 40, 82, 83, 145, 153, 227, 231, 233, 246, 260, 261, 284
  Gulf of, 5, 172, 261
  Preclassic remains in, 82, 83, 88
Honey, 227, 233, 271
Hopewell, 282, see also United States, eastern
Horse, 16, 28
House, 231, 233, see also Pit house, Settlement pattern
  mounds, 51, 237
  representation of, 79, 185, 226, 233, 268
  round stone, 280
Huasteca, see also Gulf Coast, Veracruz cultures
  architecture, 215–216
  calendar, 103
  exterior relationships of, 85, 204, 213, 214, 216
  figurines, 214, 216
  language, 7–8
  pottery, 214, 216
  Preclassic remains of, 57–58
  stone carving, 215
  and Toltec period, 214–216
Huehuéteotl, 68, 120, 129, 256, 307, see also Deity
Huémac, 204, 205, 304, see also Tula
Huéhuetl, 251, 309, see also Drum, Music
Huexotzingo, 242, 243, 274–275
Huitzilíhuitl, 240, 241, see also Mexica, rulers
Huitzilopochtli, 239, 244, 246, 250, 254, 256, 257, 260, 307, see also Deity, Mexica
Hunac Ceel, 231, see also Mayapán
Hun Cimil, see Yum Cimil
Hunters and gatherers, 4, 5, 6, 18, 31, 32

La Venta, 52–55, 61, 63, 82, 89, 282, 300,
    see also Olmecs
  architecture, 54–55, 216, 281
  caches and offerings, 55
  ceremonial center, 54
  chronology, 55, 56
  environmental setting, 52, 54
  figurines, 54–56
  population estimate, 55
  pottery, 52, 55
  stone monuments, 54
  tombs, 54
La Victoria, 42–44, 50, 288, *see also*
    Soconusco, individual phase name
  decline of, 84
  phases at, 44
Law
  Mexica, 242, 259, 263
  Texcocan, 242, 243
Lerma phase, 20–21, *see also* Early man,
    Preprojectile horizon
Lerma River, *see* Lerma–Santiago river
    system
Lerma–Santiago river system, 5, 8, 11, 73,
    76, 120, 273, 301
Lime, uses of, 57, 76, 150, 151, 168, 234,
    260, 284
Lip plug, *see* Labret
Loltún cave, 87
Loma San Gabriel culture, 219
Long Count, 3, 57, 59, 84, 93, 102, 107–
    109, 115, 117, 153, 168, 190, 192,
    222, *310*, *see also* Calendar, Calen-
    dar Round, Hieroglyphs, Short
    Count, Stela, Writing systems, indi-
    vidual site name
  beginnings of, 84, 89, 100
  distribution of, 83–84, 145, 158, 160,
    161, 168–169, 172, 178, 188–189
  system, 100, 102, 109
Lost wax (*cire perdue*) process, 254, 268,
    278, 310, *see also* Metallurgy
Lords of the Night (Nine), *see* Bolon-ti-Ku
Lunar series, 107–108, *see also* Calendar

M

Macehual, 241, 258, 262, *310*
Machililla (phase), 40, 285, 286, 288, *see
    also* Ecuador
Magnetite, 54, 58
Maguey (*agave*), 30, 31, 32, 240, 259
Mahogany, 12, 177
Maize, 57, 65, 78, 127, 156–157, 202, 235,
    243, 245, 259, 269, 277, 281, 282,
    284, 286, 290, 299, *see also* Domes-
    tication of plants, Tehuacán,
    Teosinte, Tripsacum
  in diet, 65, 168
  diffusion of, 281, 285, 292
  domestication of, 25–27, 29, 31, 32, 38,
    40, 285, 292
  in lowlands, 41–42, 80, 233
  race of

chapalote, 26, 36, 277, *309*
  nal-tel, 26, 36
  wild (*Zea mays*), 25, 26, 29
Malacate, 213, 214, 219, 220, 248, 273,
    287, *310*
Malinalco, 248
Mammoth, 17, 21
Mamom (phase), 52, 85, 86, 152, *see also*
    Petén, Preclassic period
Mani
  cenote, 85
  town, 99, 232
Manioc, 25, 41–42, 157, 284, 287, 288, *see
    also* Altamira, Root crop agriculture
Mano, see Metate
Market
  at Chichén Itza, 226
  Mexica, 245, 246
  at Teotihuacán, 124, 129
  at Tlatelolco, 260
  at Tulum, 230
Market system, 6, 260–261, 296
Mask, 65, 81, 83, 131, 137, 158, 171, 176,
    177, 178, 183, 185, 236, 272, 279
  jaguar, 54, 57, 86
Matanchén, *see* San Blas
Matlazinca, 77, 103, 248
Matzanel, *see* Protoclassic period, lowland
    Maya
Maya civilization, 154–190, *see also*
    Civilization, Classic period
  central and southern regions (Petén),
    152–182, 298
  chronology, 169
  culmination of, 167–190
  decline
    of Petén centers, 180, 182, 190–192,
      300–301
    of Yucatán, 192
  distribution, 167–169
  early centers, 156–157, 167, 169
  highland Guatemala, 148–152, 221–222
  influence
    at Oaxaca, 220
    present-day, 303
    at Teotihuacán, 137
    at Xochicalco, 199, 202
  origins and appearance of, 86, 91, 152,
    156–157, 167–168, 298–299
  scientific achievements, 168
  social organization, 165–167, 234, 237
  Toltec influence on, 220–227
  in Yucatán, 182–190, 192, 232–237
Maya Indians, 85, 93, *see also* Maya civili-
    zation
  geographical extension of, 7
  history, 99
  language, 7, 110
  life and customs, 234–237
  settlement patterns, 154–156
Mayapán, 96, 237
  as capital of Yucatán, 229, 230–234
  population estimate, 230

Mayeque, 241, *see also* Mexica, social organization

Mazapan ware, 198, 212, 227, 265, *see also* Pottery

Merchants, 93, 149, 173, 195, 230, 233, 245, 260–261, 262, 284, *see also Pochteca*, Putún Maya

Mesoamerica, 6, *see also* Nuclear America
 boundaries of, 5–7, 9 (Map 1), 37 (Map 2), 89, 118–119 (Map 3), 198 (Map 4), 213, 214, 277
 characteristics of, 2, 232, 296–297, 303
 civilization, 6, 120, 128, 277, 283, 291, 293, 296–300, *see also* Civilization
 definition of, 5–6
 exterior relationships, 79, 80, 89, 277–293
 fauna, 11, 14, 102
 flora, 11–12
 geography, climate, and resources, 1, 8–14 (9, Map 1a, b)
 languages, 7–8, 9 (Map 1a)
 and the Old World, 36, 71, 258
 Metallurgy, 192, 212, 217, 219, 227, 254, 263, 265, 268, 273, 289, 290, 291, 292, 295, 296
 introduction of, 274

Metate and *mano*, 29, 30, 31, 41, 42, 51, 55, 57, 65, 89, 158, 218, 234, 254, 278, 281, 284, 287, 290, 305, *310*, *see also* Stone, tools of

Metepec (phase), 136, 137, 139, *see also* Teotihuacán

Mexica (Aztecs), 4, 237–265, 279, *see also* Postclassic period
 archaeology, 246–254
 architecture, 245–249
 ball game, 134
 calendar, 103, 264
 commerce, 260–263
 early history, 238–240
 daily life, 99, 240–241, 258–259
 "empire" and conquests, 99, 219, 238, 262–263, 283
 figurines, 248, 265
 law and justice, 258–259
 markets, 245–246, 260
 politics, 242–245
 pottery, 248–249
 religion, 254–258
 rulers, 240, *see also* individual names
 sacrifice, 254, 256–258
 social organization, 240–241
 stone sculpture, 211, 249–251
 warfare, 241, 254, 262–263, 270
 writing, 96, 99, 110

Mezcala, 137, *see also* Guerrero

Mezcalapa River, 12

Meztitlán, 275, *see also* Independent kingdoms

Mica, 52, 58, 81

Miccaotli (phase), 76, *see also* Teotihuacán

Michoacán, 7, 8, 10, 12, 76–77, 129, 137,

217, 218, 269, 270, 274, *see also* Tarascans, Western Mexico

Microenvironment, 27, 36, 299, 302

Militarism, *see* Warfare

Milpa, see Slash-and-burn agriculture

Miraflores (phase), 45, 81, 83, 86, 148, *see also* Kaminaljuyú
 architecture, 81
 figurines, 82
 pottery, 81–82
 stone carving, 83
 stone vessels, 81
 tombs, 81, 82, 83, 86

Mirror, 6, 54–55, 58, 68, 117, 144, 145, 149, 274, 278, 287

Mississippi tradition, 281–282, *see also* United States, eastern

Mississippi Valley cultures, 279, 283, *see also* United States, eastern

Mitla, 220–221, 265, *see also* Mixtecs, Oaxaca, Zapotecs
 Postclassic period at, 221
 preceramic remains, 31
 Preclassic period at, 59–60

Mixcóatl, 204, *see also* Quetzalcóatl, Tula

Míxquic, 245

Mixteca (geographical region), 265, 269

Mixteca-Puebla culture, 4, 191, 199, 218, 248, 265, 279, 290, *see also* Cholula, Mixteca, Puebla, Tlaxcala

Mixtecs, 220–221, 231, 265–269, 275, 289
 ball game, 266, 275
 calendar, 268
 códices, 268
 figurines, 265
 influence of, 199, 202, 275
 language, 199
 lapidary art, 264, 268
 metallurgy, 254, 266
 numbers and calendar, 102, 103
 pottery, 265, 266
 writing, 265, 268
 tombs, 265, 266

Moctezuma Ilhuicamina (Moctezuma I), 238, 240, 242, 243, 259, 263, 269, 275

Moctezuma Xocoyotzin (Moctezuma II), 237, 238, 240, 245, 246, 263, 264

Mogollon, 77, 219, 277, *see also* United States, southwestern

Molcajete, 198, 213, 220, 248, 274, *310*

Momíl, 285, 287, 288

Monagrillo, 285, 286

Money, 260, 289

Monkey, 14, 52, 81, 83, 102

Monte Albán, 137, 146, *see also* Oaxaca, Zapotecs
 architecture, 146–147
 ball court, 60, 221
 calendar, 59, 89, 147
 Classic period at, 145–148 (footnote), 192
 figurines, 148

hieroglyphs, 147
Postclassic remains at, 266
pottery, 146, 147
Preclassic period at, 59, 75, 88
tombs, 59, 60, 147
urbanism, 147, 148 (footnote)
Monte Alto, 82
Montenegro, 60, *see also* Monte Albán
Morelos, 129, 199, *see also* Xochicalco
Olmecs in, 61–62
pottery, 61–62, 77
Postclassic period in, 199, 243, 248
Preclassic phases in, 61–62
Mortar
in building, 45, 57, 71, 76, 151, 155
stone, 29, 30, 83, 278
Motagua River, 10, 12, 161, 288
Mother-of-pearl, 160
Mountain Cow, 87, *see also* British Honduras
Mountain systems, 8, 9, (Map 1), 10, 12, 213, 271, 274, 278, 279, *see also* Sierra Madre del Sur, Sierra Madre Occidental
Mural paintings, 86, 117, 131, 134–135, 136, 142, 147, 161, 168, 169, 175–176, 190, 205, 225, 226, 227, 231, 236, 237, 279, *see also* individual site name
Mushroom, 82, 149
Music, 128, 176, 226, 236, 241, 242, 250, 251, 254, 258, 272, *see also* Hué-huetl, Musician, *Teponaztli,* and individual instrument
Musician, 68, 79, 176

N

Nahua, 7, 93, 202, 204, 269, *310, see also* Mexica, Náhuat, Náhuatl
Náhuat, 149, 173, 214, 239, *310, see also* Nahua, Náhuatl
Náhuatl, 3, 7, 110, 285, *310, see also* Nahua, Náhuat
Naranjo, 113, 115, 169, *see also* Hieroglyphs, Maya civilization
Nayarit, 7, 11, 76, 78, 80, 137, 145, 218, 268, 273, 278, 289, 290, *see also* Western Mexico
Needle, 30, 261, 268, 271, 273, 280, 289
Negative painting, *see* Pottery, decorative techniques, resist painting
Nemontemi, 103, *310*
New Fire Ceremony, 106, 304
New World Archaeological Foundation, 45, 301
Nezahualcóyotl, 207, 238, 242, 243, 254, 259, *see also* Texcoco
Nicaragua, 5, 10, 221, 290, *see also* Central America
Nomads, *see* Hunters and gatherers
Nonoalca, 204
Nuclear America, 5, 89, 277, 285–291, *see also* Civilization, Mesoamerica, Peru

Numeral system(s), 99–102, *see also* Calendar, Hieroglyphs
Maya, 99, 100, 102
Mexica, 102
Old World, 100

O

Oaxaca, 40, 131, 191, 260, *see also* Mixtecs, Zapotecs, and individual site name
chronology, 220, 301
Classic period at, 145–148
environment of, 11, 19, 31
geography, 10, 58
Postclassic period at, 220–221, 245
Preclassic period at, 31, 58–60
irrigation in, 58, 128
pottery of, 58
tombs, 59, 60, 147, 221, 265–266
Obsidian, 6, 56, 149, 177, *see also* Dating
eccentric, 160, 199
inlay, 131, 178, 208
jewelry, 79, 268, 271–272
and manioc graters, 40–41
polished, 6
sources of, in Mesoamerica, 56, 86, 128, 158
tools of, 10, 20, 21, 30, 41, 55, 57, 81, 82, 85, 128, 158, 219, 234, 254, 261, 262, 281, 282, 286
weapons of, 136, 257
Ocarina, 77, 254, *see also* Music
Ocós (phase), 41, 44, 51, 78, 288, *see also* La Victoria, Soconusco
Old Cordilleran tradition, 18, 20–22
Olmeca-Xicalanca, *see* Olmecs, historic
Olmecs, 46, 50–56, 213, 287, 288, 289, 290, 300, *see also* individual site name
architecture, 54–55
art, 55–56, 59, 63, 83, 281
caches and offerings, 54
cave painting, 63, 65
in central highland Mexico, 60, 64–65, 89
civilization of, 4, 40, 46, 89, 131, 134, 296–297, 299
figurines, 50, 56, 61, 62, 63
in Guerrero, 62–64
heartland, 40, 50, 52, 61, 63
hieroglyphs, 57
historic (Olmeca-Xicalanca), 50, 197, 198, 214, 221, 275
in Huasteca, 58
influence of, 58, 65, 74, 144, 152, 281, 282, 303
at Oaxaca, 59, 60
portable art, 56, 63
pottery, 50, 55, 62
relief carvings, 56, 63
religion, 55–56, 63, 65
stone monuments, 50, 63, 64
trade, 56, 60, 62, 65, 264
were-jaguar cult, 55–57, 63, 68, 83
Omichicahuaztli (bone rasp), 220, 250, 254, 271, *310, see also* Music

Onyx (*tecali*), 131, 137, 147, 161, 217, 266
Oppossum, 14, 68
Opuntía, see Prickly pear
Otomís, 103, 204, 239, 263, 271
Owl, 235
Oxkintok, 169, 182, 190
Oxtotitlán, 63, *see also* Guerrero, Juxtla-
huaca
Oxtoticpac (phase), 137, 142, *see also*
Teotihuacán

P

Pacific Coast, 36, 40, *see also* Pacific
Ocean, Western Mexico
early settlement of, 11, 12, 31
trade, 12, 273, 278, 286, 288
Palenque, 120, 154
archaeological site, 177–180
architecture, 176–178
hieroglyphic inscription, 115, 177
influence of, 180
relief carving, 177, 178, 293
tombs, 177–178
Paleo-Indian, *see* Early man
Palma (palmate stone), 144, *310, see also*
Ball game, paraphernalia
Panama, 15, 285, 286, *see also* Central
America
Pánuco, *see* Huasteca
Pánuco River, 8, 12, 57
Papaloapan River, 8, 10, 12
Paper
manufacture of, 96
uses of, 6, 96
Pasión River, 22, 85, 152, 172, 174, 190,
see also Altar de Sacrificios, Putún
Maya, Seibal
Patolli, 258, *310*
Patlachique (phase), 75, *see also* Teoti-
huacán
Pátzcuaro, *see* Lake Pátzcuaro
Pavón, 215, 216, *see also* Huasteca
Pearl, 161, 178, 254, 266, *see also* Mother-
of-pearl
Peccary, 14, 30, 52, 68
Penate, 268, *310, see also* Mixtecs
Peru, 218, 282, 285–290, 296, *see also*
Nuclear America
Petén, 12, 57, 84, 192, 193, 231, 234, 298,
299, 300, *see also* Maya civilization
agriculture in, 156–158, 167, 299
Classic period in, 152–180, 233
environment, 12, 84–85, 154–155
Postclassic period in, 195, 231
Preclassic period in, 84–88, 91
Protoclassic period in, 87, 152–153
resources of, 150, 155, 158, 168
trade in, 128, 137, 157, 158, 167–168,
173, 298
Peyote, 291
Piedras Negras, 169, 176–177, 180
hieroglyphic inscriptions, 113, 115, 160,
177, 190
trade, 177

Pilli, 240, 241, 261, *310*
Pipe, *see also* Tobacco
pan, 254, 282, 293
smoking, 213, 214, 220, 248, 271, 280,
283
Pipil, 149, 152, 221, *310*
Pit house, 29, 279, 280, *see also* House,
Settlement pattern
Plainview point, 22
Playa de los Muertos, 88, *see also* Hon-
duras
Pleistocene period, 15–21, 58, *see also*
Early man
fauna, 16–17
Plumbate ware, 151, 152, 198, 212, 214,
220, 222, 227, *310, see also* Pottery
Pochteca, 137, 233, 258, 260–261, 262,
264, *see also* Merchants, Mexica
Poetry, 7, 242
Pollen, *see* Dating
Popocatépetl, 10, 15, 199, 245
Population estimate, *see* individual site
name
Popul Vuh, 99
Port of trade, *see* Acalán, *Pochteca*,
Soconusco, Trade, Xicalanco
Position numerals, 6, 100, 102, 147, *see*
also Calendar
Postclassic period, 4, 283, *see also*
Independent kingdoms, Mexica,
Tarascans, Toltecs
in basin of Mexico, 237–265
highland Maya, 195, 221–222
lowland Maya, 195, 211, 221–237
in northern Mexico, 278–279
in western Mexico, 216–219, 269–274,
278–279
Pottery, 277, 281, 285, *see also* individual
site name, individual ware
Classic period, 129–131, 149, 151–153,
169, 190
decorative techniques
champ-levé, 117, *309*
cloisonné, 217–219, *309*
cord marking, 44, 51, 52, 281, 283,
288, *309*
double-line break, 45, 55, 58, 63, 85,
309
excising, 50, 57, 58, 61, 62, 64, 88,
287, 289, *309*
incising, 40, 44, 45, 50, 68, 78, 131,
168, 288
iridescent painting, 44, 51, 286
monochrome, 40, 45, 58, 78, 80, 85,
88, 129, 167, 230
polychrome, 72, 73, 77, 78, 85, 88,
120, 151–153, 158, 167, 190, 195,
199, 248, 265, 266, 273, 279, 280,
290
resist painting, 45, 62, 72, 73, 78, 82,
88, 120, 131, 146, 198, 214, 271,
274, 278, 283, 287, 289, 290, *310,*
see also Usulután
Río Cuautla style, 62, 68, 72, 77

rocker stamping, 44, 45, 51, 52, 55, 57, 58, 62, 64, 65, 88, 281, 282, 286, 287, 288, 290, *310*
  stamped, 137
  white-rimmed black ware, 44, 51, 52, 55, 57, 58, 61, 64–65
early occurrence of, 36, 37, 39, 40
forms of, *see Florero*, Stirrup spout, *Tecomate*, Whistling vessel
Maya phases, *see* Chicanel, Mamom, Tepeu, Tzakol, Xe
Mesoamerican–Eastern United States similarities, 281–283
Mesoamerican–South American similarities, 40, 44, 62, 218, 285–291
Mesoamerican–southwestern United States similarities, 78, 217–219, 277–281
origins, 39, 292
Postclassic period, 199, 212, 214, 219, 220, 227, 230, 248–249, 265, 271, 274
Preclassic period, 36–40, 44–45, 50, 51, 55–58, 61–65, 72–73, 77–78, 81–82, 85–86, 88
Protoclassic period, 120, 153
temper, 39, 150, 281
Poverty Point, 281, *see also* United States, eastern
Pox pottery, 40, 63, *see also* Pottery
Preclassic period, 4, 22, 278, 285, 292, 299, *see also* individual site name
  chronology, 35
  civilization, 297
  population estimate, 36
  summary of development, 35, 88–91
Preprojectile horizon, 18, 20, *see also* Diablo focus, Tequixquiac
Prickly pear (*opuntia*), 30, 31
Priest, 55, 60, 93, 96, 106, 113, 117, 129, 131, 135, 147, 177, 193, 204, 231, 234, 239, 240, 245, 256, 257, 271, *see also* Shaman
Protoclassic period, 37, 152
  in basin of Mexico, 73–120
  highland Maya, 83
  lowland Maya (Matzanel), 87–88, 152–153
Providencia–Majadas (phase), 81, *see also* Kaminaljuyú
Puebla, 8, 21, 27, 243, 258, 274, *see also* Mixteca–Puebla, Tehuacán, Tlaxcala, individual type site name
Puebla—Tlaxcala, 99, 268, 301
Puerto Hormiga, 40, 285, 286, 287, 288
Puerto Marqués, 40, 63
Pumpkin (*Cucurbita pepo*), 29–32
Purrón (phase), 38–40, *see also* Tehuacán
Putún Maya, 112, 169, 172, 173, 175, 176, 180, 182, 192, 195–196, 204, 222–227, 229, 231, 233, 261, *310*, *see also* Yucatán
Putún Itzá, *see* Putún Maya

Puuc, 195, 227, 232, *see also* Architecture, style
Pyramid, 6, 81, *see also* Architecture, individual site name
  round structure, 68, 72, 215, 216, 220, 248, 270, 280
Pyrite, 6, 68, 144, 149, 158, 180, 217, 236, 274, 278

Q

Quartz, 20, 58, 81, 137, 234, 279
Queréndaro, 218, *see also* Michoacán, Western Mexico
Quetzal bird, 14, 134, 150
Quetzalcóatl, 124, 288, *308*, *see also* Gucumatz, Kukulcán
  aspects of, 205, 256
  deity, 124, 135, 149, 205, 207, 216, 246, 248, 256, 279, *308*
  leader, 204, 205, 209, 212, 222, 246
  legendary history of, 204–207
  representations of, 205
  title, 205
Quiché, 99, 221–222, 234
Quintana Roo, 107, 190, 230
Quiriguá, 169
  architecture, 172
  hieroglyphic inscriptions, 114, 115, 172, 190
  stone monuments, 172

R

Rabbit, 11, 14, 27, 28, 31, 65, 68, 82, 103
  hair weaving, 6
Raccoon, 14
Ramon tree (*Brosimum alicastrum*), 86, 157, 233, 299
Rasp, *see Omichicahuaztli*
Rattle, 77, 79, 176, 180, 236, 254, *see also* Music
Religion, 234–236, 254–258, 271, *see also* Deity, Priest, Sacrifice
Remojadas, 145, 214, *see also* Veracruz cultures
Reptiles, 30, 52
Resist painting, *see* Pottery, decorative techniques
Río Bec (site), 182, *see also* Architecture
Río Conchas–Bravo Valley cultures, 219
Río Cuautla style, *see* Pottery, decorative techniques
Río Grande de Santiago, *see* Lerma–Santiago river system
Río Grande River, 22
Rock crystal, 254, 268, 271, 272
Rocker stamping, *see* Pottery, decorative techniques
Roof comb, 144, 158, 159, 165, 171, 172, 176, 177, 178, *310*
Root crop agriculture, 40, 41–42, 157, 284, 287, 288, *see also* Altamira, Manioc

Rubber, 6, 229, *see also* Ball game
  sources of, 12
  uses of, 254

S

Sacbé, 188, *310*
Sacrifice, 240
  human, 6, 29, 77, 81, 151, 152, 176, 190, 202, 204, 205, 225, 227, 229, 231, 235, 237, 239, 243, 245, 254, 256, 257–258, 259, 262, 264, 271, 273, 275, 280, 288, 296
  ritual, 204
  significance of, 93, 254
Salinas la Blanca, 44, 45, 84, *see also* Soconusco
Salt, 158, 168, 188, 190, 219, 227, 229, 233, 245, 263, 270, 275
Salvador, *see* El Salvador
San Blas, 11, 78, 80, *see also* Nayarit, Western Mexico
San José, 169, 192, *see also* British Honduras
San José Mogote, 58, 60, *see also* Oaxaca
San Lorenzo, 50–52, 56, 61, 63, 82, 89, 300, *see also* Olmecs
San Luis Potosí, 6, 213, 214, 215
Santa Clara (phase), 83, *see also* Kaminaljuyú
Santa Marta rock shelter, 26, 31, *see also* Chiapas
Santa Rita, British Honduras, 230, 231
Santa Rita, Honduras, 88
Santiago River, *see* Lerma–Santiago river system
Sapote (*Casimiroa edulis* and *Diospyros digyna*), 29
  wood, 165, 177
Schist, 52, 81
Scottsbluff point, 21, 22
Seal, *see* Stamps
Sedentarism, 23, 29, 30, 32–33, 36, 41, 44, 88, 277, *see also* Hunters and gatherers
Seibal, 85, 86, *see also* Altar de Sacrificios, Pasión River
  Classic period at, 174–175
  hieroglyphic inscription, 115
  location, 169, 173, 174
  outside influence at, 169, 175, 190
  Preclassic period remains at, 174
Serpent, 63, 83, 86, 124, 144, 151, 165, 171, 175, 210, 213, 239, 248, 249, 250, 290, *see also* Coatepantli, Reptile
  feathered, 124, 199, 204, 207, 208, 222, 225, 279, 280
  fire, 248, 256
  rattlesnake, 14, 209
Serpent column, 208, 226, 227
Serpentine, 46, 52, 54, 55, 56, 60, 131, 137

Settlement pattern, *see also* House, Pit house, individual site name
  central highland Mexico, 64, 68, 73–76, 120–127, 210, 246
  Gulf Coast, 55
  highland Maya, 80–82, 149–150, 151, 221–222
  lowland Maya, 154–156, 230, 233
  Oaxaca, 58, 147–148 (footnote), 269
  Soconusco, 42–45
  Tehuacán, 28, 29, 33
  western Mexico, 78
Shaft-and-chamber tomb, 79, 80, 265–266, 289, *see also* Western Mexico
Shaft tomb, *see* Colombia, Oaxaca, Tombs, Western Mexico
Shaman, 28, 68, *see also* Priest
Shell, 8, 79, 131, 160, 161, 177, 179, 180, 208, 218, 225, 236, 254, 266, 278, 293
  engraved, 58, 79, 96, 214
  in masonry, 144
  temper, 39
Shield, 135, 136, 199, 209, 215, 225, 262, 268, 272, *see also* Warfare, Weapons
Sierra Madre del Sur, 10, 12, 271, 274, *see also* Mountain systems
Sierra Madre Occidental, 11, 78, 213, 278, 279, *see also* Mountain systems
Short Count, 108, 222, 232, *311*, *see also* Calendar, Long Count
Shroeder site, 218, *see also* Western Mexico
Silver, 62, 212, 254, 266, 268, 271, 273, *see also* Metallurgy
Sinaloa, 7, 11, 199, 214, 217–219, 278, 279, 290, *see also* Western Mexico
Sinaloa River, 5
Skull, 136, *see also* Tzompantli
  burial, 29, 77
  deformation of, 180, 236, 282, 287, 288, 290
  representation of, 151, 171, 176, 225, 227, 235, 283
  as trophy, 77, 288
Slash-and-burn agriculture, 35, 89, 156–157, 190, 233, 299, *311*, *see also* Agriculture, *Tlacolol*
Slave, 227, 233, 241, 260, 261, 262, 264, 273
Snake, *see* Serpent
Soconusco, 40, 44, 51, 80, 84, 89, 91, 261, 262, 288, *311*, *see also* Trade, port of, individual phase name, individual site name
Sonora, 22, 26, 30, 278, *see also* Western Mexico
South America, 212, 270, 274, 281, 285–291
Spaniards, 232, 236, 237, 238, 245, 246, 261, 264, 273, 284, 303
Spanish Conquest, 5, 12, 50, 75, 85, 99, 172, 190, 192, 195, 202, 211, 216,

Classic period, 73, 137, 199
Preclassic period, 73, 120
power and expansion of, 120, 136–137, 148
Preclassic period at 74–76, 89, 91
religion, 129–135
stone carving, 123, 124, 134, 136
trade, 136–137
urbanism at, 117, 120, 122, 127, 128, 298
warfare, 136–137
Teotitlán del Camino, 108, 275
Tepanecs, 241, 242, 248
Tepantitla, 126, 134–135, 136, 147, *see also* Mural painting, Teotihuacán
Tepeu (phase), 151, 169, 182, 190, *see also* Petén, Classic period in
Tepexpan man, 19, 20, *see also* Early man
Teponaztli, 254, *311, see also* Drum, Music
Tequixquiac, 20–21, *see also* Early man
Texcoco, 214, 238, 239, 242, 243, 259, 260, 274, 305, *see also* Lake Texcoco
Texcotzingo, 242, 248, *see also* Nezahua-cóyotl
Tezcatlipoca, 204, 205, 212, 240, 246, 256, *308, see also* Deity
Tezozómoc, 241, 242, *see also* Azcapo-tzalco
Thin Orange ware, 120, 131, 137, 146, 149, *311, see also* Pottery
Ticomán, 71, 72, 73, 77, 120, *see also* Basin of Mexico
Tikal, 85, 86, 152, 169, 192, 234, 264, 298, *see also* Maya civilization, Petén
architecture, 155, 158–160
ball courts, 155
caches and offerings, 160–161
Classic period at, 154–167
defensive earthworks at, 165, 190
description of archaeological site, 158–165
disposal of the dead, 155–156, 161, 166
external relationships of, 168
hieroglyphic inscriptions, 107, 115, 190
housing, 154–156
population estimates, 155–156
pottery, 195
Preclassic period at, 85–87
social organization, 165–167
specialization, 165
stone monuments, 158, 161
subsistence economy, 156–158
sweat baths, 155, 165
tombs, 87, 161
trade, 157–158, 167–168
urbanism, 154, 233, 299
Tilantongo, 220, 265, 266, 269, *see also* Mixtecs
Tin, 212, 268, 273
Tira de la Peregrinación, 99, 238
Tízoc, 240, 244, 250, *see also* Mexica, ruler
Tlacaélel, 207, 242, 259, *see also* Mexica

Tlachtli, 311, see also Ball game
Tlacolol, 35, 89, 311, see also Agriculture, Slash-and-burn agriculture
Tlacopan (Tacuba), 242, *see also* Triple alliance
Tlahuizcalpantecuhtli, 207, 212, 256, *308, see also* Quetzalcóatl
Tlaloc (Cocijo), 123, 124, 146, 149, 168, 175, 185, 205, 222, 244, 246, 250, 256, 279, 280–281, 305, *308, see also* Chac, Deity
Tlalpan (phase), 64, *see also* Cuicuilco
Tlamimilolpa (phase), 124, 127, 131, *see also* Teotihuacán
Tlapacoya, 40
architecture, 74
ceramic sculpture, 65
diet at, 65
early man, 17, 19–20
phases, 64, 72
pottery, 64–65, 72–73
Tlatelolco, 239, 244, 245, 246, 260, 261, *see also* Mexica, Tenochtitlán
Tlatilco, 65, 68, 72, 73, 81, 213, 289, *see also* Basin of Mexico, Preclassic period
burials at, 65, 72
external relationships of, 58, 62, 77
figurines, 65, 68
pottery, 62, 65, 279
Tlaxcala, 99, 129, 242, 263, 265, 268, 274–275, *see also* Puebla
people of, 243, 246
Tloque Nahuaque, 243, 254, *308, see also* Nezahuacóyotl
Toad, 50, 82, 83, 144, *see also* Frog
Tobacco, 213, 281, 283
Toltecs, 214, 240, 250, 263, 275, 283, *see also* Postclassic period, Tula, Yucatán
extension of influence, 6, 199, 202, 204, 213, 214, 217, 218, 219, 220, 221–222, 263, 275
figurines, 202
legendary history, 202–207, 224, 246
pottery, 202, 212
in Yucatán, 196, 221–227, 230, 234
Toluca, 8, 11, 77
Tomb(s), 126, 264, *see also* Burial, individual site names
in Colombia, 287, 289
highland Maya, 81, 82, 83, 86, 149, 282
lowland Maya, 86–88, 91, 161, 177–178
at Oaxaca, 59, 60, 147, 148, 221, 265–266
Olmec, 54, 282
in western Mexico, 77–79, 216, 266, 272, 289
Tonalá River, 12, 52
Tonalamatl of Aubin (*codex*), 99
Tonalpohualli, 99, 103, 108, 129, 144, 147, 271, *311, see also* Calendar
Tonatiuh, 250, *308, see also* Deity